D0034458

## More Praise for *The Fair Chase*

"In *The Fair Chase*, Philip Dray tells the story, by turns appalling and inspiring, of hunting in the US and how successive waves of media imagery transformed it from simple meat procurement into a recreational activity embodying shifting beliefs about the land and its European conquerors, animals and humans, and humanity and nature. No matter how you feel about hunters and hunting, this book will fascinate you and make you rethink your ideas."

—MATT CARTMILL, author of
*A View to a Death in the Morning*

"Less than 10 percent of the population now hunts, but they still represent a large symbolic place in our national narrative. Philip Dray helps us understand why hunting *and* hunters continue to shape our ongoing debates about our relationship to wildlife, endangered species, and environmental policy. Given the dramatic changes in the management ethos of our natural resources brought on by the Trump administration, *The Fair Chase* is a timely and engaging reminder of what's at stake."

—JAN E. DIZARD, author of
*Going Wild* and *Mortal Stakes*

# THE FAIR CHASE

# THE FAIR CHASE

## THE EPIC STORY OF HUNTING IN AMERICA

———◆———

## PHILIP DRAY

BASIC BOOKS

*New York*

Basic Books
Hachette Book Group
1290 Avenue of the Americas
New York, NY 10104
www.basicbooks.com

Printed in the United States of America
First Edition: May 2018

Published by Basic Books, an imprint of Perseus Books, LLC, a subsidiary of Hachette Book Group, Inc. The Basic Books name and logo is a trademark of the Hachette Book Group.

The Hachette Speakers Bureau provides a wide range of authors for speaking events. To find out more, go to www.hachettespeakersbureau.com or call (866) 376-6591.

The publisher is not responsible for websites (or their content) that are not owned by the publisher.

PRINT BOOK INTERIOR DESIGN BY JEFF WILLIAMS

Library of Congress Cataloging-in-Publication Data has been applied for.

ISBNs: 978-0-465-06172-3 (hardcover); 978-1-5416-1673-8 (ebook)

LSC-C

10  9  8  7  6  5  4  3  2  1

# Contents

# Preface

*They say bear is tastiest in late fall because the animals have been feeding for weeks on acorns, but it was pelts my friends wanted. It was early morning when luck blessed us: a she-bear and her cubs at the edge of a swamp. We cut the canoe in sharply toward shore and muffled our paddles, and not until we beached did the three of them run, the two cubs scrambling to the top of a tree, where they commenced to whine like puppies. Mama bruin doubled back the moment she missed her offspring, and faced us, partly rising on her hind legs. Swanson brought his rifle at his shoulder, and at the flash she fell where she'd stood. We went over and were looking at her black coat, when suddenly instead of a dead bear we had a very live one, and the way George and I got out of reach was very rapid but inelegant. Swannie fidgeted too long with his gun, or so it seemed; finally he fired, and she was ours for good.*

*The boys began taking the skin, and then George decided he also wanted a cub, both of whom were still cowering in the treetop. A shot to the head brought one tumbling down.*

*Seeing this gave Rusty "bear fever," and he declared he wanted the other cub alive. With some difficulty they shook him out of the tree.*

*Once the mother bear was skinned we took the live cub with us, but the little bear would not sit still in the boat, so we let him go. He seemed tame enough then, and I stroked him on the back before he disappeared in the bushes. We floated down to Rainbow Lake, landed and George soon had a splendid trout dinner cooked . . .*

*That night when the fire was fading Old Sturgis stopped by. He must have been about eighty, smoked a long Churchwarden pipe, and owned property thereabouts: a local character. When we mentioned our encounter with the bear and the cubs he puffed thoughtfully for a moment, and said, "It reminds me of an incident up here long ago."*

*The four of us exchanged glances. We were already in our sleeping bags and bone-tired; no one was in the mood for one of his stories; but then he said, "Had to do with a panther."*

*"A panther?" we exclaimed.*

*"Solitary creatures," he nodded, loading the pipe, "but abundantly sly." I doubt he even noticed our sudden interest, or maybe he took it for granted, for he was already lost in reminiscence. "It was late in the fall, about this time of year, 1957. My brother Dick and I had come up with a new rifle he wanted to try. On our third day out we were just south of the falls when Dickie glassed a monstrous buck on the far side of the lake. When we crossed over we tracked him 1,000 yards up an old dry-wash and then not only lost him but ourselves, too. That evening Dick had to go back to town but I stayed on, determined to meet that deer again.*

*"Night fell and I made camp next to a stream, just a mile or so from where we sit now. I built a fire and slept like the dead, but sometime during the night, long after my fire had gone cold, I awoke to one of the strangest sensations."*

*"What was it?" I asked.*

*"Leaves; branches of dry leaves were being heaped upon me. I opened one eye long enough to see the panther slink off. She was trying to hide what she took for choice carrion: me!*

*"Well, I resolved not to become anyone's supper and to oppose cunning with cunning. I found a thick bough of a fallen tree and dragged it to the fire, put some leaves atop it, then went and hid behind a rock. She appeared before long, followed by two hungry cubs. Slowly she crept to within fifteen paces of the spot where she had left me covered up with leaves, and crouched down with her green eyes glaring at the log; the next instant she made a spring, struck the claws of both her fore feet into it, and buried her sharp fangs deep in the rotten wood.*

*"Boys, the look on her face when she found herself deceived! She stayed for a moment in the same attitude, quite confounded. But I did not leave her time to deliberate; I put a bullet right into her brain, and down she dropped."*

*"Jesus! What if you'd missed?"*

*"Oh, I hate to think."*

*"And what happened to the cubs?"*

*"I never knew," he said. "They're likely all grown up and lurking around here even now," he said for effect, at which we all laughed, as we inched our beds a little closer together.*

*When he'd left I asked Swanson if what the old codger had told us could possibly be true. "No," he yawned. "Go to sleep . . ."*

*Next morning we were all up just before sunrise, dressed, and after some barely warmed-up coffee walked out to the big meadow where deer were said to browse. We separated. I chose a large black walnut tree to settle under, the field slanting downhill before me and a small creek murmuring behind. Perhaps I dozed. Then as the sky lightened there came the sound of animals waking: yard dogs barking; the tinkle of a goat's bell; some lambs mewing from over the ridge; out of the woods came a snorting sound, likely an elk or a deer. But I saw no deer, only listened to a woodpecker hammering away down in the valley.*

*I watched mourning doves alight in a crabapple tree, and a squirrel run along a limb, his cheeks full. Later I glimpsed a doe and her fawn walking far off through goldenrod. She must have winded me because she moved away with the special nimbleness of her kind; and I saw with admiration how she waited, her large ears now fully rounded-out and her manner curious, slightly petulant, for the baby to come up. They seemed very smug for a moment, the two of them, trotting off without a care and leaving me there by myself. Now I looked for my gun and turned to go. It had been a fine morning hunt . . .* [1]

As a boy I devoured stories like these, occasionally beneath the covers by flashlight, enthralled by the hunter's stealthy advance into the nonhuman world, the sudden stir of leaves, and the well-made shot. All of Minnesota then seemed connected to the sport: antlered deer and moose stared down from the wood-paneled walls of local restaurants; one could buy a box of shotgun shells at many filling stations, and everywhere, even at the end of city blocks, paths led away to woods or wetlands. From an early age I heard the implied summons to wilderness in the state's enchanted nickname, "the Land of Sky Blue Waters." And it was with a sense of determination akin to pilgrimage that our first family vacation included a stop at the Hotel Duluth, where in 1929 a hungry black bear had smashed violently through a plate glass window and entered the coffee shop, the premises of which now displayed the intruder as a stuffed tourist attraction.

Despite my fascination with brute nature, casting for sunfish in Minneapolis's small city lakes with a Zebco "Junior" rod and reel was as close to it as I came; once the Beatles entered my life, my interests were permanently redirected. I never did learn to shoot, and soon after college I moved away from the Upper Midwest hunt country. It was after writing several books about prominent social justice issues, however, that I began to wish for a subject that was less overtly political, yet whose trajectory was braided firmly through our country's social, cultural, and political history.

Hunting, though it has often been a means of subsistence, is also America's oldest recreation, and thus seemed ripe for the kind of survey I had in mind. Over the past half-century, unfortunately, the subject has become something of a polarizing "red state/blue state" issue, but my hunch was that beyond the at-times vociferous rhetoric surrounding it lay a history that was in fact unifying and widely shared. My own youthful recollection of its allure hinted at such a possibility.

This book's objective, then, is to go beyond the present-day cultural battles regarding hunting, and those of gun and animal rights generally, to explore what hunting's history has to tell us—about the country's legends, its faith in manifest destiny; its evolving views on nature, wildlife, Native Americans and the concept of race; its love of sports and leisure; its notions of self-reliance and manhood—in short, about nothing less than the shaping of our national temperament.

*Introduction*

# The Nature of the Beast

IT ALL BEGAN, AS THEY SAY, LONG AGO. IN THE MID-EIGHTEENTH century, Scottish economist Adam Smith put forward a historical perspective known as the four stages theory. Humanity, he said, had advanced initially through an age of hunting, followed by an age of herding and then one of agriculture, before entering the age of commerce. Smith's theory was purely conjectural; but in 1925, Australian anatomist Raymond Dart informed the world that the fossil skull of a child with a combination of apish and human features, found in a cave in Taung, South Africa, belonged to an extinct species of hominid that "had walked upright, with its hands free for the manipulation of tools and weapons." Dart, who named the species *Australopithecus africanus*, noted that South Africa's open veldt country, where the Taung Child had been found, was inhabited by "dangerous beasts" and quite far from the forested areas that were usually the home of apes and chimpanzees. The challenges of survival in this semiarid plain had led *Australopithecus*, who had lived 2.5 million years ago, to develop bipedalism, a larger brain, and an active interest in new sources of food, the result a struggle involving "swiftness and stealth . . . a fierce and bitter mammalian

1

competition" and a "laboratory . . . essential to this penultimate phase of human evolution."[1]

Dart's claims about this missing link between man and ape, which he described in the February 7, 1925, issue of the British journal *Nature*, were not immediately accepted, but the idea that *Australopithecus africanus* had hunted and killed other animals would gain considerable credence and scientific consensus over time. Some of the baboon skulls he examined from the site had been bludgeoned, suggesting the animals were killed by a club—most likely, Dart speculated, the large leg bone of an antelope—and then butchered with other sharpened animal bones. "Man's predecessors differed from living apes in being confirmed killers," Dart wrote in a later series of papers (*The Predatory Transition from Ape to Man* [1953]). "Carnivorous creatures, [they] seized living quarries by violence, battered them to death, tore apart their broken bodies, dismembered them limb from limb, slaking their ravenous thirst with the hot blood of victims and greedily devouring livid writhing flesh."[2]

Unpleasant stuff. Yet Dart's imaginative theories proved a starting point for an extensive conversation among anthropologists over what has become known as the hunting hypothesis, the belief that early man's long experience as a hunter, said to have occupied at least 99 percent of his prehistory in contrast to his 1 percent as an agriculturalist, explains his physiological development as well as his social organization. The pursuit of ever-larger game would have necessitated not only greater individual physical and mental powers, but the ability to coordinate with others to manage the hunt itself as well as the eventual sharing and preservation of meat. The adaptation to hunting, "in its total social, biological, technical, and psychological dimensions, has dominated the course of human evolution for hundreds of thousands of years," anthropologists Sherwood Washburn and Chet Lancaster concluded in 1968. "In a very real sense our intellect, interests, emotions, and basic social life—all are evolutionary products of [this] success." Hunting not only developed civilization, Washburn and Lancaster posited, but its uniformity, for "the selection pressures of the hunting and gathering way of life were so similar and the result so successful that populations of *Homo sapiens* are still fundamentally the same everywhere."[3]

Both the hunting hypothesis and the suggestion that, on account of this heritage, modern man is hard-wired as a killer, found full articulation in the aftermath of the Second World War and the beginnings of the atomic age. Playwright, screenwriter, and amateur anthropologist Robert Ardrey produced a series of articles on the topic for *Life* magazine, as well as several books, beginning with the influential *African Genesis* in 1961. Ardrey argued that violence had been so great a part of man's makeup through the eons that it remained his key behavioral constant, a proposition that seemed justified by the upheavals of the 1960s—protests, assassinations, a genocidal war—connections made explicit in *Why Are We in Vietnam* (1967), Norman Mailer's short, hallucinatory novel about sport hunting and American machismo. The subject of the human capacity for violence—its origins and too frequent casual commission in the modern world—would also be plumed in Truman Capote's best-selling *In Cold Blood* (1966) and on-screen in such films as *Bonnie and Clyde* (1967), *2001: A Space Odyssey* (1968), *Easy Rider* (1969), *Straw Dogs* (1971), and *Badlands* (1973). "Millions of moviegoers in 1968 absorbed Dart's whole theory in one stunning image from Stanley Kubrick's film '2001,'" notes anthropologist Matt Cartmill, "in which an *australopithecine* who has just used a zebra femur to commit the world's first murder hurls the bone gleefully into the air—and it turns into an orbiting spacecraft."[4]

The hunting hypothesis has subsequently been challenged by those unwilling to ascribe modern man's violent tendencies wholly to hunting genetics while ignoring other possible explanations—social inequality, and desperation borne of injustice, hunger, or displacement. Some researchers have also rejected as overly simplistic that part of the hunting hypothesis that suggests man hunted, developing superior athletic and spatial reasoning skills, while woman cooked, gathered, and nurtured the young. If, as many believe, a large share of early man's diet was vegetable, then gathering, not hunting, was the primary activity and a major developmental aspect of our species, one in which women likely played a significant role.

The same biological and intellectual changes attributed to hunting, such as bipedalism, cooperation, and the crafting of better tools, would have also been required for the success of primitive gathering societies. Indeed, agriculture, some argue, is a greater challenge and likely a stronger civilizing force than seminomadic hunting. "It is the farmer, *not* the hunter," notes scholar Mary Zeiss Stange, "who approaches the world of nature as something over which he must seize control."[5]

Yet the sense that hunting is something we are *meant* for remains an article of faith. Hunters characterize what they do as deeply instinctual—a way of being in and with nature that offers a connection to a life force so profound it defies articulation, a feeling of renewal found nowhere else, the "bliss that passes all understanding." For the liberal Spanish philosopher José Ortega y Gasset, one of hunting's patron thinkers, man's longing to return to the hunt stems from the fact that it was as a hunter that he initially awakened to his potential mastery of the world. Every subsequent civilizing process has taken him away from that awakening, which the modern hunter reenters "by temporarily rehabilitating that part of himself which is still an animal." This can be experienced "only by placing himself in relation to another animal . . . If we want to enjoy that intense and pure happiness, we have to seek the company of the surly beast, descend to his level, feel emulation toward him, pursue him. This subtle rite is the hunt."[6]

IT APPEARS THAT HUMANS VERY EARLY ON ISOLATED FROM THEIR *need* to hunt the intense thrill of pursuing live game; from antiquity through the Middle Ages, hunting evolved as sport. In seventeenth- and eighteenth-century America, outside of a few Virginia gentlemen (such as George Washington) who rode to hounds, there was little sport hunting per se. Most was based on subsistence or profits. With the growth of cities and industry, however, the sporting impulse awoke. Promoted as a means of restoring virility and verve to urban men stuck in the doldrums of office, shop, or mill, and reflecting a new courage and curiosity about nature, American sport hunting drew on diverse influences—the "true sportsmanship" ethos of the British hunt, the deadeye heroics of frontiersmen Daniel Boone and Davy Crockett, and the forest knowledge and stealth of the Native American. Literary heroes, such as Natty Bumppo, inspired it as well, as did, eventually, such mountain men as Jim Bridger and the legendary buffalo hunter William "Buffalo Bill" Cody. Poet and philosopher Ralph Waldo Emerson, who took his first crack at a deer in the Adirondacks in 1858, termed the nation's new love of the invigorating outdoors "the joyous change."

One notable feature of the sport was its adherence to an evolving code of ethics that would eventually be known as fair chase, the idea that hunted animals must have a chance to evade or flee their pursuers, and that they were to be taken only under certain sporting rules and conditions. By the 1870s, the call of the gentlemanly hunt was something of a worldview, a faith endorsed by magazines, newspapers, and hundreds of new sportsmen's groups, and even preached from the nation's pulpits. Newly armed and outfitted Americans took to the woods.

Such editorial enthusiasm was matched by commerce. Along with sporting clubs and shooting societies came Pendleton, Abercrombie & Fitch, Remington, Smith & Wesson, and a bounty of sports-related items—from heavy boots and jackets (with deep pockets for shotgun shells) to canoes, drinking flasks, and wooden duck decoys. Also for sale were hunting excursions by rail or steamboat and the services of innkeepers, guides, and taxidermists. A robust literature of hunting stories, memoirs, and humorous tales appeared, accompanied by what would become known as "the hook and bullet press," sports-related periodicals whose news and advice covered everything from fishing lures to the kinds of retrievers best suited for grouse hunting.

Remarkably, even from the sport's earliest days in America, voices urged the need to respect and protect wildlife's seasons of procreation, and cautioned against the decimation of hunted species. In the 1880s, organized efforts coalesced through sportsmen's clubs and the advocacy of influential periodicals, most notably *Forest and Stream*, to safeguard wildlife and natural places, from which grew a broader application of restraint and stewardship—the conservation movement—as well as the political will to place limits on hunting and create America's first wildlife preserves and national parks.

The growth of the sport's popularity, its emergence as a subject in the arts—in literature, painting, and commercial applications, such as furniture carvings and wallpaper design—and the channeling of hunting's energies into a more genial "capturing" of the West through photography, paleontology, and conservation, belong to an eventful historical process. Yet hunting has largely been neglected as a topic of historical inquiry in America. This may reflect the reduced participation in the sport over the last half-century and its abandonment by elites, as well as evolving views of nature and people's changing values regarding diet, animal ethics, the use of firearms, and what constitutes recreation. Such cultural shifts allow what I call "the Age of Fair Chase," the decades between the post–Civil War era and the Eisenhower 1950s, in which sport hunting was a widely accepted pastime and family tradition, to more readily come into focus.

This book introduces many of that story's leading protagonists and relates how they and the animals they pursued came to influence American society and imagination. It asks why the sport was promoted so assiduously and taken up by so many people; why it clicked so readily with journalists, artists, scientists, and clergy. It explores the ways hunting informed advances in weapons design and the natural sciences, and tells the parallel story of the growth of animal protection societies and changing public attitudes regarding extinction, evolution, and what historian William Cronon calls "the autonomy of nonhuman nature." Finally, it examines hunting's links to notions of manhood and self-reliance, while also weighing present-day cultural battles regarding guns and animal rights.[7]

America's love affair with sport hunting led to enhanced appreciation of the great outdoors, and to public acceptance of the need for management of wildlife populations and wilderness; but it also contributed to the wholesale slaughter of birds and animal species, and nourished the myth that the hunters' dominance over living prey prepared them uniquely to be also conquerors of other men. "We are a nation of hunters and frequenters of the forest, plains, and waters," President Theodore Roosevelt once declared. "No form of labor is harder than the chase, and none is so fascinating or so excellent a training-school for war." Some hunter-conservationists, most notoriously Boone and Crockett Club member Madison Grant, extended their nature stewardship to irresponsible pseudo-scientific speculation about the alleged inferiority of racial and ethnic categories of humans.

My approach has been to not only look back, but to see where this historically beloved form of recreation has brought us. Does the legacy of hunting have anything to say about current wildlife management issues, such as the government-funded eradication of animal pests, efforts to control deer populations, the designation of endangered species, or the controversial reintroduction of large animal predators? Can the moral compass of fair chase, forged in America's rustic past, offer any direction now for environmental crises global in scale? What of the hunter himself? Has his sport been made an anachronism, replaced by newer forms of outdoor recreation? How did the respected weekend sportsman of a half-century ago become the reviled trophy hunter of today? And if hunting *has* moved from mainstream to marginal, what can be said of its devotees—the approximately 4 to 6 percent of Americans who are licensed hunters, as well as the upward of 70 percent of non-hunters who say they approve of it as a legitimate sport?[8]

Ultimately, can we ever fully understand our nation's character if we do not begin to recognize the indelible mark left upon it by our love of the hunt? *The Fair Chase* will explore possible answers as it relates the story of the country's most enduring romance.

*Chapter One*

# The Prophet

IN AMERICA'S CENTENNIAL YEAR OF 1876, THE NATION CELEBRATED, reviewed with pride its eventful first century, and decided, in this broader moment of self-examination, to at last do right by the mortal remains of its founding sport hunter: Henry William Herbert. Using the pen name Frank Forester, he had been one of the country's first outdoors writers and had almost singlehandedly awakened American interest in the hunt. To his old friends, as well as the many admirers devoted to his books, it seemed neglectful and irresponsible that he had lain for almost two decades in an unmarked grave in Newark, New Jersey.

Of course, there was the fact that he had asked to be there—in the Mount Pleasant Cemetery, adjacent to his home, "The Cedars," on the Passaic River north of town. As Herbert had been in life such an exacting person, and had left specific instructions before committing suicide in 1858, until now no one had dared question the arrangement. "Remember, when you judge me," he had written in farewell, "that of all lives mine has been the most unhappy. No counselor, nor friend, no country has been mine for six and twenty dreary years; every hope has broken down under my foot as soon as

9

it touched it; every spark of happiness has been quenched as soon as it has been handled." To make certain nobody missed the point, he had insisted that the Latin term *Infelicissimus* ("Most Unhappy") be inscribed upon his tombstone.

In many respects Herbert's life had been, as he asserted, a mess, one large regret (among several): despite his considerable intellectual gifts and his prolific output of novels, histories, biographies, and poems, he had never won serious literary recognition. Rather, his reputation rested on his sporting tales and guides to fishing and hunting, which he had published under his *nom de chasse*. Now, eighteen years after his death, his worst fears had been confirmed; his more purely literary efforts were forgotten, while his writings on the hunt were being read afresh by a new generation and proclaimed visionary in their elucidation of the pastime's pleasures and meaning. Frank Forester Clubs had formed across the country, his works read by legions of shooting enthusiasts. "It would seem that the spirit of HERBERT is still with us, and ministers to the happiness, the instruction and the well-being of his fraternity, under the magic guise of 'Frank Forester,'" noted a publisher engaged in the profitable business of keeping his sporting titles in print. "This kindly spirit let us ever cherish, if we would keep pure and unsullied the sport and sportsmanship of America, for the advancement of which he gave his finest works."[1]

It was as a kind of prophet, then, that he was remembered, a Johnny Appleseed of sport hunting, but also as something of a martyr, for the curious thing (and there were many) about Herbert was that someone who derived such immense joy from sport in nature, and so excelled at sharing that delight, was made thoroughly miserable by everything else.

The 1876 interest in Herbert's memorial, or lack thereof, arose from this mounting posthumous fame, which left continued neglect of the gravesite unthinkable. When word of his unmarked resting place got around in fall 1875, it was his New York supporters who initially rallied, convening at Astor Hall in December to organize a Frank Forester Memorial Association. Their consensus was that the proper thing would be to "translate" his remains from the unmarked plot in Newark to Brooklyn's leafy Green-Wood Cemetery, the eternal home of so many New York overachievers of the nineteenth century, and that a subscription drive be opened at once to construct a suitable monument. New York had been Herbert's first foothold in America and where his sporting articles had first appeared. "Not only did he instruct wisely in all matters appertaining to the rod and gun," the group concluded, "but there was a charm in his style and an enthusiasm apparent in all he wrote that infected his readers with the same love of the chase he felt himself."[2]

It was natural for prominent New York sportsmen to assume that so great a personage as Herbert should not be left to lie for eternity in New Jersey, when the fair lawns of prestigious Green-Wood beckoned. But New Jersey pride rose up, as they say in the Pine Barrens, like a snout-poked bear. Leading citizens convened, newspapers were enlisted, and a Newark Herbert Association hurriedly formed, brandishing its own list of influential subscribers and vowing that under no circumstance would "Our Frank" be unearthed and transported away aboard a Hudson River ferry. The trump card in this game, of course, was that the departed's own last wishes were a matter of published record, and so Newark ultimately prevailed and Henry William Herbert stayed put. In hindsight, this was a shame, since by the early twenty-first century, Mount Pleasant Cemetery, wedged between a busy freeway and rising condominiums, is largely unvisited, while Green-Wood basks in its status as a cultural icon and meticulously groomed national treasure.

So it was, however, that on the intensely sunny afternoon of May 19, 1876, the officers of the Newark association gathered for the unveiling, along with invited dignitaries and some of the author's old friends and colleagues, the ladies sheltering beneath parasols. They heard Major George B. Halsted, who had known Herbert, praise him as "a highly gifted though unfortunate genius, of highest mental culture." Major Halsted observed that while the deceased was "a miserable failure, a wretch who took his own life," and a man who forsook his noble inheritance, his own family, and his only son, and never attained the literary fame he craved, Frank Forester, the character he had created almost on a whim, had proved a brilliant success. Henry William Herbert was here interred, but Frank Forester would surely live on; for generations to come it would be *his* voice teaching America the joys of the hunt, and urging the nation into the woods.[3]

BORN IN 1807, HENRY WILLIAM HERBERT WAS RAISED IN THE English countryside near Spofforth, Yorkshire. Letitia Dorothea, his mother, was a daughter of the fifth Viscount Aken of Kildare, Ireland. His father, the Reverend William Herbert, grandson of the first Earl of Carnarvon, was a botanist, poet, illustrator, and member of Parliament; he was also a devotee of the hunt, and by reputation a very good shot. Reverend Herbert's discoveries in plant genetics were important enough to achieve mention in Charles Darwin's *The Origin of Species*. The reverend passed on to his son his faith in ecologist Gilbert White's creed, later echoed by Henry David Thoreau, that "the love of nature can make a very small place into a very large world."[4]

The extended Herbert clan had not only the habit of writing and keeping diaries, but a knack for "delighting in discovering most unusual facts." Henry's Uncle Algernon had authored scholarly speculations on the origins of Stonehenge as well as a highly regarded treatise on werewolves; Reverend Herbert had published a definitive biography of Attila the Hun. Arguably the family's best-known descendant was George Herbert, the fifth Earl of Carnarvon, who in 1922 was a financial backer and coexplorer (with Howard Carter) of the tomb of King Tutankhamen. The earl's sudden death at the Continental-Savoy Hotel in Cairo in April 1923 from an infected mosquito bite is considered the first manifestation of the "Curse of Tutankhamen," or "Mummy's Curse," apparent retribution for unwrapping things that don't have your name on them.[5]

As the second-born Herbert of his generation, young Henry was in line to become the third Earl of Carnarvon. The impediment, however, was that William's older brother, Henry George, the second Earl of Carnarvon, had a son, Henry John George Herbert, who was seven years older than Henry William and was thus the presumed heir. It was whispered from an early age that Henry John

was unsuited for higher station—that he was clumsy and "slow"—
kindling in our Henry William's mind, as one biographer put it,
"the troublesome hallucination . . . that succession to the title on his
part was not an impossibility."[6]

At age thirteen, after a genteel childhood among the rural
gentry and its horses, hounds, and private tutors, Henry William
was sent to Eton, from which, after five years, "third in his class
and with some credit as a Greek and Latin scholar," he advanced
to Cambridge. Visiting his classmates' homes, he lived to the hilt
the active, lavish life of a young aristocrat, and came to know intimately England's great estates and its sporting country life. "While
at Cambridge, he was not what is generally known as a reading
man," Herbert later offered by way of self-description, "passing
much of his time in the pursuit of field sports and athletic pedes-
trian and equestrian exercise."[7]

Upon graduation in January 1829, the young gentleman "was
a fine specimen of his race," a historian recounts. "He was tall and
erect, free from the stoop which so frequently accompanies study."
Outwardly, young Herbert seemed the master of his fate. But in
spring 1830, his "early indiscretions and college debts" resulting
from his weakness for roistering and gambling caught up with him;
at the same time, a promised share of a family trust was absconded
with by a "notorious speculator and swindler." Thus suddenly
"reduced from affluence" and threatened with bankruptcy, he fled
to the Continent. Informed that a "writ of outlawry" existed against
him, he decided to put even greater distance between himself and
his creditors as well as the shame he'd brought upon his renowned
family, and booked passage for America. His vessel slipped into
New York Harbor in the spring of 1831.[8]

This melodramatic transition in Herbert's life, his parting from
family and country, has always confounded those who've tried to
understand it. "Outlawry," such as a student running up horrendous
debts, was not uncommon among well-born youth of the period,
and Henry's father likely could have paid them. The real source of
shame and the need for flight may have been a more contemptible
social transgression, as one biographer guessed, "an offense against

the rigorous social code of his class, an offense that no paternal settlement could clear," possibly homosexuality, then still punishable
by death in England, or incest, the latter rumor whispered cruelly
by gossips among his New York acquaintances. A more charitable
account attributed his ostracism and exile simply to his "unusual
behavior," which rings true, as Herbert was widely known to be
moody and unyielding.[9]

While it has never been entirely clear what led him to put an
ocean between himself and his troubles, his choice was not unusual:
America in the early nineteenth century was "the traditional desti-
nation of wastrels and dissolute sons who were unable to live within
the strict code of the English ruling class." In the United States they
were called remittance men: youth who accepted a regular allow-
ance of some kind to stay away from England, and about whom,
in their new country, there was always an air of mystery. It was not
polite to pry into the reasons for a remittance man's presence in
America, and Herbert rarely spoke of his Cambridge years, except
to concede: "I was a careless, happy, dare-all, do-no-good."[10]

Now twenty-four years old, "shy . . . and with the repelling
reserve of his caste,"[11] the banished son set out to make a new start
in his adopted land. He was if nothing else well educated, a stellar
classicist. Perhaps he would teach, or write. He soon found work
instructing young men in classical languages and gymnastics at
the Reverend R. Townsend Huddart's Classical Institute at 5 Beaver Street, and took to writing newspaper and magazine articles
for hire, while dreaming of attaining literary fame like that of his
heroes Walter Scott and Alexandre Dumas. Self-conscious at having taken work as a teacher, he implored in a letter to his Uncle
Algernon: "I do not wish this to be mentioned at all as I am well
aware that such situations are not considered as of high standing in
England although God knows it does not matter as I do not imagine there are ten people in England who care or consider where I am
or what I am doing."[12]

He was certainly not alone in having come to the city in the
hopes of a literary life, as American publishing, then "in its lusty
infancy," held much promise. The most cosmopolitan metropolis

"The stone which he picked up in his wayside ramble . . . became a text from which he would read you an entertaining and instructive lecture . . ." The words of Henry William Herbert (a.k.a. Frank Forester) inspired generations of American outdoorsmen. (Library of Congress)

in America, with a population of 200,000, New York was seeing the emergence of the "penny press," daily nonsubscription papers, such as the *New York Sun* and *New York Herald*, that were among the first to be hawked on the street and edited to appeal to an increasingly literate public with their sensational stories, gossip, and strongly worded satire and opinion.

The first sporting magazines had also appeared—the *American Turf Register*, the *Cabinet of Natural History and American Rural Sport*, and the *Spirit of the Times*—primarily covering horse racing but occasionally field sports as well. The offices of the *Spirit* in the basement of the American Hotel at Broadway and Barclay served as "a kind of central headquarters for a huge nationwide club of outdoor enthusiasts, and its pages were a clearinghouse for a vast body of narrative, chiefly in epistolary form addressed to its genial editor." This was William T. Porter, a Dartmouth-educated giant from Vermont who stood six foot six and was known as "the Tall Son of York," or simply "the Tall Son." Any local or visiting gent who wished to "talk horse" inevitably found a welcome at Porter's office, or nearby at Frank's, a drinkers' sanctum that kept the first generation of New York deadline journalists well watered.[13]

It was a writer's market. Magazines and newspapers, eager for more and better copy, relinquished their former reliance on reprinted articles and regurgitated news tidbits from abroad; increasingly they sought fresh pieces about New York life, as well as articles and letters from the rest of the country—Ohio, Kentucky, Louisiana, or the Carolinas. "It was not a question of how to get anything published but how to obtain enough to print," one memoirist recalled of a literary flowering characterized by a decline in British and European influence and the awakening idea that American democracy need speak for itself. "I ask not for the great, the remote, the romantic; what is doing in Italy or Arabia; what is Greek art, or Provencal minstrelsy," said Ralph Waldo Emerson of the tidal shift. "I embrace the common, I explore and sit at the feet of the familiar, the low . . . Why should not we have a poetry and philosophy of insight and not of tradition? There are new lands, new men, new thoughts. Let us demand our own works and laws and worship."[14]

The printed word in ascendance, Herbert joined a colleague from Huddart's school, Alexander D. Paterson, in 1833 to launch the *American Monthly Magazine*. Contributors included attorney William P. Hawes, who wrote as "J. Cypress Jr."; Charles Fenno Hoffman, later to be famous as the author of *Greyslaer* (1840), about a real-life murder mystery in upstate New York; and author and essayist Theodore S. Fay, formerly the editor of the *New York Mirror*. Paterson departed after one year, leaving Herbert sole editor until March 1835, when Hoffman joined as coeditor; after a disagreement with Herbert, Hoffman took over the publication.

Herbert's difficulties at the magazine were of a sort that would plague him throughout his career—a lack of patience with others' opinions and a tendency to react very poorly to those who challenged his; many would-be colleagues deemed him impossible and steered clear. This was unfortunate because, as his few loyal friends and students recognized, Herbert was immensely talented, his accomplished classical scholarship and vast knowledge of history and letters matched by a dexterous prose and a fair talent as an illustrator. He was also well informed about hunting, dogs, guns, and horses; had a connoisseur's appreciation for art, furniture, and liquor; and, as a botanist's son, was versed in natural science. "The stone which he picked up in his wayside ramble, under his eye, became a text from which he would read you an entertaining and instructive lecture on geology or mineralogy," one acquaintance recalled.[15]

Haunted by his student debts, he had sworn off gambling but remained a free and easy spender, his earnings going chiefly to quality sports equipment, clothes, and books. The local literary scene of his day had a rough-and-tumble aspect and was never too refined for a good brawl. It was a time, one memoirist wrote, when a threat to horsewhip someone was meant literally. The poet William Cullen Bryant fought with a Col. William C. Stone on Broadway across from City Hall, while *Herald* publisher James Gordon Bennett, a half-mad, cross-eyed Scot, was pummeled regularly for his invasive, libelous articles when his victims met him on the street. Herbert, proud and intolerant of any perceived slight, could throw fists as readily as insults, but he was often on the losing end of such affairs, once being tossed bodily from a favorite drinking establishment. While much of the time he could be the gracious, erudite Englishman of noble lineage, his unforgiving temper was "displayed not merely towards retainers and inferiors," one friend remembered, "[but] also with equals. He would fairly force disputation and, waxing wroth at opposition, employ exceedingly coarse language and occasionally, when not wholly himself, attempt to substitute physical strength for argument."[16]

Sometimes it wasn't readily apparent what had set him off. Dime-novelist Ned Buntline once made the mistake, in friendly conversation, of regaling Herbert with a sea yarn that involved a British ship's captain's deciding it best, just before a looming battle, to order an extra emergency ration of brandy for his men. Herbert seemed amused, but the next morning, Buntline awoke to a card from Herbert suggesting that a duel might resolve the issue of whether Englishmen required brandy to defend their honor. Panicked, Buntline ran to the office of the *Spirit*, and with William Porter's help, managed to defuse the situation. Sometime later, when a stranger confused Herbert with Buntline, whom he slightly resembled, Herbert exploded: "For God's sake, don't take me for that scoundrel!"[17]

Editorial offices were the scene of numerous Herbert tantrums, as he held book publishers to be snakes, "from the least wriggling dealer in cheap obscenity to the vast baronial constrictors." However, he did produce from his capacious mind and quick pen a trove of published works. In addition to romantic novels—*The Brothers, a Tale of the Fronde* (1835); *Marmaduke Wyvil, or the Maid's Revenge* (1839); and *The Roman Traitor* (1840), he also completed substantial biographies, such as *Henry VIII, and His Six Wives; The Cavaliers of England*; and *The Chevaliers of France*. He "nursed the hope of returning to England in a nimbus of literary glory that would make people forget the past," a friend noted; Herbert, resolute in this ambition, in 1839 quit "the arduous and thankless profession of teaching" to devote himself henceforth "to the profession of letters."[18]

The books of which Herbert was proudest, however, impressed few critics. "Nothing worse than his tone can be invented," was Edgar Allan Poe's pronouncement on Herbert's prose, decrying its "pompous grandiloquence." The very genius Herbert possessed for exacting detail and the lyrical possibilities of language, often led, especially in his fiction, to overinvolved, lumbering wordage. "The heavy dews, as they were exhaled by the rising day god," ran his description of a tropical dawn in *Tales of the Spanish Seas*, "teemed with the incense of unnumbered perfumes wafted from the ten thousand vegetable wonders which had given name to that peninsula." Soon, as the sun rose,

> the land-breeze swept far seaward the rich odors from the or
> ange groves, and the vast forests whence gleamed frequently the
> snowy chalices of the superb magnolia, and the dense star-like

blossoms of the flowering dogwood, and colored the azure waters of the Gulf into a thousand tiny wavelets, which sparkled
with innumerable smiles to the bright heaven, while the thrill-
ing and prolonged notes of the emulous mocking-birds . . .
made everything resound with their rich liquid melody.[19]

Such heavy sledding belonged to the world of Walter Scott and
the romantic literary tradition, which Herbert admired; but the
style found an insubstantial welcome among Americans eager for
fresh voices, as well as for subjects nearer to their own experience.

DELIVERANCE FOR HERBERT CAME FROM THE YOUNG, GROWING
American sporting press, the origins of which lay with attorney
and Baltimore postmaster John Stuart Skinner, founder in 1819
of the *American Farmer* magazine. The *Farmer* ran pieces about
English shooting matches and bird hunting. A decade later, Skinner
introduced the *American Turf Register and Sporting Magazine*—
America's first publication wholly dedicated to sport—which covered horse racing but also hunting, as Skinner was a field sports
enthusiast. (Another of his distinctions was to have been with
Francis Scott Key in Baltimore Harbor at dawn on September 14,
1814, when Key, inspired by sight of a tattered American flag that
had survived a British bombardment, wrote the lyrics to "The
Star-Spangled Banner.") Skinner's fellow sports gazette pioneer,
William Porter, "the Tall Son," had come to New York at roughly
the same time as Henry William Herbert, and in 1831 had started
the *Spirit of the Times*, which he initially conceived of as an American version of *Bell's Life in London*, a successful English sporting
magazine. Like Skinner, Porter at first relied heavily on racing and
other sports news from England; the *Spirit* for years ran a regular
column, "The Letter Bag of the Great Western," sharing the latest
bulletins from London, the name evocative of the years when New
York papers sent reporters out in skiffs, vying with one another to
intercept docking transatlantic vessels so as to get first glimpse at
the arriving communiqués.

The *Spirit* eventually found adequate news from the "turf action" at American racetracks to fill its pages. Horse racing in America had begun on crude ovals in Virginia in the seventeenth century, but wealthy planters soon were laying out large sums for imported thoroughbred horses from England, and through careful breeding perpetuating the noblest equine bloodlines. Competition among owners was strong, the honor of having a winning horse considerable. Cash, property, even slaves, were wagered, spectators creating a festive atmosphere of balls and social gatherings at familiar "race weeks," which featured special ladies' grandstands, bars, buffets, and sideshow attractions. The Washington Race Track in Charleston, one of the best known in the South, was famous for these spectacles, and became so firmly associated with betting and the settling of scores that it served also as the local dueling ground.[20]

The antebellum era saw the sport thrive not only in plantation country but along the Eastern Seaboard, with major tracks in New York City, Washington, and Baltimore. New York's Union Course, located in what is now Jamaica, Queens, hosted some of the most prominent races; here, in 1823, the northern champion Eclipse famously defeated the South's Sir Henry. With sectional rivalry still lively a generation later, the Union Course in 1845 was the site of the battle between the southern mare Peytona, who had already won several large purses, and the northern favorite, Fashion, known as "Queen of the Turf." In a 4-mile run before seventy thousand spectators, Peytona came home victorious. It was the largest sports event in America to date and the first to be the subject of national coverage. But the continuation of a playful North-South sporting rivalry became unfeasible in the politically fraught years leading up to the Civil War; also, lingering economic pressures related to the Panic of 1837, such as a decline in the price of cotton, contributed to racing's downturn.

William Porter toured the South in 1838. His objective was to meet horse owners and collect breeding lists for publication. However, he found himself enamored by something else—the distinctive folkways, hunting yarns, legends, and outsize personalities of the region. The following year, when he and his brother George bought out Skinner's *Turf Register* and sought writing talent for both it and the *Spirit*, they decided to open their pages to the best from this new literary frontier. "Life at the West and South is a teeming theme for magazine writers," William Porter wrote, and "the cleverest and most amusing have certainly been of a sporting nature. The curious and often rich provincialisms of dialect are here most appropriate, and are most vividly brought out by scenes on the Course or in the Field."[21]

The term *sport* itself was still largely associated with the Bowery's bachelor subculture known as the fancy—young working-class men who caroused, raised hell, and gambled on cockfighting, ratting, and billiards—leading many early contributors of hunting and sport-related regional tales generally to ask that they be published under a pseudonym. Comedic writing, in particular, "was not considered literature," but rather, "the masculine humor of the barroom and race track, cleaned up a bit for printing." As a result, George Washington Harris was "Sugartail" or "Mr. Free"; C. M. F. Noland wrote as "N. of Arkansas" or "Col. Pete Whetstone"; Mississippi contributors included "Obe Oilstone," "Yazoo," and "the Turkey Runner"; and Alabama was represented by "Satchell," "Azul," and "the Very Young 'un"; while a cohort of military officers stationed in Florida published collectively as the "Cor de Chasse." Other early practitioners whose bylines were familiar in New York–based sports journals included "J. Cypress Jr.," "Old Turfman," "Nimrod," and "Acorn." Many were newsmen or well-situated figures in business or law. Porter believed that the governors of both Mississippi and South Carolina had submitted anonymously to the *Spirit* "some of the most side-splitting stories ever published in this country," but the items had been passed through so many intermediaries, even he was not entirely sure of the authors' identity.[22]

What became apparent to the Porters with these articles' appearance was that hunting stories—hunters pitted against elusive, dangerous animals in forbidding terrain—possessed unique narrative power. Fine literature they were not, but they were immensely readable evocations of both nature and humanity, as man engaged in a supreme and suspenseful test of character and endurance. Aware that their New York acquaintance Henry William Herbert was an outdoorsman, George Porter suggested that he, too, try his hand at writing some "woodland" pieces akin to those appearing in the Porters' magazines. Herbert hesitated, but warmed to the idea when George suggested he use a pen name: "Frank Forester."

For Herbert, the Porters' offer held not only the appeal of a new creative outlet and source of income, but also the chance to assume a role he enjoyed as knowing arbiter of anything that involved field sports, honor, tradition, and chivalry. (There had been an embarrassing incident during his early years in New York when he'd stuck his nose into a duel between two other men simply because he'd thought it was being managed improperly.) As for sport, he much resented the way it had been tainted as grubby and demoralizing by the aimless hustlers of the fancy, and as a physical cultist he frowned upon the way American men had grown listless and dull from the failure to lead vigorous lives. He need look no further than his own undergraduate indulgences—gambling, drinking, loss of control—weighed against the restorative virtues of nature and the hunt. "When first it was my fortune to become a dweller on the Atlantic seaboard of the United States," he later said, "the word *sportsman* was understood to mean, not him who rises with the dawn, to inhale the pure breeze of the uplands or the salt gale of the great salt bay, in innocent and invigorating pursuit of the wild game of the forest or the ocean wave; but him who by the light of the flaring gas-lamp watches, flushed and feverish, through the livelong night, until the morning star, to pluck his human pigeon over the green field of the faro table." He would have concurred with one writer's allusion to the hunter's shotgun as "the most effective of all surgical instruments" at providing "astonishing cures" for inert city men; Herbert thought to apply it to the cancer of saloons and poker dens.[23]

The May/June 1839 issue of the *Turf Register* featured his debut as Frank Forester, whose "A Week in the Woodlands, or Scenes on the Road and Round the Fire," proved to be the first of a seven-part series. The lightly fictionalized stories featured Harry Archer, his Irish servant Tim Matlock, Archer's friend Tom Draw, and Forester himself, all British expats and lovers of the hunt and country life, and were set primarily in the scenic hills around Warwick, New York. Herbert had been introduced to the area by a friend, Anson Livingston, an attorney and sportsman who served as property manager of his own family's estates. (In 1805, Anson's father, Brockholst Livingston, while serving on the New York Supreme Court, had heard a landmark hunting case, *Pierson v. Post*, in which the court ruled on appeal that a hunter's pursuit of a wild animal, in this instance a fox, did not constitute possession. Livingston dissented, insisting that it was the custom of the field that "no saucy intruder" be allowed to carry off wild game if another hunter had exerted himself in the chase.) Herbert was himself known as a bit of a "saucy intruder" to irritated local Warwick farmers who resented his freedom in leading hunting parties across their lands, although he probably seemed beyond a commoner's reproach. "Mounted on the fine hunters he loved, with dogs of choicest breed following his erratic trail, he was an attractive figure," it was said. "Erect, distinguished in appearance, with a *hauteur* and careless grace in every movement . . . he sat his horse as if, to use an old-time saying, 'he were born in the saddle.'"[24]

The Warwick stories are borne along by an infectious glow of manly bonhomie as Forester and his cohort pursue quail, snipe, rabbit, and deer, challenged by the rigors of the hunt but sustained by their shared love of the chase, good food, and fine cognac savored in the open air. "Hunters go into Paradise when they die, and live in this world more joyfully than any other men," Edward Duke of York had written in the early fifteenth century's *Master of Game*, the oldest book about hunting in the English language. It was a prophecy that Herbert and his characters brought vividly to life. Stopping by Archer's New York townhouse prior to their departure for Warwick, Frank Forester admires his friend's "cozy bachelor's exquisite snuggery," and at a rural Dutch tavern, they are greeted by the proprietor (the memorably named Beers Hard), and welcomed for a late hunter's supper. "A glass all round of tip-top champagne brandy," Forester records, "a neat snug supper of capital veal cutlets, ham and eggs, and pork steaks and sausages—a brief consultation on the best beat for tomorrow—and then to bed we went, and dreamed—I at least—till the break of day, of dead points, double shots, and game-bags swollen to the size of meal sacks." The following day, the game bags do fill rapidly, and at lunch hour, the servant Tim has laid a picnic at a spring head. "Capital was the cold fowl and Cheshire cheese," Forester reports, "and most delicious was the repose that followed, enlivened by gay wit and free good humor, soothed by the fragrance of the exquisite cheroots."[25]

Forester describes Tom Draw, whom he is meeting for the first time, as having a Henry VIII–like figure—five foot six in height and "six or seven feet around . . . with a broad jolly face . . . Such a mass of beef and brandy!" Archer cautions Forester not to underestimate him, for Draw will be fully redeemed by his skill as a shooter. He is "a rough block . . . but there is solid timber under the uncouth bark enough to make five hundred men, as men go nowadays *in cities!*"[26]

Forester's descriptions of how well heeled the hunting life could be intrigued American readers, but his exacting depictions of the hunt itself, making of it both sport and science, captivated the most:

"Fall back, Tom, if you please, five yards or so"—[Archer] said as if he were completely unconcerned—"and you come forward, Frank, as many—I want to drive them to the left, into those low red bushes—that will do—now then, I'll flush them—never mind me, boys, I'll reserve my fire—"

And as he spoke he moved a yard or two in front of us, and under his very feet, positively startling me by their noisy flutter, up sprung the gallant bevy—fifteen or sixteen well-grown birds, crowding and jostling one against the other—

Tom Draw's gun, as I well believe, was at his shoulder when they rose—at least his first shot was discharged before they had flown half a rood, and of course harmlessly—the charge must have been driven through them like a single ball—his second barrel instantly succeeded, and down came two birds, caught in the act of crossing—

I am myself a quick shot—*too* quick if anything—yet my first barrel was exploded a moment after Tom Draw's second—the other followed, and I had the satisfaction of bringing both my birds down handsomely.—

Then up went Harry's piece—the bevy being now thirty or thirty-five yards distant—cocking it as it rose, he pulled the trigger almost before it touched his shoulder, so rapid was the movement; and, though he lowered the stock a little to cock the second barrel, a moment scarcely passed between the two reports—and almost on the instant two quail were fluttering out their lives among the bog grass.[27]

The Porters understood that Herbert had created something altogether new—a hybrid of Walter Scott and Alexandre Dumas and the exacting British hunting and animal artist Edwin Landseer, all fueled by "freshness [and] humorous tang." He had transplanted the romance of the Old World aristocratic hunt to the more familiar landscape of rural America. Most important, the heavy "old mannerisms, the forced elegance of style," that had weakened Herbert's earlier writings, had "left fresh naturalness and unconscious art in their stead." The new effort was unforced, free of artifice. That the characters were men of means, and Britons in America, suggested elitism and fussiness, but Herbert was clever enough to make them as occasionally stubborn and bumbling as they were likeable. In "Frank Forester," Herbert had hit upon a literary persona that was the best possible version of himself by invoking simultaneously the inherent nobility, but also the eternal humility, of the chase.[28]

The response from readers was correspondingly ecstatic; they, too, recognized the achievement. "There is animation in the characters that makes them live, and act, and enjoy, in our presence, and with us," an excited reader wrote to "the Tall Son" in February 1840. "The graphic delineations of lake, and wood, and sky—their ever changing variety of aspect—the delightful and memory-treasured associations that must be called up with all who have delighted in Field Sports . . . the startling whirr of the pheasant and the partridge—the glorious cry of the hounds . . . the burst of the antlered buck through the brushwood . . . the sharp quick crack of the rifle, and the death halloo of the huntsman, are all admirable.

Whoever 'Frank Forester' may be, present to him, my dear Sir, the thanks, the hearty thanks of one who almost envies him the power to enjoy 'A Week in the Woodlands,' and still more the happy talent to impart its pleasures to others."[29]

1839, WHEN HENRY WILLIAM HERBERT ADOPTED THE PEN NAME Frank Forester, marked the beginning of a successful run in both his personal and professional life. This was the year he married Sarah Barker, the daughter of John Barker, the mayor of Bangor, Maine, and on August 3, 1841, Sarah gave birth to a son, William George. Two summers later, in July 1843, the couple welcomed a second child, Louisa. Relocating to Philadelphia, Herbert became a regular contributor to *Graham's Magazine*, placing him in the company of some of America's most prominent literary voices, among them William Cullen Bryant, Henry Dana, James Russell Lowell, Edgar Allan Poe (the publication's first editor), Henry Wadsworth Longfellow, and N. P. Willis. The magazine boasted forty thousand subscribers and carried consistently high-quality writing aimed at literate men and women; it was also known for its appealing engravings. Publisher George Rex Graham attracted his roster with a rate of five dollars for a page of prose, well above the usual pay scale and so welcome an innovation that it became known as "the Graham page." Many of Poe's seminal stories, such as "The Murder in the Rue Morgue," first appeared there, although Graham rejected the poem "The Raven" when Poe offered it in 1844.

*Graham's* was good to Herbert, printing his fiction and poetry under his own name and also his sporting pieces as Frank Forester, even running a lengthy and highly favorable review of the collected essays of Herbert's clergyman-botanist father. Of course, the younger Herbert's quarrelsome ways still got him into trouble during this otherwise successful period. He fell out with his book publisher, and brawled in a Philadelphia barroom with a judge who insulted Queen Victoria. "He was apt to be brusque with those he did not like, and when 'beyond his depth' through too much conviviality inclined to be ugly when opposed," it was recalled, a delicate way of saying Herbert could be a nasty drunk. When in New York he was seen occasionally at Pfaff's, the Broadway beer cellar popular with the city's artists and writers and associated historically with Walt Whitman, although cartoonist Thomas Nast, actor Edwin Booth, humorist Artemus Ward, and actress-novelist Ada Clare, "the Queen of Bohemia," were all regulars as well. Herbert could be imperious and aloof, but the Pfaffians liked him—not so much for his company but because of his great and difficult reputation: the eccentric English lord in exile, his love intrigues, infamous fits of pique, and ugly disputes with the city's publishers. There were by now dozens of stories in circulation about Herbert's peculiarities, some likely not so true, but who could resist the gossip that Henry had laid a large hunting knife on a table before commencing a meeting with an editor or had taken $500 for a manuscript, which, when examined, turned out to be one published the year before.[30]

Herbert's literary output as Frank Forester, however, never flagged. The Warwick Woodlands series appeared in book form in 1845, followed in 1851 by an edition illustrated by the author. Other hunting books—*The Shooting Box* (1846), *The Deerstalkers* (1849), and *The Quorndon Hounds* (1852)—were all, like *Warwick*, popular during Herbert's lifetime. He also produced several hunting guides: *American Game in Its Seasons* (1853), *A Complete Manual for Young Sportsmen* (1856), and *Frank Forester's Horse and Horsemanship of the U.S. and British Provinces* (1857). Another, *Frank Forester's Fish and Fishing*, went through seven editions between 1850 and 1866.

He was also an early advocate of recognized hunting seasons, and an opponent of practices that violated the ethos of gentlemanly sport, such as shooting birds anywhere but in flight, the use of artificial lights to freeze deer in place, or the use of dogs to force them into water. In 1844, he cheered the formation of the eighty-member New York Sportsmen's Club (NYSC), one of the first in America. Dedicated to preserving game, the club sought to curtail the sale of wild game at market and to impose closed seasons on fowl, trout, and deer. In its advocacy, the NYSC used a model law written by Herbert, which was adopted by some counties but was kept from becoming state law due to intensive lobbying from exclusive restaurants and hotels that bought and served wild game. Herbert warned of the imminent "extinction" of some game birds within the outlying areas of New York, unless its more affluent citizens could change their dining habits. "The ostentation, rather than the epicureanism of the rich New Yorker demands woodcock," he complained; "therefore, despite law, common sense, and common humanity, the bird is butchered at all times." Even where game laws existed, they were hard to enforce, as there were no game wardens at the time. Fortunately, colonial legal precedent allowed citizens to sue those who sold or possessed wild game out of season. As many of the NYSC members were lawyers, they had considerable success in this regard, especially since bringing such cases could begin by simply noting what "specials" restaurants added to their menu. This method of "courtroom game preservation" would be replicated by numerous eastern cities before the Civil War, putting a crimp on rural poaching and illegal hunting.[31]

Farmers constituted an aggrieved class in the world of early game legislation, often grousing that such laws arranged seasonal schedules for hunters—both sport and market shooters—to go traipsing over the countryside, but did not adequately safeguard private property rights. "It is the more vexatious on account of the impudence and incivility of persons calling themselves sportsmen," wrote one farmers' collective from Newburgh, New York, in a letter to *The Spirit of the Times*, relating that "On the first day that the law permits, they issue in droves from the dens and groggeries of our towns and villages, and not unlike the predatory Vandals . . . they ride down fences, grain and grass, killing game in useless and unnecessary quantities; and some times, in their intolerable insolence kill sheep for rabbits, and chickens for partridges."[32]

Herbert, writing in response, supported the farmers' complaints about "idling, groggery haunting poachers," but insisted these men not be mistaken for the better followers of the chase. "The true sportsman," he averred, "abhors the whole race of them, knowing that his gentle occupation is by them brought into disgrace and disrepute." He pointed out that game laws, by protecting birds' breeding cycles, ultimately benefited the farmer by sustaining a population of birds, which devoured insects. He urged the farmers to join the campaign for game laws in collaboration with "the sporting men of the cities . . . as the real interest and object of the two parties are identical."[33]

Amid Herbert's engagement with a subject he loved, however, family tragedy arose. Herbert's wife, Sarah, became ill with consumption, and after several months during which there was reason to hope her health had improved, she suddenly took a turn for the worse, and on March 11, 1844, at age twenty-three, expired in her husband's arms. "My loneliness is beyond all conception," he told a friend. "Other men can go into the bustle of a concourse to do their business but mine must be performed in the solitude of the room which she was wont to people with her sweet smile." Compounding the loss, in August, the infant Louisa "joined her mother in the future world." Herbert at first kept his son, Willie, with him, or with Sarah's parents, but soon found the situation unmanageable, and in 1846 sent him to be raised by his family in England. "Forget all about your unhappy father," he wrote the boy, "except how tenderly he loved you; and remember that, if he gave up the care of you to others, it was for your own good and to his great grief and sorrow." He never saw the child again, and over the years stopped imagining his own return to England. By 1849, he forfeited any hope that he would ever be called home to assume the title "Earl of Carnarvon," for when his old nemesis Henry John, known as Lord Porchester, died that year, he inconveniently left an heir, Henry Howard Molyneux Herbert, whom the family called "Twitters," to immediately succeed him.[34]

In 1845, a year before Willie was sent home, and possibly as some sort of quid pro quo, Reverend Herbert sent $1,500 to his son Henry's close friend Anson Livingston with the request that Livingston administer it as a trust to secure Henry a permanent place of residence in America. The money was to buy property and a house, which would remain in Reverend Herbert's name and then be passed along to young Willie, with the stipulation that Henry would be allowed full use of it during his lifetime, an arrangement designed to prevent him from selling it under the pressure of paying off debts

or raising cash for some reckless purpose. As he had never become
an American citizen, and New York State did not allow aliens to
buy property, Herbert and Livingston located a pastoral spot north
of Newark, New Jersey, on the banks of the Passaic River, and there
purchased an acre and a half where, within six months, a small cot-
tage was built, which Henry named "The Cedars."

The site was "as beautiful a stretch of hill and vale and riverside as could well be found," according to one local history; "the
river was clear and sparkling . . . and the call of the whip-poorwill
was heard on the evening air and the brown thrush sang from the
thicket." Herbert liked to ramble with his dogs in the rustic cemetery that abutted his property, oblivious to rumors that it was occasionally visited by "resurrection men," medical students looking to
obtain fresh cadavers. Bereft of his wife and daughter, having given
up his son, Herbert lived a productive if monkish existence. When
his father died in 1847, most of his correspondence with England
stopped as well.[35]

He kept a large Newfoundland dog named Sailor, and was
happy to devote a summer afternoon to reading or dozing under a
tree. His neighbors often saw him in his hunting jacket, corduroy
pantaloons, a Scottish plaid shawl flung over one shoulder, and a
pair of thick brogans on his feet, followed occasionally by a mock-
ing, hooting gang of boys. In Newark he was inclined to stop at the
Black Horse Tavern before moving on to the public library, which
he used to research his hunting and fishing guides. "Not content
with the privilege there afforded," noted one biographer, "he cut
out bodily leaves from the Encyclopaedia Britannica, evidently
unmindful of the selfishness and criminality of the act." After he
released his servants from his employ, his behavior grew increasingly strange; one visitor discovered Herbert tending a large pot of
soup that he had been boiling for twenty hours. Another found him
immobilized on his divan, which he had arranged so he could gaze
upon a large portrait of Sarah by Henry Inman that was suspended
in the main room of the house. "No sculptor could do justice to the
exquisite beauty of her neck, hands and arms," Herbert mused.[36]

There would be one last attempt at a loving companionship. In February 1858, he married Adella R. Budlong, age twenty, of Providence, whom he had met on Fifth Avenue in Manhattan the previous fall, by his account, after intervening to defend her from a pair of menacing street toughs. Adella, charmed by her gallant Englishman, moved to New Jersey to share his lodgings along the Passaic. What happened next is not entirely clear, although the best evidence is that the initial novelty of being the wife of the famous Frank Forester, who was almost thirty years her senior, quickly wore off, particularly when she realized how lonely and isolated life was at The Cedars, and how difficult its chief resident could be. She departed after only six weeks. One guessed-at explanation was that "this unlooked-for denouement" had come about because "a busy-body" had whispered to the new Mrs. Herbert that her husband did not truly love her but had married her in the hopes her family's money might pay off his debts. Herbert denied this vehemently, and his friends suspected the situation was exactly the opposite: that the girl had married the writer because of his fame and connection to British nobility, and left in disgust when she came to understand he was neither rich nor entitled.

Such rumors and suspicions were the kind of melodramatic half-truths that swirled around Herbert all his adult life; like many people, Adella may have simply found Herbert too cold and overbearing. He was "capable of intense affection," as one friend recalled, "but utterly unfitted to bring happiness to its object." What is known is that Adella, tired of a life of seclusion with the mercurial Herbert, and complaining that he had struck and cursed her, went "to visit a relative," and never returned. The jilted author briefly rallied, taking a room in a posh hotel on lower Broadway in New York from which to stage a campaign to win her back, but a formal, discouraging rejection soon arrived from Adella's attorney: there was no hope of reconciliation. Herbert, humiliated and deeply hurt, confided his desperation to a loyal former student who, on May 17, at Herbert's urgent request, had arrived to keep him company; that night, having prepared detailed suicide notes, he entered the suite's bedroom, gazed at himself one last time in a bureau mirror, and raised a gun to his head.[37]

The papers the next day were filled with the sensation and scandal of the case—a famous man's love suicide—but there was also genuine remorse for the interesting Englishman who had created not only Frank Forester, a persona for spreading the gospel of sport hunting, but also another relatively new figure: the American sportsman. Over the coming years, as the sordid details of his life and death receded in memory, it was the ardent purity of his mission that resounded. He became—to a degree he could not have imagined, and of which he might have disapproved—*beloved* for his accomplishment: "Our Frank." For a generation, from 1839 to 1858, he had tamed the outdoors and thrust America into it, while making the sporting chase an acceptable, even refined recreation, what Theodore Roosevelt would one day call "the best of all national pastimes."

*Chapter Two*

# When Good Queen Bess
# Met Daniel Boone

THE IDEA THAT HUNTING WAS TO BE ENJOYED AS AN ETHICAL AND disciplined sport did not flow only from the pen of Frank Forester. While the British and European legacy was significant, there were other key influences in early America—celebrated frontier hunters Daniel Boone and Davy Crockett and the woodcraft of their Native American counterparts, who taught the need to allow deer and other game their natural breeding cycles and access to browsing habitat. As for the sporting aspect of the chase, it needed little inventing. As early as the third century BC, Plato was distinguishing between two kinds of hunters—the "idle," who killed animals using snares and deception, and the "sacred," who relied on their own skill to track their prey. In Plato's time, great courage was required to hunt a large animal that could at any moment wheel about and make a meal of a careless pursuer, who was armed only with a bow, club, or other primitive weapon.[1] Yet it was (and remains) important to the "sacred" or ethical hunter that his prey is sentient, capable of evading and even outsmarting him.

The virtues of the ethical chase had by the late Middle Ages bequeathed a fairly involved code of honor, a dignity shared with the horses and dogs that aided in the hunt as well as with the noble beasts whose deaths were its culmination. Hunting, according to sixteenth-century English physician Andrew Boorde, was for "great men," those who "do not set so much by the meate, as they do by the pastime of kyllying it." As an axiom of the period held, "He cannot be a gentleman which loveth not hunting and hawking . . . He cannot be a gentleman which loveth not a dog."[2]

It was the British, absorbing French hunting traditions introduced in the Norman Conquest, who most transformed hunting from "a barbarous act into an act of gentility." The hunt in England from the eleventh century onward came to be defined by an array of rituals and behaviors, rules, standards, signals to hounds, and hunting cries—all to serve the sanguinary fixation with the taking of animal life, but also to ensure that in its complexities hunting remained an adventure for the privileged. Under Norman influence, England developed strict game laws, the nobility reserving the prime hunting lands for themselves; the punishments against poachers and trespassing peasants were severe. It's no surprise that folk legend came to link civil liberty with access to food, and that well-loved heroes, such as Robin Hood, boldly defied the stringent laws that kept ordinary people from taking "forbidden" prey. So objectionable was this exclusion that eventually a decree opening the king's lands to lesser nobility was made part of the Magna Carta.[3]

These elite, spirited hunters came at the sport with an intensity that allowed no half-measures, for as hunting historian William Baillie-Grohman tells us, they

knew much more than we moderns do of the nature of the beast they were hunting, of its habits and wiles, of its stratagems and ruses. They studied wild nature with a keenness unblunted by intellectual occupations, and they loved her with unstinted devotion. To see the play of the sun's rays in the forest's foliage, or to hear the song of the birds in the dewy morn delighted their senses, and they loved to listen to the brave music of their deep-toned hounds as they gave tongue in wooded glades. The chief pleasure did not lie in the slaying of the hart, but rather in the incidents that led up to it.[4]

Stories abound of royal figures so consumed with hunting they neglected their official duties. King James became obsessed (and was ultimately humiliated) by his repeated failure to kill a clever stag nicknamed "Cropear." The rotund Henry VIII frequently spent entire days on the trail, accompanying his love letters to Anne Boleyn with the gift of a freshly slain deer. When, in 1536, at age forty-four, he sustained a debilitating leg injury in a jousting tournament, he ordered special platforms built to allow him to get on and off his hunting steed. His daughter Elizabeth inherited fully his love of the chase, and at age fifteen began fulfilling the monarchial obligation by slitting the throat of a wounded stag. An illustration from 1575 shows her, as queen, honoring another tradition—the reviewing of the *fewmets*, or deer droppings, offered by a master of game for her inspection prior to a day's outing. Even at age seventy-seven, Good Queen Bess was said to remain "excellently disposed to hunting, for every second day she is early on horseback, and enjoys the sport long."[5]

The hunt was highly ritualized at all moments—even the field dressing, or "unmaking," of a killed stag, was governed by intricate rules regarding the dissection of the animal and the fair distribution of its organs to the hunters, beaters, and hounds that had been in on the kill. This ritualization lent itself abundantly to the fifteenth and sixteenth centuries' imaginative use of language. England's inhabitants, historically swept by diverse currents of language—Celtic, Latin, Norman—developed "an astonishing verbal amenability, a quite childlike open-mindedness to and delight in the new." The chief recipient of this playful linguistic obsession was the stag, the adult male deer. The accomplished hunter could name it at all stages of its life—in its first year as a *calf*; at age two, a *knobber*; at three, a *brocke*; at four, a *staggard*; at five, a *stag*; and at age six, a *hart*. An individual deer hunted by a king or queen attained high status, especially if it managed to escape, thus becoming a *hart royal*; if it fled to a distant forest, it was a *hart royal proclaimed*, meaning no one else was to give pursuit before the frustrated monarch got another crack.[6]

Best remembered of the imaginative vocabulary of the medieval chase were the "nouns of assembly"—a *sloth* of bears, an *exaltation* of larks, an *unkindness* of ravens, a *murder* of crows, a *business* of ferrets, a *parliament* of owls. Some such terms—a *colony* of ants, a *school* of fish, a *plague* of locusts—remain in use. Aspects of the chase itself were also connoted with precision. A red deer put to flight by hounds was said to be *unharbored*, fallow deer were *roused*, roebuck were *found*, a boar was *reared*, a hare was *started*. A jackrabbit was *bolted*; a fox, *unkenneled*; a badger, *dug*; a wolf, *raised*; a marten, *bayed*; and an otter, *vented*. There were also specific words for animal droppings. Deer left *fewmets* or *fewmisgings*; bears deposited *lesses*; rabbits, *croteys*; fox, *feance*; and otter, *sprayntes*. Being able to "read" these leavings has always been crucial to successful tracking, providing information about the animal's size, how recently it passed by, and what berries or browse it ate, intelligence that might well direct a hunter to a known meadow or woods nearby. In a royal hunt, deer droppings took on great significance. Gathered by a huntsman, a minor but trusted official, they were shown to the presiding noble at the traditional outdoor meal at which the participants fortified themselves for the day's ardors. Pushing his breakfast aside for a moment, the lord or majesty would inspect the *fewmets* so as to judge which were the freshest and largest, and which suggested the most impressive stag. Several huntsmen might make such presentations, and it was an honor for any subordinate to have his chosen, although he then had the challenge of leading the royal shooters to the designated prey.[7]

Abetting the huntsman were the dogs, the "natural detectives" of the chase. They were indispensable for hunting over large swaths of land, and could include bloodhounds, running hounds, leash hounds, racing hounds, greyhounds, or beagles—each specially bred for its role in the hunt and suited to specific prey or terrain. Some excelled in a sprint; others were dependable runners over distances well beyond the capacity of horses and men. With as many as thirty hounds in a pack, they were a constant source of frisky, tail-whipping commotion, and hunting guidebooks of the day are meticulous in suggesting their diet and upkeep, incentives and chastisements, as well as likely names, the better to keep order afield, for an unruly pack reflected badly on the sportsman in charge. Banger, Bouncer, Trouncer, Fuddle, Merryboy, and Truelove were popular names, although Spanker, Sootbag, Tulip, Vulcan, Ramble, and Tempest also had their vogue.[8]

By the sixteenth and seventeenth centuries, as deer became overhunted in parts of Britain, attention pivoted to the hare and the fox, other creatures known to "give good chase." The fox, initially despised as a pest but soon acknowledged as a worthy adversary, was so clever it at times seemed to be actually playing a game along with the hounds and humans pursuing it. Capable of befuddling the best dogs and horsemen over many miles of countryside, it retraced its steps, ran along streams to hide its scent, and was seen to flee atop fence rails. "Reynard," the conniving fox antihero of a series of comedic rhyming narratives composed in the Middle Ages, became (and remains) a common appellation for the animal.

Fox hunting came with a distinctive couture for participants and many specialized terms, as well as a lexicon of recognizable whoops, cries, and blasts from the horn. The commanding reality of the affair, however, was the pounding exhilaration of being atop a horse plunging at full gait through uncertain terrain—a supreme challenge for mount and rider in which sound horsemanship counted for all. Using the horses as magnificent athletes and buoyed by the "soul stirring music of nature's own choir—a fine pack of dogs," the riders, or "thrusters," displayed their quickness and equestrian skill, jumping fences and streams at a thunderous pace. The ideal, as riders expressed it, was to go over the country "as if it wasn't there," but both human and equine endurance were tested by the fact that a fox can run several hours without letup, a pace that exhausted horses and riders alike. Staying in the saddle and abreast of the other riders, not shying away from nor getting tossed off at the jumps, was a major feat, the ultimate goal to be present when the hounds finally surrounded the fox.[9]

As with stag hunting and its ritual of the *curee*—the rewarding
of the dogs with deer innards mixed with some bread or flour—the
disposition of the fox was subject to exacting custom. Its tail, or
brush, went to the first rider to arrive at the kill; first-time riders
were initiated by having drops of the fox's blood dabbed on their
face; and the fox's carcass was fed to the deserving hounds. Such
rituals had to be performed in facsimile, however, when it became
evident that foxes were not available in the numbers required to
serve England's hunters. So popular had the sport become that
vulpicide—the killing of foxes, usually by farmers who considered
them a nuisance—became a serious offence, and days when no wild
fox could be "unkenneled" for a hunt were sad occasions, requiring
the use of a "bagman," or captive fox available for release. Bagmen
known to "give good chase" were highly valued, and were carefully
rescued from the dogs and rebagged at the end of each day's hunt;
one such champion, known to his admirers as "the Bold Dragoon,"
was pursued, recaptured, and rereleased three dozen times.[10]

BRITAIN'S LOVE OF THE FOX WAS REPRISED IN THE AMERICAN COL-
onies, most notably in Virginia. It was said George Washington's
first utterance each morning upon waking at Mount Vernon was to
query a servant as to whether the weather favored a hunt, and that
once aboard his chosen mount, he "shirked not fence, nor craned
at a water jump." But elsewhere in the early United States, there
was little recognition of sport hunting. The American backwoods
hunter, though increasingly admired after the Revolutionary War,
was a loner living at world's end, often seeming to have more in
common with the animals he stalked than other human beings.
Henry William Herbert confronted this pervasive and negative
impression of hunting by insisting on the elite origins and purpose
of the chase regardless of whether one rode with the Tidewater
elite or stalked game with a musket and a hound dog. He was
instrumental in joining British and Yankee traditions, reminding
his US readers that British globe-spanning dominance was unques-
tionably derived from his countrymen's historic passion for blood
sport. "Whatever weaknesses, follies, deficiencies or vices, may

be justly laid to the charge of the English gentry and nobility," he wrote, "want of manliness, of pluck to do or to endure, is not of them." The British man's love of field sports and stoic "disregard of climate, country, toil, hardship, or exposure" had carried him and the cause of empire "to the snows of Canada, the unwatered barrens of Australia, the pestilential brakes of Africa, [and] the tiger-haunted jungles of Hindostan." Hunting, vowed Herbert, could have a similarly restorative effect on the average American, who, in his view, risked losing his soul to "the trickeries of trade," the burdens of family, and a dull job. He called out as the twin culprits the "over earnestness in the pursuit of gain on the one hand, and over frivolity in the pursuit of pleasure on the other," and asked for "more manhood and less Miss Nancyishness on the part of the young men of our Atlantic cities."[11]

Herbert's ideas weren't new, of course; they echoed the British hunting ethos of the late Middle Ages, that "hunting trains up youth to the use of manly exercises . . . (and) inclines men to good acquaintance, and generous society," as Nicholas Cox wrote in *The Gentleman's Recreation* in 1686. They also enlarged on the concern of the American founders that, as John Adams had warned, the "Revolution's moral edge" might be lost as hard work and industry created riches—affluence that would foster luxury, which could in turn produce "effeminacy, intoxication, extravagance, vice and folly." Herbert's admonishments can as well be seen as part of a trend in the early republic for reform-minded behavior, sometimes printed as tracts, warning of intemperance, the need for regular exercise, bolting one's food, and "the heinous sin of self-pollution."[12]

William Elliott, a southern sports writer and Herbert's contemporary, agreed with the Englishman's prescription of the hunt for developing manly character, but also emphasized that the rewards included the acquiring of beneficial habits afield. "The rapid glance, the steady aim, the quick perception, the ready execution; these are among the faculties and qualities continually called into pleasing exercise; and the man who habitually applies himself to this sport will become more *considerate*, as well as more prompt, more full of resource, more resolute, than if he had never engaged in it!" To hunt, one needed to enter and share the world of wild animals: learn their eating, sleeping, and mating habits; identify the sounds they made; know their tracks and the meaning of what was in their scat; and use all human capacity to read the murmurings and movements in the forest. What it involved was introducing the American man to nature, and thus reuniting him with his true self.[13]

WHILE FRANK FORESTER EVOKED THE CHARACTER-BUILDING VIR-tues of the chase and his account of the Warwick Woodlands charmed readers with its cool aesthetic, William Porter in *The Spirit* had struck a complementary lode, publishing for his national readership the lively hunting, folk-, and tall tales from the region then termed the Southwest—Arkansas, western Tennessee, Missouri, and Texas. The authors, small-town newspaper editors or professional men, formed, in Porter's view, "the nucleus of a new order of literary talent . . . a new vein of literature, as original as it is inexhaustible in its source."[14]

The emergence of the woodsy tall tale, no less than the popu-larity of Frank Forester's sport hunting narratives, rested in part on the demystification of the long-forbidding interior of the country. The westward drift of white settlement, the turning of ferocious beasts into hunted prey, the decimation or forced removal of native tribes, all worked to neutralize the wilderness. Its roaring rapids and treacherous heights had, in the hands of its ablest storytellers, become simply awesome landmarks, and it was safe to laugh at the outback's unlettered human citizens, their country dialect and odd expressions. A "feller" whose bottomland just flooded or had his privy collapse might appear "as slunk in the face as a baked apple," or "as mad as a rained-on hen." The sufferer might experience the further indignity of having a raccoon shoved down his pants and a dog turned loose after it, only to sigh in resignation, "Stranger, may I be chawed to death by young alligators."[15]

Porter had long trod carefully regarding the feelings of his southern readers, for whom the northern abolition movement had bred considerable sectional resentment; but the rustic tales of back-woods savants hunting coons, scamming Yankees and occasionally one another, the braggart storytellers and the "gynormous" critters they hunted (which inevitably "came on like screamers"), possessed an earthy charm that defused regional pride. There was "Captain Simon Suggs, late of the Tallapoosa Volunteers," a lovable swindler who wouldn't hesitate to fleece a preacher, and professed, "It is good to be shifty in a new country"; Ransy Sniffle, the raucous troublemaker of Augustus Longstreet's "The Fight"; Thomas A. Burke's satire of a stranded North Carolina nuptial party in "Polly Peablossom's Wedding"; and George Washington Harris's character Sut Lovingood and his dialect tales, such as "Chunky's Fight With the Panthers," "How Sally Hooter Got Snakebit," and "Sut Lovingood's Daddy, Acting Horse." That such stories stirred nostalgia for vanishing rural life only enhanced their appeal.[16]

There was a mild raciness to the tales. In one, a man returning home late one night from prayer meeting unwittingly climbs into bed with Nancy, a young woman who is visiting his wife, Polly. The next morning, Polly is furious and insists the matter be brought before the minister, who listens as the husband explains he made a mistake in the dark and thought he was in bed with Polly. All eyes turn to the blushing Nancy, who offers, "Well, I *thought* I was Polly, too, until next morning." In another, a southern belle enters a dry goods store and instructs the clerk that she desires a pair of gloves "just the color of your drawers there." The young man stutters: "My drawers, miss! Why I don't wear any!" Then there was the night the Devil joined a lone hunter at his campfire. The man cleverly hands a pipe full of gunpowder to his unwanted guest, and when the Devil lights it, there comes a tremendous explosion, but the Devil, his face blackened by soot, simply observes, "Damned strong 'backy!"[17]

Hunting stories, with their intrinsic capacity for embellishment, lent themselves abundantly to the form. Put a gun in the hands of a "ring-tailed roarer," and he becomes the world's premier blusterer, full of exaggeration and bravado. In Thomas Bangs Thorpe's "The Big Bear of Arkansas," Jim Doggett dismisses the wasting of bullets on winged creatures, for, "a bird any way is too trifling. I never did shoot at any but one, and I'd never forgiven myself for that, had it weighed less than 40 pounds. I wouldn't draw a rifle on anything less than that; and when I meet with another wild turkey of the same weight I will *drap* him." As for bears, "the way I hunt them— the old black rascals know the crack of my gun as well as they know a pig's squealing. They grow thin in our parts, it frightens them so, and they do take the noise dreadfully, poor things. That gun of mine is a perfect epidemic among *bar*."[18]

The American love of the tall tale was by now well established. The nation's founding kidder, Benjamin Franklin, told of whales that so loved the taste of codfish, they chased them up and over Niagara Falls. John James Audubon spread word of a wild horse that wandered from Kentucky to Pennsylvania, subsisting on pumpkins and eggs. Especially prized by hunters were tales of incredible marksmanship—placing a bullet hole in a milkmaid's pail on the far side of the Potomac, or setting weather vanes spinning on distant church steeples. William Elliott wrote of killing two bears with one blast of his shotgun. However, few could top the story of the hunter who, finding himself cornered by a bear and a moose, fired at a nearby boulder. The bullet broke in two, killing both beasts; and a moment later, a squirrel dropped out of a tree, pierced by a fragment of the blasted rock. The hunter, meanwhile, had been knocked by his gun's recoil into a river, and after swimming to shore, found his coat full of trout. Perhaps the ultimate "wonderful hunt" story told how a man hunting above the tree line glimpsed a winged silhouette overhead and fired quickly, only to cry out in mortal shame when a cherub dropped into his game bag.[19]

Many hunting tales relied on quasi-supernatural elements— bears that vanish, mysterious black stallions, pure white deer that miraculously appear. Albino deer, while rare, do exist, and retain a magical quality for those fortunate enough to behold them; shooting one is considered bad luck. The ghost of Virginia Dare, the first white child born in English North America, is to this day said to haunt Roanoke Island in the form of a pure white doe. One of the best-known myths involved a European noble, Hubert ("the Bright-witted"), an avid hunter who, on Good Friday of the year 700, was converted to Christianity after meeting a milk-white stag in the forest whose antlers formed a luminous crucifix. Subsequently he was known as the patron saint of hunters, with St. Hubert's feast day (November 3) being honored in Europe into the twentieth century. Hunters in Central Europe still observe a custom in the saint's name of placing fresh twigs in the mouths of just-killed game, signifying the return to God of the animal's soul.[20]

The story of how Daniel Boone met his wife echoed one such tale. Out alone at night, Boone was using a lit torch to "shine" deer in the dark. Suddenly, he saw two eyes. Raising his gun to fire and pushing through some underbrush a few steps closer to his prey, he found himself gazing into the face of Rebecca Bryan, a young neighbor. Frightened, she tore through the woods and, barely able to catch her breath, swore to her family that she had been stalked by a panther. Boone, smitten by the features he'd glimpsed in the light of his torch, went the next day to present himself as her suitor. A similar experience was reported by Captain Dan McCarty, a Virginia hunter who chased a fox across the lawn of a great mansion only to see it disappear inside the front door; a moment later, a pretty girl strode outside holding the fox, which was her own pet. The captain would later say that "he had in that chase caught more vixens than one," for finding the young woman's intellect much to his taste, he proposed marriage.[21]

Imagery of the elusive or uncatchable prey recurs throughout American fiction. A backwoods hunter identifies so thoroughly with an "un-huntable bar," that he takes the name "the Big Bar of Arkansas" himself and intrigues fellow steamboat passengers with his bizarre story of futile pursuit. Herman Melville's Ahab hunts the world's oceans for the obscure white whale Moby Dick. In William Faulkner's "The Bear," the eponymous prey is "not even a mortal beast but an anachronism indomitable and invincible out of an old dead time, a phantom, epitome and apotheosis of the old wildlife which the little puny humans swarmed and hacked at in fury of abhorrence and fear like pygmies about the ankles of a drowsing elephant." Such animals, larger and wiser than others of their species, glimpsed rarely, and seemingly endowed with magical powers of evasion and invisibility, lurk in the deepest woods; the hunters they obsess sometimes term them "spirit animals."[22]

The mysteries in the woods also assumed human form, such as the Harpes, a "family" of late-eighteenth-century frontier renegades considered America's first serial killers; and John A. Murel, a slave stealer who worked the Natchez Trace, often disguised as a preacher, luring slaves into running away only to sell them back to their masters or, if they proved uncooperative, stuffing their disemboweled remains into a sack and sinking it in a river. More questionably human were the Jibbenainosay, a shape-changing phantom white man out to avenge his family's murder by Indians; and the Catawampus, a ghostly half-woman, half-cougar who yet haunts eastern Tennessee.

Americans were taming the frontier, but their anxiety about wild places had not yet vanished entirely. Throughout the early nineteenth century, this fear gave birth to a fanciful zoology of slightly impossible woodland creatures—some threatening, others playful: the Guyascutus, coated with huge scales and said to eat large stones; the Haggletopelter (also known as the Side Hill Gouger), whose two shorter legs on one side of its body allowed it to run across the face of steep hills; or the Hodag, which dined exclusively on white bulldogs (one "Hodag" exhibited in Wisconsin in 1896 brought an investigative team from the Smithsonian Institution). To mention only these few would be to ignore the Wapaloosie; the Whirling Whimpus, and the Whistling Whoo-Hoo; but travelers made nervous by twigs snapping in the night could also ponder the Barking Moon Crumbler, the Cross-Feathered Snee, the Yambird Lunkus, the Squonk, the Gumberoo, and the Hicklesnoopus. The linguistic mash-up that so curiously named these things also produced such homespun terms as *absquatulate, tarnacious, rampagious, rumsquattle, cahoots*, and *flabbergasted*, the latter two of which, of course, survive to this day.[23]

William Porter printed dozens of Southwest stories in the *Spirit* during the two decades before the Civil War, and brought out two anthologies of humor writings—*The Big Bear of Arkansas* (1845) and *A Quarter Race in Kentucky* (1847); in doing so, he likely did more than any other individual "to develop and foster the humorous genius of his countrymen." The love of all this outsize, raw language, the frontier humor, and the tales' facile buncombe and exaggeration, would become staples of American culture, prominent in the words of Abraham Lincoln, Mark Twain, and Joel Chandler Harris, among others.[24]

MEN WHO LIVED PAST THE BOUNDARY OF CIVILIZATION AND derived their sustenance from hunting were, in the estimation of colonial writer John Hector St. John de Crevecoeur, "no better than carnivorous animals of a superior rank." Many settlers looked forward to a day when, because wild animals no longer roamed the backwoods, the frontier hunter might grow scarce as well. Such attitudes were largely transformed, however, by the example of the "long hunters": storied pathfinders, such as Daniel Boone, who opened the lands beyond the Alleghenies for settlement, and the buckskin-clad sharpshooters who emerged from the woods to lend their skills to the cause of war. The Brown Bess, the military musket carried by British troops in the war, was a hard-to-aim weapon designed for use by large masses of soldiers arrayed and firing together in close proximity to an enemy. The Americans' Pennsylvania rifle, with its bored and long, slender barrel, was easier to load quickly and more accurate at greater distances, and as historian Richard Hofstadter points out, was "well adapted not only to the shooting of squirrels but to the woodman's shoot-and-hide warfare." General Washington encouraged his men to wear hunter's buckskin, the better to make the enemy fear that every American combatant was a deadly marksman.[25]

Most of the Americans who fought in the American Revolution as well as the War of 1812 were not backwoods hunters, but the latter's much-praised pluck and resourcefulness emerged from both conflicts as admirable national traits. New value was attached to hunting and individual confidence with the gun. "Had we not been such good marksmen in our wilds and prairies, we should not have taught our enemies such a severe and salutary lesson," wrote Andrew Jackson. "I would conjure you, my friends, not to let your rifles rust."[26]

Daniel Boone is not typically counted among the nation's founders. Only marginally literate, he rarely sat in parliamentary

gatherings, made no eloquent speeches, and authored no founding
documents. But in the decades following 1776, perhaps only Benjamin Franklin and George Washington were as legendary. No
less than they, Boone, as early as the 1780s, had become an idealized American, one known around the world. Born into a Quaker
farm family in Pennsylvania on November 2, 1734, he displayed
by age fourteen precocious skills as a woodsman and hunter, soon
after receiving his first gun. In 1755, he served with a militia unit
in the French and Indian War, taking part in Braddock's March,
the ill-fated campaign led by British general Edward Braddock to
seize Fort Duquesne (at present-day Pittsburgh), which ended in
an Indian and French rout of the British and the death of the general. The following year, Boone married and began a family; but
he proved a restless farmer, and by 1760 was hunting and trapping,
sometimes beyond the Blue Ridge Mountains.

His ability to operate west of the farthest white settlement relied
on Boone's unique character and powers of calm diplomacy, perhaps
the fruits of his Quaker upbringing. He knew well the Indian creed
of "Much talk, no hunt," and learned to go stealthily and silently
into the woods. Although the natives occasionally robbed him of
his pelts and guns, he surrendered the items without a fight; he was
an interloper on their land, after all; better to live to hunt another
day. Similarly, he accepted their blatantly unfair "trades," such as a
pouch filled with pemmican for a new rifle. "I often went a-hunting
with them, and frequently gained their applause for my activity
at our shooting matches," he recalled. "[But] I was careful not to
exceed many of them in shooting, for no people are more envious
than they in this sport. I could observe, in their countenances and
gestures, the greatest expressions of joy when they exceeded me."[27]

Nine years later, Boone made his first extended trip into Kentucky, a place that impressed white visitors as a land of physical
splendor and boundless resources, including abundant wildlife. He
returned several times to hunt, and in 1775, led the first group of
settlers through the Cumberland Gap, eventually making Kentucky
the first land settled west of the original thirteen colonies. His success as a tracker and pathfinder proved of great interest to would-be

land purchasers back east, prompting one of them, a former Pennsylvania schoolteacher named John Filson, to interview Boone and include his story as an appendix to a book Filson published to entice settlers to buy property across the mountains. Entitled *The Discovery, Settlement and Present State of Kentucke* (1784), the book, immodest as any real estate brochure, described the bounteous new home as "the best tract of land in North America, and probably in the world." "The Adventures of Col. Daniel Boon" [*sic*] was added to personalize the experience of opening the area to settlement, using Boone's example to placate settlers' fears of wild animals and Indians.[28]

Filson initially had come to Kentucky in 1782, acquiring about 13,000 acres. At one point he owned the future site of Cincinnati, Ohio (he called it Losantiville), but he ultimately used Lexington, Kentucky, as a base, where he worked as a surveyor and teacher and performed research for his book. He mapped and queried locals about the area and became versed in wilderness living, often with Boone as his guide. The narrative he assembled of Boone's life was episodic, showing how experiences mostly brutal, sometimes kind, had taught Boone to survive and thrive on the frontier. Filson did not minimize the real dangers. Kentucky was known as "the dark and bloody ground," so named by Chief Dragging Canoe of the Cherokees for its long history of warfare between Indians and settlers. White men went hunting and vanished, some presumed eaten by wild animals, other slain by tomahawk. Several of Boone's companions were killed by Indians, as were two of his sons; a daughter was kidnapped, and Boone himself was involved in numerous skirmishes with Indians and desperate defenses of lonely frontier stockades; he also was once held captive, although his captor, a Shawnee chief, liked him so much he adopted him and was heartbroken when Boone escaped.

The appeal of Filson's saga, in part, is that Boone is no renegade frontiersman; he returns always to his family, and it is for them that he continues to push the frontier westward, while assuring readers (via Filson) that although "many dark and sleepless nights I have been a companion for owls, separated from the cheerful society of men, scorched by the summer's sun, and pinched by the winter's cold . . . now the scene is changed: Peace crowns the sylvan shade."[29]

Filson, in boosting Kentucky real estate, had inadvertently created one of the most important biographies of an American ever written. Fifteen hundred copies of his book were published in Wilmington, Delaware, in summer 1784; "The Adventures of Col. Daniel Boon," often separated out from the larger work, then ran through multiple editions in several languages: French in 1785, German in 1790. While Filson wanted Boone's example to show that courage and hard work could conquer the frontier, neither author nor subject possibly could have dreamed the extent to which Boone would become a mythic figure, a representation of the young country's hopes.

Boone remained modest and philosophical about his fame. "Many heroic actions and chivalrous adventures are related of me which exist only in the region of fancy," he reflected late in life. "With me the world has taken liberties. And yet I have been but a common man." He was cognizant of his life's great paradox: that by nurturing the process of settlement, he had contributed to the destruction of the very things he loved, the beauty and solitude of the frontier and the native peoples he respected. Boone is honored as an eminently decent man, but his fallibility may be his most winning feature. Largely ill-suited as a store owner, ginseng trader, tavern operator, and surveyor, he was careless with money and financial transactions and spent much time in court being hounded for debts, defending his land claims, or trying to explain his errant bookkeeping. It was with immense relief that in 1799, in deference to his fame, his family received the gift of 10,000 acres in Missouri, then a Spanish territory. Characteristically, he neglected to complete needed paperwork or make required improvements to the property, so when the Louisiana Purchase was signed in 1803, transferring the land to the jurisdiction of the United States, Boone and his family were briefly threatened with dispossession. It is said that his last great adventure came in 1810 when, at age seventy-six, he accompanied a group of friends and trappers as far west as the Yellowstone River, from which he looked upon the Rocky

Mountains, and that he dreamed until his death in 1820 of seeing the Pacific Ocean. "The health of the eye seems to demand a horizon," Emerson would write, a seeming epitaph for America's original hunter-frontiersman.[30]

THE MOST PROMINENT HEIR TO BOONE'S LEGACY WAS THE BRASH Tennessee hunter, frontiersman, and politician Davy Crockett. Alexis de Tocqueville sounds astonished in 1829 to note that "two years ago the inhabitants of the district of which Memphis is the capital sent to the House of Representatives an individual who has had no education, can read with difficulty, has no property, no fixed residence, but passes his life hunting, selling his game to live, and dwelling continuously in the woods."[31] Crockett, from 1827 to 1831 a member of the US House of Representatives, was, as Tocqueville understood, a new kind of American political personality. As the courtly founding generation of Adams and Jefferson receded, such commoners as Crockett, Jackson, Henry Clay, Zachary Taylor, John C. Frémont, and eventually Abraham Lincoln were those who emerged to prominence and also greatness.

Born in 1786, Crockett, like Boone, was a hunting prodigy, although as a sociable, talkative fellow, he was far more likely than the Quaker-raised Boone to boast of his prowess. With a mind that, "untaught by rigid rule, roved free as the wild beasts he hunted," he developed an appealing knack for public speaking and winning his listeners' trust, using engaging tales of his death struggles with bears and other "critters" as his political currency. He became known for quaint bits of wisdom, such as "Never sneeze because somebody else has taken snuff," and figured in the coining of the frontier's favorite expression of utter helplessness, "I'm a gone coon," signifying the wail of a raccoon treed by hounds upon learning that Crockett, a deadeye shot, was headed that way. A tribute play based on his exploits, called *The Lion of the West* (1831), featuring a Crockett-like figure named Col. Nimrod Wildfire, a loud, boastful, *rampagious* character, was hugely popular in New York and elsewhere on the East Coast, and eventually in England. In 1833 came the publication of the first "Crockett

Almanacs," collections of tall tales featuring the coonskin-capped hero and bearing such titles as "A Riproarious Fight on the Mississippi," "A Squabble with Two Bears," "Crockett Killing Four Wolves at the Age of Six," and so on. In the almanacs, Davy could do anything—pull the tail off a comet, escape a tornado by jumping on a streak of lightning, or push the sun back into motion when it got stuck. His "official" autobiography, *The Narrative of the Life of Colonel David Crockett* (he had been an officer in a county militia), published the following year, told of how Crockett met Mississippi boatman and brawler Mike Fink, "a *helliferocious* fellow, and . . . an almighty fine shot," who foolishly brags to Crockett of his marksmanship. Crockett can't pass up such a challenge and proceeds, from a distance of 150 yards, to shoot the ears off a cat. Fink responds by shooting the tails off an entire family of pigs, although Crockett points out that one pig has retained part of its tail and proceeds to shoot it off. Fink, refusing to be shown up, then takes aim at his own wife, who's standing across the yard, and "shoots half a comb out of her hair, then orders her to stand still and dares Crockett to hit the remaining half, but Davy, more the gentleman, refuses to even level his gun at such an *angeliferous* critter."[32]

The names of Boone and Crockett are forever intertwined in the iconography of the early American frontier (both were popularly revived in the Cold War 1950s, their individuality and backwoods grit a foil to the perceived threat of totalitarianism); but they were unalike in significant ways. Boone moved from civilization into wilderness; Crockett came from the frontier to conquer the world of government and society. The unassuming Boone was demure about his accomplishments; Crockett couldn't stop talking about his. He was so popular a figure in Jacksonian America that he even became the protagonist of the nation's first Kilroy-like graffito "Here D Crockett Killed a Bar," which was carved into tree trunks across the land, both before and after the hero himself fell at the Alamo in 1836. It's possible he would be less known today were it not for the heroic manner of his death. When he eventually lost political power in Tennessee in 1835, after serving an additional term in Congress from 1833 to 1835, he left the state and joined the

Free Texas movement, and was at the legendary mission in San Antonio the following March when it was stormed by the Mexican army. Depending on which version one chooses to believe, Crockett either surrendered and was executed on orders of General Santa Anna, or died a martyr inside the besieged walls, where his body was found "lying on his back, a frown on his brow, a smile of scorn on his lips—his knife in his hand."[33]

In Crockett's heroic death, in Boone's stamina and modest resolve, and in other frontier role models, such as wilderness guide and army scout Kit Carson or mountain men Jim Bridger and John "Grizzly" Adams, Americans had a rejoinder to Frank Forester's touting of the beneficial rigors of the British hunt. No one would deny the valor of English gentlemen plunging over brook and dale after fox; but what were such things, really, in comparison with the grit required of westward-looking Americans—taking black bear with knife or cudgel, risking death by tomahawk, even the tall-tale artist demystifying the alien hollows and dark wild places with self-mockery and Yankee horse sense. To this burgeoning home-spun pride there soon would be added a third element in the unique story of the American hunter: an embrace of the restorative values of the natural world.

*Chapter Three*

# "Let Us Have More Hunters"

I N THE SUMMER OF 1858, ONLY WEEKS AFTER THE DEATH OF HENRY William Herbert, some of the nation's foremost thinkers went hunting. Their guide was landscape painter William Stillman, who for months had regaled his friends in Boston's intellectual Saturday Club with tales of the Adirondacks, the pristine 9,000-square-mile expanse of mountains, forests, lakes, and streams in upstate New York west of the Hudson River. Stillman, who had studied with renowned Hudson River School artist Frederick Church, knew the mountains well, and had in mind a remote encampment on Follensbee Pond where his literate brethren might hunt, camp, and experience nature as they never had before.

The sportsmen's campout would soon become routine in American life, but for the moment it represented something fresh. Instead of going like wary pilgrims into the forest, or swooning like silly romantics at the mists around mountaintops, these doyens of law, philosophy, and natural science had come to engage with nature— to hunt, fish, breathe the air of rejuvenation Stillman had promised, and contemplate all the hours and moments of the experience.

The Saturday Club's members included Concord poet and philosopher Ralph Waldo Emerson; eminent Harvard biologist and geologist Louis Agassiz; Judge Ebenezer Hoar, witty scion of an old Puritan family; and poet Henry Wadsworth Longfellow, whose epic "The Song of Hiawatha" of a few years earlier had offered America a sentimental view of "the vanishing Indian." Several members—James Russell Lowell, Oliver Wendell Holmes, Emerson, and Longfellow—were early contributors to the *Atlantic*, which had been founded the previous year. Lowell, an exuberant man who liked to say he belonged in "a hospital for incurable children," served as the magazine's editor; Holmes had provided the publication's name. Jeffries Wyman, a physician close to Agassiz who had put himself through medical school by serving with the Boston Fire Department, also agreed to join the Adirondacks outing.[1]

Agassiz, who came to America from his native Switzerland in 1846, was a compelling lecturer who inspired students to seek answers in nature, not in books: he was known to lead them on tours of local fish markets. "I have seen him stand before his class holding in his hand the claw of a crustacean," recalled one student. "In his earnestness it seemed to be for him the center of the Creation, and he made us all share his belief. Indeed, he convinced us." Highly opinionated, Agassiz refused to accept the theories of Charles Darwin, insisting that "the animal kingdom especially has been constructed upon a plan which presupposes the existence of an intelligent being as its Author." His anti-Darwinism, his faith in polygenism (the idea that human "races" stemmed from separate creations) were in time debunked; but he was a pioneer in explaining the significance of fossil fish, the first to suggest that the earth's glaciers were the remnants of a prehistoric ice age, and was credited with breathing life into the study of the natural sciences in this country.[2]

Longfellow ultimately bowed out of going on the mountain retreat, Stillman concluding he was "too strongly attached to the conditions of completely civilized life" in his manse on Brattle Street. The lauded poet's own explanation was that he feared Emerson would accidentally shoot someone. He needn't have worried.

Emerson spent much of the vacation "under canvas," jotting notes for a poem he would write about the group's journey and encampment, while Agassiz captured lizards, Stillman sketched, and the rest of the party hunted deer with the help of the outing's several Saranac Lake guides. As the group's activities suggested, hunting as sport had gained a foothold in these mountains, had attracted artists and gained a visual aesthetic, and had realized a kinship with natural science. Dinner of fresh trout and venison was served en famille around a campfire, and all slept on beds of evergreen branches. Hoar later recalled that, for a pack of citified gents, the transition to soldiers of the wilderness had been for the most part convincing, as "our party when assembled in costume were a remarkable looking set; I think any one of them would have been convicted of piracy on very slight evidence."[3]

The ease with which they embraced the untrammeled region greatly pleased Stillman, who had been an early convert to the Adirondacks' charm. "There is a power in the mountains to shut out the world," he once wrote to a friend, describing the remoteness of the region's interlocking lakes and streams, where "my boat's keel leaves no path on the watery road." Indeed, the remote spot Stillman had selected for their camp, Follensbee Pond, came with a mystery. It was said to be haunted by its namesake, a hermit, rumored to be a British army deserter, who had lived for years at the pond and was buried thereabouts in an unmarked grave. "Many the daring hunter or trapper, laughing at every other peril," read an early guidebook's description of the place, "trembles as night environs him in its dreaded precinct."[4]

Lowell suggested the name Camp Maple for the picturesque spot Stillman had chosen, but the guides christened it Philosophers' Camp in honor of the distinguished company. "Those were symposia to which fortune has invited few men, and which no one invited could ever forget," Stillman said of the conversations around the campfire. "The forest echoed with such laughter as no club ever knew, and the owls came in the trees overhead to wonder." He would later recall it as "a gathering unique in the history of vacations."[5]

Long before coming to the Adirondacks, Emerson had written eloquently of nature as a force that offers energy and spiritual sustenance to mankind, but he had little actual experience of it, certainly nothing like the soaring pines and deep stillness of the New York mountains. "He marveled at the completeness of the circle of life in the forest," Stillman observed. "He examined the guides, and me as one of them, with the interest of a discoverer of a new race . . . To find me axe in hand, ready . . . to fell the trees, to kill the deer, or catch the trout, and at need to cook them . . . it was a form of independence which he had never realized before." In his poem about the camp, Emerson described the transformation in himself, in his friends, in his country:

> Ten scholars, wonted to lie warm and soft
> In well-hung chambers, daintily bestowed
> Lie here on hemlock boughs, like Sacs and Sioux,
> And greet unanimous the joyful change,
> Sleep on the fragrant brush as on down-beds,
> Up with the dawn, they fancied the light air
> That circled freshly in their forest-dress
> Made them to boys again.

Emerson was especially moved by the cool confidence of the Adirondack guides, whose minds and muscles seemed one with the trees and rocks and water, and whose grasp of life, at least here, prevailed over that of the elites from Harvard Square.

> No city airs or arts pass current here.
> Your rank is all reversed; let men of cloth
> Bow to the stalwart churls in overalls:
> They are the doctors of the wilderness,
> And we the low-prized laymen.
> In sooth, red flannel is a saucy test
> Which few can put on with impunity.
> What make you, master, fumbling at the oar?[6]

VACATIONING HUNTERS DRAWN TO THE ADIRONDACKS, THE FIRST real forest playground for the East Coast's urban middle and upper classes, were often surprised to learn that the hunting guides of Indian heritage were themselves recent arrivals to the mountains. Mohawk, Algonquian, and the Abenaki people of western Vermont had historically visited the area in summer to hunt, fish, and trap, and use its waterways for transport, but few had ever settled here. There were no large native villages, much for the same reason there had been minimal white settlement: the winters were too harsh, the mountains too steep, and the hunting of game and the growing of crops had proved far easier endeavors in nearby lowlands. The result was that when whites began to explore the Adirondacks in the early nineteenth century, they found no substantial Indian population to war against or displace, really few residents at all but for the rare hermit or trapper.

Arguably the first white man to enter the mountains in an official capacity was geologist Ebenezer Emmons, a professor at Williams College and chair of its Department of Natural History, who toured the region in 1836–1837 on behalf of the New York Natural History Survey, in the company of the Indian guide Lewis Elijah Benedict. Emmons's travel reports, issued over a number of years, formed the first recognized advisory regarding the area's virtues—its verdant mountains, clear-water lakes and streams, sizable lake trout, and forests alive with deer, moose, and other big game. In 1837, the professor climbed the highest peak in the region, which he named for William L. Marcy, the governor of New York. It was Emmons who suggested calling the mountains the Adirondacks, claiming it to be the name of an Algonquian tribe, the "Tatirondacks," who had once hunted in the area. The word, of Iroquois origin, literally meant "bark eater," and possibly served as a term of derision for those who were mediocre hunters: who, up against the mountains' unforgiving winters, had no choice but to chew on the skin of trees.[7]

His mission was scientific in purpose, but Emmons wrote and recorded his impressions with the awe common to early-nineteenth-century romanticism—breathtaking mountain vistas, deep gorges,

and thundering waterfalls, wherein the professor found the imma-
nence of a kindly God. "How solemn it is to move all day through
a majestic colonnade of trees and feel that you are in a boundless
cathedral whose organ notes swell and die away with the passing
wind like some grand requiem," he wrote. "God seemed near, there
in the solitude and night, and his voice seemed to be speaking to
me." Articles he published in a New York newspaper brought the
first handful of curious tourists to the area, including Charles Fenno
Hoffman, a literary colleague of Henry William Herbert's. Hoffman, who had lost a leg in a boating accident at age eleven, gam-
boled about the dramatically scenic area near Indian Pass despite
the hindrance of his wooden leg, with the help of Indian guide John
Cheney. He valiantly tried but failed to summit Mount Marcy, but
would not be denied a role as a pathfinder, and once at home published an account of his partial ascent in the *New York Mirror* in
which he insisted that the actual Indian name for the mountain was
Ta-ha-wus, or "cloud-splitter." The source of this information may
well have been Cheney, as there is scant evidence Native Americans
ever called the mountain by that name.[8]

The Reverend Joel T. Headley, who came to hunt several times
in the mid-1840s, contributed the first book about the area, *The
Adirondack, or, Life in the Woods* (1849), which developed an
emerging theme in the region's allure—the idea that nature, and
the Adirondacks in particular, had restorative powers for human
health and well-being. Headley loved to hunt, but he'd also come
seeking a cure for both bronchitis and a bad case of nerves, and in
his memoir reported that he had found in "the song of birds and
chirp of the squirrel," and in the gentle lapping waters and hushed
stands of mountain pine, that "the soul loses its sternness and fierce
excitement, and becomes subdued as a child's!"[9]

As Hoffman had with John Cheney, Headley fell under the
spell of another legendary guide, Mitchell Sabattis. A farmer from
Long Lake who had a German wife and two children, Sabattis
was a renowned hunter who had killed, by his own count, nine
panthers and twenty moose. He was a pure-blood Indian of the
Abenaki tribe; spoke French, English, and two Indian dialects;

and, as his many admirers attested, "told no lies in any of them." Born in 1823, he was the grandson of "Old Peter" (or "Captain Peter") Sabattis, who had fought on the American side in the Revolutionary War and the War of 1812, and who as an elderly man was still seen occasionally paddling his canoe through the watery network of lakes along the Raquette River, accompanied by one of his granddaughters, Mitchell's sister Hannah, who like Peter retained an Indian way of life. Old Peter, whose "knowledge of the woods verged on animal instinct," boasted that he had never slept in a white man's bed.

To Headley, Mitchell Sabattis's careful manner and keen intuition were not merely skillful but bizarre. He could "smell" deer long before they came into view, track animals based on downturned blades of grass, and silently maneuver a canoe into a trout-filled bay. "I never before saw such an exhibition of the stealthy movements of an Indian," Headley recounted.

> The lake was as still and smooth as a polished mirror, and our frail canoe floated over it as if impelled by an invisible hand. I knelt at the bow with my rifle before me, while Mitchell sat in the stern as still as a statue, yet urging the boat on by some strange movement of the paddle, which I tried in vain to comprehend. I could tell we were moving only by marking the shadow of trees we crossed, or the stars we passed over. Though straining every nerve to catch a sound, I never once heard the stroke of his paddle. It was the most mysterious ride I ever took.[10]

White hunters' trust in the local guides was absolute. On faith, visiting Boston clergyman William Murray consented to let his guide "Honest" John Plumley, take them both toward a thunderous waterfall and then down and over its sheer vertical drop, an experience Murray later cited as life-changing. Another guide, Alvah Dunning, was known for his curious utterances and an "ignorance that could not be dispelled," such as his stubborn insistence that the earth was flat. It was the policy of his citified clients to sit mum in

their part of the canoe while Dunning ventilated; no good would
come from contradicting him, and his company was worth tolerat-
ing for his uncanny ability to find game.[11]

ALTHOUGH THE GROUP AT THE PHILOSOPHERS' CAMP WAS SUBSIST-
ing in part on freshly killed venison, Emerson didn't at first share his
cohorts' keen interest in the hunt, nor was he comfortable with the
idea of personally shooting an innocent creature. Certainly this was
not the first time he had pondered the matter, for hunting as sport
had troubled some of its practitioners as early as the seventeenth
century, when Englishman Nicholas Cox worried that men would
be "transported with this pastime, and so ourselves grow wild,
haunting the woods till we resemble the beasts which are citizens of
them"; and Emerson's Concord protégé Henry David Thoreau had
deeply probed and written of the question. A devoted naturalist,
Thoreau acknowledged that hunting was likely an impulse intrinsic
to man, and admired hunters for their closeness to nature, for living
lives touched by that which was savage and wild. He never abandoned his curiosity about the methods of the chase and the behavior
of man and prey, and gladly accepted gifts from Concord hunters
of carcasses that he could dissect and examine. He also could not
resist collecting his neighbors' hunting stories. Yet he grew increasingly ambivalent about the practice's moral implications, writing of
an 1853 moose hunt in Maine, "I went as reporter or chaplain to the
hunters."[12]

Thoreau's philosophical compromise ultimately was to think of
the chase as a stage in a man's development: boy hunters would,
as he had, succumb in time to nature's more understated rewards.
"Such is oftenest the young man's introduction to the forest, and
the most original part of himself," he wrote in *Walden*. "He goes
thither at first as a hunter and fisher, until at last, if he has the seeds
of a better life in him, he distinguishes his proper objects, as a poet
or naturalist it may be, and leaves the gun and fish-pole behind . . .
No humane being, past the thoughtless age of boyhood, will wantonly murder any creature which holds its life by the same tenure
that he does."[13]

The author of these words would have undoubtedly recognized his friend Emerson reclining in Stillman's boat as the artist rowed him to the middle of Follensbee Pond each evening at sunset so Emerson could watch the tops of the pine trees wave in the breeze. Stillman, observing his passenger, caught glimpses of Emerson's upturned face as the poet mentally voyaged on one of his "serene excursions into the upper air." But would Thoreau have known the Emerson who, meditating as the boatman sat on his oars, heard from across the lake the raucous noise of the dogs pursuing a deer, and suddenly exclaimed, "Let us go after the deer!" Wrote Stillman of the moment: "That survival of the earliest passion of the primitive man, the passion of the chase, overcame even the philosophic mind of Emerson, once exposed to the original influences, and he recognized his ancestral bent." When they arrived across the lake, however, they learned that Lowell had already shot the deer.[14]

His interest now aroused, Emerson dedicated himself to the pursuit of the animals, and with the guides' help tried two ordinarily surefire methods—hounding, or having dogs drive deer into bodies of water, where they were easily shot; and jack-lighting, in which hunters at night glide close to the shore, where the deer come to eat the lily pads, and light a torch or a lantern, the glow of which, like "a new-fangled moon," both fascinates and freezes the deer, illuminating their eyes and making them easy targets. "I must kill a deer before we go home," Emerson confided to Stillman, "even if the guide has to hold him by the tail." Both methods were already considered by many to be less than ethical and would be outlawed eventually, but even with these advantages, Emerson failed to kill anything. Two years later, he had not disowned the impulse that had seized him on the lake, endorsing hunting and fishing, along with other recreations, in *Conduct of Life* (1860). "Out upon these scholars," he quipped of his usual Cambridge crowd, "with their pale, sickly etiolated indoor thoughts! Give me the out-of-door thoughts of sound men, thoughts all fresh and blooming."[15]

Stillman later would dismiss Walden Pond, where Thoreau took his famed plunge into nature's solitude, as "the barn-door backwoods in which he acted the recluse . . . a pinchbeck royalty with a lunch-basket from his father's farm hardly hidden behind his throne." By contrast, it was Emerson, the artist insisted, who had at the Philosophers' Camp experienced a truer and deeper connection. So had the others. Agassiz, Lowell, Hoar, et al. were sufficiently taken with the experience to form an Adirondack Club with an intent to buy 22,000 acres to build a retreat that would include the Follensbee site. But the coming of the Civil War soon ended the prospect of annual reunions. Stillman, the project's leader, was appointed consul to Rome by President Lincoln. The others moved on in turbulent times. *The Philosophers' Camp*, the name Stillman gave to a painting he executed of the scene, is the outing's best-known survivor, showing Agassiz and Dr. Wyman dissecting a trout on a tree stump, Emerson standing alone, and others shooting at a target; the image has become, like the event itself, an icon of the era's desire to surrender to nature as both practical and spiritual refreshment. When, a quarter of a century later, Stillman happened to return to the site, he found that "not the slightest feature remained at the grove where wit and wisdom held tournament a generation before. In some Eastern countries," he reflected, "it is the custom to break the bowl from which an honored guest has drunk. Nature has done this service to Follansbee Water."[16]

THE SCENIC AND SPIRITUAL QUALITIES OF THE ADIRONDACK wilderness embraced by the Stillman group, as well as the therapeutic virtues celebrated by Joel T. Headley, would find a new generation of boosters among the hunters, anglers, and health-seeking tourists who began to pour into the region after the Civil War. The movement had its figurehead in the Reverend William H. H. Murray, a Congregationalist minister at Boston's Park Street Church, whose chief message to his congregation (and to the readers of a popular guidebook he produced, *Adventures in the Wilderness; or, Camp-Life in the Adirondacks*), was that for far too long the Adirondacks, a virgin wonderland within easy travel of New York and Boston, had been a well-kept secret. "It is estimated that a thousand lakes, many yet unvisited, lie embedded in this vast forest of pine and hemlock," he wrote enticingly. He held its beauty to be comparable to

Switzerland's, noting that thousands of Americans "are in Europe today as tourists who never gave a passing thought to this marvelous country lying as it were at their very doors."[17]

Murray was a popular figure at Park Street, his voice likened to "the music of deep-toned bells" and his sermons occasionally drawing standing-room crowds. But though he wore a clerical collar, "he was too vigorous and ebullient to be hemmed in by genteel requirements of the pulpit or fussy restrictions on personal conduct," and having made no secret of his great love of hunting, became known as "the shooting pastor" after once arriving at church fresh from a morning's trek with a shotgun under his arm. He wore the appellation with pride, for he identified with a new kind of clergyman, one who placed his faith in "muscular Christianity," which assailed the common perception that men of the cloth were underfed weaklings; they cited Moses and Jesus as examples of "vigorous outdoorsmen," and celebrated a God who was not judgmental and stern regarding humans at play, but who smiled upon their zeal for recreation, fitness, and fresh air.[18]

The concept had been forged in part by two books arrived recently from across the Atlantic—Thomas Hughes's 1857 classic, *Tom Brown's School Days*, which linked manly behavior with faith and portrayed the playing field as the molding press of male character; and Charles Kingsley's 1855 *Westward Ho!* The latter, a historical novel in which the Protestant English challenge the excesses of the Spanish Inquisition, was so popular that a Devon village took the title, including the exclamation mark, as its name. Boston abolitionist Thomas Wentworth Higginson, already known for combining Christian goodness with physical courage in putting his own body on the line to oppose enforcement of the Fugitive Slave Act, proposed in an 1858 *Atlantic Monthly* article a unity of physical and spiritual well-being. As the soul resides in the body, he insisted, sound maintenance of the latter was itself a worthy religious endeavor. In the essay "Saints and Their Bodies," he warned that boys inclined toward the ministry would "wither away like blanched potato-plants in the cellar," while other, more rugged youth, their bodies developed in outdoor work and play, stood

ready to seize life's opportunities. "Go out under pretense of shooting on the marshes or botanizing in the forests," Higginson urged.
"Go to paint a red maple-leaf in autumn . . . meet Nature on the
cricket ground or at the regatta; swim with her, ride with her, run
with her, and she gladly takes you back once more within the horizon of her magic, and your heart of manhood is born again."[19]

Murray, whose regular visits allowed him to know the Adirondacks well, contributed tall tales and regional essays to local newspapers, many with colorful titles, such as "A Ride with a Mad
Horse in a Freight-Car" and "Jack-Shooting in a Foggy Night."
His enticing guidebook, *Adventures in the Wilderness*, appeared
in 1869. Prior to the Civil War, vacations had largely been the pre-
rogative of the well-to-do, who escaped crowded cities in summer;
however, Americans of an emerging middle class (who would never
have felt welcome at Newport or Saratoga Springs) were increasingly able and motivated to effect a getaway. In contrast to the
invigorating experience waiting in Murray's wilderness, the nation's
older resorts, spas, and mountain houses, favored by the affluent,
soon became associated with idleness and tedium.

Going hunting was a splendid recreation—an *exercise* of faith,
the muscular Christians held—but there were also practical benefits, for urban dwellers of the period were plagued by persistent
respiratory ailments caused by buildings' poor ventilation and
the dust of ground manure on city streets. And Murray warned
his congregants that the fast pace of city life itself would make an
individual's nerves "like so many red-hot wires under the skin."
Urban reformers tried to address some of these problems with play-
grounds and swimming piers for children, gymnastics programs
at the YMCA, picnics, and church excursions, but for Murray the
only genuine cure and revitalization lay in complete immersion in
wilderness.[20]

The appeal of the Adirondacks for their ability to ameliorate
respiratory ailments and improve one's overall health would in
time lead to a regional industry of "cure cottages" and sanitariums,
such as the famous clinic at Saranac Lake, where thousands flocked
for "a month's experience among the pines" in hope of ridding

themselves of consumption, dyspepsia, melancholia, or simple ennui. Some hostelries catered to lack of appetite, where, Murray enthused, "The combination of pure mountain air and venison steak was said to cause the most delicate ladies to gain a pound a day." In 1869, physician George M. Beard coined the term *neurasthenia* to describe a deficiency of spunk that left men aimless, indecisive, and fearful. Afflicting primarily "brain workers," such as business and professional men, it was brought on by an overdose of civilization, and was an especial threat to manhood and virility, although the diagnosis was also made of women who suffered from emotional stress or overwork. (William James termed the condition "Americanitis.") The prescription, of course, was a vigorous engagement with nature. "Let us have more hunters and more hunting in America," Fordham University medical professor James J. Walsh, advised, "and we shall have far fewer nervous breakdowns."[21]

If Murray's popular book about hunting, fishing, and enjoying the Adirondacks sinned, in the view of some, it was not necessarily because its descriptions were false or excessive (although there was some of that); it was because as America's first how-to guide to outdoor life it was *far too usable.* Murray had recklessly added a substantial section entitled "The Wilderness: Why I Go There—How I Get There—What I Do There—And What It Costs," enumerating such details as how much to pay a guide ($2.50 a day), the weather and wild animals one could expect to encounter, and what clothes to bring. Worse, it explained all the rail and stagecoach connections involved, and offered extended commentary on hotels, hunting lodges, and even small private guest houses, such as "Mother Johnson's," where "you find such pancakes as are rarely met with."

The book was sold in every emporium, kiosk, and train depot in the Northeast and sped through ten editions in only four months. "Murray's Fools" was what the locals called the armed hordes of citizens who began to ascend the Hudson, staggering from the railroad under the weight of their tents, fishing poles, and newly purchased shotguns, all with Murray's sinister guidebook peeking from their knapsack. Once in place at their campsites, fathers used their store-bought hatchets to chop campfire wood before their proud families, while raucous parties of young city folk swam, sang, and tramped the lanes, scaring most wildlife to higher ground. Some of the resorts became so crowded with aspiring hunters that assigned hunting spots on the lake were chosen by lottery the night before.

Murray's literary star was not burning quite so brightly back at his church on Park Street, however, where his celebrity had begun to stir resentment. As "Adirondack Murray," as he was now known, he had appeared in magazine ads for the region and given well-paid speeches out of town about muscular Christianity and the lure of the woods, which struck some of his congregation as *un*-Christian. Others, who'd taken his advice to go to the Adirondacks for health reasons, were heard to grouch that the lauded balsam and pine vapors had failed them. There was also grumbling that Murray had expressed a willingness to accept Irish immigrants as parishioners. He lost his pulpit at Park Street in 1875 and in 1878 left the ministry.

A quintessentially American character, Murray had the perfect message at the right moment, knew how to pitch it, and took readily to the role of nature's Pied Piper; nor did he neglect the related business opportunities that arose. However, he made the mistake of believing his Midas touch would work elsewhere, and his overconfidence led to some questionable financial decisions and projects that failed to pan out—breeding race horses, opening an oyster restaurant in Montreal, and marketing a new breed of buggy he called the Murray Wagon. It was said he remained good-humored through it all, loved his family, and eventually attained the ultimate (if ironic) glorification available to a nineteenth-century American, appearing as himself in Buffalo Bill's Wild West.[22]

AT THE SAME TIME THE ADIRONDACKS WERE ATTRACTING THE nation's health-seekers, outdoorsmen, muscular Christians, and deer hunters, they were beginning to export something—the aesthetic of the hunt—to Americans and the wider world. Through the efforts of the painter Arthur Fitzwilliam Tait, popularly disseminated as lithographs, the romance and hunting scenes associated with the area's lakes and mountains became some of the most viewed artwork of the nineteenth century. Tait, born in Liverpool in 1819, was the son of a shipping magnate who, due to financial reversals, sent young Arthur to live on a local farm owned by an aunt and uncle. Here the boy developed his lifelong love of animals and the outdoors and, showing skill with a brush, was apprenticed to learn lithography, a newly invented form of reproduction in which an original painting is copied onto a stone treated with lime, from which can be produced numerous quality prints. It was a method ideally suited to the new purposes of advertising, handbills, and home decor created by the Industrial Revolution. Many of his early efforts were lithographs of the youthful British railway system. Trains, introduced in England in 1830, quickly became a source of national pride, and the public, smitten with these twin innovations of affordable decorative art and rail travel, snapped up his and other artists' renderings of locomotives, viaducts, and other railroad tableaux.

Inspired by a traveling exhibit of George Catlin's pictures of American Indians, however, and having concluded that for an artist interested in nature subjects the English countryside offered little to compare with the endless vistas of the New World, Tait began eyeing emigration to the United States. When in 1850 a first cousin, George Danson, a theater scenery painter and part-time designer of fireworks displays, received a commission to stage a simulation of the eruption of Mount Vesuvius in Hoboken, New Jersey, Tait tagged along on the ocean crossing as Danson's assistant. Permission for the simulation was ultimately denied by the authorities, but Tait was now in New York and free to turn to his own work. He was apprehensive that "Americans were indifferent towards art, preferring mirrors," but there proved to be substantial commercial interest in art as decoration, no doubt encouraged by the plentitude of affordable lithographs. Buyers, largely uneducated in classical themes, preferred homespun subjects, lightly sentimental and well painted. Hunting, with its inherent narrative of pursuit and danger and involvement of landscape, animals, and men, was naturally compelling.[23]

There was much precedent for this. Pictures of animals and scenes of the hunt drawn on cave walls were among mankind's first

A hunter and fisherman share their joy at the ample bounty of American game in Arthur Fitzwilliam Tait's *Good Luck All Around*. (Library of Congress)

artistic representations, and while there's some question whether the images depict the animals man hunted or the beasts he feared, the markings speak to a fundamental bond between man, art, and animal. Images joined words in the world's first book on the sport of hunting, the 1387 *Le Livre de la chasse* by Gaston Phoebus (published in England in 1406 by Edward, the second Duke of York, under the title *Master of Game*), a volume of eighty-eight exquisite miniatures of animal prey, hunting dogs, and horses, accompanied by a text that scolds the hunter who would "take his game falsely" through the use of traps and nets. Maximilian I of Austria was the first to insert himself into tales and images of the hunt, producing six vividly illustrated books of his successes afield; these images included, in 1504, the first picture of a gun, or "fire-tube," being used on big game.

Every age has had its dominant masters of hunting art and illustration—from the sixteenth century's Florentine artist Stradanus and genre painter Hans Bol, to the gifted Johann Elias Ridinger, the eighteenth century's finest engraver of horses, hounds, and hunting scenes. Nineteenth-century French realist painter Gustave Courbet hunted when visiting his rural village of Ornans, and executed a number of renowned canvases of *le chasse*—pastoral themes, such as *Thicket of Deer at the Stream of Plaisir-Fountaine*, or more poignant views of the sport's brutality in *The Kill of Deer* or *The Booty (Hunting with Dogs)*.

Artists through the ages, from seventeenth-century Flemish painter Peter Paul Rubens to nineteenth-century American sculptor Augustus Saint-Gaudens, have been inspired by Diana, the Roman goddess of the hunt. Saint-Gaudens's golden sculpture of a lithe Diana aiming her bow and arrow once dominated the skyline of lower Manhattan from atop Madison Square Garden, although the best-known depiction is Titian's sixteenth-century portrayal of the myth of Diana and Actaeon, in which Actaeon, a great hunter, inadvertently surprises the virgin Diana and her nymphs bathing nude in a forest stream. Indignant, she takes away his power of speech so he cannot tell what he's seen, but Actaeon, hearing the call of his hunting party, cannot resist and cries out; Diana, in retribution, turns him into a stag that is devoured by his own hounds.

Edwin Landseer, a British colossus of nineteenth-century hunting art, integrated animal emotion as well as human society of both aristocrat and commoner. He conjured hunting's ritualized nature, the nobility of dogs and horses, and the beauty of fallen prey. The tension between nature's sublime beauty and its injustice and abject brutality runs through much of his work, as in *A Random Shot*, his painting of a fawn attempting to nurse from the body of its dead mother, killed by a reckless hunter. In 1851 he created one of history's best-known and most beloved animal portraits, *The Monarch of the Glen*, an illuminated portrait of a powerful, humanized stag posed triumphantly against the backdrop of the Scottish Highlands. The immense popularity of his prints, and the steady patronage of Queen Victoria, established him and the Highlands as icons of the age, and underscored Britain's legacy as the home of the venery arts.

As early as Stradanus in the sixteenth century, the popularity of
hunting depictions as cheap prints had made them potentially lucrative, and over the centuries hunting art—from Landseer to Tait
to a twentieth-century promotional Smith & Wesson calendar—
has proven one of the most explicit examples of virtuosity slipping
unnoticed into the collective culture through extensive commercial
reproduction. Hunt-related images were ubiquitous in nineteenth-
century America, appearing on whiskey labels, musical scores,
pitchers, plates, and the fabric of boys' pajamas. Sideboards, common in the dining rooms of middle-class homes, were often carved
with elaborate hunting tableaux, a decorative link between the hunt
and the hearth.

Tait's manner of depicting animals was far less anthropomor-
phic than Landseer's, and unlike the works of the master, who was
drawn to melodrama or magnificence, Tait's canvases seem more
like candid snapshots, showing weekend gentleman hunters, sometimes called "shantying New Yorkers," in quotidian settings—
preparing to depart the camp for an early hunt, as in *A Good Time
Coming*, stalking deer, crouching in a duck blind, at repose cleaning their guns, or scenes suggesting an unknown outcome from the
meeting of man and nature, such as a fly fisherman midstream in
*An Anxious Moment: A Three Pounder Sure.*

His work eventually came to the attention of Nathaniel Currier and his brother-in-law James Ives, "printmakers to the American people," who reproduced forty-two Tait paintings between
1852 and 1864. As a trained lithographer himself, Tait could paint
with the medium's limitations in mind; this allowed him to antici-
pate better than other artists how to make his own work most successful in lithographic form. An 1866 painting he executed of baby
chicks became one of the first widely sold color prints, known as
chromo-lithographs, and tested his critics' tolerance for sentimentality. But when some derided him as "the chicken painter from
New York," none other than author Harriet Beecher Stowe came
to his defense, reminding readers that the typical American did not
care for classical art "half as much as [for] one of Tait's pictures
of chickens picking at a worm or some hens in a barnyard, which

Painter and lithographer Frances Flora Bond Palmer, who produced dozens of images for Currier & Ives, including the popular *Partridge Shooting* (1865), was likely the first woman in America to support herself (and her family) as an artist. (Library of Congress)

put him in mind of the pleasant old days, when he was a boy." She expressed impatience with "the scornful style in which some self-important art critics have condemned or ridiculed efforts [like Tait's] that are bringing beauty and pleasure to so many thousand homes that otherwise poverty would keep bare." Affordable copies of Tait prints, advertised in the *Spirit of the Times* and other publications, soon decorated hearths across America and ran in illustrated periodicals.[24]

An equally prolific nature artist of the era was Tait's countrywoman Frances Flora Bond Palmer, considered the first woman to support herself as an artist in America. Fanny, as she was known, and her husband, Edmund, a lithographer, started out producing images of British monuments, churches, farms, and railway viaducts, her efforts hailed by one newspaper for "a boldness and freedom not often exhibited by a female pencil." Coming to the United States in 1844, the couple struggled against more entrenched competition. Edmund opened and operated a tavern in Brooklyn, while Fanny tried her hand at everything from giving singing lessons to serving as a governess. She eventually returned to a career as a commercial illustrator and lithographer, obtaining work with Currier & Ives. Sporting scenes of hunting were a great specialty (Edmund, along with his dogs, served as models), as were trains, tableaux of gardens and rustic homes, and cozy winter images of sleighs and young people skating on ponds. Her best-known work is probably *A Midnight Race on the Mississippi*, a dramatic depiction of the 1854 race between the celebrated steamboats *Natchez* and *Eclipse*.[25]

Edmund, said to have grown overly fond of drink, died in 1859 after falling down a flight of stairs. To support her children, including a son who was sickly and a daughter who was a young widowed mother, Fanny, now the sole breadwinner in the family, increased her efforts for Currier & Ives, ultimately producing 170 lithographic prints, more than any other single artist affiliated with the firm. Such output did not come without risk to her health. From a lifetime of bending over her work she developed a dowager's hump, an outward bending of the upper vertebrae of the back, before dying of tuberculosis in 1876.

While some Currier & Ives artists, such as Tait, enjoyed independent artistic reputations, Palmer, alone of her sex in an industry in which largely anonymous artists created corporate artworks intended chiefly to be ornamental, long remained an obscure figure despite her extensive body of work. As one recent chronicle of the Currier & Ives era concludes, "It is likely that during the latter half of the nineteenth century more pictures by Mrs. Fanny Palmer decorated the homes of ordinary Americans than those of any other artist, living or dead."[26]

American interest in hunting was thus reinforced from its earliest stages by both the talents of such fine arts painters as Catlin, Tait, William Ranney, Alfred Jacob Miller, and others, but also by widely available, inexpensive generic prints and other commercial representations. The hunt's suggestion of the bounty and sustenance of the natural world, as well as the vivid drama of human and animal struggle and the sporting thrill of danger and predicament, led to its becoming enshrined as a popular visual decorative motif, at once evocative of the world's mysteries yet reassuring of man's dominance.

*Chapter Four*

# Hunters Go West

AMERICAN SPORTSMEN WHO CAUGHT THE HUNTING BUG IN THE Adirondacks had considerably less access in the years before the Civil War to the Great Plains and Rocky Mountain West. The distances involved were formidable, as would be the provisioning of any such adventure and the potential risks of encountering hostile native tribes. The allure was great, however, as the frontier held not only larger and more challenging big game but the rewards of venturing into areas few whites other than trappers and mountain men had seen, let alone hunted. With the rapid expansion of railroads, the growth of settlements, and the suppression of the Indians, the West in the thirty years following the Civil War would receive a substantial number of sporting tourists from back east, loaded with guns, gear, and expectations of buffalo, elk, and other big game. As the region became a theatrical reflection of itself, these visitors were often met at railheads by all manner of "expert" hunting guides, many with the inevitable names "Buckskin Louie," "the Remington Kid," or "Half-a-Horse" Jones. Some were for real; all promised good hunting.

But that was all in the future. At first, beginning in the 1830s, those who braved the frontier for sport were often writers and artists, intrepid lone adventurers, or wealthy men of means. Their experiences, when turned into books, artworks, articles, or passed-along narratives, worked powerfully on the imaginations of those who would follow in their wake.

One of the first vivid accounts came from the pen of Washington Irving, America's greatest living author, whose tales were often set in New York City or the Hudson Valley. The highly regarded Irving had only recently returned after having lived in Europe for seventeen years. Not only would the story of his journey west be among the first written by an American, but readers were eager to know what the author of the famous *Rip Van Winkle* and other well-loved tales would have to say about his growing young country after so long an absence, especially the western plains, as they were considered by all the site of future national expansion. His *Tour on the Prairies* (1832), one of three books he wrote about the frontier, was widely anticipated well before its publication.

Set in Oklahoma Territory, which Irving traversed with a detachment of US troops and other dignitaries in fall 1832, the book shares the impressions of a New York gentleman abashed at the limitless beauty of the open plains and the rigorous experience of subsisting on wild game. Chronicling his own transformation, Irving writes that "man is naturally an animal of prey, and, however changed by civilization, will readily relapse into his instinct for destruction . . . I found my ravenous and sanguinary propensities daily growing stronger upon the prairies." Charmed by campfire stories of bear hunts and the sight of grizzly claws worn as ornaments by Indian hunters, a "trophy more honorable than a human scalp," Irving succumbs to the joyful authenticity of roughhewn men taking sustenance from the land and marvels at how it sends "youthful blood into a flow." Watching the accompanying soldiers thrive on the exertions of the chase, he rues that "we send our youth abroad to grow luxurious and effeminate in Europe," when a "tour on the prairies would be more likely to produce the manliness, simplicity, and self-dependence most in unison with our political institutions."[1]

The first buffalo he pursues has "an aspect the most diabolical," with "eyes [that] glow like coals . . . a perfect picture of mingled rage and terror." Irving manages to kill it by riding alongside and shooting the animal with a pistol at close range, but within moments he is crouching next to and pondering with sudden regret a creature, now dying in the grass, that a minute before, as it raced away, had been so magnificently alive.

> I am nothing of a sportsman: I had been prompted to this unwonted exploit by the magnitude of the game and the excitement of an adventurous chase. Now that the excitement was over, I could not but look with compunction upon the poor animal that lay struggling and bleeding at my feet. His very size and importance, which had before inspired me with eagerness, now increased my compunction. It seemed as if I had inflicted pain in proportion to the bulk of my victim, and as if there were a hundred-fold greater waste of life than there would have been in the destruction of an animal of inferior size.[2]

Contrition may have helped spoil Irving's appetite when he attempted to savor his first meal of buffalo soup and buffalo flank, for "the soup was peppered most horribly, and the roast beef proved the bull to have been one of the patriarchs of the prairies: never did I have to deal with a tougher morsel."[3]

His own taste for hunting dimmed somewhat by his experience killing a buffalo at close quarters, Irving begins to express hesitation about the sport, and when the entourage stops to pursue a band of wild horses, he chooses not to try his hand with a lariat; rather, he watches in admiration the spectacle of such magnificent animals roaming free. "As I was slowly ascending a hill, a fine black mare came prancing round the summit and was close to me before she was aware. At sight of me she started back; then, turning, swept at full speed down into the valley and up the opposite hill, with flowing mane and tail and action free as air. I gazed after her as long as she was in sight, and breathed a wish that so glorious an animal might never come under the degrading thralldom of whip and curb, but remain a free rover of the prairies." Regrettably, other horses have been captured, and it grieves Irving to see how, once placed in harness, they quickly adapt to life as man-serving beasts.[4]

The tour teaches him to view with similar regret the impending white incursion into and settlement of these plains. Savoring the land's yet unspoiled virtue, he conspires to remain for a few extra moments at their campsite each morning after the outfit has breakfasted and saddled up to begin that day's march. "I loitered in the rear of the troop," he explains, "disposed to linger until the last straggler disappeared among the trees, and the distant note of the bugle died upon the ear . . . that I might behold the wilderness relapsing into silence and solitude."[5]

Another influential memoirist/hunter of the period, whose background could not have differed more from Irving's, was Frederick Gerstaecker, the son of itinerant opera singers, who arrived in New York in 1837. Unusually a German immigrant who had come not to buy land, farm, settle, or pursue a trade, Gerstaecker was intent on adventure and large game. During a four-year odyssey of tramping through much of New York State, Ohio, and ultimately Texas, Arkansas, and Louisiana, his diary his sole companion, he recorded his impressions of the chase, the American landscape, its wildlife, and many of its raffish human citizens. In lieu of maintaining a regular correspondence with his mother back home, he occasionally sent pages torn from the diary. Later gathered and edited, they appeared in 1845 as *Wild Sports in the Far West*, one of the most intimate and compelling accounts ever published of a hunter's life in the United States.

Gerstaecker was thrilled by the New World—where "roasted pigeons flew into men's mouths" and the train from Albany to Utica cut "the air with the speed of an arrow." Having none of Irving's reserve about the taking of wild animals, even relishing the close contact with prey, he wrestled bears and slayed them with a knife, even crawling on hands and knees to roust them in their hibernating caves. Living off the land, at times near starvation, he was often reliant on his next kill for food, once reluctantly shooting a tiny fawn that naively ran to him in wide-eyed curiosity because "hunger was not to be cajoled."[6]

Grotesque forms of death seem to shadow him. In one narrow cave, he sees petrified footprints of animals that had for millennia used the confines for shelter, and a few chambers farther on is horrified to come upon the skeletons of a man and a bear, lying within 3 feet of each other—"an Indian," Gerstaecker concludes, "who had bravely attacked the bear single-handed, and had fallen in the struggle, the skeleton of the bear proving that he had sold his life dearly."[7]

Traveling the backwoods of the South, he is shocked to see more Indian remains strewn liberally about. At first he is bewildered by their presence, until he learns that he is passing along the Trail of Tears,

> a part of the route by which some years ago a numerous body of eastern Indians, having given up their lands to the United States on condition of receiving equally good lands in the West, were conducted by the parties who had engaged to provide for them on their journey. Many a warrior and squaw died on the road from exhaustion . . . and their relations and friends could do no more for them than fold them in their blankets, and cover them with boughs and bushes, to keep off the vultures, which followed their route by thousands, and soared over their heads; for their drivers would not give them time to dig a grave and bury their dead.[8]

The potential to find ignominious doom in the American backwoods becomes far more personal when, while hunting with a companion, an Englishman named Erskine, they corner a fierce bear that slashes at their hunting dogs with its massive, talonlike claws. Unable to get a clear shot, Erskine hurls down his rifle and rushes in with his knife, stabbing the bear deeply in the side and bloodying him. But in pain the bear strikes one final time, and in a moment both man and bear lie dead. Having heard the commotion, friendly Indians hasten to the spot and use their tomahawks to dig the human victim a shallow grave. "I could not avoid a shudder at the quiet coolness of the whole proceeding," Gerstaecker wrote, "as the thought struck me, that the same persons, under the same circumstances, would have treated me in the same cool way, had I fallen instead of Erskine. Like me, he was a lonely stranger in a foreign land, having left England some years before, and his friends and relations will probably never know what has become of him. Thousands perish in this way in America, of whom nothing more is heard."[9]

WITH HIS GUN, RUCKSACK, AND VAGABOND WAYS, GERSTAECKER was something of an anomaly. Most of his fellow European hunter-adventurers who surfaced in New Orleans, Omaha, or Council Bluffs in the early nineteenth century were gentlemen who'd crossed the ocean seeking the personal testing and adventure only the New World could proffer—grizzlies, wildcats, the thrill of an Indian buffalo hunt—but unlike him, were relatively well outfitted. Gentry of middling rank in Britain found they could comport themselves as absolute lords in the primitive economy of the barely settled West, and frequently traveled with many of the comforts of home (in at least one instance, a full-size bathtub), as well as a retinue of naturalists, taxidermists, and weapons handlers. There would be many such characters . . . too many, in the view of some Americans.

Easily the most flamboyant was William Drummond Stewart, a Scottish noble who had served as an officer in the Napoleonic Wars. Grown bored with life in fashionable London, and eager to put behind him an entanglement with a neighbor's servant that had inconveniently produced a son, he arrived in Saint Louis in 1832. There he gained an audience with William Clark, one of the leaders of the Lewis and Clark Expedition of 1804–1806, now a superintendent at the new US Bureau for Indian Affairs and the city's most well-known citizen. He also befriended William Ashley of the Rocky Mountain Fur Company, who in 1824–25 had originated the custom of the fur trappers' mountain rendezvous. Each summer for a fortnight in the lush Green River Valley of western Wyoming, this combination swap meet/bacchanal brought together trappers, mountain men, and Indians to bet on horse races and feats of strength, arrange marriages (of short or long duration), talk shop, and barter goods. After talking with Clark and Ashley, Stewart decided to structure his hunting expedition around a visit to the Rocky Mountains and the 1833 rendezvous.

The star of the "rondy," as the meet-ups were known, was the mountain man, the quintessential western outcast, who lived a free, filthy, exultant life trapping and hunting, alone with his mule and musket, under the open sky. "To some of the children of cities it may seem strange, that men with no object in view should continue to follow a life of such hardship and desperate adventure," Francis Parkman wrote by way of explanation, "yet there is a mysterious, resistless charm in the basilisk eye of danger, and few men perhaps remain long in that wild region without learning to love peril for its own sake, and to laugh carelessly in the face of death." One priority for the long-distance hunters and trappers at the rondy was to stock up on handy items to go in one's "possibles bag," anything from a sharpening stone to a flint or a yard of cloth, anything that one might possibly need to survive the winter. There would also be the selling of furs and peltries and the trading of gewgaws and foofaraw, ornamental trinkets that had high status value as gifts on the frontier because they were machine manufactured. Most important, a full year's worth of visiting, gossip, and the settling of scores—what passed for mountain society—would be consumed in the space of ten or fourteen days. So popular and essential were these yearly events, anyone who failed to show up was assumed to have "gone under" (died) or "lost his hair" (been murdered and scalped by Indians).[10]

In the 1830s, it was understood that a trip as Stewart contemplated into the western interior, with its vast emptiness, hostile indigenes, and wild animals, would be a momentous experience—life-changing, at least, life-ending if one was incautious or unlucky. Yet it had everything to offer in its abundant big game, jaw-dropping scenery, and the unlimited freedom to choose one's own path, a singular adventure set in what the world had come to think of as a hunter's paradise. For Stewart, who had fathered an illegitimate son but was homosexual, it represented something more: a flight from stifling repression. Although in Europe laws against sodomy were becoming less strict, England remained in the grip of what can only be characterized as homophobic hysteria, with punishments so severe they did not exclude death on the gallows. Stewart, like many elites of his day, idolized Lord Byron, the fearless aesthete who had found sexual and emotional freedom (as well as escape from his creditors) by getting far away from the strictures of Regency England. Per Byron's example, Stewart had sought the mystery of the Ottoman Empire and known the pleasures of the seraglio; but the American West held the prospect of excellent big game hunting, and also, in ways more important for Stewart, liberation.

"Any man who headed west knew that months or even years might pass before he saw a white woman again," Stewart biographer William Benemann observes, "and while many of those men entered into relationships with Native American women that lasted a few minutes or many years, others formed emotional and physical relationships only with other men—white, Indian, and Metis," the latter the mixed-race children of French voyageurs and Native American women. The braves of the Crow Nation, whom the French called *beaux hommes*, were especially known for their striking good looks; an opinion easy to confirm, given their propensity for going about bare-chested and with little wardrobe beyond a loin cloth and buckskin leggings slit down the sides.[11]

The *berdache*—which had originated as an Arab term (*bardaj*) to denote a kept boy or male prostitute—became in the argot of the early French visitors *bardashe*, Native American males who exhibited numerous types of gender-variant behaviors and dress, and who had been encountered in North, South, and Central America since the 1600s. "When they crossed the Mississippi," writes Benemann, "men who had been reared in communities that taught them that sodomy was the most grievous of unpardonable sins encountered Native American cultures in which homosexuality in the phenomenon of the *berdache* was not just permitted but ritualized. The

American West for these men became the land of the special dispensation, and many who journeyed there discovered a prelapsarian paradise, an Eden filled only with Adams."[12]

Stewart was to commence the most significant relationship of his life at the 1833 rendezvous, where he was introduced to the youthful Metis hunter Antoine Clement. Born of a Cree mother and an Irish Canadian father, he was a stunning composite—a blue-eyed Indian with a muscular build, delicate nose, and long reddish-brown hair. Western artist Alfred Jacob Miller, who painted numerous images of Clement and Stewart together, referred to him as "that wild child of the Prairie." Antoine's skill as a hunter was so nuanced he could graze a bullet off a buffalo's skull just enough to stun the animal so that it would stand perfectly still for several minutes, allowing Miller to move in close to complete a sketch.[13]

Stewart and Clement were a complementary match—a lean, handsome European sophisticate and a buckskin-clad man of nature. But unlike many privileged nabobs of the chase who came west, Stewart rarely held himself aloof. He accepted the physical deprivations of life on the frontier and the numerous threats posed by animal and man, making it a point to hunt, climb, shoot, and ride in the toughest of circumstances and with the roughest company. He allowed the environment and the rough society of the mountain men to remake him, as Benemann observes; for Stewart, it seemed "that everything that had come before—his privileged childhood in Perthshire, his venturous adolescence in the Fifteenth King's Hussars, his debauched manhood in smoky London gaming rooms—all that had died in the Rockies."[14]

Miller, a Baltimore native, had moved in 1836 to New Orleans better to make do with his meager income. His meeting with Stewart in spring 1837 was fortuitous. Captivated by one of the artist's paintings he saw in a shop window, Stewart sought him out, saying, "I like the management of that picture and the view," and then offered to bring Miller along on an upcoming expedition to a rendezvous. Miller never fully shared his patron's love of trail life, but he recognized its significant artistic potential, and he, too, was smitten by the lush Green River Valley's soft natural light and the layered 100-mile vistas of sagebrush prairie, brown hills, and distant snow-capped peaks. The prolific Miller would make his name painting the superb artistic subjects of the fabled rendezvous, held amid serpentine rivers meandering through fertile valleys and peopled with the abundant pageantry of frontier and native hunting cultures. He drew buffalo hunts, camp life, and mountain men and Indians at rest, in a muted, intimate style, not dissimilar from the work of his contemporaries George Catlin, who spent eight years in the West in the 1830s, and Karl Bodmer, who accompanied the naturalist Prince Maximilian of Wied-Neuwied up the Missouri River to its headwaters in 1833. Miller's work has an intimate, languid quality; his *Return from Hunting*, *Roasting the Hump Rib*, and *Sir William Drummond Stewart Meeting Indian Chief* are convincing as scenes of everyday life sketched as they occurred.[15]

Like Washington Irving, historian Francis Parkman, and other whites who ventured west in the 1830s and 1840s, Miller understood that his efforts were of anthropological importance, that he was seeing and recording a fading world. The ways of the great nomadic hunting tribes, as well as the fur- and peltry-based economy of the mountain men, were in the preliminary stages of collapse, doomed by the coming onslaught of white settlement. His art expresses well the situation's poignancy and the singular beauty of the region and its inhabitants.

In 1839, Stewart's older brother died, making him a baronet and requiring him to return to Scotland to secure his holdings. He sailed home from New Orleans with a menagerie of western animals, including several buffalo, to the delight of the newly crowned Queen Victoria. Her and Prince Albert's interest in the Scottish Highlands helped pique the fashion for English sportsmen to go there hunting, and Stewart shrewdly had a hunting lodge erected on his property to rent to affluent holiday shooters. A small group of Indians, including Antoine Clement, had also made the journey with Stewart. To provide sufficient cover for Clement's presence in his household, Stewart appointed him his valet, although, predictably, "the wild child of the prairie" soon tired of the pretense; he disliked wearing kilts and bristled at the requirement that he appear servile to his lover. According to Miller, Clement did on occasion, possibly at Stewart's bidding, dress in an elaborate chief's outfit, delighting and frightening household visitors and chambermaids. The local gentry seem to have been successfully kept in the dark about Stewart's lifestyle arrangements, but voices of concern and disapproval were raised when Antoine and some of the other Indians brawled in a village pub. Eventually, Stewart decided that his partner needed to go home, and that his own familial obligations in Scotland had kept him from his beloved Rockies for long enough. Selling off one of the family properties to raise quick cash, he began planning a spectacular return to America, and to the mountain rendezvous, for 1843.

The mountain man event had waned in recent years, as changing fashions in men's clothing back east—largely a switch from beaver hats to ones made of silk—diminished the demand for beaver pelts. The last and most recent rondy had taken place in 1840, and the tradition seemed set to disappear, but for Stewart's determination to revive it one final time. The result was what historian Bernard DeVoto has called the West's "first dude expedition, with staggering luxuries, a handful of rich American bloods as paying guests, full newspaper publicity—the grand style ornate."[16] William Sublette, who helped Stewart plan the adventure, described it more prosaically as "Some of the armey, Some professional Gentlemen, Come on the trip for pleasure, Some for Health . . . doctors, Lawyers, botanists, Bugg ketchers, Hunters and men of nearly all professions."[17] Jefferson Clark, the son of explorer William Clark, and Clark Kennerly, the explorer's nephew, tagged along, as did Jean-Baptiste Charbonneau, son of the legendary Sacagawea, the young Snake woman who had guided Lewis and Clark to the Pacific. Because Miller could not make the journey, Stewart invited bird naturalist and artist John James Audubon to come in his stead; but after initially expressing interest, Audubon withdrew, possibly because he grew to suspect natural science might be the least of the outing's priorities.

Whatever Audubon and others thought or imagined about Stewart's collection of buckskin dudes, the 1843 Stewart-led

rendezvous—two weeks of fishing, hunting, trading, and horse racing, joined by trappers and a group of Snake Indians at a pristine
glacial lake near present-day Pinedale, Wyoming—proved an outstanding good time. There was plenty of bear and buffalo hunting,
gambling and games of chance (to which the natives were devoted),
and feasting on brisket of venison and fresh buffalo hump roasted
over a prairie hearth. Stewart had spared nothing and seemed
eager to be conspicuous, having managed to bring along an enormous crimson tent, a rubber dinghy, and a Scottish servant named
Corbie, as well as a friction machine, the kind of device Benjamin
Franklin had once used to make his discoveries in electricity. While
his teamsters probably questioned Stewart's lugging such a device
across country, it proved its worth many times over when an impol-
itic situation arose between Stewart and a tribe of Brule Sioux. A
delegation of armed, unsmiling Brule had ridden into Stewart's
camp, upset because they believed his entourage was to have honored their village by coming for supper; the whites' nonappearance
was a huge show of disrespect. Stewart was able to defuse the situation after offering to show the Brule the great magic of the elec-
trical machine. Eventually they seemed to forget the broken dinner
invitation, exulting that "the dose of lightning was great medicine."
Stewart and his relieved colleagues could only agree it was that.[18]

Stewart's dude hunting expeditions; Miller's paintings; books
by Washington Irving, Francis Parkman, and Frederick Gerstaecker—all were harbingers of the coming white appropriation of
the West, a massive transformation that was geopolitical, military,
social, and cultural. The region's peoples, and certainly its most significant protagonists, from Wild Bill Hickok to General Custer to
Buffalo Bill Cody and Sitting Bull, would be overtaken by the swiftness of this change. Many would live simultaneously in two worlds,
experiencing hardship and danger in the rugged West while serving a parallel existence as performers enacting their own real-life
heroics—in Hickok's and Cody's examples literally on the stage;
in Custer's, as a public emissary of the Indian Wars and the western big game hunt. It was a weird consciousness, which in some
manifestations (such as Indian warriors playing Indian warriors in

Bowery theaters) could begin to seem quite surreal. Hunting would prove a unifying theme across the decades, in ways both good and bad; it linked the Plains hunting tradition of the natives to the subsistence needs of the early settlers and railroad crews, and the sporting interests of intrepid visitors seeking big game. Disgracefully, however, beginning in the 1870s, it opened the West to the legions of market hunters who sought neither sport nor sustenance but rather hides and money, and who would so decimate western wildlife their efforts came to be perceived as not only a threat to the survival of the American buffalo, but part of an unofficial US policy of Indian genocide.

*Chapter Five*

# Forest and Stream

IN SPRING 1874, A GROUP OF YOUNG GENTLEMEN WERE SEEN WALK-ing very fast together in New York City's Central Park. Their embrace of strenuous physical activity, it was reported, had been necessitated by the stifling sameness of the workaday world. "They now declare that walking a mile in nine or ten minutes is a delightful excitement, when a month or so ago a lounging gait across the street was declared by them to be 'a horrid bore,'" a news item explained, "and they are not only surprised but delighted to find what an amount of 'go' was in them." The gents' example offered hope that the "increased morbidity of disposition, the result of mental exhaustion so common, possibly brought on from our commercial application, will in athletic exercises find its cure." It also bespoke more generally the growing interest in outdoor sports culture that flourished in the generation following the Civil War. While backroom amusements of the urban demimonde, such as cockfighting, dogfights, and ratting contests, did not disappear, they were increasingly seen with disfavor by newspapers and called out by reformers as debased blood sport, associated with wagering and intemperance. Newly popular recreations, including swimming, hunting, rowing, and hiking, as well as organized team sports, offered by contrast bracing physical activity. There were also newsworthy participatory competitions, such as the America's Cup Race, founded in 1851. The following year, intercollegiate sports was inaugurated when Harvard and Yale held a rowing match. Baseball's National League formed in 1876; the American League, in 1882. The League of American Wheelmen, a cycling club, was organized in 1880; the U.S. Lawn Tennis Association, in 1881. Walking races, known as pedestrianism, were held in Madison Square Garden, and long-distance challenges, such as walking from Maine to Chicago, were staged. There was burgeoning interest in cricket, canoeing, gymnastics, and archery, while quad-wheel roller skates, invented in 1863 by James Plimpton, became an affordable social activity for the young. By century's end, many towns had built cavernous roller rinks to accommodate the craze.[1]

National sporting journals were not idle, nurturing the growth of sporting clubs and hunting societies across the country with such names as the Hound Dog Club or North Trail Rod & Gun, or at the high end, New England's Myopia Hunt Club, established in 1882. One hundred such organizations had formed in 1874–1875, and by 1878, the number had tripled. Two were named for John James Audubon; five, for Frank Forester; two, for Charles Hallock, editor of *Forest and Stream*, the newest and most popular sports sheet; and eight, for *Forest and Stream* itself. They fostered enthusiasm for sport hunting along with a respect for prey animals and wilderness; some clubs were already cautioning members about the overconsumption of wildlife.[2]

For those unable to escape the confines of the city, several new institutions offered wholesome environs and physical sport. The Young Men's Christian Association (YMCA), founded in England in 1844 and organized in the United States in 1851, offered gymnasiums for physical exercise, lectures, socials, and other activities designed to divert young unmarried men from the lures and snares of urban life. The "Y" idea spread to most major cities, and by the early 1890s there were 261 YMCAs; at one such facility in Springfield, Massachusetts, a physical education instructor named James

Naismith introduced the game of basketball. A related development was the liberal German physical fitness movement, the Turner clubs, imported to America after Germany's failed Revolution of 1848. Convening at local *Turnvereinen* (athletic clubs), these organizations emphasized athletic conditioning, as well as social, political, and cultural activities, based on their motto: *"Mens sana in corpore sano"* ("A sound mind in a sound body"). By 1894, there were 317 Turner societies in America totaling some forty thousand members, as well as a large number of German-American *Schützengesellschaften* (shooting clubs), whose members ferried to the New Jersey Palisades or other suburban precincts on weekends for marksmanship contests and picnicking.

It was an era of *joining*, the sporting organizations paralleling a similar interest in fraternal lodges, seventy thousand of which, totaling 5.5 million members, were registered by 1897. Among these were the Odd Fellows, the Improved Order of Red Men, the Ancient Order of Hibernians, the Loyal Order of the Moose, and the Benevolent Protective Order of Elks, as well as elite ventures such as Boston's Somerset Club, Chicago's Bohemian Gymnastic Society, and Philadelphia's Rittenhouse Club. The lodge idea had emerged in part from the Civil War's harsh lessons about family loss and vulnerability as a result of sickness and death. In lieu of a government safety net, many lodges offered health and death benefits to members; but they also revived the collegial all-male intimacy of army rituals and ranks, pomp, and costume that had disappeared at the end of the war. Not surprisingly, many groups took the form of militias or rifle clubs, with plumes and swords, sashes and rituals, and such names as Hartford's Putnam Phalanx and San Francisco's California Wing Shooting Club. Training with guns, rifle sports, and hunting excursions fit naturally into military tradition and martial exercise. The fundamentals of hunting live game, such as "glassing" a large meadow with binoculars, moving stealthily through dense woods, seeking an evasive "foe," bore obvious similarities to war.

Hunting, through the boosterish coverage by *Forest and Stream*, *Outing*, the *American Sportsman*, and the daily press, as well as

advertisements enticing enthusiasts to the Adirondacks and other
regional hunting grounds, soon took hold as one of the country's
more alluring pastimes. It was, as Herbert, Murray, and others had
urged, an ideal alternative to the drone of office and factory work
and the pressures of urban life, as well an escape from the femi-
nized household. In addition to its virtues as a balm for body and
soul, hunting offered a link to the nation's rigorous heritage. "The
masculine ruggedness displayed so heroically at Valley Forge, the
Alamo, and Gettysburg had somehow been eroded by the combined
forces of urbanization, over-civilization, and . . . (the) notion that
woman had achieved a questionable hegemony in white, bourgeois
culture," notes historian Philip Terrie. "Americans feared that their
young men were becoming effete, refined, and delicate." To those
young men's ears, Herbert's words now had the rousing effect of
sustained blasts from a hunting horn. Ashamed at how badly they'd
lapsed, they hastily slung away pipes and slippers and other accou-
trements of ease and, heavily armed, decamped for the wilderness.[3]

There was a boyish exhilaration in donning buckskins and
sleeping rough, the rail or steamboat trip to the forest or hunting
trailhead undertaken with male friends and animated by cigars,
whiskey, and talk; the warmed-over hunting tales swapped and the
merits of various dogs and rifles debated, and the collective relief
and even a laugh at the city's less fortunate citizens left behind,
"probably now half stewed, fried and wasted, blinded with dust and
dirt, and breathing an atmosphere impregnated with the fumes of
putrefying garbage."[4]

Once he was outfitted and turned loose in the wilds, much was
expected of the gentleman hunter's ethics and bearing. His sport,
after all, was conducted largely in private, in isolated woods and
glens far from the gaze of others. This meant that while a flask was
acceptable to ward off the effects of rain and cold (Frank Forester
recommended it), the sportsman was not by his behavior to contrib-
ute in any way to the occasionally whispered suspicion that hunters were simply "carousing topers whose chief aim in seeking the
field or stream is to enjoy a drinking bout with their companions."
Nor were frustration or impatience in finding game or reckless

shooting to spoil the mood. True sportsmanship, *Forest and Stream* reminded readers, "is not in the inevitable certainty of success—for certainty destroys the excitement, which is the soul of sport, but it is in the vigor, technique, and manhood displayed, in the style, the dash, the handsome way of doing what is to be done, and above all, in the unalterable *love of fair play*."[5]

THE ADVENT OF *FOREST AND STREAM* AND OTHER SPORTING PUBLICAtions owed a roundabout debt to the original living emblem of recreational sport in America, its first national celebrity, boxer John L. Sullivan. "His Fistic Holiness" had emerged from bare-knuckle fighting to help usher in the modern era of professional prizefighting, becoming the first American heavyweight champion in 1882. A man who knew how to give the sporting press good copy (he was said to have coined the expression "The bigger they come, the harder they fall"), Sullivan took a much-publicized nationwide tour in 1883–1884 in which, over the course of 250 stops, he challenged local amateurs to face him and offered a cash prize to anyone who could last four rounds. He did not lose a single fight, often dispatching opponents within seconds. "I never thought any man could hit as hard as he does," remarked one James McCoy of McKeesport, Pennsylvania. "But I can say what few men can: that I fought with the champion of the world." Enrollment in America's neighborhood boxing gyms blossomed during his reign.

Sullivan was among the first pugilists to train on a punching bag (invented by a boxing instructor at the New York Athletic Club, reusing a leather football), and adopt both the use of boxing gloves and the Marquis of Queensberry rules, which outlawed gouging, hugging, and wrestling. While his rugged masculinity appealed to a nation concerned about modern comforts' sapping the strength of its men, Sullivan's well-known love of drink and his fierce Irish American loyalty—he went out of his way to visit mining towns where Irish laborers were employed, and once refused to toast the health of Queen Victoria—provided an added pinch of character. He surrendered the heavyweight championship in 1892 to "Gentleman" Jim Corbett, the only loss of his career, but his legend was enduring enough that former president Theodore Roosevelt was honored in 1909 to accept a gift of Sullivan's lucky rabbit foot during his departure for an African hunting safari.

Sullivan's fame had been scripted in part by the adoring coverage of the *National Police Gazette*, founded in 1845 with a strong interest in urban crime and outlaws; the publication, in anticipation of later tabloids, such as the *National Enquirer*, amused readers with its decidedly purple prose. One regular column detailing the lives of the lost and desperate was titled "Some of the Wrecks of Humanity Borne Upon its Ensanguined and Turbid Tide Towards the Ocean of Eternity." It was also the unofficial organ of the American boxing scene, giving generous coverage of "the fistic arts" and in-depth portraits of and interviews with its leading stars, particularly Sullivan.

The *Gazette*'s pioneer status is unquestioned, but in retrospect it was a coarse forerunner to the many alternatives that appeared after the Civil War, a new generation of periodicals made possible by lower printing and publishing costs, low postal rates, and the growth of national advertising and subscriptions. The number of magazines published in America zoomed upward from 700 in 1865 to 3,300 in 1885, an expansion that, reflecting hunting's popularity, included an "unquenchable public thirst" for accounts of outdoors adventures, as well as how-to guides for everything from the fundamentals of fly-tying to wild turkey calls. But in terms of style and intelligence, it was a long way from the sensationalism of the *Police Gazette* to the urbane flagship of the sporting press, *Forest and Stream*, founded in 1873 by Charles Hallock.

He was the scion of an old East End, Long Island, family that dated its arrival in America to 1640; one ancestor had been a governor of Nantucket and Martha's Vineyard; several had taken part in the Revolution; and a distant relation, Major General Henry W. Halleck, known derisively as "Old Brains," was General Ulysses S. Grant's chief of staff in the Civil War. Young Charlie, born in 1834, showed an early inclination for the chase. Sent to live on an uncle's farm, he regularly slept outside in a tree house, preferring it to his bedroom indoors, and later, at Hart's Classical School in

Connecticut, was allowed to store his gun in the principal's office. "I was the only student who had the privilege and I frequently brought in a bag of pigeons, partridges and quail," said Hallock. "When the meadows were flooded in the spring I shot muskrats galore from a pungy skiff."[6]

After college, he edited newspapers in New Haven and New York; took hunting trips to the Rockies and to Labrador, the latter of which he described in *Harper's Weekly*; and under the name "Lariat" wrote a series of hunting sketches for the *Spirit of the Times*. He worked for and had a proprietary interest in the New York–based *Journal of Commerce*, although he was ousted from his position in 1861 over "political troubles," likely having to do with his secessionist views. These sentiments emerge in his antebellum hunting pieces from the South, in which whites are depicted as valiant, clear-eyed gentlemen; and slaves, as fawning ignoramuses, good only for driving game out of the woods. "As the chase dogs dart hither and thither in wild excitement," he writes of a hunt for feral cattle on a coastal island, the black beaters, led by "Sambo" and "Picaninny Joe," are threatened with a whipping, scolded for being "a chattering flock of lunatic crows," and instructed to remind "old marm Sallie" to have lunch ready when the hunters return, "for we shall be as hungry as wolves."[7]

In February 1863, at the height of the Civil War, Hallock acted on his Southern sympathies, and headed overland through Virginia to reach the Confederacy. There he assumed the editorship of the *Augusta (GA) Chronicle*, and in the spring, wrote a quickie biography of General Stonewall Jackson, who had died in May from wounds received at the Battle of Chancellorsville. Early July brought major reverses in the Confederacy's fortunes: General Robert E. Lee was turned back in Gettysburg; Vicksburg fell to Grant; and in October, Hallock disappeared, running the Union naval blockade to reach Bermuda, ostensibly to procure paper and other supplies for the *Chronicle*.

Other Southern papers were indignant. "He talked big, cursed the Yankees, drank whisky, and kept up a *good appearance* generally," moaned the *Raleigh Progress*. "We suspected then that he came as a spy, and we are not at all surprised to find our suspicions turn out correct." But from his Caribbean perch, Hallock redoubled his support of the Confederacy, warning in an article in the *Royal Gazette* against the people of the South indulging "even a shade of despondency." The question of whether the South believed or forgave him soon became immaterial with the Confederacy's collapse. In 1866, after three years' exile in Halifax under British protection, he returned to New York upon the death of his father, and by 1868, was back behind an editor's desk at *Harper's Weekly*. In the city throughout the war, there had been a current of Northern, or Copperhead, support for the Confederacy, so while some acquaintances no doubt disapproved of the choices Hallock had made, his example was not unusual; and postwar New York would prove to be a place of business, not lingering sectional rancor.[8]

In founding *Forest and Stream* in 1873, he at last had full control of a publication, one that he could use as a mouthpiece for his own deeply ingrained conservatism and love of field sport. Rarely has there been a new periodical introduced better suited to its moment. Under the steady editorial hand of Hallock and later Yale-trained scientist George Bird Grinnell, *Forest and Stream* would for decades be synonymous with American sport hunting—encouraging the thrill of good sport as well as a respect for etiquette afield; providing technical information about guns, gear, and where to find game; and giving voice and substance to some of the nation's earliest concern for wildlife and forest conservation. In the first issue, published in August, Hallock promised "to inculcate in men and women a love for natural objects, and to cultivate a high moral tone in this department of literature." The magazine would take no interest in the underworld of urban sporting and animal fighting or baiting. "Nothing that is regarded as 'sport' by that low order of beings who in their instincts are but a grade higher than the creatures they train to amuse them, will find place or favor in these columns," he vowed.[9]

*Forest and Stream* would go on to editorialize consistently for adherence to the principles of fairness in hunting: no one was to "shine" or "jack" deer with a bright light, send dogs to chase them into lakes or rivers, or employ the technique of "crusting"—shooting deer when they were immobilized in winter drifts (a scene powerfully rendered by French artist Gustave Courbet in an 1866 canvas *Hind Forced Down in the Snow*). Winged creatures were only to be shot as they flew, never on the ground, and the hunter was not to scatter shot aimlessly into a flock, but always aim at an individual bird. "Hunting disciplined violence by constraining it within a complex, nuanced web of texts, customs, rules, and institutions that defined elite hunters as sportsmen," the scholar Monica Rico writes of the era. This new breed of gentlemen hunters observed legal hunting seasons (as they were established), and scorned market hunters, who slaughtered game in large numbers and sold their pelts, hides, plumage, or meat for commercial gain. "I kill no bird unless it has a chance for its life on the wing, and no four-footed game except in its season of health, and possessed of all the advantages which God has given it for escape," had said James Fennimore Cooper's protagonist Hawkeye, in a succinct expression of what would come to be known as the ethos of fair chase.[10]

What is remarkable about the early issues of *Forest and Stream* is how swiftly Hallock struck an octave between the mystical and the utterly pragmatic, rhapsodizing about God-inspired scenery in one sentence and explaining which shotgun to buy in the next. Within this capacious editorial world thrived numerous affections—for the refined traditions of the British hunt, the flinty American pathfinder, the woodcraft of the Native American, and the history of the hunting arts back to the Middle Ages.

The magazine also admonished the hunter to know natural history, updating the notion of inspired Yankee scientific curiosity that dated to Jefferson's collection of mastodon bones; Franklin's lightning rod; and the backwoods traipsing of naturalist John Bartram and his son, William, whose rapturous *Travels*, an account of exploration set in the Southeast and Florida, became one of the most-read books of the nineteenth century. *Forest and Stream* readers thus learned of albinism across animal species, intelligence in dogs, and the life cycles of conifers. The genius of turning hunters into armchair natural scientists was that it lent gravitas and legitimacy

to the sport while addressing the basic fact that all hunters truly did
need to engage knowledgably with the phenomenal world—wind,
temperature, light conditions, and time of day, as well as the habits
of prey animals.

For *Forest and Stream*, it became an important article of faith
that domestic game laws, which Hallock advocated, were not to
be confused with the restrictive class-oriented British governance
of game and property. He understood that regulations "involved
the difficult task of showing to a republican country the real difference between the aristocratic game laws of olden times, which were
intended for the few grand land owners, and the modern game laws,
which . . . protect and breed game for the reasonable good of all the
people." In furtherance of this objective, Hallock was behind the
creation of the International Association for the Protection of Game
and Fish, which boasted 250 sportsmen and naturalists representing
all the United States and parts of Canada. "Laws for the preservation of wild animals are a product of civilization," observed sportsman Charles Whitehead. "The more civilized a nation, the broader
and more humane will be these laws." However, in an era before
such laws were widespread in America, before the federal government moved to preserve wildlife and habitat, it was often endeavors
by private sportsmen that led the way. Hallock pursued the latter
method as well, helping in 1871 to found the Blooming Grove Park
Association, a 12,000-acre tract in Pike County, Pennsylvania, that
offered a clubhouse, sleeping cottages, and a 1,000-acre deer park
that supported ample populations of animals, fish, and birds for its
hunting members. The leading partner at Blooming Grove, which
also saw some of the first systematic forestry practices in America,
was Fayette S. Giles, a wealthy jeweler who had hunted in Europe
and admired the large protected forests there, such as at Fontaine-
bleau, outside Paris.[11]

Whether their efforts were public or private, sportsmen were
among the first to perceive that collective restraint on the part of
hunters would be required, one of the first inklings of the coming of
the modern conservation movement. As early as October 1873, the
third month of his magazine's publication, Hallock was cautioning

readers about the overharvesting of buffalo and the sinful waste of buffalo meat in the taking of hides. He even aimed his editorial guns at the Reverend William Murray, the man who had introduced him to the Adirondacks—not for the usual alleged "crime" of ruining the mountains with tourism, but for taking fish and game out of season. "Among all true sportsmen," Hallock scolded, "there is a bond of sympathy, one touch of which makes the fraternity akin, and within this charmed circle, Mr. Murray ha(s) not yet been admitted."[12]

AS EARNEST AS WERE THE PUBLICATION'S ENTREATIES ABOUT ACT-ing on the perception of wildlife as a natural resource, its larger message was one of overflowing enthusiasm for sport hunting. Whether one's taste ran to possum, squirrel, magnificent elk in their western grazing lands, or frost-breathing timber wolves at Lake Superior, the continent teemed with prey. Bighorn sheep navigated the heights of the Rockiess, the ghostly panther stalked the swamps of the lower Mississippi; all awaited the intrepid sportsman. One could even go to the Everglades and, from a skiff, shoot alligators.

The sporting press worked to promote the idea of a national hunting fraternity, never failing to keep readers informed about the guides, suppliers, hoteliers, and taxidermists who waited at the remotest boat launch or jumping-off point to enable good sport. All belonged to the family of like-minded souls devoted to the chase. This universe extended to those who had nothing to sell—railroad conductors, coach drivers, deputy sheriffs, and farmers—all of whom stood ready to advise on local hunting conditions, roads, and accommodations. Hallock liked to poke fun at the citified types who took to the woods, calling them "embryo sportsmen in velve-teen and corduroys of approved cut," but it was he who sent them thither.[13]

In 1879, Hallock got into the hunting lodge business himself, creating a Farm Colony for Sportsmen in far northwestern Minne-sota, a place he thought of as a hunter's paradise. He built a hotel there, the Hotel Hallock, and with the assistance of Minneapolis railroad magnate James J. Hill, "the Empire Builder" of the Great Northern, arranged for the construction of a railroad depot. Soon the crossroads hamlet he'd chosen had the look of a small Midwestern town. Hallock promoted his sportsman's Eden as a community where wildlife behaved more like residents than prey. "Bands of elk came within a few miles of town," he wrote. "Once a moose ran directly through the village . . . a black bear came up out of the bottoms to play with the school children at recess; a couple of pet bears were kept on hand for the Swedes to practice boxing on."

Many visitors did score outstanding bags. One party from Pennsylvania claimed two elk, five deer, seven wolves, and seven moose—a remarkable feat, given that the latter is a difficult creature to track and kill. Although Hallock's published encomiums brought many sportsmen to the area, over time the location proved too inconvenient for return visits; the autumns were bitter cold and of short duration, and even the prospect of moose proved an inadequate draw. The end of the venture came when the hotel burned to the ground.[14]

Despite such occasional setbacks, Hallock's vision of this American hunting cornucopia remained upbeat. The Midwest was "fine hunting ground for elk, bears, wild turkey, and partridges"; the South saw "coon and opossum very abundant." On the Pacific coast, "the sturgeon hold high carnival, (and) plenty of accomplished and gentlemanly anglers act as guides, who are *au fait* in all that pertains to rod and gun." In Florida, "for a trifling charge negroes . . . will keep the piscator supplied with bait"; while in Minnesota, "it is entirely within bounds to say ducks can be found by the million." Typical *Forest and Stream* updates on the availability of local game reported, such as one for August 26, 1875:

"New Jersey–Beach Haven, August 23—Willets, marlin, peeps, yellow legs, robin snipe and plover are quite plenty. Last week "Mohawk" and "Homo" made big bags.

"Maryland–Snow Hill, Worcester County, August 21—Birds are plentiful on the beaches, and are being slaughtered in immense quantities.

"Delaware–Kills Hammock, Kent Co., August 24—Young ducks and all the different varieties of beach birds are here in plenty now. Take cars from Philadelphia to Dover, via Delaware Railroad."[15]

Hunting might strike a man as an appealing idea at any time of day, perhaps as he sat gazing dully out his office window; but to act on the impulse and get oneself into the woods with a gun and in a position to track wild game (and to savor all the restorative feelings involved), required buying no shortage of things—a rifle or shotgun, a decent knife, duck decoys, wild turkey lures, waterproof boots, a hammock or camp bed, lanterns, pocket flasks, and much more. A map and a guidebook were essential, if not a list of places one might hire an actual guide. Such items could be had at the many new sporting goods stores that had materialized, most located along Broadway in Lower Manhattan. There was Thomson & Sons; Peck & Snyder; W. Holberton's Complete Outfits; Hanks & Ogilvy; and, on Maiden Lane, Abbey & Imbric. At the art shop Williams, Stevens, and Williams at 353 Broadway, viewers might pause to admire works by Arthur Tait, William Ranney, and others. Remington & Sons at 283 Broadway sold shotguns and pocket revolvers, while Fowler & Fulton at 300 Broadway carried "wading moccasins and rubber stockings, the best thing in the world for snipe shooting in wet meadows." Francis O. de Luze & Co., 18 South William Street, stocked an assortment of dog biscuits.

These emporia were forerunners to the ultimate New York sporting goods store, opened in 1892 at 36 South Street by David Abercrombie. By 1900, the founder had brought in Ezra Fitch, a wealthy customer, as partner. The business thrived but the partners didn't get along, and Abercrombie soon departed, leaving behind only his memorable surname. In 1909, Abercrombie and Fitch issued an opulent 456-page catalog, and by 1913 was calling itself "the Greatest Sporting Goods Store in the World." Four years later, the company took possession of its own twelve-story building at Madison Avenue and Forty-fifth Street, which boasted a golf school (with a resident teaching pro), a rooftop pool where an instructor gave fly-casting lessons, and a basement gun range. The store became an obligatory stop for American big game hunters headed to Africa, to supply one's expedition with bush jackets, pith helmets, bug spray, and other necessities.

Of course, hunting trips weren't all about crouching in the rain, waiting for a turkey or antlered buck to come by. Many hunted in great style, with real dishes and glassware, a liquor cabinet, a rug, and a tent with waterproof flooring, as well as a cook and other servants. The inspiration also flowed in reverse, as hunters brought the look and feel of the woods into the house, with mounted heads, animal rugs, a racked shotgun, hunt motifs carved into furniture, and an innovation soon associated with the American middle-class home—"the den"—a room decorated with a masculine theme and understood to be a kind of private retreat.

Thus, through the articulate voice of *Forest and Stream*, through decorative art, men's weekend habits, and changes to homes' interior design, hunting became more than just a popular diversion. It was a way of life, or more accurately, it became integral to the American way of life, a pastime in rhythm with the seasons, as traditional and familiar from one generation to the next as granddad's double-barrel, connecting us to the delights and rigors of the natural world, assuring us of our manhood, and of life's great promise.

MEN WERE THE PRIMARY ACTORS IN THE BURGEONING OUTDOORS movement, but the appeal of "a sound mind in a sound body" quickly came to include women and children. Given the already visible ill effects of gritty industry and workers' slums on human health and vigor, children were clearly at risk. Like their parents, they were denied the regimen and rhythms of village life, farm chores, extended family, and sunshine and breathable air. The Fresh Air Funds, initiated by the *New York Times* in 1872, arranged summer getaways for kids from homes without means, on the principle that "the evil which must result to the city from allowing so many of its children to grow up in the narrow confines of courts and alleys without ever a day's experience of the health-giving and purifying influences of the country does not need a prophet to predict."[16]

A fair amount of anxiety regarding children's development came from their own parents, who projected onto them the fear of growing up weak and ineffectual in a more frenetic, competitive world. While some continued to insist on a child's strict obedience to authority, there was a developing appreciation among middle-class families, which tended to be smaller, of childhood as a distinct and separate realm, and a fresh emphasis on newly idealized traits—independence, resourcefulness, and a righteous way of conducting oneself in public. Hunting, a highly disciplined sport that challenged young people physically as well as temperamentally while teaching them martial skills, was seen as an ideal way to improve boys' character. This interest was stirred also by advertising and children's literature. Much as a generation of sportsmen had been sent afield by the hunting narratives of Frank Forester, so young readers were nurtured on the frontier adventures of "Captain" Mayne Reid, an Irishman who had arrived in the United States in the 1840s and later became the western world's most prolific and popular author of juvenile adventure stories. He worked in Philadelphia and New York as a journalist, knew (and drank with) Edgar Allan Poe, and enlisted to fight alongside the Americans in Mexico, where he was badly wounded at the Battle of Chapultepec. Convalescing back in London, he wrote plays and began producing well-crafted novels featuring child protagonists and celebrating youthful daring and intrepid curiosity. His best-loved volume was *The Boy Hunters* (1851), a tale of three young brothers—a daring hunter, an aspiring naturalist, and the story's narrator—who, at the behest of their disabled father, a natural scientist, venture into the American frontier in search of a rare white buffalo. The notion of celebrating children as hunters was unique to America—there was no such precedent in Europe—but the book's formula of youth on a cross-country hunting or adventure jaunt set a pattern for a veritable library of children's "buddy" books, culminating in the early twentieth century with the hugely successful Rover Boys series and the adventures of the Bobbsey Twins. At the same time, the ideal of young people, particularly boys, learning to hunt at the side of father or another family elder became entrenched American tradition.[17]

Character-building organizations also emerged to shepherd youth and make them fit to be useful, successful adults. The Boy

*On the Wing,* by artist William Ranney, was an early representation of a celebrated theme in American genre painting, the passing on of a love of hunting from father to son. (Courtesy of the Blanton Museum of Art, University of Texas at Austin)

Scouts of America (BSA) was the most famous of these, but there was a bounty of alternatives, most now long forgotten—the Knights of King Arthur, the Men of Tomorrow, the Epworth League, the Princely Knights of Character Castle, and girls' spin-offs that were forerunners to the Campfire Girls and the Brownies. To "put into a boy's hands a gun, rifle, or rod" was a frequently cited goal. Commentators both in print and in the pulpit, such as the Reverend William Forbush, promoted a rustic setting as the "place where the boy will develop" necessary "savage virtues," while one boys' camp in Pennsylvania promised to take "pale, petted and pampered objects of maternal solicitude" and turn them into outdoorsmen, "bronzed and ruddy with insatiable appetites." R. M. Ballantyne, the author of *The Gorilla Hunters* (1861), a juvenile literary favorite in the style of Mayne Reid, took the man-building program a step further by recommending that boys be "inured from childhood to trifling risks and slight dangers [and] ought never to decline to climb up a tree to pull fruit merely because there is a possibility of their falling off and breaking their necks."[18]

For somewhat different reasons, the hunt was also actively promoted to women, not only for their own enjoyment but because their presence helped define sport hunting as a respectable, even refined calling for gentlemen. The involvement of "white, upper-class women hunters," as historian Eric Mogren writes, served to "distinguish recreational hunting from lower-class market and subsistence hunting, demonstrate its legitimacy as a suitable pastime for social elites, distance it from other lowbrow amusements, and generally lend sport hunting a veneer of Victorian civility, sportsmanship, and restraint."[19]

Many of the sporting journals ran regular "ladies" columns encouraging the active outdoor life for "the fairer sex" and hailing female athletic accomplishments of note. A notable example was the *Harper's Weekly* cover of August 25, 1883, which featured a fashionably dressed woman, identified as "Miss Diana" (an allusion to the Roman goddess of the hunt), lowering her shotgun after having fired across a forest stream at a large antlered buck. "The young lady who made the successful shot, and thus killed her first deer, is well known in New York society," the magazine explained, "and were her name to be mentioned, many readers of the *Weekly* would say, 'Why, I know her well; but I never heard that she was a good rifle-shot.'" The article stressed that Miss Diana had rejected the option of killing her deer as many lazy Adirondack hunters did by having dogs chase it into a lake where it could easily be run down in a boat, but had sportingly waited for her prey to rise from the water on the opposite bank before squeezing the trigger. "She preferred to take the chances of a long shot at a moment when one more bound would have lost the deer to sight amid dense underbrush," *Harper's* praised, noting the likelihood that Miss Diana "will return to the city in the autumn bearing other antlered trophies to add to those already won."[20]

Sensation had surely been intended by putting on a magazine cover a stylish woman killing something with a shotgun, but the image was not inaccurate; female hunters *were* encouraged to join the chase. There was naturally some pushback against this trend, as hunting has since time immemorial represented to men a potential hiatus from wives, mothers, children, and the domestic sphere generally. This was the basis for the prejudicial superstition that a woman accompanying a hunt brought bad luck, or at least made tracking game difficult, what with her physical neediness and inability to not talk. Women who went on male-led hunting trips frequently discovered that once on the trail, even as they were urged to join the shooting, there existed a tacit expectation that they would be wifely and supportive while managing to look appealing, and not mind cooking and cleaning up. "She paddles like an Indian [and] sends a bullet into the heart of a deer without a touch of 'buck fever,'" observed an appreciative Boston *Herald* of the typical woman hunter in 1903. "She can construct a lean-to, and build and light a smudge in front of it with the best of the men, [yet] she is still so charmingly feminine that the best men flock around her as devoted slaves. Of course to be so masculine in action and yet so true to her womanly self in mind and appearance, this camping-out girl of the day needs clothes and plenty of them." It was the alleged wardrobe excesses of lady hunters that so disturbed Charles Hallock, who never forgave "Adirondack" Murray for urging women into the mountains, as now "the whole New York wilderness was littered with parasols and bits of lingerie."[21]

Of course, not all women hunters were fashionable "Dianas" just off the train from Grand Central; many were self-taught marksmen who, like Annie Oakley, the star trick shooter from Buffalo Bill's Wild West, had from a young age known how to kill their family's dinner. A few were outrageous characters, such as scout Martha Jane Cannary, known as "Calamity" Jane, an extreme but admirable example, who knew Wild Bill Hickok; rode with George Armstrong Custer; and lived, drank, handled a gun, and swaggered much like her male peers. General Custer (he had been a brevet major general in the Civil War, and although now a lieutenant colonel, was out of respect and custom still addressed by the former rank) was a man whose approval was famously hard to attain, but who during his years on the frontier grew to respect Calamity's and

Sporting publications of the Gilded Age often encouraged and publicized women's participation in the hunt, as their presence in the field was thought to exemplify the pastime's refined character. (Library of Congress)

other women's trail skills. He once was amused to be shown up by a Miss Talmadge, the seventeen-year-old daughter of a guest in his camp, who after being warned condescendingly by the general that a buffalo hunt was dangerous, proceeded to bring down two of the fleeing animals with her rifle from horseback.

Conditions in the West helped induce many women to take up the sport. Officers' wives stationed at remote frontier posts saw it as one of the few means of spending time with their husbands, and, like them, pursued the sport as a needed diversion as well as a means of supplementing army rations. Frances Roe, who accompanied her husband to Colorado in 1871 and chose to live the same rugged life he did, wrote dismissively of other garrison wives "who yawn and complain of the monotony of frontier life . . . who sit by their own fires day after day and let cobwebs gather in brain and lungs. If they would take brisk rides on spirited horses in this wonderful air, and

learn to shoot all sorts of guns . . . they would soon discover that a
frontier post can furnish plenty of excitement."[22]

Grace Gallatin, wife of the naturalist Ernest Thompson Seton,
traveled and hunted extensively with him in the West, where, as her
husband recalled, "She was a dead shot with a rifle, often far ahead
of the guides, and met all kinds of danger with unshrinking nerve."
There was Elinore Pruitt Stewart, a Wyoming homesteader whose
*Letters on an Elk Hunt* was excerpted in the *Atlantic Monthly*; also,
Finetta Lord, who killed a grizzly bear near her family's Montana
farm; and Alberta Claire, "the Girl From Wyoming," who rode a
horse 10,000 miles across the United States and described her hunting adventures in the pages of *Outdoor Life Magazine*. Common
in Western archives today are historical images of girls as young as
seven or eight holding a shotgun in one hand and a passel of dead
squirrels or rabbits in the other. One account of the Old West tells of
a farm wife so handy with a gun that she could survey the chickens
pecking around her yard, and without leaving her doorway, neatly
blow the head off the individual bird chosen for that night's table.
Women also heroically protected their family's barnyard with their
guns. In 1875, Kansas's *Russell County Record* alerted its readers to
the example of Mrs. D. Homer Jennings, who had become fed up
with her chickens being carried off by a hawk. Hearing her rooster
squawk suddenly while she was sitting at dinner, she rushed outside
in time to see her winged nemesis, and "quickly brought the gun
to her shoulder and fired, and down came the hawk, as dead as a
mackerel."[23]

One of the most enterprising western female hunters was Martha Maxwell, an Oberlin graduate who had moved to Colorado
with her husband and family in 1860. She not only developed a keen
eye for taking prey, but was an innovator in the male-dominated
world of animal trophies and taxidermy. Posing creatures in lifelike
tableaux, or dioramas, Maxwell attained national renown when
her menagerie was exhibited at the 1876 Centennial Exposition in
Philadelphia.

The preparation and display of animal trophies is likely as old as
the chase itself. Julius Caesar's descriptions of Gaul in the century

before Christ mention that the antlers and horns of oxlike aurochs were hung from houses or left at shrines; and portraitist Charles Wilson Peale discovered at his American Museum in Philadelphia in the 1790s that a mastodon bone attracted far more viewers than a gallery of paintings. For Martha Maxwell, stuffing animal specimens grew out of her use of birds and animals as decorative features in home décor. She appointed her own parlor liberally with her homespun taxidermy, until it became such a local curiosity that she was asked to exhibit her efforts at a Boulder agricultural fair in 1868. Heartened by the response, she began considering expanding the exhibit; needing specimens, she went out and killed them herself. From small creatures, such as birds, squirrels, and chipmunks (which she called "lightnin' on legs"), she soon graduated to larger game, such as antelope, which she learned could be lured close by tying a red kerchief to her gun, as the animals suffered from a fatal curiosity.[24]

"The sight of a new specimen always affected her, as the smell of alcohol is said to affect an inebriate," noted her sister and biographer Mary Dartt Thompson, "and she would sacrifice any amount of personal comfort, and put forth any degree of extra effort to obtain and preserve it."[25] On a visit to San Francisco in 1873, Maxwell visited Woodward's Gardens, a well-known attraction that was part natural history show and part amusement park, boasting an aquarium, skating rink, live animal exhibits, and comical taxidermy in which stuffed specimens were posed in humorous "human" tableaux, such as monkeys dancing or playing cards. Impressed, she returned home and began experimenting with new methods of taxidermy. She long had had reservations about the usual technique of packing an animal skin with straw, as the results were often unrealistic and in the worst examples leaned toward the grotesque. Lifelike perfection was the goal. With the aid of a local blacksmith, she devised a means of creating inner skeletons or mannequins, using animal bone and wire. She then covered the wire forms with wool, cotton, and other materials to attain the appearance of musculature, before sewing on the skin, a process that made the subject appear animated. Having been inspired by her trip to Woodward's

Gardens, in 1874 she opened her own Rocky Mountain Museum, containing examples of her taxidermy as well as several live animals, including bear cubs, squirrels, and a rattlesnake.

Asked by the State of Colorado in 1876 to create an exhibit to represent the state at the Centennial in Philadelphia, she mounted an elaborate exhibit of five hundred animals, 80 percent of which were birds, on a realistic landscape of sagebrush plains and mountainside. Deer browsed by a small creek that flowed from a mountain and gathered in a tiny lake, around which Maxwell positioned turtles, fish, beaver, and ducks; on the mountain ridges stood bears and cougars, while ruminating on the plains were buffalo, elk, and antelope. "Woman's Work" read a banner posted overhead, which was seen by many of the nearly 10 million fairgoers who visited the exhibition that summer and fall.

*Forest and Stream* had a site at the fair as well, a simulated "Hunter's Camp" like a scene from an Arthur Tait painting, complete with a lean-to, cook fire, and upturned canoes, which the magazine touted as "life at the beginning . . . a reminder of the world's youth when it was content to play and be happy." But it was Martha Maxwell's exhibit that was the more viewed and talked about, the lifelike appearance of the animals in her menagerie so extraordinary, visitors could not resist poking them or yanking their tail. Expecting the "Colorado Huntress," as a local newspaper had dubbed her, to be an Amazon, fairgoers who met the artist were surprised to encounter a small, modestly dressed woman who stood not five feet in height. She was described by a reporter as "shy as one of her own weasels," but she was savvy enough to sell *cartes de visite* of herself dressed in western garb and holding a shotgun.[26]

Martha Maxwell's pioneering efforts in habitat display were largely unheralded in her lifetime. An exhibit of orangutans entitled *A Fight in the Treetops*, by William T. Hornaday, one of the nation's leading taxidermists, was shown at a scientific meeting in 1879; his *Bison Group*, mounted at the National Museum of Natural History in 1887, was called revolutionary for "presenting the animals in natural poses and even replicating the look of the prairie setting," but Maxwell, as her sister Mary would point out in a

letter to Hornaday, had already demonstrated the power and effi-
cacy of this approach. Diorama may well have been a format that
grew logically and organically in several places at once; naturalist
Jules Verreaux and later artist Carl Akeley refined and excelled at
it, and unlike that of her male counterparts, Maxwell's work never
appeared in public museums. But even if she was not the inventor
of the technique, she surely deserves recognition as a gifted early
practitioner.[27]

In a sense, even if she had stolen *Forest and Stream*'s thunder
at Philadelphia, the theft was nonetheless a kind of tribute to the
magazine. The national enthusiasms for hunting, for natural science, for the West, which the journal had lovingly nurtured, were
well represented by the fact that a physically unimposing wife and
mother from Colorado had, with a shotgun and some ingenuity,
placed herself at the vanguard of the venery arts and won public
acclaim.

For Maxwell, unfortunately, life in the years following Philadelphia became an often futile quest to recapture the excitement
of her six months at the exposition and find a permanent home for
her large collection. She was unable to interest a museum or gallery
in purchasing it. Increasingly alienated from her husband and family after being so long separated, she relocated to the East Coast,
where she attempted to operate a museum of her own—first in New
York City, then Boston and Washington, and finally as a summer
attraction at New York's Rockaway Beach. For a time, she ran a
boardinghouse to raise cash and occasionally sold off individual
items from her animal groupings. When she died in 1881, a daughter from whom she had long been estranged came east, and after
briefly attempting to keep the museum open, began to dispose of
the remaining collection. After many years of shipment, storage,
and exposure to sand and salt air, many of the specimens were in
such poor condition they had to be thrown away.

Coincident with the opening of major natural science museums
in the 1880s, including the American Museum of Natural History,
taxidermy was beginning to gain respectability as an art wedded
to science. It would, however, assume a profound new importance

within a few years of Maxwell's death. Sharp concern had been raised that some species of American wildlife—the buffalo, the passenger pigeon—were endangered with a sharp decline in their numbers and possible extinction. The latter term—*extinction*—was as yet unfamiliar to most Americans, but its meaning was hugely significant to natural scientists. With such consequences looming, taxidermy, it appeared, might soon become more than a mode of representation; it would be a means of immortalizing that which could no longer be. This unprecedented moral dilemma would seriously test *Forest and Stream* and the nation's sport hunting cohort—fortunately, those perhaps most uniquely prepared to address it.

*Chapter Six*

# Arming the Hunters

HENRY WILLIAM HERBERT ONCE PREDICTED THAT BY THE END OF the nineteenth century, rifles and shotguns would be obsolete in America; by then, he assumed, the game they were designed to shoot would have become scarce. He said this in the context of his advocacy for conscientious game laws, but while he wasn't far off the mark about the threat to wildlife, he misjudged greatly the resilience of the American firearms industry. New methods of salesmanship and promotion, the advent of replaceable parts and mass production, and the popularity of the breech-loading rifle, as well as arms sales to European armies, would sustain and grow the business throughout the late nineteenth century. Gun makers often complained that a well-made gun lasted too long without requiring replacement (i.e., additional sales), but as the sport shifted west, hunters demanded new guns to meet its changing conditions. The Great Plains and the Rocky Mountains provided an ample basis for innovation, with manufacturers designing lighter-weight guns to allow better mobility in rugged terrain, increased power against larger game, and improved means of rapid fire.[1]

The influence of hunting on product development in American gun manufacture began in the colonial era—in New England, Philadelphia, and also in the South—although it surged notably with the development of the Pennsylvania rifle (later known as the Kentucky rifle) by German American gunsmiths located at Lancaster, Pennsylvania. At 51 to 71 inches in length, these guns were believed to offer greater accuracy than the old, cumbersome flintlock musket. Another innovation, the percussion cap, introduced in the 1820s, simplified reloading by replacing the flint, powder, and pan mechanism with a small capsule filled with fulminate of mercury; when struck by the hammer, the compound exploded down a tube into the barrel, igniting the main powder charge. In addition to making reloading more efficient, the caps were impervious to dampness.

The Kentucky rifle ruled the frontier in the years following the War of 1812. It was respected as a superior hunting weapon and even celebrated in song for giving Americans a winning edge at the Battle of New Orleans in 1815, but the gun became less practical as America headed west. Due to its length, it was awkward to carry on horseback, let alone fire from the saddle; some pioneers worried that it lacked the power to drop such western denizens as a buffalo or grizzly bear. And all muzzle-loading guns, even the Kentucky, required far too much time to reload. The shooter had to place a flint in the hammer, cocked so as not to fire; load the gun from the muzzle end with black powder and a ball of lead shot; shove the powder and lead down the barrel, using a ramrod; fill the flash pan with a small amount of powder or insert a percussion cap; and finally, free the hammer from the safety notch—only then could the gun be leveled and fired. This routine might also require a shooter to rise from his place of cover. If he hadn't already spooked the animal he was stalking, he had only one shot to make the effort worthwhile before he'd have to repeat the process. An increased rate of fire and reloading arrived eventually with the introduction of the self-contained metallic cartridge, which held projectile, powder, and primer all in a fixed casing.

Such technological fixes as the percussion cap and the metal cartridge were accomplished through advances in industrial practice. The use of interchangeable parts, famously demonstrated before an army board in 1798 by inventor Eli Whitney, who randomly scrambled the parts of six muskets, then assembled and fired each one, made feasible the efficient repair of guns and revolutionized the factory methods of production. This leap forward in technical competence that modernized gun manufacture during the first half of the nineteenth century, was met by another major advance around the time of the Civil War: the introduction of the breech-loading rifle, which allowed for the rechambering of bullets through the rear of the gun, eliminating the numerous steps required of muzzle-loaded weapons. A related advance was the appearance of the repeating rifle, a breech-loaded weapon that either manually or automatically fed new shells from a magazine into the firing chamber.

Despite the clear advantage of the breech-loaders, federal authorities were slow to relinquish muzzle-loaded guns. As historian John W. Oliver suggests, while the South struggled to produce enough rifles of any kind to arm its new recruits, the North lacked a means of testing new weapons prototypes.[2] Perhaps federal hesitation about arming troops with repeating rifles had to do with the concern that soldiers would then stay at a remove from the fight: many officers retained a faith in close combat, or the threat of it, as a means of demoralizing an enemy and forcing him from the field. Bayonet and sword wounds accounted for little of the physical damage suffered by Civil War soldiers, but a field of gleaming bayonets could always be relied on to strike fear in the hearts of defending infantry.[3]

The Sharps breech-loading rifle, designed by Christian Sharps and patented in the mid-1850s, made its mark in abolitionist warfare in Kansas, where the guns, shipped in boxes labeled "Bibles," became known as "Beecher's Bibles" after the Reverend Henry Ward Beecher, an ardent abolitionist, declared they possessed "moral agency." Soon after, Sharps carbines contributed by Northern abolitionists armed John Brown and his followers in their 1859 attempted seizure of the federal arsenal at Harpers Ferry.

Although slow to make their way to frontline troops during the Civil War, breech-loaders and repeaters did show up throughout the conflict. These included a seven-cartridge Spencer, able to fire fifteen shots per minute, and in fewer numbers, the Henry Rifle, a fifteen-cartridge lever-action repeater designed by New Haven weapons maker Benjamin Tyler Henry. This first lever-action rifle gave a single shooter the impact of several muzzle-loading soldiers firing at once, and was devastating in raking oncoming troops in battle. The Confederates despised it as a death-dealer, calling the Henry "that damned Yankee rifle that is loaded on Sunday and fired all week long."[4]

At war's end, the dominant gun makers were Colt, Remington, Sharps, and Smith & Wesson. Oliver Winchester, a New Haven textile manufacturer, bought up the Spencer patents to eliminate them from the market, and hired gun designer Benjamin Henry to further develop his lever-controlled rifle under the Winchester name. The result was one of America's most iconic guns, the Winchester '73, the "Gun That Won the West," a twelve-shot lever-action repeater that was deemed "an excellent gun for the Plains, where one's game may be a jack-rabbit one minute and a deer the next." It was soon joined by the Sharps Buffalo Gun, the Colt pistol known as "the Peacemaker," the Remington Rolling Block Rifle, and the 1873 Springfield "Trapdoor," all designed for lightness and rapid fire and, in the case of the Sharps, maximum "knockdown power." The Sharps entered western legend in June 1874 at the Second Battle of Adobe Walls, near Hutchinson, Texas, when professional buffalo hunter Billy Dixon used the gun to kill a Comanche horseman at a distance of 1,500 yards, or about nine tenths of a mile. Later, the Winchester Model 1892, a fifteen-shot lever-action rifle, became one of the country's most popular hunting rifles, sold in record numbers up until the Second World War. Another Winchester, the Model 1894, with an eight-shot capacity and a .30/30 cartridge, was the legendary 30/30 beloved by generations of American sportsmen—the first sports rifle to use smokeless powder, which crucially improved a hunter's ability to see the game at which he'd just fired and better protected his cover in case a second shot was needed.[5]

Gun makers' marketing accompanied every step of this technological advance, linking weapons to the taking of big game as well as defense against "hostiles," outlaws, and wild animals. Sporting magazines, calendars, brochures, and lithographs all reinforced this idea—that men, and women, would best meet the rigors of the frontier with a trusted firearm, one's truest and perhaps *only* friend in a pinch. Befitting their "personalized" role, many had names that grew almost as legendary as their owners: Calamity Jane relied on her "Hunter's Pet"; Theodore Roosevelt cradled "Big Medicine"; Buffalo Bill carried "Lucretia Borgia," and his friend Texas Jack Omohundro swore by "the Widow"; but there were endless variations, such as "Old Meat in the Pot," "Hair Splitter," "Deadeye," "Sure Shot," and so on.

The Colt 1873 Single Action Army Revolver allowed a hunter engaged in a horse-mounted chase to retain control of the reins with one hand while firing several rounds in quick succession with the other, a vast improvement over trying to fire a rifle accurately from aboard a galloping horse. Another important benefit of both the revolver and the lever-action rifle was that the new guns undermined the Indian strategy of swiftly closing the distance on a panicked trooper or settler as the latter struggled to reload. A survivor of an attack on a wagon train along the Bozeman Trail recounted:

> The Indians began the offense in the old way by circling around, making feints at charging, and all the tricks wherein they were devilishly proficient, for the purpose of drawing our fire at a long range, and then charging in on empty guns. They kept drawing a little nearer until perhaps their patience became exhausted and (then) made a simultaneous dash on all sides. Coming within the limits of rifle range the Henrys began to play a tattoo the like of which they had never heard before . . . to say that the Indians were astonished at the storm of lead that met them would be but a weak expression.[6]

Prominent among gun manufacturers for his sales acumen was Samuel Colt. He introduced prescient marketing and promotional methods—business historians say he coined the phrase "new and improved"—and was shrewd enough to patent his own signature, a facsimile of which was engraved on some of his guns and appeared routinely in advertisements. He also bought access to the powerful with elaborate gifts of personalized Colt weapons, fine liquor, and other favors, and was innovative in deploying expert endorsers and paid lobbyists. Significantly for the subsequent mass sales of hunting weapons, he also initiated the concept of product placement, commissioning famed western artist George Catlin to execute a series of twelve paintings showing Colt weapons in use, as seen in the popular 1851 lithograph *Catlin the Artist Shooting Buffalos with Colt's Revolving Pistol*. He also paid writers to produce articles for magazines in which a Colt weapon played a heroic, predicament-saving role.

Born in Hartford in 1814, Colt was smitten at a young age by tales of steamboat inventor Robert Fulton, and by his teens had become a prodigious tinkerer with water-related devices and pyrotechnics. Serving aboard a merchant ship in the 1830s, he observed that the spokes of the ship's wheel were caught by a clutch that held them in position after each turn. He later adapted the method to a wooden revolver, known as a pepperbox gun, in which the three barrels would rotate, each moving into position for firing after the previous one had discharged. After a stint as a medical pitchman, performing demonstrations of laughing gas (nitrous oxide), he returned to work on his weapon designs, abandoning the pepperbox scheme and focusing instead on a gun with a single barrel that remained stationary and was automatically reloaded by a rotating cylinder. Building on Eli Whitney's innovation of interchangeable parts (what had become known as the "armory" or "American" system), Colt envisioned something even greater: a means of assembling the revolver speedily by hand through the repetitious functioning of several workers. "The first workman would receive two or three of the most important parts and would affix these and pass them on to the next who would add a part and pass the growing article on to another who would do the same, and soon until the complete arm is put together," he explained in an 1836 letter to his

Contemporary illustrations of turkey shoots, like this one by Charles Deas in 1838, often featured diverse groups of spectators and participants, young and old, suggesting the contests' unique popularity among nineteenth-century Americans. (The Athenaeum)

father, describing the basis of the modern assembly line. Colt's weapons—the 1851 Navy Revolver, the Colt Walker, the Dragoon and Baby Dragoon, and the Peacemaker all became hugely popular, although his aggressive salesmanship caught up with him in the run-up to the Civil War, when it was found he was selling guns to Southern interests. Embarrassed, he quickly terminated the sales, and attempted to deflect criticism by having himself commissioned a colonel in the Connecticut militia and offering to field a regiment of men, all of whom, he promised, would be 6 feet tall and armed exclusively with Colts.[7]

With so many powerful new guns coming onto the market, it was not surprising that there would emerge an interest in publicized contests to judge the relative merits of the various models, as well as the skills of competing shooters. This enthusiasm had grown up with the country, dating to the impromptu backwoods matches Daniel Boone felt obliged to lose to his Indian acquaintances, and the venerable custom of the village turkey shoot, in which contestants paid to fire either at penned turkeys or, later, paper targets, the winner taking home a prize bird. The competitions became more sophisticated and the ranges longer after a wave of German immigration about 1850 brought a revival of the medieval *Schützenfest*, or shooting tournament. The Americanized version saw employees of factories, shipyards, and members of Turner clubs and other organizations form "target companies," or *Schützenbunden*, to facilitate team training and prepare for competitions. There were talented *Bunde* riflemen, although the target companies' picnics were notorious for becoming too carnival-like to allow much actual sharpshooting. One such fete in Lake Hopatcong, New Jersey, in 1892 grew so loud with the sound of guns and fireworks that Delaware Indians living nearby complained, donning war paint in symbolic protest.[8]

Certainly the most consequential shooting society to emerge during this era was the National Rifle Association (NRA), in 1871. Its founders—former Union army officer and New York National Guard captain George Wood Wingate and Colonel William Conant Church, the publisher of the *New York Sun*—had both observed with concern the relatively dismal level of marksmanship exhibited by Union soldiers during the Civil War. Not that the Confederate troops had proven themselves far superior. The South liked to cite its rural background and the lore of the long-hunters in boasting of its inherent gun expertise, but the facts of the war did not bear out the claim; North or South, Americans were "a nation of 'duffers' as far as general exactitude of aim went." Part of the problem may have been the rapid recruitment of young men into both armies, as well as the not uncommon sentiment among officers that a talent for shooting was something a man either did or did not possess; it could not be taught in the short gap between the troops' recruitment and their being required at the front. On the Northern side in particular, many city-bred recruits had rarely, if ever, held a gun larger than a pistol. After the war, former Confederate officers claimed to have frequently found dozens of brand-new federal rifles, unfired and possibly abandoned, strewn on the ground, following major engagements.[9]

A more recent inducement, one closer to home, came with the Orange Riot of July 1871, one of the most violent outbreaks of street violence in New York City's history, in which National Guard units protecting an Irish protestant parade along Eighth Avenue fired indiscriminately into a heckling crowd of brick- and stone-throwing Irish Catholics, killing as many as sixty people. Like other urban confrontations of the nineteenth century, bloody violence often resulted from the inability of militia or police, when hemmed in by an unruly mob, to remain calm and *not* fire their weapons. The Orange Riot reaffirmed Wingate and Church's determination that an inadequately trained armed force—whether in the field of battle or arrayed against a mob in a city street—was lethally dangerous, to itself and to others.

Wingate and Church set out to rectify the situation. They asked Union general Ambrose E. Burnside (a hero of the Battle of Antietam whose distinctive facial hair had inspired the term *sideburns*) to serve as the NRA's first president, and with the support of New York governor John T. Hoffman, received $25,000 in matching funds from the state legislature to buy land for a rifle range. Locating a seller was difficult because many people assumed that a range for competitive shooting, like a horse racetrack, would attract gamblers and criminals; on Long Island, however, a farmer named Creed was willing to part with a desolate area of brambles and stubby grass, a place so barren locals referred to it as "Creed's Moor." The NRA's founders quickly collaborated on the first book of rules governing rifle contests, and Creedmoor, as it came to be known, soon became a gathering place for past and current military shooters interested in improving their skills.

ALMOST IMMEDIATELY, THE NASCENT AMERICAN RIFLE MOVEMENT received an unexpected challenge. Rifle competitions were already popular in Britain—there was a well-known range at Wimbledon—and for many years England and Scotland had traded victories.

Then, in 1873, Ireland won. The Irish, emboldened, took out a notice in the *New York Herald*, challenging the amateur marksmen of America to meet them in fair contest. The NRA was not confident it could compete; Creedmoor hosted only a modest Amateur Rifle Club run by Wingate and Alonzo Alford, president of the Remington Arms Company. Should national pride lead the Americans to accept, there was also a significant technical concern: the British shot at targets as far as 1,000 yards distant, whereas American target companies and the *Schützenbunden* fired at targets no more than 200 yards away. The Amateur Club had recently pushed some of its targets back to 500 yards, but that was only halfway to the British range. Still, as *Forest and Stream* observed encouragingly, it was impossible for America to spurn the challenge, since the Irish were "coming 3,000 miles over here, under the very shadow of the Stars and Stripes, and calmly challenging the whole United States to a contest of skill with *our national weapon*." The magazine spoke without hesitation, and for many Americans, in proudly claiming the rifle—like the one carried by Daniel Boone, by the "embattled farmers" of Lexington and Concord, by Buffalo Bill—as a beloved family member, virtuous and loyal in battle as well as in the chase.[10]

The makers of Remington and Sharps firearms, eager to appear as patriotic sponsors, stepped up to pay the Amateur Club's required $500 ante, while vowing to produce the finest weapons possible for the American shooters. The contest would in part address a technological question, as the Irish team would use European muzzle-loading guns, which were considered more accurate at long distances, whereas the Americans relied on the newer and more convenient breech-loaders. It seemed unlikely an American team that had to be pieced together from scratch might beat the champions, but Wingate and others expected that even a decent showing would help promote interest in the sport here at home.

Things got off to a less-than-rousing start when a call for the country's legendary backwoods marksmen to step forward and shoot for the United States produced few candidates. Eventually, thirty men drawn largely from the New York City region tried out at Creedmoor over the spring and summer of 1874, with local newspapers and the public increasingly caught up in following the qualifying contests. Ultimately, a team of six was chosen: a lawyer, a civil engineer, a retired merchant, two gun factory foremen, and a person described simply as "an old rifleman." "While [the Irish] have been practicing under scientific teachers, and popping away at a bulls-eye in a carefully constructed gallery," wrote the *Chicago Inter-Ocean*, "our boys have been shooting buffaloes on the plains or taking a wild turkey on the wing . . . It will be a contest between trained efficiency and native skill, between the dainty hand of the city and the rough grasp of the woodsman."[11]

In September, the Irish team arrived amid great fanfare, and was feted and shown the sights of the city. The two teams practiced side by side, reporters scrutinizing the preparations and speculating each day in their columns about the practice scores being posted. In the finals, the participants would fire at 3-foot-square bull's-eyes 800 and 900 yards away, and finally at a target set at a distance of 1,000 yards. At the longer distances, the shooting was more art than science, as even the best gun lost some control over its projectile at that range. As the bullets were susceptible to crosswinds, the Americans' greater familiarity with the grounds was expected to offer a slight advantage.

On the day of the match, September 26, 1874, more than five thousand fans descended on Creedmoor, clogging the local railroad connections and overflowing onto Farmer Creed's once barren scrubland, which now, on its day of glory, had become, via the *Herald*, "a beautiful piece of grass one-half mile long and 1/8 mile wide."[12]

For excitement the match did not disappoint. It was extremely close throughout, with missteps on each side. One Irish shooter, J. K. Milner, mistakenly scored a bull's-eye on the wrong target, a hit that was scored a miss; an American, T. S. Dakin, drank too much champagne in making lunchtime toasts to his opponents, and as a result shot poorly in the afternoon round. Two Yanks distinguished themselves, however—Henry Fulton, who had the best overall score and nailed ten bull's-eyes in a row at the 1,000-yard distance; and John Bodine, a veteran hunter and former colonel in the New York militia, who came to the firing line at the tournament's end, with the score 931 to 930 in favor of the Irish and everything resting on his reply. To the horror of spectators, when Bodine paused for a moment to accept a drink of ginger beer offered by a friend, the bottle shattered. The physician for the Irish team rushed forward to inspect the glass splinters in Bodine's right palm, and suggested a postponement. But Bodine, "a tall, gaunt man with bronzed face and iron gray hair," wrapped a bloodstained handkerchief around the wound and insisted on shooting. Steadying himself before a hushed crowd and lying forward in a prone position, he hit the bull's-eye at 1,000 yards, worth four points, to move the United States ahead to 934 and victory. Bodine was thereafter known as "Old Reliable," a fitting nickname that, in his honor, later turned up as a stamped "autograph" on the top barrel flat of a Sharps breech-loading model.[13]

"The contest at Creedmoor yesterday is without parallel in the annals of any nation," boasted the *Herald*, which printed diagrams of shots-on-target for each of the two teams' individual shooters. As its boosters had hoped, the victory accomplished something not a dozen Charlie Hallock editorials could, elevating shooting contests from a working-class pastime to a scientific, intellectually demanding, and internationally recognized sport.[14]

The excitement spilled over into broad popular interest in the shooting arts. Rifle clubs for men and women were formed; commercial rifle ranges opened; tunesmiths, honoring the heroism at Creedmoor, composed "The American Rifle Team March" and "The American Rifle Team Polka"; and within a decade, fifty colleges fielded rifle teams (the federal government providing the schools free ammunition). The NRA did its part by working with authorities to make surplus military weapons available to the public, and by the early twentieth century, the group was leading national high school and collegiate gun training programs and competitions. One of the greatest enthusiasms was for marathon shooting for accuracy—sometimes of live pigeons, but increasingly glass balls or clay pigeons sprung from a trap—as well as elaborate trick shots, such as using a hand mirror to aim and fire at a target over one's shoulder. Many of the best marksmen and women, such as the

A hunting prodigy as a child, Annie Oakley became a professional trick shooter, the featured star of Buffalo Bill's Wild West, and one of the most popular Americans of her time. Sitting Bull called her "Little Sure Shot," a name that caught on with promoters and fans. (Library of Congress)

gifted Captain Adam Bogardus; dentist turned sharpshooter William "Doc" Carver; or, the biggest star in terms of ticket sales, Ohio prodigy Annie Oakley, who starred for sixteen years in William Cody's successful pageant Buffalo Bill's Wild West. The program for one version of Cody's show identified "The Bullet" as a "pioneer of civilization."[15]

It was an age fascinated by record-making feats, technical precision, and human endurance. Bogardus, a Chicagoan who made his reputation in the late 1860s and early 1870s with such difficult stunts as shooting targets hurled into the air as he rode past in a buggy, took on all challengers and established numerous records—100 pigeons released and killed consecutively without a miss, 500 birds killed in nine hours, 981 glass targets shattered out of 1,000 tossed. Touring England in 1875, he mopped the floor with all the local champions, the London sporting press eking out a small morsel of home pride by mentioning that his gun had been manufactured in Birmingham. So perfect was his aim, the press even noted that his pigeon victims died more efficiently and humanely than they might at the hands of any other shooter. Back home in 1879, he was still setting records, blasting 4,844 thrown targets out of 5,000. "He was a champion of champions," acknowledged one competitor, "willing to shoot anywhere . . . at pigeons, blackbirds, snow birds, blocks of wood, glass balls, anything so it was in the air and moving."[16]

But others also excelled: in 1883 a Dr. A. H. Ruth hit 984 of 1,000 targets; Annie Oakley racked up scores not as high yet impressive enough to win national acclaim. Doc Carver, who boasted of being the world's best rifle shot, seemed to deserve that reputation after an 1886 marathon in Minneapolis where he plunked 59,340 glass balls out of 60,000. In contrast to Bogardus's workmanlike attitude, Carver strove to present a stylized western persona. At six foot four, with flowing red hair and a prominent jaw, he was an imposing figure and natural star, billed as "the Most Handsome Man Who Ever Held a Gun." His record was secure for only three years, however, as a Captain Bartlett nudged him aside by banging 59,720 composition balls, which were smaller than glass balls, out of 60,000 hurled. Carver's apologists explained that he had begun to suffer from eyestrain after so many years of squinting up at things tossed before him.

Oakley's act had been developed with her husband, Frank Butler, who assisted her in her numerous trick shots, such as hitting several targets tossed into the air before any fell to the ground. Another well-known sharpshooting couple was the Famous Topperweins; husband Adolph ("Ad") and his wife Elizabeth, known as Plinky. One of the longest-running vaudeville acts in American history, remaining on the road for forty-two years, Ad and Plinky did all manner of tricks—shooting objects off one another's head; backward shots; shooting an apple off a poodle's head; hitting multiple targets in the air; and Ad's specialty, what he called "shooting art," in which he fired a careful pattern of bullets into a wood or tin surface to create portraits of Indian chiefs and other representations.

In San Antonio in 1907, Ad shot at 72,500 targets over a ten-day period, smashing 72,491. Not to be shown up, Plinky in five hours nailed 1,952 birds out of 2,000. Her famous onstage composure was said to have cracked only once, when a pure white pigeon fell wounded and fluttering its life out at her feet, crimson blood staining its soft white down; horrified, Plinky walked off the stage and vowed to never again fire at live targets.

Her outburst was no doubt brought on by the highly emotional public debate surrounding the sport of shooting captive pigeons. The contests were frowned upon even by many sport hunters, who considered them cruel and unethical, but they were hard to regulate in part because they were popular with older, well-to-do shooters— men who enjoyed firing at live targets without the physical exertion of a field hunt. The sport was rapacious at sweeping up birds for its use. Pigeons were easily captured, and when released from traps, they were swift to rise but slow in flight, yet unpredictable enough to offer a challenging moving target.

First appearing in England about 1750, bird-shooting contests arrived in the United States in the 1830s. They frequently involved substantial purse prizes and discreet wagering, which guaranteed the sport's elitism. In New York, such business leaders as James Gordon Bennett Jr., financier August Belmont, Cornelius Vanderbilt, and mine magnate J. G. Heckscher often joined top competitors at the shooting line. Henry Bergh, the New Yorker who started the American Society for the Prevention of Cruelty to Animals (ASPCA) in 1866, and was the public face of the anti–pigeon shooting campaign, knew most of these affluent men, but in his view, the fact that the participants were New York gentry made no difference; they were as guilty as the "sports" who gathered in the rat pits with their grimy dollars in hand. "To take an immortal work of the Deity," said Bergh of the pigeons sacrificed, "and after assembling a crowd of spectators, deliberately tear it to pieces merely for fun, is, in my opinion, a double crime, by reason of its disastrous reaction on human character."[17]

The matches of the era's champions, such as Captain Bogardus and Doc Carver, were popular spectator events, with the scores meticulously charted and printed in the next day's papers. Each pigeon's "escape" from the trap—straight up, to the left, or right, or close to the ground—determined its fate, and was recorded in detail:

> A driving bird; well-killed.
> A quartering bird to the right; missed.
> A quartering bird to the right; killed quickly. A capital shot.
> A well-killed driving bird.
> A towering bird; shot dead.
> A strong driver; well hit.
> A driving bird; hit hard, but escaped.
> An incoming bird; splendidly killed.
> A quartering bird to the left; wounded, but was gathered
>     and killed.
> A crossing bird to the right; missed.
> A strong wheeler; a dead shot.
> A streamer; well-killed.

Even reporters accepting of the shoots didn't hesitate to criticize contests that used inferior or unhealthy pigeons. Birds weak from hunger or dehydration resulting from long confinement often staggered lamely from the opened trap, or managed to barely spread their wings in a feeble attempt at flight, making for very poor sport. And the intensity of the betting occasionally bred match-fixing and dirty play, such as sabotaging opponents' guns or mutilating birds so that, on release, they would present erratic targets. Charles Hallock, who complained bitterly about the shooting of captive birds, noted that the passenger pigeons used were so mistreated in transit that "twenty percent of them died, and when the survivors were turned loose at the shooting line they were too tired to take wing, and so the starters would throw a baseball at them to make them rise." Released birds that did manage to fly free were often targeted a second time by amateur shooters lingering just outside the boundaries of the event, where neighbors complained of having to gather up the tiny corpses, or collect mortally wounded birds "with legs shot off, wings shattered and bills broken." That *Forest and*

Gentlemanly Henry Bergh, "the Angel in Top Hat," took to New York's streets to personally enforce the protections of the American Society for the Prevention of Cruelty to Animals, which he founded in 1866. (Library of Congress)

*Stream* and Bergh would be allies in this fight was not exceptional; sport hunters were ardent lovers of horses and dogs, animals protected by the ASPCA, and, like Hallock, tended to disapprove of captive wing shooting. Where Bergh could not stop this "cruel and demoralizing pastime," he and his agents at least tried to ensure that all wounded birds were put out of their misery as quickly as possible.[18]

James Gordon Bennett of the *Herald* became enraged after an incident in early January 1872, when Bergh's agents broke up a shoot on Manhattan's Upper West Side at which Bennett himself was one of the competitors, along with Bogardus and another star of the sport, Ira Paine. As Bergh had a unique, longish face upon which a dour expression seemed permanently fixed, Bennett dubbed him "the Knight of the Rueful Countenance." Mayor A. Oakey Hall piled on, calling Bergh "a mere charlatan, a notoriety seeker, and also a malicious man." One letter in the *Herald* questioned Bergh's patriotism, asking,

Does Bergh . . . intend to leave us defenseless? Men are not
born marksmen. Accuracy can be secured only by practice,
and certainly no method is better calculated to insure accuracy
than these much-decried pigeon matches. Since we can no longer practice upon Indians and wildcats . . . let us accept the
necessity that involves the lives of so many of the feathered in-
nocents. The killing in itself may be granted cruel. But if the
results inure to the benefit of man, why cavil?[19]

The *Times*, which often opined on behalf of the fledgling
ASPCA, countered that rifle sports at the Creedmoor range, involving paper targets, would adequately address the national interest in
maintaining or improving marksmanship, and at the same time give
"our young men . . . something better to shoot at than the pigeon-
matches which Mr. Bergh has felt called upon to put a stop to in the
interest of humanity." It was none other than Bogardus, the greatest
shooter of his day, who stepped in to salvage the sport's dignity. In
1877, he introduced a trap system for hurling glass balls into the air,
the balls ridged on the outside so bullets would not simply bounce
off. Some versions came stuffed with feathers so that the moment of
impact resembled the killing of a bird in flight. The sport was further transformed a few years later, when in 1880 a Cincinnati inventor named George Ligowsky created the clay pigeon, a disk-shaped
ceramic "flying target" that soon entered standard use.[20]

AS THE STAR OF THE SHOOTING LINE BOGARDUS SOON HAD TO MAKE
way for Annie Oakley, who had kept clear of controversies involving pigeons on her way to becoming the biggest draw in Buffalo
Bill's Wild West and one of the most admired people in America.
Long before she entered the limelight, she was Phoebe Ann Mosey,
born August 13, 1860, in Darke County, Ohio, where she took up
hunting at a tender age to help feed her family; a natural shot, she
killed her first bird at age six and her first squirrel at age eight. After
her father, Jacob, froze to death in a blizzard, the family's situation
deteriorated to the point that she was farmed out first to a county

home and then to an abusive foster family. By the time she was a teenager and reunited with her family, she was a successful market hunter and a deadeye shot, selling quail and other edible prey to small-town markets. A superb hunter, she could kill most game with a clean shot to the head, thus sparing the meat, and likely knew the trick of "barking squirrels": shooting the creatures off of trees with the concussion of a bullet sent close to their body, thus preserving the pelt, a practice at which Daniel Boone had also excelled.

Wild West audiences beheld a tiny woman under five feet tall who skipped into the arena dressed in tasteful but modest skirts and blouses, carrying what appeared to be a very large gun. She quickly won their applause with a combination of girlish wholesomeness and awesome technical proficiency. As someone once said of Oakley's fellow small-town Ohioan Victoria Woodhull, "She was born in the West, and has all the dash and spirit of that breezy country." Intensely competitive at the shooting line, Oakley scowled when she shot poorly and gave a little backward kick of excitement when she did well.

Sitting Bull appeared long enough in Cody's show to develop a great fondness for Oakley, whom he affectionately called "Little Sure Shot." She refused the money he tried to give her for a signed photograph, but accepted the old chief's offer to make her an honorary member of the Hunkpapa Sioux. He stayed only a short time with the tour, western writer Larry McMurtry suggesting Bull was saddened not by Oakley's unwillingness to return his attentions but by the "white people's cities . . . and their lack of concern for the poor," although it's also easy to imagine he simply tired of the show's pervasive shtick.[21]

Despite her huge fame, Oakley, who never completely left behind the trauma of her impoverished childhood, lived frugally, retiring to her quarters after each performance with her husband, Frank, and keeping to herself. Of her image and reputation, she was likewise protective. The Hearst press at one point concocted a story that she had been arrested in Chicago for stealing a pair of pants from a black man so she could buy cocaine, a yarn so absurd she

Buffalo Bill Cody and his renowned Wild West costar Sitting Bull. The authentic pageantry of Cody's exhibition was greatly enhanced by the presence of the legendary Sioux chieftain and other real-life western figures turned performers. (Library of Congress)

might have laughed it off; instead, she sued for libel all fifty-five newspapers in which the story had appeared, collecting from all but one, with Hearst itself paying her $27,000.

A quiet but fervent patriot, when the Prince of Wales told her "America should be proud of you," she replied without a beat, "I'm proud of America." At the onset of both the Spanish-American War in 1898 and the US entry into the First World War in 1917, she wrote to Presidents McKinley and Wilson, respectively, offering to train, arm, and lead her own corps of fifty female sharpshooters. Both times, Washington politely refused, but she and Frank did visit army bases during the latter conflict to demonstrate precision shooting to new recruits. She reminded newsmen that on a Wild West tour of Europe, she'd once obliged Kaiser Wilhelm II by shooting the ashes off the end of his cigar. If only she'd missed by a few inches, she rued, the world might have been spared the war and all its suffering.

The celebrity of such figures as Oakley and the popularization of competitive and trick shooting, as well as the consumer needs of hunters and steady sales to the world's armies and police, all powered the American firearms industry's growth. It benefited also from its own knack for promoting guns as valued, necessary accessories, even, in the case of hunting, family "acquaintances" to hand down from one generation to the next.

With the partially successful activist effort to ban live pigeon shoots, the country had seen the first public campaign to restrict the wanton taking of animal lives. Similar crusades would soon be mounted against the market-scale slaughter of buffalo and the touristic shooting of the animals from moving trains, as well as the ravaging of southern plume and songbird populations. The focus of reform was not guns per se—their status appeared secure—but on whether such activities were needlessly destructive of wildlife, and, as an affront to the American ideal of sportsmanship, insulting to basic human decency.

*Chapter Seven*

# Sportsman's Paradise

IN 1878, IN VIRGINIA CITY, NEVADA, A GROUP OF HUNTERS DROVE A captive coyote by wagon to the edge of the desert. A coyote has less vanishing speed than a fox, the animal most favored as prey in a staged hunt, but it does not lack for cleverness. The plan was that the coyote, once released from its box, would be given a head start of a few miles, the dogs would be set loose, and the men would commence the chase on horseback. The slat was lifted on the box and the freed coyote ran off, but he managed to elude both the hounds and the hunters and, by making a long circuit, returned to the wagon and climbed back into the box. The men repeated the attempt, but with the same result. The sun was getting hot and a lot of dust had been raised, for nothing.

Confounded, the hunters were discussing the coyote's strange behavior when a violent gust of wind suddenly lifted a hunter's hat from his head and sent it flying. Spurring his horse, the man set off immediately in pursuit, joined by several of his companions. "The chase was as exciting as any fox run ever seen in the state," according to one newspaper account, as the hunter finally "overtook and captured his hat four miles from the starting place."[1]

The American West, like the sagacious coyote, had an endless capacity to shock and surprise hunters and settlers alike. It was where sport hunting would take on new dimensions, new character, in keeping with the region's majestic heights and far horizons. Journeys were weeks and months in duration, the seemingly endless sagebrush lands sparsely populated with nomadic indigenous peoples and the odd trading outpost or army garrison. There were arid plains littered with the bleached bones of animals perished of thirst, and conifer forests so dense that inside them it was night at noon. One encountered spiders that stung and some that bit, grasshopper swarms, snakes, and black wasps as big as birds, among other creatures that grew larger with each telling. Kansans swore to the existence of a pelican 8 feet from wingtip to wingtip, a goose 6 feet 4 inches long, and an otter that measured 5 feet 7 inches. A Mrs. Zion and her friend Mrs. Higgins, fishing in Big Creek, landed a 30-pound snapping turtle, a report soon eclipsed by word of a turtle taken from the Arkansas River that weighed 50 pounds and "belonged in a museum," but was instead "utilized for soup."[2]

In several places, there was wonder at the "biblical" phenomenon of raining fish and frogs, until someone discovered that it occurred when cyclones passed over a shallow stream and vacuumed the creatures up into the clouds before showering them back down. As there was no scientific weather forecasting, storms came on in full ferocity to slam unsuspecting Plains communities. It was a time when people walked or rode long distances from home to track stray cattle, mend fences, hunt, or simply visit the next town. The unlucky lost fingers and toes to frostbite, perished in blizzards, or simply vanished.

Hunters in particular often succumbed to the urge to press on, to cross just one more ridge, anything not to return home empty-handed. And each spring the thaw revealed their corpses, huddled where they'd died—in crevices, hollows, or between boulders—anywhere a last bit of shelter had been sought. Of course, because hunters tracked game assiduously, staying with a promising animal trail no matter where it went, pursuit could be treacherous in any season—a wrong step at the edge of a fast-moving river,

There was no lonelier or more disorienting place for a novice western hunter than the silent, endless prairie after both game, and one's companions, had vanished. Alfred Jacob Miller portrays the dilemma in *The Lost Greenhorn*. (Courtesy of the Walters Art Museum, Baltimore)

soggy ground that became deadly quicksand, an avalanche, a rock fall. Some hunters went missing for years before their remains were found—the precise explanation for their disappearance and demise unknown and left to the speculations of their sorrowful kin. "I knew an estimable man who went out alone after buffalo," recalled western memoirist Col. Richard Irving Dodge, who regularly cautioned his officers and troops against hunting unaccompanied on the Plains. "Three weeks afterwards his remains were found in the bottom of a deep chasm, into which he had fallen and broken his leg, and where he had perished miserably by starvation." A macabre case came to light in 1923, when the skeletons of a man and a moose were found entwined together deep in the woods of northwest Montana. The hunter had mortally wounded the moose, it appeared, but the animal had managed to rise up and trample its attacker before collapsing. The man's vintage, barrel-rusted Sharps that lay nearby suggested the incident had occurred a very long time before, perhaps in the 1870s. There was no local recollection of a hunter's disappearance from that period, only the irrefutable evidence that hunter and moose had "laid in their last sleep, side by side," for at least half a century.[3]

Frontier hunters took seriously the fact that big game animals such as wolves, cougars, bears, moose, elk, and even deer were capable of fighting back. The grizzly was the ultimate threat. With its acute sense of smell, it is difficult to approach undetected; yet shooting a grizzly from a distance reduces the chance of a kill shot, and they are known to charge even when mortally hurt. Hunters who came too close often met with unhappy results. Arthur M. Stiles of the United States Geological Survey and Charles B. Penrose, a Philadelphia hunter, were in northwest Montana in 1907 when Penrose shot and killed a grizzly cub. In his excitement to inspect his trophy, he forgot about the likely proximity of the mother bear, and set his rifle against a tree. The grief-stricken mother suddenly rose up before him, all teeth, claws, and fury; he managed to reach his gun and fire three times, but not before she struck him a mighty backhand that pitched him to the bottom of a ditch. She then clambered down after him and began ripping his upper body to shreds with her powerful claws, an attack that ended only when she "sickened with her own wounds and, staggering, fell dead at his feet." Having heard the commotion, his friend Stiles arrived on the run to find him unable to stand and begging for water. "Stiles, I am all in," Penrose said. "I have had a fight with a bear."[4]

Cougars, apparition-like in their stealth, ranged over a wide expanse of western territory, "wandering pirates," in the memorable phrase of *Outing Magazine* editor Caspar Whitney, as likely to stalk a hunter as to be stalked *by* him. Stories of savage attacks by the creatures had long been told by campfire light. "There is something about the look of a cougar on business bent, with its greenish, staring eyes, that produces a most uncomfortable sensation," Whitney reported. "I have had many trying experiences of one kind and another, and hunted many different kinds of game, but none ever harassed my soul as the cougar has." With the coming of rifle-bearing hunters to remote parts of the West, the cougar lost some of its verve, according to Theodore Roosevelt, who as a ranchman knew them as livestock thieves; they became more inclined to flee at the sight or sound of an advancing human than to pounce. However, their ability to move without perceptible sound, appearing and reappearing mysteriously, and their liking for the taste of deer (which made them man's unbidden competitor), all contributed to the cougar's daunting reputation. Hunters experienced with the big cats soon learned the wisdom of catching them just after they had fed, possibly on an animal carcass left as bait, as they were then less inclined to run and more likely to seek to evade the dogs by going up a tree, where they could be shot or roped. But even this course was not without risk, as in their determined last defense, they frequently killed or gashed the hounds that cornered them. Roosevelt, while hunting in Colorado, engaged in a one-on-one tussle with a cougar, which ended with his knifing the animal to death.[5]

Large ruminants, however docile they appeared, were also not to be trifled with. Sportsman Roger D. Williams, who while hunting in the Black Hills nailed a buck deer with a well-placed shot, made the rookie mistake of rushing forward too eagerly to claim his prize. The "dead" animal suddenly leapt to its feet, charging with antlers lowered and "eyes gleaming like coals of fire." In desperation Williams clubbed his attacker with the butt end of his gun, but the rifle broke in two; he then grabbed the deer by the antlers, but felt himself losing the struggle to a foe accustomed to using those sharp appendages as weapons. He was saved by his two hunting dogs, which, racing in, leapt on the dying buck; both dogs were badly hurt and Williams came away with facial cuts and shredded clothing.[6]

An incident from the 1870s recorded by George Bird Grinnell, then the natural science editor of *Forest and Stream*, offered a macabre version of Williams's experience. A young half-breed hunter went alone to hunt buffalo and mysteriously did not return. Friends who searched for him discovered his horse and weapons, but the man was nowhere to be seen, and eventually he was given up for lost. A year later, the same hunters saw a buffalo cow with a strange object on her head. "They chased and killed her," Grinnell wrote, "and found that she had on her head the pelvis of a man, one of the horns having pierced the thin part of the bone, which was wedged on so tightly that they could hardly get it off. It is supposed that this bone was part of the missing young man, who had been hooked by the cow, and carried about on her head until his body fell to pieces."[7]

DANGER WAS INTEGRAL TO HUNTING, WHICH WAS ITSELF INTEGRAL to the frontier. All who came west brought ample powder and shot expressly for that purpose, for hunger was a constant and keeping one's larder full a daily preoccupation. Trappers, prospectors, explorers, and settlers, like the Native Americans they encountered, came to rely on a smorgasbord of wild game. There was an ordering of favored meats, with buffalo and venison considered choice, followed by antelope steaks and chops from bighorn sheep. Plover, quail, and grouse were esteemed as "toothsome" birds, bunnies were filling, gophers could make a meal in a pinch, while some new arrivals developed a taste for grilled beaver tails, almost pure fat but salty and delicious. Nothing that walked, flew, crawled, or swam was beyond the appetite of the hungry hunter—there's at least one account of a man strangling a skunk—nor did the age of the prey particularly matter. White hunters were often willing to share the Indians' belief that all animals, young and old, had been provided for their nourishment by a benevolent god; as it happened, buffalo calves and yearlings were more tender anyway. Dog could be satisfying if one didn't mind gnawing on a recent companion; in less than ideal circumstances, one's own horses and mules were dinner. Pack animals offered the additional advantage, in an emergency, of being shot and used as breastworks. General Custer once proudly told his wife, Elizabeth, known as Libbie, that his Crow scouts remained loyal to him because "they had heard that I never abandoned a trail, [and] that when my food gave out I ate mule. That was the kind of a man they wanted to fight under; they were willing to eat mule, too."[8]

White people generally disdained eating dog, but would partake if the dish was offered by native hosts, as it was to the latter a great delicacy. The duty of slaughtering the tribe's most plump young dogs when their turn came on the menu fell to the women of the tribe, as writer George Ruxton, who once witnessed the procedure, explained:

> With a presentiment of the fate in store for them, the curs slunk away with tails between their legs, and declined the pressing invitations of the anxious squaws. These shouldered their tomahawks and gave chase, but the cunning pups outstripped them, and would have fairly beaten the kettles, if some of the mountaineers had not stepped out with their rifles and quickly laid half-a-dozen ready to the knife. A coyote, attracted by the scent of blood, drew near, unwitting of the canine feast in progress, and was likewise soon made *dog* of, and thrust into the boiling kettle with the rest.[9]

Other native dietary habits also affronted white sensibilities. Where an Indian hunter had gone several days without food, freshly hunted animals might be devoured immediately, without preparation and almost in their entirety, including heart, lungs, stomach, liver, and bowels. For between-meal nourishment, native bow hunters developed a knack for dropping small birds from trees without bloodying them by using a blunt-tipped arrow; the tiny creatures would then be quickly opened and crisped whole over a fire and munched down in one or two bites—a kind of prairie fast food. At a western military outpost, Colonel Dodge was smitten by a visiting chief's daughter, a girl of fourteen, "a vision of loveliness . . . ripened by the Southern sun to perfect woman." But after a day of exchanging hopeful glances, he was horrified when, without taking her affectionate gaze from him, she reached into the carcass of a cow and removed 8 to 10 feet of the animal's intestines, which she wound around her arm and, feeding one end into her mouth, and "without apparent mastication swallowed the whole disgusting mass. I returned sadly to my tent," Dodge wrote, "my ideal shattered, my love gone; and I need hardly add that this one Indian love affair has satisfied my whole life."[10]

For white and Indian hunters alike, buffalo, because of their size, were of necessity butchered in situ. Buffalo tongue was the West's great delicacy, and it was almost always the first thing removed, extracted by slitting the lower jawbone. Then the hide was opened down the spine, and the prime cuts—the small hump on the animal's neck, the larger hump, and the hump ribs—were taken. The "fleece," the fat separating the spine and ribs, was considered choice, as were the side ribs and the abdominal fat. "Feed fair!" was the (mostly) futile caution mountain men issued to their mates as the orgy of eating commenced. "All traces of Anglo-Saxon civilization vanished instantly," reads one account. "The blood . . . spilled down the trapper's face, arms, and body . . . [the buffalo's liver] was seasoned with gunpowder, or by squeezing the gallbladder's contents over it, and then consumed without further preparation." One favored way to prepare buffalo was to cook it *en appolas*, on a stick with alternating meat and pieces of fat; another was to make *boudins*, intestines that had both ends tied to keep the fat in, and which lengthened as they cooked and were delicious when crisp. "As the generous fat dripped on our clothes we heeded it not," recalled hunter Lewis Garrard of a buffalo rib dinner, "our minds wrapped up with the one absorbing thought of satisfying relentless appetites; progressing in the work of demolition, our eyes closed with ineffable bliss."[11]

Perhaps no wild creature of the West inspired hunter admiration like the black-tailed deer—beautifully proportioned with noble face and head, in motion swift and graceful. Its weakness was its powerful curiosity. "He is never quite satisfied with the evidence of any one sense, except his nose," Dodge explained, "and if an enemy approach against the wind, yet close enough to be heard, he will spring to his feet, make a few bounds away from the noise, then stop and look around for the cause. This is the sportsman's opportunity, and nine-tenths of the black-tails bagged are killed in that pause."[12] Similarly, the antelope, the fastest land animal in North America, had grown to be so confident in its ability to outdistance predators that it paid a price by responding too leisurely when men showed up with guns. Naturally inclined like the black-tailed deer to indulge its curiosity, the antelope could be distracted by waving of a red bandana or other diversion, an inclination hunters quickly learned to exploit. Caribou, which American hunters encountered in the far north, would scatter at the sound of a gunshot but then return to see why one of their number was not rising from the ground, offering a second opportunity to the clever shooter who had managed to remain nearby, out of sight.

Hunters found no such inclination among moose, an animal the French voyageurs who encountered them in the northern wilderness called *l'original*, as befitting its gangly and prehistoric appearance. All animals hunted by man eventually learn to flee before him, but for some creatures, such as moose and wild turkey, no education is necessary; gifted with a preternatural distrust of *Homo sapiens*, they rarely stick around to see why man comes or what he wants. Elk could also be notoriously difficult to hunt on open ground, despite their considerable size; unlike buffalo, they do not flee in a straight direction but zigzag, go in a circle, change course. A man pursuing a fleeing elk on horseback in unfamiliar terrain could readily become disoriented.

Among all these creatures, the buffalo, dubbed "Monarch of the Plains," reigned as the supreme lure of western hunting. The animal's great appeal as the object of the chase was its majestic appearance; its romantic association with the landscape and indigenous hunters; and the ultimate challenge of riding at top speed alongside a fleeing creature of such immense size, which might unpredictably turn and gore rider or horse. It was, historian Bernard DeVoto believed, "the consummation of the sportsman's life," in whom it stirred "an emotion equivalent to ecstasy." So keen were European big game hunters to shoot a buffalo, many were crestfallen, upon arriving in New York, to learn the animals were not available immediately at hand, say, in Westchester or New Jersey.[13]

Even God could not compete against buffalo fever. The story was told of a minister who had managed to assemble a group of frontier hunters for Sunday mass, but in midsermon, buffalo suddenly

Tait's 1862 lithograph, *Life on the Prairie: The Buffalo Hunt*, echoed George Catlin's iconic 1830s scenes of Indians hunting buffalo from horse-back, but now it was mounted white men who gave chase. (Courtesy of the Yale University Art Gallery)

appeared in the valley below, prompting the congregation to jump to its feet and depart with horse and gun, "leaving Mr. Parker to discourse to vacant ground." Later, it was noted that he, too, seemed to enjoy the buffalo repast. "All around them they saw manifest the splendor of creation," writes William Benemann of these men, "and they could not help but feel themselves a part of something that was exactly as it was supposed to be." There was a simple reward, as one hunter put it, in turning in for the night "with my saddle for a pillow, the green sward for a bed, the star-lit and eternal vault for a canopy, and for a lullaby the melancholy howling of innumerable wolves."[14]

Yet dozing by the fading embers of a frontier campfire brought its own risks. The lone hunter learned to sleep with his rifle butt between his face and upper arm, like a pillow, the muzzle between his legs, his arms folded across the trigger lock and breech, so that if awakened suddenly by animal or human intrusion, he might sit up, ready to shoot. As explorer Jim Bridger felt obliged to warn new arrivals, "The grace of God won't carry a man through these prairies. It takes powder and ball."[15]

SOLDIERS GARRISONED AT REMOTE FRONTIER OUTPOSTS WAGED another life and death struggle: the fight against boredom. Except in locations where the Indian threat mandated the building of a stockade, these sites were often less proper forts than a jumble of buildings hurriedly thrown up with little thought of their permanence, and made lonely by their isolation, long harsh winters, and constant anxiety over the possibility of native ambush or harassment. The routine drilling and preparation for confronting an enemy who rarely materialized bred paralyzing ennui; as did the frequent assignment to "fatigue" duty—hammering new structures together, laying bricks, and other menial jobs.

The opportunity to hunt and fish was one of the few diversions from such pressures, and an immensely appealing one. "The West offered no Broadway theaters, no Delmonico's, no elegant casinos," notes historian Brian Dippie, "but it did offer the antelope, the deer, and the mighty buffalo. [Whatever] its drawbacks, in short, the West was a sportsmen's paradise." As one enlisted man informed *Forest and Stream*, "enjoyments aside from hunting are few," while another acknowledged, "hunting and fishing is about all we do here." The joy of sport aside, soldiers welcomed the chance to supplement the camp larder.[16]

General Custer's wife, Libbie, upon seeing the barren Plains for the first time, worried about what one might possibly find to eat—but her concern and appetite were soon vanquished by the ample supply of a small wading bird known as the plover. Three soldiers with double-barrel shotguns could easily shoot and collect a sack full of eighty or more of the birds within minutes, to be broiled over the coals of a campfire. "They were so plump that their legs were like tiny points coming from beneath the rounded outline that swept the grass as they walked," Libbie wrote. "No butter was needed in cooking them, for they were very fat. How gladly we gathered around that hamper when the command halted at noon!"

The troops also found the sage grouse delicious eating, and so slow and easy to hunt that they called it "the fool hen."[17]

Hunting for sport or sustenance, however, was not available to every enlisted man. Few soldiers owned personal firearms, and army rifles were often unsuitable for hunting game; the army could also be tight-fisted as to how its ammunition was allocated, and, as ever, small hunting parties wandering away from base on their own did so at some risk. But military leaders eventually came to see the hunt as a form of martial training. "The successful hunter, as a general rule, is a good shot, will always charge his gun properly, and may be relied upon in action," cited officer Randolph B. Marcy. "Short excursions about the country," he advised, would allow soldiers to "acquire a knowledge of it, become inured to fatigue, [and] learn the art of biv-ouacking." On the other hand, men "confined to the narrow limits of a frontier camp or garrison, having no amusements within their reach," he cautioned, "are prone to indulge in practices which are highly detrimental to their physical and moral condition."[18]

By 1881, under a direct order from General Sherman, the army approved of the hunting of game by the troops, and went so far as to commission an official army shotgun, a .20-gauge model from the Springfield armory, to be distributed to enlisted men at posts west of the Mississippi along with instructions and a supply of ammu-nition. The soldiers welcomed the change, but most had already demonstrated the ability to produce significant bags even without the proper equipment. In 1874 at Fort Sill, a detail of twelve men sent out to help stock the post's larder for Christmas dinner killed 156 turkeys, almost three times the number shot by a party of offi-cers. Troops assigned to provision General Custer's 1,200-person wagon train to the Black Hills that same year were said to have killed one hundred deer per day.

As Custer himself told the Eastern readers of one of his many hunting letters to *Turf, Field and Farm*, published under the pen name "Nomad,"

> To attempt to give anything like an accurate or full account of
> the game we encountered would be impossible. You may rest

assured we were not restricted to Hobson's choice. From a buffalo steak to a broiled quail we indulged *ad libitum*. Beginning at buffalo as the largest, we had buffalo, elk, black-tail deer, antelope, turkey, geese, duck, quail and several variety of snipe. When we added to this list wolves—of at least three varieties, and with which the market was overstocked—beaver which was to be found upon almost every stream we crossed, with here and there a wild-cat or panther, it will be seen that he must have been a sportsman of most fastidious taste who failed here to find abundant and choice sport.[19]

Custer, because he is so thoroughly identified with the manner in which he died, is remembered as a rash and vainglorious militarist, but he was a person of diverse interests—literate, scientific, and political. When back east, he sought the company of artists, writers, actors; he envisioned a postarmy career as a businessman, or in politics; and he was a published writer on hunting and military affairs. His articles in the magazines *Turf, Field and Farm* and *Galaxy*, about the Indian Wars, his weapons, dogs, horses, and most memorable hunts, made him a favorite read for hunters everywhere. Passionate about the chase, he was also a diligent amateur taxidermist and student of natural history.

By his own account, the pinnacle of Custer's frontier hunting career came in 1875 with his taking of a grizzly bear, which he killed with the help of Bloody Knife, one of his scouts, and two other men. Custer considered bears generally to be "the highest rung on the hunters' ladder of fame," and his prize likely became the mounted bear head that adorned his study at Fort Lincoln near Bismarck, North Dakota, from which the Seventh Cavalry departed on its fateful march to the Little Bighorn in summer 1876. There was also a large bear rug on the floor where Custer liked to sprawl after hours of writing or examining specimens; he would light and tend the fireplace and, with his hands clasped behind his head, admire his many trophies of the chase adorning the walls and the mantle—a buffalo's head, a queue of stuffed rabbits, a mountain eagle, foxes, a great white owl, and numerous sets of antlers from which were suspended gloves, whips, sabers, and a sword he'd captured in the Civil War that bore the inscription "Do not draw me without cause; do not sheathe me without honor."[20]

So central was hunting in Custer's life that looking for hostile Indians seems at times to have been a secondary concern. Frontier photographs of the general find him frequently not in uniform but in hunter's buckskin, surrounded by his beloved pack. Libbie recalled that one of the amusements of a Custer encampment was listening as the dogs—he kept as many as forty stag and fox hounds—all howled at once in an attempt to match the keynote of the army bugler. As Custer assured his readers, "the music of a well-arranged pack, when earnestly settled to their work, possesses far more enticing charms to my ear than those claimed for the latest opera."

He liked to say he was the best shot in the army (a view diplomatically shared by his subordinates), taking special pride in his ability to kill even a fast-fleeing antelope at a considerable distance. He also coveted the challenge of mounted buffalo hunting—the ridership it demanded, and the skill to fire a gun with accuracy from atop a moving horse, while guiding one's mount to avoid crevices or prairie dog holes that might injure the animal and pitch the rider headlong. "I know of no better drill for perfecting men in the use of firearms on horseback, and thoroughly accustoming them to the saddle, than buffalo-hunting over a moderately rough country," Custer wrote. "No amount of riding under the best of drill masters will give that confidence and security in the saddle, which will result from a few spirited charges into a buffalo herd."[21]

Custer had himself been introduced in rough fashion to these difficulties. It was 1867, he was new to the West, and he was hunting antelope when he spied a conspicuous black dot, a solitary buffalo, moving slowly along a nearby ridge. He gave chase with revolver drawn, and after 3 miles came abreast of his prey, which at once commenced a determined sprint for its life. "It may be because this was the first I had seen, but surely of the hundreds of thousands of buffaloes which I have seen since, none corresponded with him in size and lofty grandeur," he recalled. "Repeatedly could I have placed the muzzle against the shaggy body of the huge beast, by whose side I fairly yelled with wild excitement and delight, yet each time I would withdraw the weapon, as if to prolong the enjoyment of the race." Suddenly, while Custer "was already thinking of the triumph with which I would enter camp, carrying with me the choicest portions of *my* buffalo . . . ," the animal went on the offensive, swerving toward Custer, which threw the general so severely off-balance he inadvertently shot his own horse through the neck, killing it.[22]

Finding himself on the ground, Custer looked up to meet the gaze of the buffalo, which had stopped as though to analyze the sudden shift in the hunt's fortune. "Whether the buffalo was dumbfounded by the changed aspect of affairs, and looked upon the lofty tumbling he had just witnessed as a new and dangerous kind of tactics, with which he would do well not to trifle, or considered my condition then and there as being sufficiently helpless and humiliating, I know not . . . Taking one look at me, [he] contented himself with one threatening, scornful shake of the head, and departed . . . leaving mc in possession of the field, but in all other respects *sorely* defeated." Custer's predicament was not uncommon. Mounted hunters who charged into unknown parts after fleeing elk or buffalo and came up empty-handed often reported the same progression: intense focus, exhilaration, then a frustrated halt or tumble into a barren world suddenly gone silent, lacking familiar sign or landmark, where one felt not only foolish, but quite lost.[23]

ANOTHER, MORE SERIOUS SETBACK ARRIVED LATER THAT SAME year, when Custer's dedication to his mission of finding and destroying Indians, and his willingness to obey orders, both came under harsh scrutiny. He had been sent to remote Fort Wallace, Kansas, to coordinate protection for railroad construction crews beset by Indian attacks, but finding the fort inadequately provisioned against a rise in cholera on the frontier, he left without orders to march 225 miles to Fort Harker to procure needed medical supplies. From there, again on his own initiative, he detoured by train to Fort Riley to see Libbie. For these unauthorized meanderings, he was charged with leaving his command and the misuse of government personnel

The army's best-known Indian fighter, George Armstrong Custer, revealed a developing literary side in chronicling sport hunting and wildlife on the western frontier for curious readers back East. (Library of Congress)

and supplies on private business. Worse, he was accused of abandoning two troops who had been bushwhacked by Indians, and ordered the shooting of soldiers suspected of being deserters, one of whom died after Custer delayed getting him a doctor's attention. Made to face a court-martial at Fort Leavenworth, he was found guilty of five of the eleven counts against him and suspended from military service for one year without pay.

This was the other Custer—not the larkish hunter and aspiring chronicler, but a man known to be often a tyrant to his troops, and willing to bend and even evade army regulations when it suited him. Professional jealousy may account for some of the dislike many fellow officers harbored for him—he'd been promoted frequently for gallantry during the Civil War, hailed as "the Boy General," and even featured on the cover of *Harper's Weekly*—but it was his ego and mendacity that especially grated. When *My Life on the Plains*, a collection of Custer's *Galaxy* articles, was published, the Seventh Cavalry's Captain Frederick Benteen, who served under Custer, slyly suggested the book might be more accurately titled *My Lie on the Plains*, for "the falsity of much of it is as glaring as the sun at noonday." But Custer had admirers in high places, including General Philip Sheridan, commander of US forces on the Great Plains, and William Tecumseh Sherman, soon to be commanding general of the army. Sheridan was a great fan of Custer's since the Civil War. Like General Ulysses S. Grant, who had been rapidly promoted by President Lincoln during the war because of his willingness to seek out the enemy and engage him, Custer was valued by Sheridan and Sherman for his readiness to fight, his courage and derring-do. There was mounting impatience in Washington with the progress in putting down Indian resistance, and although Custer "was harsh to and hated by his men, as well as by most of his fellow officers," Larry McMurtry notes, "he was, nonetheless, the kind of man Sherman was looking for: one to whom fighting came first," and he was reinstated to duty after only two months. As Sherman vowed of the challenge in the West, "These Indians require to be soundly whipped, and the ringleaders in the present trouble hung, their ponies killed, and such destruction of their property as will make them very poor."[24]

Custer understood what he was being asked to do. But the scorched-earth strategy Sherman had used in his March to the Sea would not be effective here. In conquering the South, federal troops had laid waste to buildings, farms, towns, and enemy installations; most of the indigenes of the western plains, on the other hand, were wanderers. They rarely if ever presented a stationary target, nor did they stand and fight pitched battles as had Confederate forces. Their métier was the ambush from boulders or bushes; a sudden rush with tomahawk, gun, or bow and arrow; a theft of horses; and then a quick flight. Frontiersmen learned to guard against such surprises. A common subterfuge was to create two campsites—one with a fire for cooking or warmth, another some distance away, kept dark, for sleeping and tethering horses. "I do not mind getting killed," hunter and Custer scout Charley Reynolds once said, "but I should hate to have somebody come along next year and kick my skull along the sand and say, 'I wonder what fool this was, who built a fire in the country and then slept by it.'"[25]

One Indian tactic whites were warned about was the appearance of two or three apparently wayward braves on the next ridge, their true purpose to lure overeager troops into a reckless charge. Such had been the tragic undoing of Captain William J. Fetterman on December 21, 1866, sent out of Fort Phil Kearny in northeast Wyoming to punish a small group of Indians who had attacked the fort's "wood train." Against explicit orders not to pursue the enemy, Fetterman followed a decoy led by the Oglala Sioux warrior Crazy Horse over a height known as Lodge Trail Ridge. Fetterman had once vowed, "Give me 80 men and I would ride through the whole Sioux nation." In fact, all eighty-one of Fetterman's troops perished with him, for when they topped the ridge, they beheld what must have seemed like "the whole Sioux nation"—as many as one thousand Sioux, Cheyenne, and Arapahoe adversaries. Fetterman and his men were horribly slain; only the corpse of the company bugler remained intact, his gallantry in using his horn as a weapon having won his killers' respect. The massacre was at the time the worst single US military loss in the West.[26]

The winning of the frontier, it was said, was "not about how to defeat the Indians but how to catch them." Custer knew where to catch them: he would attack when they were in their semipermanent winter encampments, when snow and cold made travel nearly impossible. At such times, the natives tended to become lax, believing US troops were also likely stationary. Another advantage to the assault on a home village was that, as soldiers rushed in, warriors would be distracted by the urge to protect their families; they would resist, certainly, but they were not trained to fight as a coordinated defensive unit to begin with, and here would be particularly disoriented. Amid the violent chaos of a raid on an Indian village, Custer believed, the cooler heads of disciplined soldiers could best even a much larger number of Indians.[27]

Before dawn on November 27, 1868, he and his men surprised a sleeping Cheyenne village on the Washita River in western Oklahoma, killing or capturing an unknown number of Indians, perhaps as many as 120 men, women, and children. The soldiers burned their lodges and, in what must have been an especially gruesome spectacle, shot several hundred Indian ponies to death after driving them into a nearby meadow. The tribe's chief, Black Kettle, known to be friendly to whites, was killed along with his wife while trying to flee across the river.

Newspapers at the time, and most historians, regard the Battle of the Washita, a surprise assault on unsuspecting men, women, and children thought to have been on their way toward their reservation, to have been a massacre. But for military authorities hard pressed to show they were gaining ground against western tribes, the "victory" offered renewed confidence in Custer as the country's ablest Indian fighter.

AFTER THE RAILROAD REACHED DENVER IN 1870, MORE SPORTS-men, journalists, politicians, and well-heeled hunters began to come west. Custer, the war hero, big game hunter, and minor literary celebrity, was often besieged by visitors. Some merely wanted to shake the hand of the famous "Boy General"; from these, Custer sometimes hid in a closet or privy while his house servant made excuses for him; others sought him out for hunting advice or as a guide. As the army's prosecution of the Indian Wars was an ongoing topic in the eastern press and in Congress, which provided funds and other support, he, like other military leaders, was frequently called upon by higher-ups to meet and escort touring VIPs on their hunting expeditions; given the threat of Indian attack, many of these hunts required military protection. For Custer, who enjoyed hamming up his role as a frontiersman, it was a pleasurable way to meet and show off for powerful men of business, politics, and publishing. Even America's "Master of Ballyhoo," P. T. Barnum, who joined him to kill buffalo in summer 1870, said he had to admire Custer's showmanship.

In late 1871, at the last-minute behest of the White House, General Sheridan arranged for Custer to host another special hunt, this time for Russia's Grand Duke Alexis, son of Czar Alexander II. Americans of the nineteenth century were ambivalent about most European royalty, but the Romanovs were popularly viewed as exemplars of Old World monarchial refinement and chic. Russia also enjoyed special regard at that moment because it had supported the Union during the Civil War, the czar warning other European nations that if they intervened on the side of the Confederacy, Russia would consider it a hostile act. US Navy admiral David Farragut, the victor at the Battle of Mobile, known for issuing the command "Damn the torpedoes, full speed ahead!" had visited Saint Petersburg in 1867, and since then the idea of a reciprocal social and diplomatic tour by a suitable Russian dignitary had been contemplated by both countries.

The winter of 1871–1872 happened to be a convenient time to send the twenty-one-year-old Duke Alexis Alexandrovitch on an extended vacation, as his girlfriend Alexandra Zhukovskaya was pregnant, and his father, the czar, had forbidden marriage on the grounds that she was a commoner. (The child, a son also named Alexis, was born while the duke was in America.) The duke was understandably heartsick for much of the trip, although his spirits lifted when he learned that he was adored by thousands of American women. Blond, six foot two, with matinee idol looks, Alexis was a powerful-looking man (he was known to have once rescued a child from drowning), and, needless to say, quite rich. Ladies along the tour route—New York, Chicago, Saint Louis, and Denver—beseeched him with letters and invitations, some proper, others not so much, while crowds gathered to catch a glimpse and a New Orleans paper rhapsodized:

> *Alexis! O Alexis!*
> *It seems so very queer.*
> *How you can so perplex us*
> *With your yellow beard and hair!*
> *So set the girls on fire,*

*So make the men perspire,*
*A. Romanoff, Esquire,*
*You handsome polar bear!*[28]

On November 21, 1871, Alexis arrived in New York harbor aboard the *Svetlana*, a flagship of the Russian navy, where he was welcomed with a parade and celebration that seemed to last for the entire two weeks of his stay. Balls, the opera, boat excursions, lunches with dignitaries great and small filled his official schedule. He sat for the famous photographer Mathew Brady. At Council Bluffs, two thousand well-wishers turned out, including several classes of schoolchildren and their teachers. In Chicago, he handed Mayor Joseph E. Medill a $5,000 donation for victims of the recent Chicago Fire, as well as forty letters written to him by local women seeking financial help, to which the duke had attached small contributions. When his train from Chicago to Saint Louis passed through Springfield, the weight of hundreds of spectators caused the roof of the station to collapse.

He conducted some official business, placing an order for $250,000 worth of Smith & Wesson arms for the czar's military, and visited Washington, where he met President Grant and General Sheridan. Alexis assured the president he enjoyed seeing America and meeting its people, but confided that his one remaining wish was to go buffalo hunting on the Great Plains. Western artist Albert Bierstadt had already tipped the Grant administration that the duke was keen on such an adventure, and had also sent word to General Sherman. The White House immediately offered to finance and arrange such a trip, and Sheridan sent word to Custer, who agreed to assist.

Through the scout Bill Cody, Sheridan also arranged for Spotted Tail, a Brule Lakota tribal chief, to lead his people in performing traditional Indian dances and ceremonies for the duke in exchange for twenty US wagonloads of coffee and tobacco. Spotted Tail was a renowned warrior but more recently had become a peacemaker, advising his and other tribes that making war against the whites was pointless, and Sheridan felt he could trust him to keep his braves in line and not steal horses or play any tricks on the

Russian royal party. Sheridan joined the duke and his entourage at
Omaha, then rode with them by train to North Platte, where they
were greeted by Custer and Cody; they then proceeded to a special
hunting camp that had been established by the federal government
on nearby Willow Creek, 40 miles south of Fort McPherson.[29]

As Sheridan had arranged, one evening Spotted Tail, his fellow
chiefs Black Bear, White Bear, Fast Bear, Conquering Bear, Cut Leg,
Little Eagle, and Red Leaf joined their tribesmen to perform for
the duke, who sat transfixed. As the whites looked on, the natives
staged sham fights, hurled lances, displayed their skills with bow
and arrow, and danced to the traditional beat of a tom-tom while a
chorus of squaws and maidens vocalized.

While the duke would surely have been told about the fame of
his host, General Custer, he was at the same time meeting a man
destined, even more than Custer, to become the celebrated embod-
iment of the American West and indeed one of the most popular
individuals in the world. William Cody, born in 1845, was the son
of Isaac Cody, a state legislator active on the side of a free Kansas
in the heated slavery debates of the 1850s. Isaac had died in 1857 in
part from wounds received in a politically motivated beating; and
Bill's older brother was killed accidentally when his horse reared
and fell on top of him, so the future western star began supporting
his family at a tender age, working as a helper on wagon trains.
While his fantastical claims to have shot and killed an Indian at age
eleven and to have been a Pony Express rider were likely "facts" he
concocted later or were inserted in his biography by dime novel-
ists, Cody did accomplish some impressive feats while a young man,
such as completing a marathon assignment as a messenger in which
he rode 322 miles in twenty-two hours. He also became known for
his hunting skill and virtuoso horsemanship, a favorite trick involving dismounting and then hopping back onto a swiftly moving
horse from the rear. At age eighteen, he was a scout for the Union
Army in the Civil War's western theater, and by 1867, was earning
$500 per month hunting buffalo to maintain the commissary for
rail construction crews of the Kansas Pacific Railway. He favored
a converted breech-loading Springfield that threw a heavy shot and

was accurate enough to drop a buffalo at 600 yards. Cody claimed to have personally slain 4,280 of the animals over an eighteen-month period. "It was at this time that the very appropriate name of 'Buffalo Bill' was conferred upon me by the road hands," he later recalled. "It has stuck to me ever since, and I have never been ashamed of it." General Sheridan had heard of his prodigious skills, but developed a special interest in the young man after the July 1869 Battle of Summit Springs, Colorado, in which Cody joined an army raid that freed a captured white woman.[30]

The *New York Herald* reporter covering Duke Alexis's tour described Cody as "seated on a spanking charger . . . with his long hair and spangled buckskin suit," and noted that "white men and the barbarous Indians alike are moved by his presence." As McMurtry would write of Buffalo Bill, "It is hard to overestimate how far a man can go in America if he looks good on a horse." Custer similarly sat his mount so handsomely he was considered "a Centaur" in frontier vernacular, "so lightly poised and so full of swinging, undulating motion" on his charger, recalled his wife, "it almost seemed the wind moved him as it blew over the plain." Custer, perhaps feeling a bit upstaged by Cody, had lost no time abandoning his uniform for a suit of buckskin, while the young duke also managed to wrangle some western garb. Witnesses recalled the stunning image of "the Duke, Custer, and 'Bill,' all hardy hunters" riding off together in search of prey. Alexis had been given Cody's Buckskin Joe, a "buffalo horse" trained to gallop alongside a fleeing bison at top speed and shift tactically along with its evasive movements. Under Custer's tutoring, the duke practiced running at and shooting imaginary buffalo, after which, as it was understood Alexis would get the first kill; Custer rode with him into a herd, chose a large bull, and directed Alexis to fire. The duke shot the animal with a revolver at close range, then put it to death with a rifle; in a grand moment of exultation, having crossed two continents and an ocean for the privilege, he then dismounted and chopped off the felled animal's tail as a souvenir.[31]

Cody later told a different story: the duke had been unable to kill a buffalo with a revolver that had been presented to him when he'd visited a Smith & Wesson factory back east, so Cody had graciously lent him his own trusted "Lucretia Borgia." The newspapers had fun muddling the various accounts, one suggesting that Cody, unbeknownst to the duke, had secretly brought down the buffalo by shooting it from the opposite side; another, a version of an old threadbare hunting yarn, claimed that the duke had initially thought some of the army mules were buffalo and had slaughtered several before his mistake was pointed out to him, after which he was led to a buffalo that had been tied in place and beat it to death with a club. Regardless of how the duke's success came about, he was exuberant, even gathering the startled Custer in a bear hug. Of one thing there was universal agreement—that the ducal party's tradition of having a basket of champagne handy and celebrating each of his highness's kills with a round of raised glasses was extremely virtuous.

Everything about the duke's visit—he was royally feted in Denver and was last seen shooting buffalo from the windows of his train at it headed back east across Kansas—spoke of the role of hunting in glamorizing the lure of the West as a sportsman's paradise. From the sympathetic fraternization with real Indians to the rubbing of shoulders with actual heroes Custer and Cody, the region was seen, through Alexis's experience, to be capable of appealing to the world's most demanding and sophisticated tastes. It offered rugged adventure in a harmless and colorful simulacrum of itself, a "West" in which visitors, too, became momentary actors in a locale that was simultaneously authentic and theatrical. Such events as Alexis's tour, faithfully covered by the *New York Herald* (whose publisher, James Bennett Jr., had himself indulged in a Custer-led hunt) went a long way toward promoting to the average hunter the abundance of and access to big game; this western adventure waited at the tumbleweed station stops where a buckboard wagon met your train, a once-in-a-lifetime experience for those with gumption and a gun.

*Chapter Eight*

# Buffalo Bill, Custer, and Texas Jack

IT HAS BEEN SUGGESTED THAT THE IDEA FOR BUFFALO BILL'S WILD
West originated with the spectacle staged by Spotted Tail's troupe
for Duke Alexis on the Nebraska plains in winter 1872, and that Bill
Cody, who watched it, was inspired by the natives' performance to
create the show that capped his long and illustrious career. There's
possibly some truth to that, although the notion of the West as theater, the wilderness canned, dates back at least to the 1830s, when
the play *The Lion of the West* about the exploits of "Col. Nimrod
Wildfire" (Davy Crockett) stormed theaters on both sides of the
Atlantic. In that same decade George Catlin, artist of the western
hunt, suggested that a museum and park celebrating the American Indian be built in the nation's capital. The idea was rejected by
Congress (Catlin may not have helped his cause by gaining an audience with President Andrew Jackson and using it to complain about
Jackson's Indian removal policies), but the artist did eventually open
a show at the Stuyvesant Institute on Broadway in New York City,

featuring native performers who demonstrated war dances and precision shooting with bow and arrow.

At around the same time, wild animal performances were being popularized by Isaac Van Amburgh, an eccentric American animal trainer known as the first man anywhere to put his head in a lion's mouth. Deeply religious, Van Amburgh cited God's assurance that man had been granted dominance over "the brute creation." All animals were cowards at heart, he averred; even the most ferocious tigers, bears, and lions could be intimidated. "You have to face them boldly and show them now and then what you can do, and it's all over with their terribleness," he explained, alluding to a method he'd devised he called "the Silent System," which seems to have consisted of his beating with a crowbar his more defiant co-performers and thereafter glaring at them until they behaved submissively. In archival photographs, Van Amburgh's cold, ghostlike gaze remains unsettling even after more than a century; one can't help feel for the creatures made to endure it.[1]

P. T. Barnum, who began his show business career exhibiting Joice Heth, an elderly black woman Barnum claimed was 161 years old and had swaddled an infant George Washington, also decided to enter the compelling theater of animal entertainment. In late summer 1843, he announced a "Grand Buffalo Hunt," claiming to have imported a herd of magnificent buffalo from New Mexico along with several lasso-twirling "border men" who would chase the animals on horseback and rope them. The event, near the ferry landing in Hoboken, New Jersey, was open to the public, free of charge. On August 31, twenty-four thousand eager New Yorkers crossed the Hudson, exceeding even Barnum's expectations. The show, however, was a disaster, as the buffalo proved to be a small herd of scrawny yearlings that became spooked immediately by the crowd and crashed through a cheap restraining fence. "The breaking loose of the animals amongst the crowd of auditors caused much confusion, and some ludicrous mishaps," reported the *Herald*, including the death of one young spectator who fell from a tree. Barnum did well, however, having made a lucrative arrangement with the ferry operators, and walked off with a profit of $3,400.[2]

If Barnum had a literary soulmate, it was Ned Buntline, a dime novelist and gadfly who is credited with "creating" Buffalo Bill Cody. Born Edward Zane Carroll Judson, Buntline spent a year in prison for leading a Know-Nothing mob in the Astor Place Riot of May 1849, was driven out of Saint Louis for stirring up anti-German violence, was almost hanged for killing a jealous husband in a duel, and was accused of desertion during the Civil War. He was also a devoted hunter and sportsman, a "true knight of the trigger." Early in his career he wrote a realistic piece about life on the Bowery entitled "The Mysteries and Miseries of New York," and thereafter made his living as a prolific writer of adventure stories that often involved exaggerated versions of his own exploits. "He undoubtedly had in him the makings of a big man, but he sadly misused the ingredients," one biographer reflects. "Brave and daring, a sincere patriot, and a staunch and generous friend . . . he spoiled these sterling traits by loud mouthings and a braggadocio manner that made him appear like one of his own cheap heroes."[3]

In 1869, Buntline went west, seeking a story about the North Brothers—Frank North and his younger brother Luther—legendary hunters, army scouts, and participants in a recent Indian skirmish, the Battle of Summit Springs, which had made the news because it involved white female captives. Renegade Cheyenne Dog Soldiers had been raiding local settlers and had abducted the two women, Swedish immigrants Susanna Alderdice and Maria Weichell. The army launched an assault against the Indian camp, and Frank North had slain the dastardly chief behind the kidnappings, Tall Bull. Unfortunately, a squaw killed Susanna Alderice as troops swept in to save her, but the soldiers did manage to free Maria Weichell.

When Buntline located the North brothers, they waved off the prospect of being written about in a magazine, and directed him instead to the army scout Bill Cody, who had also been in the raid and was nearby sleeping under a wagon. When introduced, Bill's first impression of Buntline was of a "stoutly built" man in a blue military coat with "about twenty gold medals and badges of secret societies" pinned to it, which, ever the sharpshooter, Cody couldn't help but imagine would be "a good mark to shoot at." Buntline, in turn, recognized a handsome hero-in-the-making when he met one. Bill submitted patiently to Buntline's questions and described his part in the fight at Summit Springs; however, once Buntline had perfected his story of the battle, it was Cody, not Frank North, who had killed Tall Bull. (This was likely untrue, although Cody did apparently come away from Summit Springs with the dead chief's horse.) The resulting article, "Buffalo Bill: King of the Border Men," which ran in the December 1869 issue of *New York Weekly* (a publication Buntline owned), was a hodgepodge of western captivity tales, knife fights, and villainous Indians, featuring Cody, the North Brothers, as well as, for good measure, some unrelated exploits of the gunfighter "Wild Bill" Hickok, a friend of Cody's.[4]

A rash of Buntline-authored "Buffalo Bill" dime novels followed, leading to the premiere of a stage version in 1872 at New York's Bowery Theater with J. B. Studley in the starring role; the show was a huge hit, eventually spinning off related productions, imitations, and burlesques. These popular western plays were the closest most Americans would ever get to the frontier, and eastern audiences, understanding that the show was a mash-up of fact and fancy, lustily cheered each bogus heroic.

When the real Buffalo Bill made his first visit to New York, he was received as a conquering legend, politely doffing his hat and making brief, modest remarks to theater crowds between acts. Unlike "the typical desperado of the West, bristling with knives and pistols, uncouth in person," a witness reported, Buffalo Bill was an "agreeable, well-mannered man, quiet and retiring in his disposition . . . in all respects, the reverse of the person we had expected to meet." As his cabinet photographs from the period reveal, Cody was a fine-looking man, "tall and somewhat slight in figure, though possessed of great strength and iron endurance; straight and erect as an arrow." Publisher James Gordon Bennett Jr., who had met Cody on a western hunt, became his most influential New York fan, the *Herald* eagerly running with the Cody myth Buntline had spawned. Buntline, not one to miss a chance, churned out more Cody stories, a task made easier by the fact that his flesh-and-blood subject continued to generate excellent copy. On April 26, 1872, in Loup Forks,

Nebraska, Cody and a squad of army scouts surrounded a group of Indians who had stolen horses from the Union Pacific Railroad and killed several of the thieves; for his actions, Cody was awarded the Congressional Medal of Honor.[5]

Even while the first Buffalo Bill theatrical was running in New York, its producer had approached Cody about taking over the role of the lead character himself. The frontiersman politely demurred, claiming stage fright, but Buntline then got involved and urged him to reconsider, writing several times during the summer and fall of 1872 to assure Bill, "there's money in it, and you will prove a big card, as your character is a novelty on the stage." There was indeed good box office to be had, far more than one could earn shooting buffalo. In Chicago that December, Cody finally did step before the footlights, appearing along with Buntline and his friend, hunting guide "Texas Jack" Omohundro in *Scouts of the Prairie; or, Red Deviltry, As It Is*, a melodrama hastily dashed from Buntline's pen. In the mode of most frontier dramas, the play featured a knife fight, a prairie fire, a tribal maiden friendly to the whites (played by Omohundro's stunning actress-wife, Giuseppina Morlacchi, who claimed to have introduced the cancan to America), and plenty of wicked Indians. The pear-shaped Buntline, looking entirely miscast next to the statuesque Buffalo Bill and Texas Jack, further alienated the audience by breaking character midplay to lecture on temperance.[6]

*Scouts of the Prairie* was roasted by theater critics, yet managed to play to packed houses on the marquee value of Buffalo Bill. Buntline was soon edged offstage and replaced, with much coaxing from Cody, by "Wild Bill" Hickok. Custer had once described the lean, angular Hickok as "one of the most perfect types of physical manhood I ever saw," which is saying something, as Custer was not usually generous with such observations; however, Wild Bill proved even less believable as an actor than Buntline, and made himself unwelcome by abusing the extras and threatening to shoot (for real) some of the Indians in the cast.[7]

Frontier shows in which real frontier heroes reenacted their actual deeds were unique to the American theater of the nineteenth

century. Like reality TV of our own time, the shows appealed largely
to low- or middle-brow audiences that enjoyed the frisson of seeing
authentic pugilists, politicians, feathered warriors, or border men
such as Cody and Hickok perform, for the most part awkwardly, as
themselves. The payoff was the chance to see dramatizations of real-
world events portrayed by the nonactors who had in fact carried
them out, who wore the same clothes, spoke the actual names of the
Indians and criminals they'd killed, and often used, as stage props,
the genuine guns, knives, hatchets, or other implements involved.
Cody would later work a human scalp into his act, which happened
to be the actual scalp of the actual Indian whose death (and scalp-
ing) he had both committed and was reenacting. Keeping things
lively, the principals between theatrical seasons returned to the
western settings of their real-life heroics, frequently bringing back
new tableaux as fodder for the stage. "It is not every day that one
can see on the stage a real border scout fighting over again his battles," noted the *Herald* of the phenomenon. "As we look on the actor
and remember that it is no merely mimic performer, but a man who
has passed through similar scenes . . . the interest is doubled and the
realism of the scene forcibly impresses itself on the spectator."[8]

IN 1874, GEORGE ARMSTRONG CUSTER AND THE SEVENTH CAVALRY
were ordered to enter the Black Hills stronghold of the Sioux
Nation, an expedition destined to change the region forever. For
while the pattern of whites ignoring treaty guarantees in the interest
of settlement, railroads, and mineral wealth had by now become
routine, the crisis looming in the Black Hills was far more charged:
it was one of the last Indian redoubts of the northern plains, a
sacred home and bountiful hunting ground whose people called it
"the Heart of Everything That Is," and who were adamant about its
defense.

The area had in fact been vouchsafed to the tribe by General
Sherman and the United States at the Second Treaty of Fort Laramie in 1868. That treaty ended Red Cloud's War, in which the canny
chief had wreaked havoc on the isolated government outposts along
the Bozeman Trail, frightening off or slaughtering many of the

troops and settlers who set foot there, including the hapless Captain Fetterman and his men, massacred outside Fort Phil Kearny in 1866. The treaty guaranteed the Sioux a "great reservation" that included the Black Hills and the part of South Dakota west of the Missouri River, as well as an "Unceded Indian Territory" in the Indians' rich hunting lands of the Powder River area of northeastern Wyoming and southeastern Montana; the area was to be off limits to all whites except government agents.

On July 22, 1874, all 1,200 men of Custer's expedition departed Fort Abraham Lincoln near Bismarck, under orders to locate a site for a future military fort and find an efficient route to the southwest; but the group had a purpose not officially acknowledged: to ascertain whether the region held substantial deposits of gold. The retinue included naturalists, or "bug hunters," as the soldiers called them; two prospectors; a geologist; a medical staff; and three newspaper reporters, one from New York City. Because of the prohibition against whites entering the region, few if any had gone there (some who had were not heard from again), and as a result there was much to see and learn.

Scout Luther North and Yale-trained naturalist George Bird Grinnell were among those who'd joined the expedition, Grinnell noting prophetically as the venture got under way that the threat of a gold rush in the Black Hills "will mean an Indian war I expect, for the Sioux and Cheyenne won't give up this country without a fight." Their tent was near Custer's, and after dinner they were often invited to join his campfire. North thought the general sociable and "a very enthusiastic hunter," but, as he "was always telling of the great shots he made each day . . . he didn't seem to care much about hearing of anyone else doing good shooting."[9]

Custer's avidity for hunting had grown in recent years. "I have done some of the most remarkable shooting I ever saw, and it is admitted to be such by all," he had informed Libbie from the western Dakotas in 1873. Almost single-handedly, he reported, he was keeping his regiment's larder full, having bagged forty-one antelope, four buffalo, four elk, seven deer, two white wolves, one red fox, and "geese, ducks, prairie chickens, and sage hens without number." He noted he had also captured a wildcat and porcupine alive for shipment to the Central Park Zoo. He reserved greater passion for an elk he felled, "a fine large buck-elk . . . weighing clean, eight hundred pounds, and with the handsomest pair of antlers I ever saw, and such a beautiful coat." Custer's hounds had pursued the wounded elk into a river, where they'd climbed on him and bitten his ears. "The combat in the water was one of the finest and most exciting hunting scenes I ever witnessed," mused Custer, who like many hunters of the era savored the spectacle of a battle to the death between species—dogs on a cougar, kitten versus rooster, elk goring a bear, even a rabbit tussling in the grass with a snake. "Oh! for a Landseer to have grasped and preserved the exciting features of that combat."[10]

One day, North and Grinnell were off hunting away from the troop column when three black-tail deer, likely spooked by the advancing soldiers, ran directly toward them, crossing a ridge less than a hundred yards away. That evening Grinnell presented a choice piece of venison to Custer, saying, "Captain North did some very good shooting, he killed three running deer with three shots." Custer, with a lack of interest, replied, "Huh, I found two more horned toads today." On another occasion, Grinnell, North, and Custer were riding at the head of the command when they came to a pond across which a duck was shepherding seven or eight ducklings. Custer dismounted, saying, "I will knock the heads off a few of them." Grinnell gestured to North that he should join in the shooting. Custer fired and missed; then North shot and clipped the head off one of the ducks. Custer fired again and missed, and again North succeeded in shooting off a duck's head. Custer gave North an unhappy look, but the same thing happened a third time. The awkwardness of the moment was relieved when an officer rode up to say that some of the shots were coming close to his troops. "We had better stop shooting," Custer said. He "got on his horse and rode away without saying a word to me," North recalled, "but I don't think he liked it very well." Soon Custer killed his first grizzly bear, and his restored confidence spilled out in late-night talk around the fire; when North happened to mention his relief that a large Indian village they had stumbled upon earlier that day had been abandoned, Custer waved the remark away, declaring, "I could whip all the Indians in the Northwest with the Seventh Cavalry."[11]

In addition to North and Custer, there was another fine shot along on the trip, scout "Lonesome" Charley Reynolds. A professional buffalo hunter and friend of Buffalo Bill's, Reynolds was a private man, who, as Grinnell recalled, "preferred to go off and hunt or trap by himself rather than to spend his time in the dreary little frontier towns where cards and whiskey were the sole diversion." A story he told of having run away from home as a boy and being raised in part by a mysterious old hunter he'd encountered in the woods sounded fantastical, yet his talents as guide and hunter often *did* seem unnatural. Indians who knew him believed the source of his powers was a set of illustrated natural history books he owned, which gave him "special medicine, which when used, induced animals to come to him." A good-looking man with large blue eyes set in a wide, honest face, he never married and, as Libbie Custer recalled, was too shy to even raise his eyes when he spoke to her. The general, however, entrusted him with some of the Seventh's riskiest missions, and in late August 1874, he asked Reynolds to carry out news of great importance: the expedition's geologists had discovered traces of gold.[12]

Custer's letter describing the gold find was restrained, but even the muted announcement created excitement, leading newspapers to declare a new El Dorado. "Rich Mines of Gold and Silver Reported Found by Custer," blared a headline from a Yankton paper in the Dakota Territory, while the *Chicago Inter-Ocean* reported of one Black Hills site: "From the grass roots down it was 'pay dirt.'" Intensely interested parties headed to the region at once, even as the Sioux cried foul and demanded that the United States honor the Laramie pact and deter the gold diggers from entering. But the few efforts by soldiers to expel the thousand or so prospectors who had flowed in proved futile. "If the whole army of the United States stood in the way," Ohio senator John Sherman observed, "the wave of emigration would pass over it to seek the valley where gold was to be found."[13]

The Grant administration found itself under pressure to resolve the issue quickly and to open the region for mineral exploitation and settlement. Since 1869, the year he took office, Grant had advocated a Peace Policy of avoiding further bloodshed against the Indians while seeking officially to bring them into the American fold. Church groups, missionaries, and other humanitarians had taken a hand in improving the distribution of government assistance at the often corrupt various Indian agencies, and had worked to encourage farming, Christianity, and education. But now Grant faced a dilemma: with miners and settlers demanding admittance to the Black Hills, he needed to convince the Indians to void the terms of the Laramie pact, when there was little incentive for them to do so. There was behind all this a truth evident for years, really since the Indian Removal Act of 1830: that it was disingenuous of whites to wonder whether Indians could or would assimilate. Whites wanted the Indians' hunting grounds, their land, and whatever lay under it, pure and simple—and the Indians, whether farmer Indians, nomadic hunters, book-reading Indians, or Stone Age savages—all must make way. In May 1875, when Spotted Tail, Red Cloud, and other chiefs were invited to Washington to discuss their possible surrender of the Black Hills, for which Grant offered to give the tribes $25,000 and help in relocating to the Oklahoma Territory, Spotted Tail cheekily replied, "If (Oklahoma) is such a good country, you ought to send the white men now in our country there and let us alone."[14]

That fall a federal commission came to the Black Hills to try to renegotiate access to the area with the individual Indian agencies, federally supervised centers of local tribal governance, but the natives remained uniformly opposed to the idea. Sitting Bull, the Sioux's charismatic war leader and spiritual chief, and his fiery lieutenant Crazy Horse, refused to attend, and their followers continued to roam and hunt the Black Hills and the Unceded Territory, threatening miners and other arriving whites. With hope of a settlement gone, the Grant administration could only look away as more prospectors flooded into the Sioux lands. From a policy perspective, it could only wait until the situation devolved into open conflict, at which time the United States would be released from the promises it had made at Laramie. In November, the US government took the next step, warning that unless the Indians returned to their agencies by January 31, 1876, the army would force them to do so.[15]

IN EARLY SPRING, WHEN THE CAMPAIGN AGAINST THE SIOUX IN THE Black Hills began, there was a new face among the local US military leadership, General George Crook. A six-footer of trim military build, with steel blue eyes, he sported a large sprig of whiskers that made him look like a permanently surprised preacher. Among his peers he was thought "more Indian than the Indians." He did admire Native Americans, and was generally liked by them in return for his honesty. A favorite of President Grant's and a former West Point classmate of Philip Sheridan's, Crook was a plain, reserved man who had previously engaged the Nez Perce and the Apache, against whom he had been effective as both a fighter and a mediator.

At times it seemed he would prefer not to be dealing with them at all, for when he "was not chasing Indians . . . he was chasing wild animals through great reaches of the vast western plains and mountains." As his aide-de-camp John C. Bourke would recall, "Duck, geese, turkeys, sage hens, prairie chickens, pike, pickerel, catfish, trout, salmon and whitefish; elk, deer, moose, antelope, mountain sheep, bears, wolverines, badgers, coyotes, wolves . . . all yielded tribute to his rod or rifle." Even when deep in hostile country, Crook was "prone to slip away for a day or two of hunting, his only company 'Apache,' his favorite mule." As he was skilled enough at the chase to always bring in a swelling bag, "all fears for his safety were forgotten in the great banquets that ensued."[16]

The strategy for driving the rogue Cheyenne and Sioux back to their agencies in the Black Hills involved a three-pronged US assault: Crook would move north from Fort Fetterman in Dakota Territory close to the Wyoming border; General Alfred Terry would arrive from Fort Lincoln in the east, accompanied by Custer and the Seventh Cavalry; and Colonel John Gibbon's men would march from the west at Fort Ellis, near present-day Bozeman, Montana.

Crook's men made contact first on March 17, in snow and freezing weather, when six companies of cavalry under Colonel Joseph J. Reynolds surprised a village containing between sixty-five and one hundred lodges. In what became known as the Battle of Powder River, the troops drove the Indians away, burned their wigwams and possessions, and made off with their herd of about a thousand ponies. However, Reynolds was slow in securing the village, allowing numerous Indian fighters to escape and take up hidden positions in nearby cliffs, which they used effectively to shoot down at the troops. As it was far too cold for an extended standoff, the soldiers—some already suffering from frostbite—had no choice but to withdraw, leaving US dead and wounded on the field. The Indians quickly reclaimed most of their horses. Crook, having initially gotten the jump on the enemy, rued the lost opportunity.

In late May, he again ventured into the field, with one thousand cavalry and army scouts as well as two hundred civilians—mostly hired teamsters (including Calamity Jane, disguised as a man), along with miners, prospectors, and others eager to take advantage of the army's protection to glimpse the Black Hills' mineral potential. On June 14, the force was joined by more than three hundred of Crook's Crow and Shoshone allies, led by Old Crow, Medicine Crow, and Good Heart.

Three days later, on a march down the valley of the Rosebud River, Crook divided his troops into multiple columns to limit the amount of dust raised, but native warriors already knew of the invading force and were waiting in a narrow canyon just north of his position. Crook had allowed his Indian allies to hunt buffalo the day before, and the sound of their guns may have alerted the enemy to the army's presence; the morning of the seventeenth he made another curious decision—having his troops rest in place in their order of march, even though they were well within enemy territory and imminent engagement was likely. The troops' alignment complicated the US response when Crook's Indian scouts suddenly rode pell-mell down the valley into camp, shouting, "Sioux, heap Sioux!" Crook had to hurriedly swing his troops into position as the attack came on.

It was said that 1,800 warriors had left the Red Cloud Agency to join the forces already living in the Unceded Territory under the leadership of Sitting Bull and the daring Crazy Horse. Many of the natives had been drawn to the Powder River area by the splendid hunting there and the possibility of rallying to defend their homeland; some of those initially reluctant to leave the agencies may have been angered by Crook's earlier assault at Powder River or cowed by Sitting Bull's shaming of the agency Indians who subsisted on government largesse. "You are fools to make yourselves slaves to a piece of fat bacon, some hard-tack, and a little sugar and coffee," Bull had said. Historical estimates of the number of warriors facing Crook range from one to five thousand, the higher number no doubt reflecting white witnesses' shock at finding themselves badly outnumbered; but it is doubtful there were more than two thousand present. What *was* clear was that Crook had been caught off guard and "had been struck a blow much harder than he had believed the Indians capable of delivering." For their part, the Indians, realizing they'd surprised the soldiers, were much invigorated, and pressed their advantage with gusto, charging isolated pockets of troops and dismounting to fight with tomahawk and club. Other braves raced back and forth across the narrow valley hanging low on their horses' necks, shooting from below, thus denying a target to US sharpshooters.[17]

Unlike most frontier battles, the Indians did not deploy their usual hit-and-run tactics, but dug in for an extended fight. "There was ammunition enough expended on our side to have killed the entire Sioux race," a trooper later wrote, for the confrontation lasted almost six hours, an eternity by standards of Indian warfare. So much time elapsed that a surreal incident took place: suddenly "a herd of buffalo ran through the Sioux line of battle," as a US soldier remembered, "and after remaining some time between the lines, apparently much bewildered by the heavy firing, finally charged down upon us, and passed within one hundred yards of our left flank." Crook, though blindsided by the initial attack, had the presence of mind when the Indians finally broke off not to pursue them as they retreated up the Rosebud, a likely feint intended to

lead the soldiers into what would have been a replay of the Fetterman Massacre, but on a much larger scale. One Indian combatant
later judged that if Crook had taken the bait, "it would have been
like throwing his men into the grave."[18]

Crook instead withdrew to Goose Creek, at the headwaters
of the Tongue River, which he renamed Camp Cloud Peak, to
rearm, tend to his wounded, and await reinforcements. Newspaper accounts—there were journalists in the expedition—questioned
him for having his progress halted by the Indians and for the fact
that his troops' very survival rested on the bravery of his Crow
and Shoshone scouts. "[Crook] seems to have formed his estimation of the Sioux from his experience of the Apaches," opined the
*New York Herald*, "and the surprise which he suffered on June 17
was the first awakening from this delusion." Absent Crook's native
allies, who spread the alarm and then turned to fight the attackers,
giving the men in blue time to assemble for battle, the US forces
might have sustained heavy losses. "All these shortcomings," concluded the *Herald*, "may be attributed to the fact that before 1876
no general officer of the army had occasion or opportunity to learn
how to fight the Sioux." Like the Comanche in Texas, the Sioux
were seen as particularly tough, ruthless antagonists, an impression
reinforced by the ferocity of Red Cloud's War a few years earlier.[19]

The criticism Crook endured did not suffice to drag him away
from Goose Creek, however. "Characteristically," writes a biographer, "he responded by withdrawing into himself and burying his
self-doubt in the familiar rhythms of field and stream." The camp
was "situated on a lovely mountain stream, fresh from the snow,"
recorded Bourke, a location that seemed "to have been anticipated
by the beavers, they having constructed a dam, causing water to fall
most gratefully to the ear at all hours." There were, Crook and his
men found, ample "uneducated" trout here, ranging from a half to
two and a half pounds, that would rise to take a grasshopper as bait.
Indeed, in what felt even to those present to be a queer transformation, the Crook expedition's bloody encounter with thousands
of Indians along the Rosebud became, within days, a dreamlike
hunting idyll, "an orgy of hunting and fishing" set in a welcoming,

peaceful locale. Whether Crook was still brooding about his poor showing on the Powder River in March (he'd demanded the commanding officer, Colonel Reynolds, face a court-martial), the recent setback on the Rosebud, or simply found distasteful the whole military enterprise in which he was now engaged, he perhaps quite naturally turned to more familiar, more manageable prey.[20]

Bourke said later that his own notebooks for the period "seem to be almost the chronicle of a sporting club, so filled are they with the numbers of trout brought by different fishermen into camp, (and) for those not inclined to fish, a variety of game birds and elk, deer, bear, mountain sheep, and of course buffalo awaited slaughter by any officer or enlisted man with a taste for blood sport and the courage to go into the surrounding hills." Crook's Indian allies also made themselves at home, constructing "wonderfully comfortable hovels with willow saplings and their twigs, and enjoy(ing) existence with a lazy relish . . . In the evening they sit under their sylvan shelters and sing in monotonous chorus until overpowered by slumber." A scout in Crook's service later estimated that fifteen thousand fish were caught by the troops and officers during the seven-week encampment, Crook personally landing seventy in a single day.[21]

To his credit, Crook did presently undertake some scouting expeditions with small, hand-picked groups of aides, but gazing through field glasses over the Black Hills, he saw nothing to suggest the movement of Indians. And invariably these trips included hunting for fresh game. One of the outings lasted so long, the camp sent out a search party to locate the general and bring him back.

The press compared Crook ensconced at Goose Creek unkindly to General McClellan's having been bogged down by indecision before Richmond, and historians ever since have pondered why so normally feisty a commander as Crook would spend weeks of the army's summer campaign against the Sioux hunting instead of looking to reengage the hostiles. One tactical explanation is that Crook still had not shaken off the ominous scene on the Rosebud and the overwhelming enemy numbers he'd glimpsed pouring down on him; he seems to have decided he must wait on reinforcements, for in response to a message from Sheridan, instructing him to "hit them again and hit them hard," he wrote, "I wish Sheridan would come here himself and show us how to do it. It is rather difficult to surround three Indians with one soldier."[22]

On July 10, another telegram from Sheridan reached Camp Cloud Peak. This one carried devastating news: Custer, his officers, and 242 men of the Seventh Calvary had all been killed on June 25 in an engagement with Sioux and Cheyenne to the north along the Little Bighorn River. Coming upon a larger-than-expected Indian village and exposing his forces before a coordinated US attack could commence, Custer's Seventh had been isolated and then slaughtered by hundreds of indignant warriors who had swarmed out of their camp, crossed the river, and closed up on the surrounded whites at what would become known as Last Stand Hill. Word of Custer's fate, Bourke noted, made "every lip quiver and every cheek blanch with terror and dismay . . . Grief, revenge, sorrow and fear stalked among us." Too many beloved comrades had been lost, including the ever-loyal Charlie Reynolds, who despite an invitation from an eastern friend to attend the Centennial Exposition in Philadelphia, had elected to stay and accompany Custer's march that summer. At the battle, he sacrificed himself to disrupt an Indian charge and protect a frantic retreat over the Little Bighorn River by troops under Major Marcus A. Reno. "Here, boys," Reynolds was heard to call to his scouts, his last words, "let us try to stop these Indians and give the soldiers a chance to cross."[23]

Crook finally did move from Camp Cloud Peak and won a minor skirmish against the Sioux at a place called Slim Buttes, but as far as the Sioux were concerned, the American campaign had been lost at the Battles of the Rosebud and the Little Bighorn. These were great victories for the Sioux and their allies, a credit to their determination and Sitting Bull's leadership. But they proved, in retrospect, to be not only Custer's but also the natives' "last stand." The US government, stunned and indignant over the Custer massacre, lost no time in arresting some of the Indian leaders of the summer's fighting, while in Washington, Congress rushed through a law eviscerating all Sioux rights to the Black Hills. Now, as Spotted Tail had warned, more whites would come; they *always* came; and Sitting Bull had already led his dwindling group of Sioux resisters away to Canada.[24]

FOR MILITARY PEERS WHO KNEW CUSTER'S BOLDNESS AND OVERweening self-regard, the fate he and his troops met was a tragedy, but one many would have foreseen. To the larger nation, the shock was twofold—that, at what many had assumed to be a late stage in the Indian Wars, US forces could suffer so devastating a defeat, and that the dashing hunter and cavalry man who'd graced the cover of *Harper's Weekly*, whose literate articles appeared in New York magazines, who had never failed to vanquish his enemies, had himself been utterly swept from the earth. With such a popular subject and setting, the project of turning the massacre into a saga of combined heroism and martyrdom began almost immediately; the newspapers, Libbie Custer, and various western artists and scribes would have their roles, but important too were the efforts of Buffalo Bill Cody, who was now a well-traveled veteran of the conduit that turned frontier hardship into entertainment and filled seats in Bowery theaters.

On July 17, 1876, with the nation still staggered by the Seventh Cavalry's demise, Cody took part in the Battle of Warbonnet Creek in Nebraska, where he killed and scalped a Cheyenne chief named Yellow Hair (whose name was often mistranslated as Yellow Hand, including by Cody himself). According to a news account, Buffalo Bill, serving as an army scout to protect two couriers from a wagon train in danger of being ambushed by a Cheyenne war party,

> instantly sprang to his horse (and came) down off the hill. Yellow Hand, a young Cheyenne brave, came foremost, singling Bill as a foeman worthy of his steel. Cody coolly knelt, and taking deliberate aim, sent his bullet through the chief's leg and into his horse's head. Down went the two and, before his friends could reach him, a second shot from Bill's rifle laid the redskin low.[25]

Cody recalled that "before he had fairly touched the ground I was upon him, knife in hand, and had driven the keen-edged weapon to its hilt in his heart. Jerking his war-bonnet off, I scientifically scalped him in about five seconds . . . As the soldiers came up I swung the Indian chieftain's top-knot and bonnet in the air, and shouted: 'The first scalp for Custer!'"[26]

As with most reports of Cody's legendary deeds or, for that matter, almost any story of Indian warfare in the West, it can't be known for certain exactly what happened. However, the description offered by the paper agrees with what is known of Cody's style of Indian fighting—the calm preparation, the shooting of an enemy's horse first so as to unseat and disorient the rider. And Cody did obtain Yellow Hair's scalp and other personal items, because he promptly boxed them up and sent them to his wife, Lulu, who was living in Buffalo, Wyoming, suggesting she arrange to have them put on display in the window of a local department store. Although there is no evidence to suggest Yellow Hair was at the Battle of the Little Bighorn, Cody the following year began reenacting his deed onstage as "Custer's Revenge, or, the First Scalp for Custer." The powerful, ritualistic act of retribution in which the audience shared was enhanced by the fact that Cody displayed and incorporated into the show the actual scalp he'd lifted from the chief's head, as well as other items that had belonged to him. (Whether out of respect for his victim or recognition of the scalp's importance to his box office, Cody maintained close watch over it, keeping it in a portable safe in his private railway car when the troupe was on the road.)[27]

"Custer's Revenge" helped cinch Cody's place as the undisputed star of the theater of the American West, but greater work lay ahead: the abandonment of traditional staging of heroic tableaux in favor of a large outdoor western pageant, Buffalo Bill's Wild West. The success of the 1872 performance of Spotted Tail and his people before Duke Alexis (and the fact that the Indians had been good sports about the whole thing), may have been on his mind a decade later, on July 4, 1882, when Cody put on a western-theme party called the "Old Glory Blow Out" in his hometown of North Platte, Nebraska. It featured mock fights between Indians and settlers, trick riding, daredevil stagecoach antics, shooting with gun and bow and arrow, and athletic demonstrations of the lariat. The event was a hit, but more important, Cody was inspired; he envisioned turning the sprawling pageant into powerful theater, to be staged on a grand scale. It was an imaginative leap of which only someone with his dual appreciation of western spectacle and big city box office was capable.

The name "Buffalo Bill's Wild West" pointedly did not contain the word *show*, *revue*, or *vaudeville*; it was none of those. What spectators would see would be a replication of the settling of the West, as little varied from reality as could be managed, with roping, native dancing, re-enactments of legendary battles, crimes, shootouts, and romantic reunions—more an immersion, an experience to be lived. The props, lariats, and stagecoaches were all genuine; the Indians, especially the Indians, would be real. What Native Americans thought of working as paid extras in what was, for them, the restaging of their own near extinction, cannot easily be guessed, although the production did celebrate Indian prowess and customs, and it was said Cody was a considerate employer, often paying train fare and other expenses for any native extra who grew homesick.

Such a thing—a vast, moveable pageant with scores of actors, other performers, and hired hands—would not have been possible a generation before. Now, with people concentrated in cities, staged spectacles could attract large paying audiences; interstate railroads could transport horses, sets, and costumes hundreds of miles overnight, and telegraph lines sped news of rave performances. Those same wires also carried word of sensational events in the West— bank robberies, Indian attacks—that might become a gripping Wild West reenactment within days, even hours, reinforcing the show's immediacy.

Among its set pieces, Cody's success with "Custer's Revenge" made imperative a larger spectacle of the Last Stand itself. For the important role of Custer, Cody cast Buck Taylor, a poster-ready hunk from Texas who had worked as a cattle herder. Buck and his brother Bax, orphans whose father had been killed in the Civil War, had come north with a cattle drive and were hired by the North

Brothers to work on the Nebraska cattle ranch they owned with Cody. Buffalo Bill saw potential at once in Buck, who was six foot three and ruggedly handsome, with broad shoulders and a thick mustache, superb at roping and riding, his only eccentricity being that he lived almost entirely on pie, which he ate four or five times a day. Taylor's acting was if anything even more wooden than Hickok's or Buntline's, but "The Last Stand" became a much-touted part of Cody's spectacle, with Buffalo Bill himself appearing as a potential rescuer of the doomed Seventh Cavalry just at the moment Custer/Buck Taylor fell dead and the tragic words "TOO LATE!" appeared on a backdrop. Custer most likely had lost the Battle of the Little Bighorn because he'd surged ahead without adequately protecting his flank and been overwhelmed by the Indians' superior numbers, tactics, and motivation; but Cody's version tended to echo a popular "abandonment" narrative of the Last Stand: that Custer and his valiant troops had died because expected reinforcements had failed to arrive.

Cody billed Taylor as "the King of the Cowboys," and his publicist Prentiss Ingraham in 1887 wrote a fictional biography of the boy that became a series of dime novels, such as *Buck Taylor, the Saddle King*, helping to introduce the type as a staple of western literature. This process was fully realized in 1902 with the appearance of Owen Wister's hugely popular novel *The Virginian*, which introduced the expression "smile when you say that" and other tropes, and refined the cowboy hero into the plainspoken, quietly capable loner who would serve as protagonist in countless western films and long-running TV series.

Of course, none could compete with Cody himself. His entrance on a magnificent white charger, trained to rear up on its hind legs as Bill doffed his hat in a sweeping gesture, opened every Wild West spectacle. Unlike some of the other performers, Buffalo Bill did little shooting. While he was regarded with awe for his ability to kill buffalo from horseback (Luther North swore he once saw Bill drop sixteen of the animals on the run with sixteen shots), he was not much for standard target shooting or marksmanship. In some versions of the show, he did a trick shot with targets connected to piano keys so that with a spray of bullets he could "play" "Yankee Doodle," but the gag was possibly rigged, and by and large he left such things to the experts.

Aside from its virtuosic elements, what lent the spectacle's extravagant pageantry its immense appeal was, in large part, its utter poignancy, the knowledge that what it portrayed—the free spirits of the open country, the hunting tall tales, the Indians, the mountain men and trappers, the cowboys and the vast cattle spreads, even the "most unlovely race of beings" known as hide hunters—was already in the process of being replaced by almighty Progress. The Wild West, with its blank-firing six-shooters and its fake stagecoach holdups, as well as its flesh and blood participants like Buffalo Bill, enabled spectators to witness one of mankind's greatest final adventures, the conquest of the last western frontier, whose rougher aspects were now safely obsolete. In the show's dramatic finale, "The Assault on the Settlers' Cabin," Buffalo Bill arrives at the last moment to save a frontier family from annihilation, restoring, to loud cheers from the bleachers, the virtue of hearth and kin to the national saga; the rough edges of the western experience have been celebrated, but it is civilization that is welcomed in the end.[28]

One of the high points of Cody's exhibition was its 1887 trip to Queen Victoria's Golden Jubilee in London, where the "Wild West" did a six-month run in a temporary stadium that held twenty thousand in a grandstand and fifteen thousand standing. Spectators beheld a real buffalo hunt, a wagon train of pioneers ambushed by Indians and rescued by Buffalo Bill, various rope and riding tricks, and Annie Oakley's shooting, with interludes enlivened by the oom-pah of a thirty-six-piece band. Following the show, visitors could tour the Indian Village behind stage, where the ninety Native American performers lived, and meet Wild West stars, such as the now-genial Sioux warrior Red Shirt, who had been at the Battle of the Little Bighorn, as well as Walking Buffalo, Black Elk, Moccasin Tom, and Cut Meat, and also chat with real cowboys, Mexicans vaqueros, and others. Heads of state arrived; Queen Victoria came twice (it was said she admired Cody, but was most impressed by the fine-looking Red Shirt). The Indians called her "Grandmother England" and enjoyed the spectacle of the "shining wagons" in which her entourage rode. To Nicholas Black Elk, an Oglala medicine man, "she looked like a fire coming." The queen was smitten enough in turn to invite the Native Americans to tea at Windsor Castle, where she confided, "If you belonged to me, I would not let them take you around in a show like this." In response, the visitors, touched by the queen's remark, "sent up a great cry," Black Elk remembered, "and our women made the tremolo."[29]

The Wild West followed its tours in England and Europe with a long, lucrative run on Staten Island, as well as at the Columbian Exposition of 1893 in Chicago. In the spirit of the internationally flavored Chicago fair, Cody added Syrian and Arabian horsemen to his "Congress of Rough Riders," which already included Cossacks, gauchos, and vaqueros. When the troupe played an extended engagement before twenty thousand spectators in Ambrose Park, Brooklyn, in 1894, a critic raved that "to miss seeing his Congress of Rough Riders of the World, in their most wonderful and daring feats of horsemanship, which, by the way, are perfectly natural, and contain no circus play, is to miss one of the finest educational exhibitions ever given." So clamorous by now was the demand for the Wild West that dozens of competing western pageants appeared and began to circulate, but Cody's spectacle always remained the gold standard: in the quarter-century between 1883 and the First World War, it was estimated to have been seen by 50 million people around the world. At the time of his death in January 1917, one scholar ventures, "probably more people throughout the world had seen Cody in person than any other man or woman who had ever lived."[30]

An intriguing coda to Cody's life's work was his last creative endeavor, an attempt to bring the great saga of the West to the screen. This was an obvious move; his Wild West, with its stock characters and dire predicaments resolved heroically at the last possible moment, was a clear precedent and direct inspiration for the pioneering western-themed films that began to appear as early as

1903. Cody's own ambitious film project, which he called Indian War Pictures, was to be a series of movies depicting the key battles and confrontations between the army and the Indians in the taming of the West, with Cody reenacting yet one more time his heroics at the Battle of Summit Springs and the Battle of Warbonnet Creek, among others. Although no viewable prints of these films survive, it is said that many re-created sequences went well.

The enterprise stumbled, however, when the army's technical consultant, Lt. General Nelson A. Miles, a stickler for authenticity, insisted that the last reel, the December 1890 massacre at Wounded Knee, be filmed on its exact historical location. This infamous slaughter of between 150 and 300 Indian men, women, and children, mowed down by US troops after having fled into a ravine, was in 1913 barely history, and the local Indian extras grew uneasy when Miles, for accuracy's sake, arranged for the presence of hundreds of soldiers bearing Hotchkiss guns, rifles, and wagons of ammunition. The natives were also outraged that the reenactment would occur almost on top of the graves of their relatives, and some braves warned Cody that they would carry loaded weapons during the filming in case white troops got carried away. Master legend maker Buffalo Bill, it appeared, had at last met a set of incontrovertible facts he could not subdue into standard heroics or myth, and under the influence of the natives' great emotion and the filmmakers' uncertainty, the resulting footage suffered—both for what it showed and for what it pointedly ignored.

The production was further marred by Cody's tacking onto the film's ending several scenes of Indians engaged in useful activities, such as farming, attending school, and working in offices, fitting themselves to be Americans like everyone else, which he had had to agree to insert so as to gain the federal government's approval to hire natives to appear in the film. But as Cody's biographer Louis Warren has pointed out, viewers of early movie westerns, not unlike the audience at a Wild West, wanted to see the Indians vanish, not reappear in a tedious anticlimax as upstanding citizens. Titled *The Indian Wars Refought*, the silent movie had the further misfortune to be released in August 1914, just as war was beginning in Europe, and although the sixty-nine-year-old Cody tried his practiced hand at promotion, riding onstage at the Denver premiere astride his white horse and doffing his hat as he had thousands of times, the film did poorly in both Denver and New York, the only two cities in which it was shown. Perhaps in part overshadowed by current events, it not only soon disappeared from the nation's theaters, but vanished for good; many film historians believe that all prints were confiscated and destroyed by the government, displeased by the painful depiction of US troops in action at Wounded Knee.[31]

*Chapter Nine*

# The New Type of Goodness

HENRY WILLIAM HERBERT'S ENACTMENT OF THE BRITISH GENTLE-manly hunt had nurtured the sport as an American pastime; William Drummond Stewart's multiple visits to the West had awakened curiosity about the customs of the mountain rendezvous and the tribes of the northern Plains; Duke Alexis had brought a taste of imperial Saint Petersburg to the buffalo-hunting grounds of Nebraska. There was a stark exception to all this transatlantic civility, however, and its name was Sir George Gore—eighth Baronet of Manor Gore, near Sligo in northwest Ireland. In the mid-1850s, he commenced a big game hunt across America like none ever before seen, an event that became so notorious it would serve as a touchstone for the earliest efforts at curbing hunting and wildlife preservation.

A bachelor whose passion was for the chase, Sir George had learned of Stewart's western experiences and, using connections he had with the American Fur Company, mounted an expedition that reached Saint Louis via New York in March 1854. Back in Ireland, he was that unpopular type, the absentee landlord who collected rents on his lands while living in England, so perhaps he had grown inured to criticism, for he proved to lack all restraint in marching (and shooting) his way across the American landscape. His expedition included a pack of thirty-two greyhounds and eighteen foxhounds, a staff of taxidermists, forty teamsters, a chuck wagon, seventy-five rifles, numerous shotguns, all manner of powder and ammunition, two wagons of fishing gear (accompanied by a fly-tying specialist), a brass bed, a steel bathtub, a cabinet of wine and brandies, several wardrobes, a portable commode, a library of classic books beginning with Homer, an inflatable raft, and—for trading purposes—cloth, beads, candles, and 250 gallons of whiskey. Various scientific instruments were also in the baggage, including a telescope and a special odometer on two wheels that was pulled along to measure the distance traveled. Resembling an invading army more than a hunting party, it formed one of the largest caravans to ever traverse the Great Plains, or so it appeared to eight-year-old William Cody, who watched the spectacle pass through Leavenworth, Kansas, on its way west.

Gore proceeded at a leisurely pace, at one point even constructing a private fort where he remained for nine months. His custom was to rise late, about ten or eleven a.m., breakfast and bathe, be out hunting by midday, and remain afield until dark. His doggedness was admired, but his guides saw in him a so-so horseman and average shot, and they thought him too lordly at times, as when he hired a gang of Indians to build a road over a mountain so he could go fishing. For two years he was methodical, crossing and recrossing 6,000 miles of Wyoming, Montana, the Dakotas, and Colorado, bringing death to 2,500 buffalo, 1,600 elk and deer, 105 grizzly bears, and scores of smaller game. "Forty guns a-blazin' and a-barkin' from sun up to sundown till the ground wuz fair covered with dead and dyin' critters," was how hunter and trapper Jim Bridger recalled the adventure.[1]

Sir George and Bridger made an odd couple, the Oxford-educated baronet and the illiterate mountain man apparently bonding over an appreciation of Shakespeare, which Gore read aloud to Bridger each night as they sat beneath the stars, drinking and smoking by Gore's campfire. Bridger had probably covered more of the West than any other white man, trapping beaver and hunting elk, antelope, and buffalo. He was one of the first whites to visit the wilderness that would later become Yellowstone National Park—although given his notoriety as a teller of tall tales, his descriptions of the Yellowstone region's geysers, steaming springs, and other geological wonders were at first not credited. Perhaps it was his love of a good yarn that left him vulnerable to Gore's readings of Shakespeare, as Bridger was so taken with their musical language, he learned to recite long passages by heart, and at the end of his employ traded two oxen for the books from which Gore had read.

Far less amused with Sir George were the local Indians, who complained to federal Indian agency representatives about the groaning size of the Irishman's game bag. They demanded to know how such decimation of their sources of subsistence could be permitted, when they could be punished for killing a single cow belonging to a white settler. The protest reached Alfred Cumming, US superintendent of Indian affairs, who had issued Gore his passport to hunt in Indian Territory. "The Indians have been loud in their complaining at men passing through their country killing and driving off their game," Indian agent A. J. Vaughn had written to Cumming, relating that Gore had himself admitted his group's food larder did not require such massive amounts of game and that most animals were killed for sport. "What can I do against so large a number of men coming into a country like this so very remote from civilization, doing and acting as they please, nothing I assure you beyond apprising you of the facts on paper." Not only was Gore apparently massacring game in large numbers, but he reputedly had his hand in some murky frontier business: when some of his expedition's horses were stolen by Blood Indians, Gore traded some forbidden items (likely guns, ammunition, or whiskey) to a band of Crows to help him retrieve them. Cumming sympathized with the natives and briefly there was talk of the United States confiscating the baronet's trophies of pelts, antlers, and stuffed heads and using the proceeds from their sale to compensate the aggrieved parties. Unfortunately, having granted Sir George a permit to take game, the legality (not to mention the appearance) of stripping him of his

trophies would have been problematic, and ultimately the government took no action.[2]

The only significant discomfiture Gore was made to endure
came when he departed the country in 1856. Alexander Culbertson,
a senior trader with the American Fur Company and husband of
Natawista, a Blood Indian, had learned that Natawista's brother,
Big Plume, had been wounded in a skirmish with Gore's men over
the stolen horses. When Gore sought to sell off his extensive baggage and equipment before departing for England, Culbertson
offered a pittance for the lot. Sir George, unwilling to be insulted,
refused to negotiate further and instead ordered all his expedition's
wagons, its scientific equipment, books, and furniture set afire. He
then directed that any surviving iron be sunk so deep in the Missouri River that it could never be salvaged. The West breathed a
collective sigh of relief when so difficult and entitled a man finally
loaded up the last of his myriad animal trophies and sailed away.

While Gore's exploits in the West brought him enduring
infamy—a roadside marker in Colorado still recalls him as "an
Irish Baronet bent on slaughter of game"—tales of his American
shooting odyssey fired the imagination of other British nimrods.
One was Windham Thomas Wyndham-Quin, fourth Earl of Dunraven and Mount-Earl, an Irish big game hunter. A true "sport of
all sports," he had hunted in Africa and the Mediterranean, but his
passion for America's big game had been stoked by his childhood
reading of the books of Captain Mayne Reid. "My boyish brain-
cells were stored to bursting," he said, "with tales of Red Indians
and grizzly b'ars; cabelleros and haciendas, prairies and buffaloes,
Texans and Mexicans." Arriving in the West in spring 1872, he
hired Texas Jack Omohundro and Buffalo Bill Cody as guides and
began living his youthful dream. "We were about the dirtiest, most
blood-stained, hungriest, happiest, most contented, and most dis-
reputable crowd to be found anywhere in the great territories of
the West," he reported. Moving about with none of the pseudo-im-
perial trappings of the Gore expedition, Dunraven hunted widely
throughout the West and Canada.[3]

Then, one winter evening at the elite Corkscrew Club in Denver, he heard tell of an area northeast of the city, called Estes Park, breathtaking for its scenery and renowned for good hunting. Despite its being late December, he hurried there and immediately felt he knew why he'd come to America. "It was a paradise," he wrote. "Mountain sheep, black-tail and white-tail deer in abundance, and an occasional mountain lion or bear . . . beavers and otters were plentiful, and the streams were full of trout." The place, named for Joel Estes, who had founded a modest claim in 1859, had few inhabitants, although a few years before Dunraven's coming, an Estes employee, Griff Evans, had hammered together some tourist cabins and opened one of the first dude ranches in the West, offering guided hunts, access to fishing, and scenic tours. Dunraven, taken with the idea of creating a game reserve for his own use and that of other British hunters, embarked on a plan to obtain extensive acreage in Estes Park. Under the Homestead Act of 1862, an individual could file a claim for 160 acres of land free or at minimal cost, with the promise to "qualify" or "prove up" the claim with basic improvements. Dunraven, however, was prohibited from doing so because he was not a US citizen, and in fact sought many more acres than a single claim could provide. In spirit, too, of course, his ambition to aggregate a large holding went against the act's Jeffersonian ideal of enabling individual yeoman farmers.[4]

In his favor, however, the homesteading bureaucracy was deeply backlogged at the moment due to high demand, and as a result there was a lack of oversight of individual claims. Clever petitioners, especially those with money and connections, might game the system with the help of land brokers and attorneys. Investing $40,000, Dunraven turned to the common ruse of having intermediaries file straw claims on his behalf. Soon, he and his representatives possessed 6,000 acres in Estes Park. As historian Peter Pagamenta reports, by the time other arriving settlers grew wise to these machinations, a Colorado newspaper had identified the nature of Dunraven's purchases as "one of the most barefaced land steals of this land stealing age."[5]

Despite such terrible press, Dunraven no doubt considered his corner-cutting to be for the greater good; for unlike most homesteaders, he had minimal interest in developing the land: he wanted it for its pristine perfection, to save paradise. Ultimately, however, he could not evade the growing local and national resentment toward foreign, particularly British, investment in American land. Various dukes, lords, sirs, and at least one marquis—derided as "land gods" by the American press—along with British corporations had by the 1880s accumulated as much as 20 million acres of western land. So thick was the region with British nobility, the story was told of two hunting parties in the hills of Wyoming, one led by a Lord Rodney and the other by retired British Army major Lovatt Wise, sharing a jolly good laugh after each mistook the other for hostile Indians.[6]

A sobering 1892 press report averred that British holdings in the United States were larger than the country of Ireland, news deeply unsettling to Irish emigrants who feared that the absentee landlordism then prevalent in the Irish countryside would somehow transplant itself to the American West. The Irish American's worst nightmare was that having fled tenancy at home, he might find himself re-enslaved to the very same land owner in the New World. Attempted state legislation to curb British investment was often vetoed or quickly repealed because railroads and business valued it, but in the case of Estes Park, Dunraven's trickery, rumors about his homosexuality and effete lifestyle, and of course the desired aspect of the locale ultimately caused his specious land claims to be challenged and denied. He settled for building a luxury hotel in the park.[7]

Signs that American patience with the Dunravens and Stewarts and Sir Georges of the world was wearing thin surfaced in the criticism of Colonel William C. McCarty, a British nobleman, who in late 1874 announced his intention to lead a major hunt from Texas to Oregon and back to the Rockies and the plains of Kansas. It would last about seven months, from May 1875 to January 1876, and target elk, wild turkey, buffalo, bear, antelope, and cougar. Forest and Stream termed McCarty's project "the Big Hunt."

The colonel assured American sportsmen through the magazine's pages that he would not seek to slaughter game indiscriminately or destroy animals out of season, but by now, frustrated with the never-slackening British presence in the West generally and the sense that hunter-tourists vanquished game stocks already grown scarce, readers voiced their contempt for the idea.

McCarty's group would be shooting game before it was in season, said some; it would also likely kill far more game than it could possibly need for its own larder, as surely trophies would be taken, destined for the walls of English manor houses. US diplomat and author Adam Badeau went so far as to dispute the sacred notion that hunting bred nobility into the English character, insisting that "to be forever planning and inflicting death and pain, even on animals, cannot be refining. The English nature is coarse in itself, but sport renders it more so." Subscriber William C. Mead suggested that because British game laws were more restrictive, English hunters came to the United States to exploit its more democratic hunting environment. As a result, British sportsmen wandered freely, gun in hand, through the American West, where they easily forgot their better nature and "recklessly slaughter our choicest game for the barren pleasure of telling of great deeds and wonderful prowess." He reminded fellow readers that "it is notorious that not one-tenth of the game killed upon these hunting excursions is ever put to any better use than as manure," and suggested the overkill was as bad a crime as poaching. "If marksmanship is to be tested, let it be upon the insensible targets at Creedmoor," Mead concluded. He recommended that, going forward, hunting itself be viewed as a form of animal abuse and brought to the attention of the American Society for the Prevention of Cruelty to Animals (ASPCA). As demonstrated by the antipigeon shooting movement, in which the ASPCA played a central role, the idea that animals were sentient beings and did not deserve to be mistreated was consonant with the emerging sensibility that limits were necessary on hunters and others who took animal lives in sport, whether for reasons of species preservation or immoral cruelty.[8]

HENRY BERGH, WHO HAD FOUNDED THE ASPCA IN NEW YORK IN 1866, looked to Britain not for its hunting mystique, but rather, its exemplary reform efforts on behalf of nonhuman creatures. It is worth revisiting how policies of humane consideration for animals took hold in Britain, for the story informs the way the concept later advanced in America and continues to influence today's ongoing discussion of animal consciousness and animal rights.

Challenging the enjoyment of bearbaiting, ratting, cockfighting, and other sporting pleasures in Elizabethan England was no easy task. The public had deep feelings for them, particularly distinguished fighting bears, many of which might be considered some of the world's first animal celebrities. Shakespeare mentions the ursine champion Sackerson, and there were others, such as Tom of Lincoln, Ned of Canterbury, and Blind Robin. Henry VIII, like his daughter Queen Elizabeth a keen follower of the sport in which a chained bear fended off multiple canine assailants, had a bearbaiting pit constructed that seated one thousand spectators.

Ratting also had its champions—Tiny, a dog that killed three hundred rats in fifty-four minutes fifty seconds; Jacko, said to have killed a thousand rats in one hour forty minutes; and the terrier Billy, who became so famous for his exploits in the London rat pits (he once killed a hundred rats in five minutes) that he was preserved by a taxidermist. "Nature herself, I fear, fixes in man a kind of instinct to inhumanity," wrote Montaigne. "Nobody takes pleasure in seeing beasts play and caress one another, but no one fails to take pleasure in seeing them dismember and tear one another to pieces.[9]

Cockfighting was said by its apologists to be a means of teaching men courage by witnessing the cocks' fighting tenacity, even unto death. Such adult depravity made possible the child's game of "cock-throwing" or "cock-shying," an English schoolyard tradition honored every Shrove Tuesday, whereby a rooster was tied to a stake and used as a target for a stick- and stone-throwing competition, or buried in the ground with only its head visible, the greater the challenge. In an equally barbaric form of entertainment, a monkey was tethered to a pony, and dogs were released to assault the monkey, which, to observers' amusement, would simultaneously cling for its life and fend off the lunging dogs from atop the crazed, frightened pony.

Bearbaiting, cat and dog tossing, and other sports were criticized by the Puritans as early as the sixteenth century, not solely for these recreations' harm of living creatures, but for their social corruption—their appeal to the worst of human nature. This two-pronged concern with brutality toward animals illuminated William Hogarth's *The Four Stages of Cruelty* (1751), engravings that depict the degeneration of a youthful animal-tormentor, Tom Nero. Tom first appears as a boy abusing a dog; next, as a cruel wagon master beating his horse; then, as a heartless robber and seducer who murders his pregnant mistress. The final panel shows Tom, who's been executed for his crime, on a surgeon's autopsy table, one of his organs having rolled off the table onto the floor, where it's being sniffed at by a dog. Hogarth, who deplored "the barbarous treatment of animals, the very sight of which renders the streets of our metropolis so distressing to Fellowship," had prints published on the cheapest paper possible so that they might find their way into the hands of London's toiling classes.[10]

Hogarth's work was evidence of a dawning animal rights sentiment in eighteenth-century England that echoed in the world's first book on animal protection, the Reverend Doctor Humphrey Primatt's *A Dissertation on the Duty of Mercy and Sin of Cruelty to Brute Animals* (1776). Four years later, philosopher Jeremy Bentham unseated for good the rickety edict by René Descartes that animals were soulless machines, their cries of pain no different than the sounds of creaky gears, when he proposed a new ethical basis for the human regard of animals: "The question is not, Can they *reason*? nor Can they *talk*? But, Can they *suffer*?"[11]

The Puritans had already brought, a full century before, the world's first antihunting protest. Killing wild animals for food was, no doubt, part of God's plan, they agreed, but as sport, hunting offended God and was contemptuous of his creation. "How many Gentlemen be there," queried one Puritan minister, "of whom when they die, all that can be said is this, They were born, they did eat, and drink, and play, and hunt, and hawk, and lived like so many wild Ass-colts, never minding any thing that concern'd God's glory, or their own salvation . . . and so died, and dropt into Hell?"[12]

Parliament was first called upon to respond to the question in 1822, when member Richard Martin, with the support of London clergy and the influential antislavery advocate William Wilberforce (who had waged his own fight against bullbaiting), ushered in a law on behalf of horses and cows, known as Martin's Act. "Humanity Dick," as he was lampooned, was in his late sixties when he took up the cause. Lord of a 200,000-acre Irish estate so large, it was said, that from his front door he could be driven 30 miles before reaching his own gatehouse, Martin was fond of hunting and shooting; he also was a survivor of duels and had the scars to show for it. And like his later American counterpart Henry Bergh, he took particular exception to the ill treatment of horses in his campaign for animal protection. They were overburdened, ridden or driven by drunkards or incompetents, then let die in the street or sent to the knackers to be turned into food for pets (the origin of the saying "going to the dogs"). What especially angered him was the practice known as bearing rein, designed to keep a horse's head up as it trotted, to give it a more attractive bearing. The restrictive rein inhibited circulation and denied the horse the ability to lower its head for greater pulling power when going uphill; and on a downhill slope it inhibited the animal's vision and agility at stepping over obstacles and holes.

Concerned the new law would be ignored if not enforced, Martin prosecuted several cases of animal cruelty himself and also often paid the fines of the accused drivers or workmen, as he was less interested in punishing people than demonstrating that the law would be used. In 1824, he and Wilberforce helped found the Society for the Prevention of Cruelty to Animals (SPCA), the world's first such entity. Princess Victoria became a patron in 1835, and in 1840, as queen, added the word "Royal" to the organization's name.

Jeremy Bentham and "Humanity Dick" ushered in new sympathy for "the brute creation," while romantic sensibility sentimentalized wild nature. The early decades of the nineteenth century saw numerous reissues of what many consider the first modern book of natural history, *A General History of Quadrupeds*, by English engraver Thomas Bewick, originally published in 1790 and, at five hundred pages, with Bewick's marvelous woodcuts, as stunning as it was definitive. The popularity of Bewick's work was indicative of a larger shift in how man viewed animals—not just as dumb beasts but as creatures created of the same cloth as mankind. These cultural changes were embodied in the work of Edwin Landseer, who depicted the human character of animal emotion, the close bonds between man and beast, and the tragic beauty of hunter and prey. Landseer's painting of a dog faithfully guarding his master's humble coffin, *Old Shepherd's Chief Mourner* (1837), became a popular print and sold widely. Reformers also began to focus some of their efforts on children, as it was seen that young boys were often the most casual of animal abusers. "Animals were quickly recognized as promising didactic instruments," writes historian Harriet Ritvo of the period, "and works of both juvenile natural history and moral fiction were loaded with uplifting messages about the need to treat them kindly." Two of the best-known products of this tendency were "Mary Had a Little Lamb," written in 1830 by Mrs. Sarah Josepha Hale, and "I Love Little Pussy," attributed to the poet Jane Taylor, both published and frequently republished in mid-nineteenth-century songbooks. In the spirit of *Old Shepherd's Chief Mourner*, a British humanitarian group in 1858 began promoting the story of Greyfriars Bobby, a Skye terrier said to visit his master's grave every day in Edinburgh's Greyfriars Churchyard. The story became so well known that a statue of Greyfriars Bobby was erected there in 1873, and the site still draws tourists.[13]

Two epochal events in the realm of natural science also influenced changing attitudes regarding animal suffering—the discovery in 1856 of the fossil remains of Neanderthal Man in a valley near Düsseldorf, Germany, and the 1859 publication of Charles Darwin's *On the Origin of Species*. Darwin's achievement was the more incisive, overturning millennia of guesswork and unknowing with a reimagining of biology on par with Newton's explanation of the universe according to the laws of gravitation. Both developments crystallized the idea that humans lay on an evolutionary continuum with beasts, for as Darwin wrote, "We have seen that the senses and intuitions, the various emotions and faculties, such as love, memory, attention and curiosity, imitation, reason etc., of which man boasts, may be found in an incipient, or even sometimes in a well-developed condition, in the lower animals." Not surprisingly, the era also saw the beginning, on both sides of the Atlantic, of the modern vegetarian movement, the term entering common usage in 1847 with the founding of the Vegetarian Society in England. In America, Sylvester Graham, a Presbyterian minister, advocated a vegetable diet to improve physical health as well as spiritual virtue and mental sharpness. He feared it was his countrymen's heavy intake of meat that led to their generally substandard physical health, and advised that eating animal flesh was beneath humankind, a vice on par with drunkenness or sexual depravity.[14]

All this attention to the sentience and essence of animals would ultimately fuel an acrimonious debate in England over vivisection—the dissection of a live animal—one which eventually spilled over on both sides of the Atlantic into a broader argument about violence toward animals and human pacifism as a response to the horrors of the Great War. To be sure, important advances in science, such as William Harvey's discoveries about blood and circulation, came through animal experiments, but such breakthroughs were the exception; it is more likely that Harvey's success inspired thousands of needless vivisections. The late nineteenth century also saw the spread of the use of anesthesia and painkilling drugs, enabling humans to experience dental and other surgeries without sensation, thus enhancing the notion that pain was something avoidable. In response, England in 1876 enacted the Cruelty to Animals Act, the first legislated restrictions anywhere on the role of animals in research.

The Cartesian conceit that animal cries of pain were simply the sounds of a creaky machine had always strained credulity. People performing experiments would have had to will themselves deaf and blind to not be aware that living animals experience pain just as we do, a point Voltaire stated eloquently in 1764 in an assault on Descartes's views. "You discover in him all the same organs of feeling as in yourself," he asserted. "Answer me, mechanist, has Nature arranged all the springs of feeling in this animal to the end that he might not feel?" Voltaire's challenge went unanswered for nearly two centuries. But in 1903, when British antivivisectionists published *The Shambles of Science*, an exposé of alleged cruelty at the medical school of University College, London, the issue was dragged into the open. One of the cases described was that of a little brown dog used in multiple experiments, in violation of the 1876 law, and then euthanized. However, William Bayliss, a doctor who felt he'd been libeled in *Shambles*, sued the antivivisectionists, sparking a protracted court case that Bayliss eventually won, but which nonetheless cast the matter broadly before the public. The arguments were passionate on both sides, the anti's holding up the heroic example of British author Anna Kingsford, who had once offered her own body for vivisection in the stead of a helpless animal.[15]

On September 15, 1906, with sympathizers George Bernard Shaw and suffrage leader Charlotte Despard on hand, the International Anti-Vivisection Council unveiled a drinking fountain in Battersea Park, memorializing the "brown terrier dog" killed in the misbegotten experiment and castigating the university laboratories for subjecting it and 232 other dogs to months of suffering. An inscription on the monument read: MEN AND WOMEN OF ENGLAND: HOW LONG SHALL THESE THINGS BE? It was a bold moment for the antivivisectionist cause, but one harshly answered soon after by medical students protesting the statue's "libelous inscription." In the so-called Brown Dog Riots, local trade unionists, antivivisectionists, and other progressives fought to protect the likeness of the martyred terrier from the outraged young physicians, who managed to partially destroy it with a sledge hammer. In 1910, Battersea removed the monument altogether, saying its continued protection was an undue burden.

HENRY BERGH, WHOSE EFFORTS WERE DIRECTED TOWARD HALTING the mistreatment of domestic and draft animals in the streets of New York City, did not oppose hunting per se, although his work

raised ethical awareness of animal suffering generally, as well as
threats to certain species. Born in Manhattan in 1813, he was the
son of shipyard owner and ship designer Christian Bergh, who, it
was said, was so determined to die as he'd lived, an honest man, that
in 1843, "on his deathbed, it troubled him to think that he might die
before his physicians were paid," and that Henry "was compelled
to draw a check to their order to calm the steadfast sprit in its last
moments on earth." Henry, a member of New York society, was
also an aspiring writer; however, his book of tales and sketches, as
well as a number of poems, found little love among critics. "Look at
that! They have literally skinned me alive," he wrote his publisher
after a poem was trashed by a London reviewer. His plays, including one called *A Decided Scamp*, fared no better, the *New York
Tribune* drama correspondent writing, "It is queer that a person of
so tender a heart as to cause the arrest of a huckster for piercing the
fins of a turtle should himself be pronounced guilty of a dramatic
murder." Bergh the reformer was known for a willingness to laugh
at himself—he enjoyed collecting unflattering political cartoons of
which he was the subject—but the dashing of his artistic hopes was
a disappointment he felt deeply.[16]

In 1862, President Lincoln appointed him vice consul to the
czarist court in Saint Petersburg, a post that Bergh held for two
years, and by his own account, it was there that his activism on
behalf of nonhuman creatures began. Having witnessed numerous
incidents of routine brutality toward draft animals in the streets
of Saint Petersburg, he finally could stand no more, and one night
demanded the arrest of a driver he saw beating his horse. The police
refused to help, an unfriendly crowd gathered, so Bergh thought
best to leave. The next day, he returned, however, dressed in his
official uniform with all appropriate badges and ribbons, and locating the same driver, used his diplomatic authority to have him taken
into custody.

Returning to America, he stopped in London to meet and con-
fer with the Earl of Harrowby, president of England's RSPCA, and
once home in New York began developing his plans and drawing
up a declaration of principles. On February 8, 1866, he spoke at

Clinton Hall about the need for an organization to protect animals from abuse, terming the issue "a moral question in all its aspects . . . that the blood-red hand of cruelty shall no longer torture dumb beasts with impunity." From the start, the project was blessed by support from prominent elites—Peter Cooper, August Belmont, John Jacob Astor Jr., Horace Greeley, Edwin Booth, Thomas Nast, and the Reverend Henry Ward Beecher—and by April, the state had granted a charter for the founding of the American Society for the Prevention of Cruelty to Animals. In 1867, Bergh secured from the New York legislature a strong anticruelty law, which ensured that "Every person who shall by his neglect, maliciously kill, maim, wound, injure, torture or cruelly beat any horse, mule, cow, sheep or other animal belonging to himself or another, shall upon conviction be adjudged guilty of a misdemeanor." Those who abused the law could be arrested and fined, and Bergh, who took to patrolling the streets, was allowed under the terms of the law to make arrests, as were his aides, who came to be known as "Berghmen."[17]

Bergh's moral rectitude, the "new type of goodness" one journalist credited him with having invented, was at one with the expanding moral and ethical consciousness of the age. But the tall, dignified, well-tailored Bergh, though the picture of refinement, was no meek, beseeching type of reformer. Having grown up around shipyard workers, he was as streetwise as he was confident of his strength, and his stern, direct manner often caught people by surprise. He had little patience with those he called "cruelists," and numerous teamsters made the mistake of assuming the gent who was haranguing them would not back up his words with physical force. Of course, the former diplomat was also capable of tactful appeals. "Now, gentlemen, consider that you are American citizens living in a republic," he might tell a group of cattle drovers. "You make your own laws; no despot makes them for you. And I appeal to your sense of justice and your patriotism, oughtn't you to respect what you yourselves have made?" Urging commuters to get off a crowded Broadway tram so as to lighten the load being pulled by one sickly looking horse, he'd suggest, "If we are a civilized and Christian people, let us show it now and walk."[18]

His initial concern was for horses, which were ubiquitous in New York City as draft animals and everywhere abused; the saying "Horses are cheaper than oats" characterized the nonchalance of many wagon and trolley car drivers, and made Bergh furious. "Calloused drivers met his interference with coarse ridicule and mimicry of his polite clipped accents of reproach," recalled his biographer Zelma Steele, "[but] ridicule gave way to respect as men found that the fashionable 'toff' would not flinch at threats or brickbats, nor consider it beneath him to bring hay and water with his own manicured hands to a horse fallen on icy streets."[19]

Through the efforts of a Boston cohort, George T. Angell, founder of the Massachusetts Society for Prevention of Cruelty to Animals, an organization patterned after Bergh's, the battle was taken upon this side of the Atlantic against the bearing rein. Angell and Bergh both published pamphlets to discourage the practice and arranged for signs to be posted at the bottom of steep hills that read SLACKEN YOUR REIN, to remind drivers that horses would need all their strength to ascend. Angell even bought in bulk and distributed to wagon and carriage drivers free copies of *Black Beauty*, the 1877 Anna Sewell best seller that described vividly the discomfort of the bearing rein from the horse's perspective. Sewell's book, with its unique animal narrator, became known as "the *Uncle Tom's Cabin* of the horse," and proved a rallying cry for the humane treatment of horses and the concept of all animals as sentient beings. As a concerned matron reminds a carriage driver in Sewell's book, "they cannot tell us how they feel, but they do not suffer less because they have no words."[20]

Thus, through trials on the streets and sidewalks and sometimes in the courtroom, Bergh, with his tailored suit, top hat, and walking cane, became a familiar (and sometimes dreaded) New York sight where teamsters and horses congregated. He commissioned a cleverly designed drinking fountain with three troughs arranged at different heights—one for horses, one for dogs, and one with cups on chains for use by humans. He also introduced a hoisting contraption that could lift large fallen animals and a special ambulance wagon to carry them to where they could be cared for. Passersby accustomed to seeing dead horses left to rot in the gutter looked in awe upon such innovations, one New York clergyman noting in praise of Bergh's efforts, "That ambulance teaches a better sermon than I can."[21]

EASTERN SPORT HUNTERS WENT TO THE AMERICAN FRONTIER FOR the thrill of pursuing animals unlike any they'd ever known—grizzly bear, cougar, buffalo, antelope, and bighorn sheep. But in the years 1860–1880, the West began to reveal a whole other category of big game, all unknown to modern man—prehistoric creatures, strange and monstrous, whose fossilized remains lay in creek beds, exposed in cliff faces, and sometimes announced themselves with a loud clunk from under the blade of a farmer's plow. In England, naturalists, after the researcher Richard Owen, had begun in the 1840s to use the term *dinosauria*, meaning "terrible lizard," to describe fossilized land reptiles. So abundant and accessible were the dinosaur finds in the American West that many hunters, settlers, soldiers, and prospectors became casual collectors of the relics, while a second wave of "hunters," America's first generation of paleontologists, flocked to the ravines and dry washes of the region with picks, shovels, and investigating teams in tow. Unfortunately, the mysterious items they found were not fascinating solely for telling of the earth's great age, but for their mute testimony to the fact that fauna could disappear, even that it had gone extinct in some instances through overhunting by prehistoric men. This dawning realization had unsettling implications for sport hunting, and like the Darwinian revolution, helped give impetus to the birth of the conservation movement.

Curious objects had been unearthed and pondered over for centuries. In Europe, religious doctrine had long inhibited inquiry into their scientific origin. In America, while the finds were subjected to freer speculation, they were still influenced by the lack of any system of knowledge or context. In 1712, New England cleric Cotton Mather declared mastodon remains unearthed in upstate New York to be those of an antediluvian giant; Benjamin Franklin, examining a mastodon's tooth and jawbone found in Ohio in 1764, could only helpfully offer, "'Tis certainly the wreck of a world we live on!" while President Thomas Jefferson asked Lewis and Clark to keep an eye out for the creature as they began their expedition to the Pacific in 1804, for he believed it still roamed the American West. But with such little scientific conception of extinction or of deep time, and the persistent distraction of biblical faith, how were even qualified inquirers to begin describing the phenomenon of mysterious earlier species encased in the ground? What explained the disappearance of these once-living things? Why would God breathe life into creatures, only to then extinguish it?

Just as the writings of Charles Darwin enabled people to better perceive a connection between man and nonhuman animals, so they also legitimized greater curiosity and discussion about humans' place in what could only seem a receding canyon of time, a prehistory so vast it defied comprehension, as increasingly bolder scientific estimates dared push back the probable origins of the world and its living things. It was Darwin's suggestion that Europe was already too extensively settled to allow researchers to find fossils sufficient to support his claims about evolution, but that the arid American West, its treeless prairies and exposed mountainsides, likely held the greater potential. And with the building of towns and especially railroads, archaeologists and paleontologists could now reach places never before accessible.

The modern age of American paleontology is often dated to 1858, when the skeleton of *Hadrosaurus*, a large, pear-shaped creature that walked on two legs, was found at Haddonfield, New Jersey, and analyzed by Joseph Leidy of the Philadelphia Academy of Science. A decade later, it was put on display in Philadelphia, the first assembled and mounted dinosaur in the world. New York geologist Ferdinand Hayden, meanwhile, explored the trans-Mississippi West in the 1850s and was the first to describe the geology of the Great Plains and the Badlands. Local Sioux bestowed upon him the name "He Who Picks Up Rocks Running," for his tireless gathering of the "stone bones" that some natives believed were those of a celestial "Thunder Horse" that rode across the sky and into the earth on stormy nights.

In August 1869, Yale University professor Othniel Marsh went west to search for dinosaur relics. Marsh, occupant of the nation's first academic chair in paleontology, had been sent a story from an Omaha newspaper about a western railroad construction crew finding mysterious old bones, purportedly those of a prehistoric man, while digging a well. From the brief description, Marsh couldn't determine what they really were, but was intrigued. Leading a team of his best students to a remote part of Nebraska, near a place called Antelope Station, he convinced a train conductor to make an unscheduled stop near the site of the well; here, he and his under-graduate diggers found not human remains but several examples of *Protohippus*, a three-toed, dog-size creature from the Pleisto-cene era that is a relative of the modern horse, as well as parts of a prehistoric pig, camel, and turtle. Marsh's further analysis of the find allowed him to create a timeline showing that at least some horses were native to North America and had not all been intro-duced by the Spanish in the 1600s, as was commonly believed. The pronouncement received considerable attention, Darwin himself noting that Marsh's delineation of the ancestry of the horse was the strongest support of his theory of evolution. Marsh, tickled to have unearthed scientific truth at his first western dig, exclaimed, "What untold treasures must there be in the whole Rocky Moun-tain region."[22]

One of Marsh's student helpers was a young undergraduate zoology student named George Bird Grinnell, who would go on to obtain a PhD in paleontology from Yale, become the natural sci-ence editor of *Forest and Stream*, and have an outsize impact on the ethics of western hunting and the birth of the conservation move-ment. As the team excavated buried remains of extinct turtles and other mammals, Grinnell, who was an avid hunter and had come prepared to shoot wild animals, began to appreciate that he and his cohorts were engaged in another, more significant, kind of hunt. If the "game" they were pursuing was extinct, what did that say about the present, and the seemingly ample wildlife of the West? Could the buffalo—the abundant "Monarch of the Plains"—go the way of the fossil specimens the Marsh expedition was unearthing?

The effort to answer Grinnell's questions would be directed chiefly by Marsh and a counterpart turned competitor, Edwin Drinker Cope of the Academy of Natural Sciences in Philadelphia. The two men, bound by their common interests, would come to dislike one another so thoroughly their scientific duel became known as Bone Wars. Cope, the distinguished scion of a wealthy Quaker family, possessed somewhat more ambition than scientific training, and was driven by the possibility of discovery; Marsh, large, bearded, with the unmistakable mien of the scholar, had convinced his wealthy financer uncle to sponsor the founding of the eponymous Peabody Museum at Yale, which professor Marsh was keen to fill with the results of his western digs. In additional excavations in Nebraska, Colorado, Wyoming, and Kansas between 1870 and 1873, many in stratified sediment along the "shoreline" of prehistoric lakes and streams, Marsh found mastodon remains, prehistoric turtles and rhinoceroses, rodents, birds, and many curious unknown animals—some of massive size and fearsome countenance. Buffalo Bill encountered Marsh during these expeditions and recalled the scientist's exuberance over his team's geological finds, exclaiming "Gad!" each time a promising fossil came to light. In Kansas, his digs located prehistoric sea serpents he called mosasaurs, as well as the pterodactyl, a flying reptile with a 20-foot wingspan.[23]

Cope meanwhile focused on the Bridger Basin and Bitter Creek areas of southwestern Wyoming, where in 1872 he found fifty new species of lizards, snakes, birds, four-footed mammals, fish, and turtles. He also worked the ridges of Como Bluff, which offered up so many ancient relics, it became known as "the dinosaur graveyard." Between the two men, their "big game hunt in deep time" netted hundreds of tons of bones and fossils that were ultimately brought to the Smithsonian Institution or to Yale, representing 142 species of dinosaurs (only 32 of which are now deemed to be legitimate separate identifications).[24]

The natural competition between Cope and Marsh grew as they invariably intruded on each other's turf in the West and made (or were alleged to have made) side arrangements with field workers and guides to sabotage the other's digs. The standoff escalated sharply when Marsh humiliated Cope publicly by sharing the fact that the latter had claimed discovery of a reptile (*Elasmosaurus*) that he depicted backward in drawings, having confused its head with its tail. When Marsh later tried to use his greater influence with the federal bureaucracy to claim some of Cope's bones, Cope unleashed a vicious personal attack on Marsh in the press, accusing him of plagiarism and financial wrongdoing. While their competition drove both men to great accomplishments, it also engendered some hasty science, as they rushed to assert the discovery of new species so as to establish priority. The long-running dispute eventually exhausted them both, physically and financially; both died nearly penniless and alone, Cope in 1897 at the age of fifty-six; Marsh at sixty-eight in 1899, with only $186 to his name. Cope literally took the fight to the grave, donating his cranium to science and daring Marsh to do the same so posterity could establish whose brain had been the largest. Marsh ignored the provocation, although it is said Cope's skull yet awaits the resolution of the challenge, snug in a box at the University of Pennsylvania.

LEWIS GARRARD OF CINCINNATI, WHO CAME WEST AS A YOUNG man in the 1840s, was riding with a companion in Texas one day when they both abruptly slowed their horses, having noticed a large glittering surface on the horizon. "What a beautiful lake," his friend exclaimed. They continued to admire the body of water as they rode toward it, but after some time became puzzled why it appeared "to be receding at our approach." They suddenly realized they had utterly deceived themselves: the object in the distance was not a lake at all, but a herd of buffalo.[25]

Such stories abound in writing about the nineteenth-century west, for on the flat, arid Plains there was perhaps no sight so compelling as the undulating black carpet of thousands of these large ruminant animals. Estimates of their presence in North America in the seventeenth century range from 30 to 60 million, and it is thought they once roamed much further than the western prairies, from the Carolinas and parts of New York and Pennsylvania to Texas and west to the Sierra Nevada. In 1612, English sea captain Samuel Argoll, unloading supplies on the Virginia coast, was invited by natives up the Potomac River to an area not far from present-day Washington, DC, where two buffalo were killed and impressed Argoll with their "wholesome" taste. Nineteenth-century southern hunting and fishing writer William Elliott reported that in 1712, herds of buffalo could still be found within 30 miles of Charleston, along with black bear, wildcats, panthers, and wolves. In the 1870s, British and European hunters who arrived in New York disappointed to learn that buffalo did not roam in New Jersey weren't entirely wrong in their bearings; they simply were two centuries late.[26]

It was a different story on the Great Plains, where in the decades immediately following the Civil War, it was common to see herds of buffalo said to be 50 miles long and 25 miles wide and thought to contain several million animals. "Much has been written about their enormous abundance in the old days," George Bird Grinnell would write, "but I have never read anything that I thought an exaggeration of their numbers as I have seen them." With the arrival of transcontinental train travel, passengers told of going 120 miles without leaving the company of an unbroken herd. "The engineers tried the experiment of running through these passing herds, but after their engines had been thrown from the tracks they learned wisdom, and gave the buffalo the right of way."[27]

The animal had a reprieve from the gross slaughter that awaited it while beaver pelts remained the frontier's chief export. Back east, the beaver hat, made from felted beaver fur, was much in fashion and demand, and, in any case, buffalo robes were too heavy to make long-distance shipment profitable. By the 1850s, however, the beaver hat was out of favor, replaced by the silk hat (which likely saved the beaver from extinction), and when thousands of miles of rail were laid by the Union Pacific in the northern plains and the Kansas Pacific in the South, it became feasible to bring even bulky goods to market. In 1870, new methods of tanning were introduced that allowed buffalo hides to be more readily transformed into leather goods, and to be preserved closer to their source. Previously robes had been taken generally only in cold months, when the buffalo's coat grew shaggy and full, and as a result, they were not harvested by market hunters in the warmer months, which included the animals' birthing season. However, the new processing methods allowed a shift from robes to hides and enabled year-round business. As the lucrative nature of the trade in buffalo hides became apparent, market hunters demanded guns that could allow a buffalo to be brought to earth from ever greater distances. In response, manufacturers introduced, among other new weapons, the Sharps Buffalo Gun, which, mounted with a telescopic sight and capable of bearing a heavy charge, could drop a large animal at 1,000 yards. All these developments augured poorly for the buffalo.

In part, the beast was doomed by genetics. Evolution having denied it the large, sharp horns with which its better-endowed ancestors warded off predators, the buffalo encountered by nineteenth-century hunters had as defense chiefly its tremendous size and ability to run. This worked with some effectiveness when its lethal enemies were wolves, coyotes, and Indians stalking on foot with bow and arrow, but with the advent of the horse-mounted hunter, and later the long-range rifle, the animals had little chance. As herd creatures, in response to danger they would draw together in a tight group, awaiting the movement of a dominant female cow to instigate flight—the buffalo stampede of legend. But the buffalo was "slow in comprehending the existence and nature of the dangers that threatened his life," observed zoologist William Hornaday, "and, like the stupid brute that he was, would very often stand quietly and see two or three score, or even a hundred, of his relatives and companions shot down before his eyes, with no other feeling than one of stupid wonder and curiosity."[28]

This herdlike obstinacy was widely noted. The animals in utter futility would shove against the sides of a standing train because they wanted to get to the other side of the tracks, or continue to walk into quicksand although dozens of their brethren were already sinking in it. "More than once I have lain on a hill above a little herd of buffalo," Grinnell recalled, "shot down what young bulls I needed . . . and then walked down to the bunch and, by waving my hat and shouting, driven off the survivors, so that I could prepare the meat for transportation to camp."[29]

Native Americans used a buffalo killing method known as the surround, in which the herd was gently led by a special "buffalo caller," an exalted quasi-religious character in the tribe, to enter a cul-de-sac, to be then pushed along by other men, women, and children into an increasingly smaller and narrower enclosed space, so that means of escape were closed off. Such communal hunting had been practiced on the plains since prehistoric times in the pursuit of mammoths, mastodons, and larger versions of modern-day bison and wolves. If a precipice was convenient, there was no need to expend energy in stabbing or bludgeoning the animals, as they could be driven off the edge of a cliff, to be killed or crippled by the fall. Some of these sites, known as buffalo jumps, were used repeatedly over hundreds of years; some are roadside tourist sites in the West today, and many have been painstakingly excavated. They contain not only buffalo bones, arrowheads and spear points, but also signs that semipermanent Indian encampments were established below the jumps for the purpose of processing the game.

While the fame of the Indians' sustainable use of the buffalo is likely exaggerated—they could, like whites, occasionally be wasteful in what they chose to take and leave of a slaughtered buffalo—Native Americans did a better job at utilizing every morsel, horn, and hair of the animal to make blankets, shirts, moccasins, lodge coverings, and quivers; even the hooves were boiled down to create a glue used to adhere bird feathers to war bonnets, and the animal's sunbaked waste, called buffalo chips, served as a fuel source in treeless regions where firewood was unattainable. Because Indians respected the buffalo as their seasonal subsistence, they were in the practice of culling the herd with a degree of restraint, leaving reproductive members unharmed to spawn future generations. In contrast, unlike natural predators, such as wolves, that prey upon the weakest members of a herd, white market hunters chasing robes and hides sought out those animals that appeared most fit, thus destroying the natural rhythm by which reproduction and herd survival were sustained.

The hide men roamed from Texas through Kansas and Nebraska as far as the Canadian border in teams of shooters and skinners, working the herds. A man firing from a stand might kill as many as a hundred buffalo an hour, a pace so rapid that, in warm weather, when the metal barrel became too hot, he might have no choice but to urinate on the gun to keep it cool. Business soared: robes in good condition sold for $5 apiece; buffalo tongues packed in a barrel were $24 per dozen; hides, stacked by the tens of thousands at western railheads for shipment east, went for between $2.25 and $3.25 apiece, depending on size. Some excerpts from the diary of Matt Clarkson, a member of a team of buffalo hunters, offer a vivid reconstruction of the trade's routine:

1867—"We saved every tongue so as we would know how many we killed . . . In all we killed 22,000."

1872—"We made a camp on the Smoky and I went to killing just for the hides. It was the 22nd of September and was too warm to save any meat. When Charley came up I had killed 1,900 buffaloes and hauled the hides to Grinnell station."

1872—"We went north about 30 miles and made camp for about 40 days. We killed 2,400 buffaloes and a number of antelopes. Then we went northwest over on the Republican. We camped at the Big Spring . . . about 30 days and killed about 800 buffaloes."[30]

Echoing such details, the *Rocky Mountain News* reported in 1873 that "on the south fork of the Republican [River] . . . were counted 6,500 carcasses of buffalo from which the hides only had been stripped. The meat was not touched and was left to rot on the plains; in fact, the plains were literally dotted with putrefying buffalo carcasses." A party consisting of sixteen men "stated that they killed 28,000 buffalo during the past summer, the hides of which, only, were utilized."[31]

Well-meaning state laws to deter market hunting on such a scale were mostly ineffectual, given the immense territories to be patrolled. The only meaningful deterrent to market hunters was

"the loss of one's hair," to be killed and scalped by vengeful Indians angry at the hunters' intrusion onto their lands and depletion
of their food source. Yet, as horrific as these killings were, they did
little to slow the larger project, which came to involve an estimated
twenty thousand shooters and skinners.[32]

More offensive to eastern sensibilities was the much publicized
frontier excess of shooting buffalo from trains, which occurred
both spontaneously on normal passenger runs and also on special
excursion trips sold expressly for the purpose. An English visitor on a westward-bound train remarked, "We saw no buffaloes
alive, though endless skeletons lay on each side of the track, and
we passed several dead bodies in various states of decomposition.
Many more are missed than hit: but when they are wounded there
is no means of stopping to dispatch them; so they die in misery
along the line." On designated shooting excursions, the train would
halt when the guns ceased so that passengers and employees could
alight and remove the choicest cuts from the slain animals, as well
as trophies, such as tails, horns, or heads. In one account, a cornet
band traveling aboard the train disembarked to play rousing patriotic tunes as passengers "rushed forth to see our first game lying
in his gore." Among genteel passengers it was considered polite, if
ladies were among the shooters, for gentlemen to insist in the face
of any uncertainty that it had surely been the shot from the gun of a
fair "Diana" that had effected the kill.[33]

The buffalo had one some small measure of revenge. The West's
burgeoning telegraph network ("singing wires" to the Indians) was
essential for railroad operations, enabling trains to stay on schedule. On the treeless plains, however, the buffalo discovered the joy
of scratching themselves vigorously against telegraph poles; this
sometimes disrupted transmission, causing telegraph service to be
suspended. To combat the problem, the telegraph companies began
in the late 1860s to insert sharp brad awls in the poles, but the awls'
edges only seemed to enhance the animals' pleasure. "They would
go 15 miles to find a brad awl," according to a later newspaper
account. "They fought huge battles around the poles containing

them, and the victor would proudly scratch himself into bliss until the brad awl broke or the pole came down."[34]

THE FREEDOM OF BOTH MARKET AND RECREATIONAL HUNTERS TO decimate the western herds was made possible, encouraged, and sometimes directly abetted by the frontier army, whose unofficial policy was to clear the West of buffalo as a step toward eliminating the native peoples who relied on them. Denied their traditional sustenance, the Indians, it was believed, would be forced to rely on government handouts and accept residence on reservations, thus making way for white settlement and agriculture.

"I think it would be wise to invite all the sportsmen of England and America there this fall for a Grand Buffalo hunt, and make one grand sweep of them all," General William Sherman wrote to General Philip Sheridan in spring 1868. "Until the Buffalo and consequently the Indians are out we will have collisions and trouble." While sport hunters certainly did their part, it was the hide hunters' efforts Sheridan most extravagantly praised, noting that they "have done in the last two years, and will do in the next year, more to settle the vexed Indian question than the entire army has done in the last 30 years." His Civil War experience in mind, he added, "They are destroying the Indians' commissary; and it is a well-known fact that an army losing its base of supplies is placed at a great disadvantage . . . Let them kill, skin, and sell until the buffaloes are exterminated." Years later, Sherman more than seconded Sheridan's remarks, thanking market hunters for "having in so short a time replaced the wild buffaloes by more numerous herds of tame cattle, and by substituting for the useless Indians the intelligent owners of productive farms and cattle-ranches." Nowhere had this program of elimination been legislated or formally ordered; but neither was there any government effort, such as interrupting the transport of hides from frontier railheads, that might have restrained the buffalo profiteers.[35]

General George Custer always had somewhat different thoughts about this. He was so confident in the potential of military force

against the indigents—and the verve of his own Seventh Cavalry—
that he rejected out of hand the idea that the army could not win
the Indian wars without eradicating the buffalo. On at least one
occasion, he tried to humorously conflate the two, exhorting his
troops with regard to a nearby buffalo herd, "Boys, here's a chance
for a great victory over that bunch of redskins the other side of the
hill. Major B, you will take charge of the right flank, I will attend
to the left. General Sheridan and the infantry will follow direct over
the hill. Ready! *Charge!*" But credible observers on both sides of the
argument ultimately recognized the strategic devastation of stealing the historical food source upon which Native Americans relied.
Charles "Buffalo" Jones, a veteran frontier hunter, later scoffed at
the idea that Custer or anyone's army vanquished the Indians. "The
buffalo hunters conquered the whole Indian race. As soon as the red
man was compelled to beg or starve, then his proud heart broke,
and he pled for mercy at the feet of the paleface." As Sitting Bull
lamented, "A cold wind blew across the prairie when the last buffalo fell, a death-wind for my people."[36]

A handful of frontier army officers were the first to speak out,
writing to Congress about the catastrophe they were watching
unfold and imploring its representatives to act. On March 13, 1871,
Representative R. C. McCormick of Arizona introduced the first of
several bills aimed at halting the buffalo's demise, explaining that
he had personally witnessed the value of the animal as a food source
in December 1870, when he and one hundred other rail passengers
were stranded for ten days in a blizzard; they owed their survival
solely to its "tender, nutritious, and palatable" meat. His bill went
nowhere, not even being reported back from committee, but discussion of the issue was picked up by the press, *Harper's Weekly* complaining that of the buffalo,

> a comparatively small percentage is killed for food or fur. Trav-
> elers shoot into the herds from coaches and railway cars, with-
> out expecting to secure the game, which they seldom do more
> than wound. This is all very well for the wolves, coyotes, and
> ravens, but it is neither wise nor sportsman-like. . . . Indeed, it

would seem that strenuous efforts are being made to exterminate the buffalo within the shortest convenient time.[37]

In January 1872, Colonel William B. Hazen, stationed at Fort
Hays, Kansas, called upon Henry Bergh of the ASPCA to use his
influence to agitate Congress to protect the buffalo, "a noble and
harmless animal, timid, and as easily taken as a cow, and very
valuable as food for man." Hazen pointed out that the buffalo ate
a dry grass that would not be suitable for cattle, and denounced
the "necessity" of slaughtering them to deprive the Indians of food
as a fallacy, "as these people are becoming harmless under a rule
of justice." Hazen's plea was seconded by Lieutenant Colonel A.
G. Brackett, stationed at Omaha, Nebraska. As for the sport of
killing buffalo, Brackett wrote, "all the reports about fine sport
and good shooting are mere gammon. It would be equally as good
sport . . . to ride into a herd of tame cattle and commence shooting indiscriminately." Bergh and his colleagues in ASPCA, who
decried "the useless and inhuman torture and destruction of . . .
unoffending animals, roaming on the public lands," did suggest
that Congress establish an agency whose purpose it would be to
protect the buffalo. Nothing concrete came from his effort, but
the next month, in February 1872, the Senate finally stirred to life:
Henry Wilson of Massachusetts backed a buffalo protection bill
and Cornelius Cole of California introduced a resolution directing
the Senate's Committee on Territories to inquire into the need to
protect western animals from slaughter; in the House, at the same
time, McCormick reintroduced his proposed legislation from the
previous year.[38]

This groundswell of concern to keep an entire animal species
from disappearing was unprecedented, and by summer, the western press was openly critical of buffalo slaughter. The *Denver Tribune* calculated that "25,000 bison were killed during the month
of May, south of the Kansas Pacific Railroad, for the sake of their
hides alone, which are sold at the paltry price of $2 each on deliv-
ery of shipment to the Eastern markets. Add to this 5,000—a small
estimate—shot by tourists and killed by Indians to supply meat to

the people on the frontier." That same year appeared an important book, William Edward Webb's *Buffalo Land: An Authentic Account of the Discoveries, Adventures, and Mishaps of a Scientific and Sporting Party in the Wild West*, with graphic illustrations showing the "Wanton Destruction of Buffalo." An early harbinger of the cause of wildlife conservation, *Buffalo Land* offered a searing indictment of the American people's wasteful, shortsighted avarice toward a bountiful resource. The next year, Grinnell took up the matter in *Forest and Stream*, warning that without speedy reforms, "these shaggy brown beasts, these cattle upon a thousand hills, will ere long be among the things of the past."[39]

The need for limits, let alone such a remote concept as extinction, was hard at first for most people to grasp—including members of Congress. Only a decade before, the idea that any amount of hunting or trapping could seriously and permanently deplete animal populations would have been thought absurd; the number of buffalo in particular appeared inexhaustible. "Our animal fortune seemed to us so enormous that it could never be spent," Henry Fairfield Osborn, president of the American Museum of Natural History, would later write. "Like a young rake coming into a large inheritance, we attacked this noble fauna with characteristic American improvidence." The most ready to comprehend and respond to the crisis were such thought leaders as Grinnell and Osborn and many of the sportsmen who routinely perused Grinnell's journal, as their time afield familiarized them with the fact that wildlife populations are vulnerable and may fluctuate. Most of these readers had also been informed of the need for game laws, observed seasons, and ethical hunting.[40]

Perhaps the closest Congress came to curtailing excessive market hunting of the buffalo was its response to the January 1874 legislation offered by Rep. Greenbury L. Fort of Illinois. Fort highlighted a distressing economic irony: the government, in allowing the tribes' natural food source to be vanquished, now had to pay to provide them beef cattle and other food and supplies. When concern was voiced about allowing the Indians to continue to rely on their own sustenance, Fort lost patience. "Shoot the buffalo, starve the Indian to death, and thereby civilize him!" he demanded. "I would suggest that a shorter and more humane way would be to go out and shoot the Indians themselves—put an end to their existence at once, instead of starving them to death in this manner." The House, perhaps moved by the depth of Fort's feeling, passed the bill, and by late June, it moved on to the Senate where, after a brief debate, it also won passage. President Grant, still under the sway of the notion that protecting buffalo would only prolong what little remained of Indian autonomy, pocket vetoed the bill over a lengthy congressional adjournment. Two years later, after news of the buffalo's increased decline, Fort pushed his legislation anew, but although it again passed the House, this time it foundered in the Senate and went ultimately to the place Congress sends things to die—a committee— and the issue was never heard of again.[41]

In the West, the disaster continued to unfold. The forces of destruction—market shooters, sportsmen, agricultural settlement and the demand for pasturage, and guns in the hands of slaphappy excursionists—seemed unstoppable. When the Union Pacific was built between Omaha and Cheyenne in 1866–1867, it divided the great western buffalo into a southern herd located mostly in Kansas and Texas, and a northern herd, substantially larger, at home in the Dakotas and Montana. The Kansas group was butchered between 1870 and 1873; the Texas buffalo, between 1874 and 1878. The years 1871 to 1875 saw hunters slay about 2,500,000 buffalo in the Kansas territory alone. The northern herd held out longer, but was greatly diminished by 1882.

With such indiscriminate slaughter, the perpetrators eventually killed off their own livelihoods. As the historian Michael Punke reports, a Montana dealer who in 1881 had without difficulty acquired 250,000 hides, by 1883 could lay hands on no more than 10. In 1882, Northern Pacific Railroad sent 200,000 hides east for tanning, enough to fill seven hundred boxcars; in 1883, it shipped 40,000; and by 1884, the railroad made its final shipment of buffalo hides, all of which fit in a single boxcar. Many of the hunters were forced to sell their powerful Sharps rifles, which, with the buffalo now gone, were deemed "too much gun for other game."[42]

The plains themselves had grown eerily silent, the few extant herds greatly thinned in numbers and increasingly scarce. As Grinnell observed, changes in behavior and appearance overcame the individual animals; from being continually hunted and denied the leisure to graze, they developed a panicky anxiety about humans, and also became sleeker and swifter afoot from having lost the security of membership in the herd. Some observers refused to accept that which seemed implausible; they wondered—in a way that could only bring a rueful smile from Grinnell—who these weaker, more easily spooked, "long-legged, light-bodied" newcomers were, and pondered where the "regular" buffalo could have gone and how soon they'd be back. Hornaday of the Smithsonian indulged no such conjecture, for like Grinnell, he knew the answer all too well. He went west in 1886 not to find out what had happened to the buffalo, but to count how many remained, and to gather a few specimens so that future generations of Americans might know what the "Monarch of the Plains" had looked like.[43]

*Chapter Ten*

# "Times Have Changed, and We Must Change Also"

THE STUDIO PHOTOGRAPH OF THEODORE ROOSEVELT IN A BUCKSKIN hunting costume, rifle at the ready, remains one of the most iconic images of the American conservation movement. That he looks ready to kill something is no affectation; Roosevelt was a gung ho hunter all his life. Yet his legacy is so much larger, as was the principled example he lived, of the compatibility of hunting wildlife and the protection of wildlife and wilderness. It was a synthesis that would define not only his efforts, but the nascent conservation movement that he came to symbolize.

Born in 1858 in New York City, he was the son of Theodore Roosevelt Sr., a founder of the American Museum of Natural History; the museum charter was approved in 1869 in the front parlor of the family brownstone on East Twentieth Street. His uncle Robert Barnwell Roosevelt, a US congressman and an ambassador to Holland, was a renowned expert on fishing and fish culture, an early advocate of fish hatcheries, as well as the founder of the state's Fish and Game Commission, for which he served for twenty years as commissioner. A dedicated outdoorsman, zealous reformer, socialite, and bohemian who counted Oscar Wilde as a friend, Uncle Robert seems, at least in certain respects, a kind of rough draft of his more famous nephew.

Theodore's father, in response to his son's childhood asthma, urged the boy toward an outdoor, athletic life. The son was duly swept up by the works of James Audubon, William Bartram, and Alexander Wilson, as well as the boy-hunter novels of Mayne Reid, and came to know the books of Frank Forester, although he looked askance at Forester's aristocratic fussiness about purebred hounds, cognac, and the nomenclature for groups of ducklings. "He was a true Cockney," was Roosevelt's judgment, "who cared little for truly wild sports, and he was afflicted with that dreadful pedantry which pays more heed to the ceremonial and to terminology than to the thing itself." Roosevelt, by contrast, would cultivate the twin modes of frontiersman and exacting naturalist. Taken at an early age with birds, whose vivid colors transfixed him and whose cyclical and millennia-old habits of migration he found endlessly intriguing, he considered them "messengers from prehistoric times." To improve his ornithological study and sketching, he sought tutoring in basic taxidermy and, at age twelve, shot a number of winged specimens while on a family trip to Egypt. He hunted and developed his expertise as a natural scientist in the Adirondacks, but a truer apprenticeship began in 1884, after his young wife, Alice Hathaway Lee, died in childbirth. Brokenhearted, he put his nascent New York political career on hold and, with no certain date of return in mind, left the East to grieve alone in the Badlands of the western Dakotas.[1]

As for many a tenderfoot, one of the first impulses Roosevelt acted on was to shoot a buffalo, and over the next several years he added numerous other trophies—a bighorn sheep, a 1,200-pound grizzly bear, as well as a mother bear and her cub. He also invested about $80,000, half of his inheritance, in a cattle ranch, much of which he lost over the hard winter of 1886–87, when tens of thousands of cattle across the region froze or starved to death. While a touring correspondent for the *Pittsburgh Dispatch* found him "a pale, slim young man with a thin piping voice and a general look of dyspepsia about him . . . boyish looking . . . with a slight lisp, short red moustache and eye glasses . . . a typical New York dude," Roosevelt was determined to attain a rugged manhood that would require no caveat about his big city origins or his being a son of privilege. He became a western ranchman by sheer force of will, developing passable skills as a rider and hunter, once even leading a posse to capture three armed thieves who had made off with his rowboat during a spring flood. His exuberant love of the chase was integral to his identity, and he honored it with his wardrobe, ordering a fine buckskin outfit made in the mode of his heroes Daniel Boone and Davy Crockett. This was the suit he posed in, complete with moccasins, rifle, and sheath knife, to promote his 1885 book, *Hunting Trips of a Ranchman.* The image couldn't help but appear dubious to anyone who knew his upbringing, and later, when he became famous for his hunting, critics would mock him as a boy who never grew up, or as someone with an inordinate need to kill living things. Of course, it would never have struck Roosevelt himself that he looked the poseur: the photograph was a sincere representation of his belief not only in what he was, but the kind of person he thought all American men should aspire to be.[2]

His hunting was prodigious. He took pride in shooting large tallies of birds and other fauna and securing significant trophies, some of which, as a naturalist, he termed "specimens." But to Roosevelt, the hunting of wild creatures and the taking of animal hides and horns was always about something greater—a primal reconnect with the natural, precivilized world and "the free, self-reliant, adventurous life, with its rugged and stalwart democracy." Hunting was not merely recreation but a transformation, one with stages of apprenticeship, youthful testing, and eventual self-mastery. Much as it had been a tonic for him, he thought this influence essential for ensuring the character of others, as it "cultivates that vigorous manliness for the lack of which in a nation, as in an individual, the possession of no other qualities can possibly atone." Expanding on Forester's view of hunting as a means of reinvigoration, Roosevelt posited that the fate of the country, its will to explore, to conquer, and, if necessary, defend its interests, rested on broadly inculcating

Theodore Roosevelt
came to believe that
sport hunting offered
young men not only
the physical benefits
of "the strenuous life,"
but the opportunity to
develop "manly" traits
of courage and resolve.
(Library of Congress)

among its people those values imparted by the chase. Such views
were complemented by his abiding affection for the prosaic virtues
of the frontier itself, the white-coned mountains, towering pine forests, and 100-mile vistas of the West, a display of natural wonder
he thought divinely inspired and suited to a nation of great destiny.[3]

Roosevelt's path to prominence in the cause of wildlife preservation began, strangely enough, with a comeuppance he experienced at the 1885 publication of *Hunting Trips of a Ranchman*.
The book was for the most part well received, but one very mixed
review came from George Bird Grinnell, now the editor of *Forest
and Stream*, who had replaced the brilliant but intemperate Charles
Hallock. While commenting favorably on Roosevelt's skills as a
New York state politician and his interest in the West, Grinnell

suggested that as a newcomer to the region he had missed some of its subtleties. "We are sorry to see that a number of hunting myths are given as fact, but it was after all scarcely to be expected that with the author's limited experience he could sift the wheat from the chaff and distinguish the true from the false," Grinnell wrote, allowing that the book's naïveté lent it a certain charm.[4]

It was this damning-with-faint-praise that got under Roosevelt's skin most, and the indignant author immediately presented himself at the *Forest and Stream* offices to demand an audience with his critic, whom he had never met. After a lengthy conversation, he was honest enough to acknowledge that in Grinnell, who like him came from an old and affluent New York family, he had met his better, at least as far as the West was concerned—a man, after all, who had ridden with Custer, lived among the Cheyenne, and dug for relics under the gaze of Othniel Marsh. The styles of the two, who soon became friends, proved complementary, Grinnell an older, more sophisticated, methodical, less restless version of Roosevelt, who awoke each day eager to grab life by the lapels.

Out of their conversations and correspondence grew the idea for the founding in 1887 of the Boone and Crockett Club. The purposes of the organization, to comprise hunter-naturalists, were to "promote manly sport with the rifle," create an exchange of information about big game and where it could be found, spread the ideals of ethical hunting and an interest in natural science, and advocate for wildlife preservation and related legislation. Members were required to have shown their mettle by harvesting a grown male specimen of at least three big game animals native to America. The group's initial membership was limited to one hundred, as well as celebrity associate members such as Francis Parkman, Owen Wister, Henry Cabot Lodge, Albert Bierstadt, and Generals Sherman and Sheridan. "Although hundreds of sportsmen's associations with a similar goal were already in existence," notes conservation historian John F. Reiger, "too many of them were concerned only with local wildlife conservation or spent more time talking about protecting game than in actually working for it." One immediate opportunity for the organization resulted from the newly federally enacted Dawes Severalty Act, which broke up large Indian reservations for the purpose of making individual property allotments to Native Americans; the act also made available millions of acres of former tribal lands for purchase by non-Indians. The Boone and Crockett Club, whose roster included elite sportsmen from New York's financial industry, jumped at the chance to secure some acres as game refuges.[5]

"All hunters should be nature-lovers," declared Roosevelt, chosen as the club's first president, in paraphrase of the organization's purpose. "It is to be hoped that the days of mere wasteful, boastful slaughter are past and that from now on the hunter will stand foremost in working for the preservation and perpetuation of wild life, whether big or little." The group's constitution forbade certain kinds of trapping; shooting game as it swam in water; jacklighting deer with torches at night; or crusting, the slaughtering of animals immobilized in deep snow. Hunting was deemed integral to managing wild animal stocks by culling those animals that might otherwise die of starvation or interfere with the breeding cycles of younger creatures. The killing of predators was also seen as a possible means of stabilizing vulnerable prey species.[6]

Within a decade of its founding, however, with the worsening crises of species displacement and loss, the club was forced to pivot dramatically. "Founded as an association of amateur riflemen," Grinnell recalled, "it became apparent that large game was disappearing so rapidly that unless measures were taken . . . there was danger many specimens would be exterminated. Thereby (its) purpose . . . became gradually modified . . . and grew to be a club more interested in conservation than killing." The new emphasis on restraint was soon visible. "Those who used to boast of their slaughter are now ashamed of it," he said, "and it is becoming a recognized fact that a man who wastefully destroys big game, whether for the market, or only for heads, has nothing of the true sportsman about him."[7]

In a sense, it was the sport hunter's own ethos of civilized hunting—what the Boone and Crockett Club termed *fair chase*—which had brought them here. The good hunter's appreciation of wild places, his respect for the game he hunted, for the rules of fair play and observed hunting seasons, all had led directly to this looming project, as daunting as it was grand: scientific game management and conservation.

WITH HIS BLUSTERING PERSONALITY, WILLIAM T. HORNADAY WAS as kin to Roosevelt, strong-willed, tenacious, and similarly a naturalist from childhood. Born in Indiana in 1854, he came from far more humble origins, but had the talent and good fortune to gain an apprenticeship in 1873 as a taxidermist with Henry Augustus Ward in Rochester, New York, a former student of Louis Agassiz and head of Ward's Natural Science Establishment, the nation's leading clearinghouse for scientific specimens. After only six months on the job, however, the precocious young man announced his intention to go on a collecting trip to Africa, inspired by Paul du Chaillu, a French-American zoologist and explorer who, in 1859, the same year Darwin's *On the Origin of Species* appeared, had been the first person to venture into Africa's interior and confirm the existence of pygmies and gorillas. Du Chaillu's book *Explorations and Adventures in Equatorial Africa* (1861) riveted a generation of aspiring adventurers like Hornaday with its hair-raising reports of encounters with mysterious beasts. "It has been my fortune to be the first white man who can speak of the gorilla from personal knowledge," Du Chaillu wrote. "I can also vouch that no description can exceed the horror of its appearance, the ferocity of its attack, or the impish malignity of its nature."[8]

On account of his youth, Hornaday's family was able to intervene and keep him from going to Africa, but he was soon off with a friend on a self-sponsored collecting trip to Florida, Cuba, and the Bahamas; in 1876, he made his way to South America and by 1877–1878 was in India and Ceylon, the beginning of a dynamic career as zoologist, nature writer, and conservationist. A man for whom it was impossible to relax behind a desk, he preferred always to be out in swamp or jungle, or on the prairies of the Great Plains. An avid statistician and obsessive student of nature, he developed a special affinity for the American buffalo, and could, writes historian

Douglas Brinkley, "in a quick glance . . . identify the precise home range of a buffalo—for example, Nebraska or Manitoba or Oklahoma—by the constitution of its dung." A stickler for zoological precision, Hornaday once lobbied to have the name of the city of Buffalo changed to Bison, New York.[9]

In the 1880s, when serving as chief taxidermist and director of the United States National Museum (later absorbed into the Smithsonian Institution), Hornaday was tasked with advising as to the exact number of buffalo remaining in the West. He had done a preliminary survey of this kind focused on the year 1867, based on informal surveys of western farmers and frontier officers; in that year he determined there were 15 million of the animals west of the Mississippi; however, reports arriving at his office by the mid-1880s were so remarkably below those 1867 data that he resolved to go west and see for himself. By the time he completed his travels in 1887, he estimated that 1,091 buffalo remained in the United States, indicating, based on his 1867 numbers, a net loss of 14,998,909 buffalo over twenty years.[10]

"It will be doubly deplorable," Hornaday wrote:

> if the remorseless slaughter we have witnessed during the last twenty years carries with it no lessons for the future. A continuation of the record we have lately made as wholesale game butchers will justify posterity in dating us back with the mound builders and cave dwellers, when man's only function was to slay and eat.[11]

Like Grinnell, who had handled the remains of long-vanished species, Hornaday's research and travels in the West gave him a unique vantage point from which to look down into the abyss of extinction. There was perhaps little that could be done for the buffalo, but other animals—antelope, elk, bighorn sheep, even white-tailed deer—might also soon be at risk.

While Hornaday set himself the task of locating and nurturing small, remnant herds of buffalo, Charles "Buffalo" Jones was also seeking to gather or buy small herds—not only for safeguarding, but for managed propagation. Jones had been inspired to act in March 1886 as he traveled across the Plains of Kansas and northern Texas in the wake of a devastating blizzard (the same weather that killed most of Theodore Roosevelt's herd). Domestic cattle had died off in large numbers, frozen in their tracks; buffalo, however, habituated to the region and its fierce winter upheavals, had survived. "Why not chain this great giant?" Jones wondered. "Why not domesticate this wonderful beast which can endure such a blizzard . . . why not infuse this hardy blood into our native cattle, and have a perfect animal, one that will defy all these elements?" Jones began his quest to create an animal that would be the ultimate Plains survivor by cross-breeding buffalo and domestic cattle, dubbing their potentially hardy offspring *cattalo*. Unfortunately, the gleam was mostly in the eye of the human experimenters. The buffalo bull was willing to fertilize a domestic cow, but the domestic bull evinced a pronounced lack of interest in the buffalo cow. And almost all the surviving results of mixed-breeding efforts were female.[12]

In the meantime, Hornaday, with help from Roosevelt, was nurturing a small buffalo herd at the Bronx Zoo (which had opened in 1894 with Hornaday as director) for eventual reintroduction in the West. The highlight of this effort, which included their founding in 1905 of the American Bison Society, came in 1907, when the zoo's buffalo group was sent by rail to the National Wichita Forest and Game Reserve in Oklahoma. The reserve had come into being in part through the friendship of Roosevelt and Chief Quanah Parker, the half-breed son of Cynthia Ann Parker, perhaps the frontier's most famous white female captive; Quanah Parker had defended his adopted Comanche homeland and led a brutal war of resistance, but in 1875 he had agreed to "walk the white man's road," surrendering with four hundred of his followers and entering the reservation at Fort Sill. He proved an able tribal spokesman, once hosting a dinner for Roosevelt, and by invitation riding in the latter's inaugural parade in 1905. (Roosevelt, who became president in 1901 upon the assassination of William McKinley, was elected to the White House in his own right in 1904.)

On October 17, 1907, Parker was present at an emotional event in the town of Cache, Oklahoma, when the fifteen "Hornaday" buffalo arrived. The zoo director had personally overseen their development and feeding, and had named several for famous Indian chiefs. As befitting so momentous an event—America's first animal reintroduction—the buffalo were loaded onto a train with comfortable paddocks usually used for show horses, and switched lines at Grand Central Station for its journey west to Oklahoma. Parker wiped tears away when he saw buffalo once again against the backdrop of the low familiar hills, recalling long-ago times when, as another Indian once said, "the country was one robe." Within a few years, the reintroduced Oklahoma herd there had grown to thirty animals. The Bison Society and the Boone and Crockett Club followed up with bison reintroductions in Nebraska, Montana, and at Wind Cave National Park in South Dakota. In Montana, the National Bison Range, founded in 1908 north of Missoula, came to include almost 19,000 acres, and represented Washington, DC's first purchase of land expressly for use as a wildlife refuge. So promising was the program of reintroducing buffalo to the plains that by 1909, the federal government had 158 buffalo at its various reserves, at Yellowstone, and at the National Zoo in Washington. By fall 1911, Hornaday proclaimed the crisis of buffalo extinction averted.[13]

The saving of the buffalo from extinction had been heroic, but there was something dismal about celebrating America's grand total of 158 of the once abundantly populous animals. As western cartoonist and poet J. R. Williams reflected:

> One of the saddest sights today
> Is watching a buffalo cow chew baled hay,
> In a pen, in a zoo, like a sardine can;
> It's a lump in the throat of an outdoor man.[14]

No one, least not the irascible Hornaday, was about to rest on the accomplishment. In 1913, he published *Our Vanishing Wildlife: Its Extermination and Preservation*, a strongly worded chastisement to Congress and the nation that warned that the human indifference that had nearly doomed the buffalo imperiled all animal species. "When game was plentiful, I believed that it was right for men and boys to kill a limited amount of it for sport and for the table," he wrote, "but times have changed, and we must change also . . . It is time for the people who don't shoot to call a halt on those who do, and if this be treason, let my enemies make the most of it!"[15]

HORNADAY'S MESSAGE FOUND A SYMPATHETIC RESPONSE AMONG readers attuned to President Roosevelt's and Congress's early-twentieth-century conservation measures aimed at protecting wilderness and establishing national parks and refuges. The Roosevelt administration's record in this regard is stunning: the federal protection of 230 million acres of land and creation of 150 national forests, 51 bird sanctuaries, and 5 national parks. A regrettable aspect of Hornaday's strident views, however, was that they frequently included harsh criticisms of racial and ethnic minorities for their alleged inability to comprehend or obey the strictures of game laws and fair chase. To men like those of the Boone and Crockett Club, who saw themselves as wildlife's managerial class, the unenlightened methods of less principled hunters held the alarming potential to bring down the entire edifice of wildlife protection. Some of this anxiety was attributable to a Charlie Hallock–like nostalgia for the days when hunting as sport seemed the domain of white elites, but there was nonetheless a long list of scapegoats—African American hunters in the rural South only recently allowed to compete for game with whites; Italian immigrants who disregarded bag limits and seasons; market hunters who continued to slaughter for profit; and the pot hunters in the country's outback to whom compliance with city-made laws was nothing less than an injustice.

Where did fairness reside? Could a family that had been taking animals along with timber, wild roots, and mushrooms from a forest for generations suddenly be criminalized for doing so? Must the laws serve only sportsmen who liked to find the forest unsullied when they arrived for their weekend hunt? In the post–Civil War South, hunting and fishing offered the freedmen a means of augmenting their subsistence; success with rod and gun granted that much more independence from whites. For whites, though, this was another annoying reminder of blacks' changed status, a fear suggested by the Thomas Eakins painting *Whistling for Plover* (1874), in which a young black man, who appears to be neither guide or servant, aims in the viewer's direction. The threat of depleted wildlife became in this context an excuse for white hand-wringing over the passing of the antebellum South. "These ills of modern growth were all unknown in those olden times," *Forest and Stream* lamented in 1876 of the "cocked hat gentry" that were no more. Why,

> then the gentleman had little to do beyond a general outlook over his plantation, which was governed on moderate principles. His was an easy-going existence . . . riding fearlessly, laughing joyously, living easily, with no care on his mind, no strain on his nerves, he extracted all the bloom from the peach, all the sweetness from the flower . . . shooting over his dogs, following his pack across the country; we see in him a class that does not exist now, and he stands alone in his individuality.[16]

White bitterness over emancipation and the loss of the plantation world were rarely expressed so candidly. More often the white "concern" was that blacks were now helping themselves to more than the "lower" forms of wildlife for which they had cultivated a taste in slavery—"darky game," such as rabbits, raccoons, small birds, and possum. Some of these creatures were so unworthy of the chase, they didn't even require a gun. "When de possum is kotched he will cull up, he is den put on de end ob a pole, he stays all culled up an' holds on tight," former Mississippi slave Robert Baird told a white interlocutor, who rendered Baird's account in dialect. "Yo' can throw day pole 'cross yo' shoulders an' go home an bake dat possum on de hot coals in de fire place wid seet 'taters an coffee. Dat is a eatin'." Inevitably, shortages in Virginia and the Carolinas of deer and other large game were blamed on "the terrible incubus of blackness," which was said to hover above the hunting grounds in the form of a "constant stream of loafing Africans," each "the possessor of an old army musket and two or three mongrels, who will chase anything from a squirrel to an antlered buck." Sportsman Charles "Bobo" Askins, writing in *Recreation Magazine* in May 1909, worried that as southern blacks killed "throughout the year without mercy, without discrimination, without restraint . . . by and by the last of our migratory songbirds will go down into Dixie and never return."[17]

In every such nostalgic utterance about the South's bygone days, however, there was a contradiction; for during the time of slavery, a skilled, woods-savvy black guide who knew how to track game was a boon to his white owner. In some places it was believed that blacks, like Native Americans, were closer to an animal state of existence, and shared a special kinship with wildlife and thus knew where to find it. Due to the Negro's traditional lack of ammunition, alleged white hunters, he had been forced to husband it carefully, and as a result became a superior marksman. These myths, and the reality that slaves may well have known the secret ways of local field, forest, and fauna better than their white masters, inspired the confidence that a black guide increased the odds of a successful hunt. Former slaves were often sought as hunting guides by visiting northern sportsmen. Theodore Roosevelt was a repeat client of Louisianan ex-slave, soldier, and cardsharp Holt Collier, who was so proficient a hunter that it was said he'd killed more bears than Davy Crockett. Thus, blacks in the context of the southern hunt, much like African Americans generally, existed in white perception as at once both devilishly clever schemers and childish oafs: they were bumblers who "kotched" and dined on "possum," but also talented hunters with preternatural woodcraft skills.

Similar resentments surfaced in attitudes toward "foreign" or immigrant shooters. Novelist Owen Wister, scion of a prominent Philadelphia family and author of *The Virginian*, saw his beloved adopted West as a bastion for white men, a place that bred a singular courage and self-sufficiency, but the East as a decadent place, "debased and mongrel with its hordes of encroaching alien vermin." His friend, western artist Frederic Remington, confided to Wister that it was the "Jews, Injuns, Chinamen, Italians, Huns—the rubbish of the earth I hate. I've got some Winchesters and when the massacring begins, I can get my share of 'em, and what's more, I will." Even Hornaday reserved special indignation for newly arrived immigrants from southern Europe, whom he decried as rule-breakers and despoilers. The typical Italian, he explained, was by nature a scavenger, a "human mongoose," lacking the American hunter's integrity and sense of fair play. "It seems absolutely certain," he said, "that all members of the lower classes of southern Europe are a dangerous menace to our wildlife." His suggested remedy was that states deny aliens the ability to own or carry firearms, and prohibit southern European immigrants in particular from hunting until they had been naturalized American citizens for ten years. "Wherever there are large settlements of Italians and Hungarians . . . they swarm through the country every Sunday and shoot at every thing they see," he warned. "Let every state and province in America look out sharply for the bird-killing foreigner. The Italians are spreading, spreading, spreading . . . If you are without them today, tomorrow they will be around you." That fear appeared justified in 1906 when Seely Houk, the deputy game protector of Lawrence County, Pennsylvania, was murdered by an Italian Black Hand group resentful of his efforts to control their hunting.[18]

Hornaday's arguments struck a chord among fair chase hunters. They perceived of themselves as a link between civilization and barbarism, and the integrity and character of the chase deserved defending. Wherever these were undermined—by market hunters and poachers, shooters willing to disregard seasonal restrictions and bag limits, or by "slob hunters" who carried drink and boisterousness to the woods and disrespected wildlife—the virtue central to the sport hunting ideal, and the image of its adherents, was endangered.

The need for the federal government to get involved and adjudicate hunting rights and devise a conservation policy became manifest with the development of Yellowstone, America's first national park. Preserving a place or places from the onrush of settlement and agriculture, railroads and industry, was an appealing idea to many, but the practical challenges of turning the sprawling 2-million-acre Yellowstone ecosystem in western Wyoming into a serviceable public park meant the federal government could no longer be only an observer of such evolving processes in the West. Yellowstone National Park was created in 1872 by President Ulysses S. Grant to safeguard the area's myriad geological curiosities, although by the 1880s, the caretaking objectives had largely shifted to wildlife protection, perhaps thanks in part to Grinnell's 1877 public suggestion that the area be used as a "reservation" and to sustain the variety and abundance of regional fauna, including buffalo.

One initial problem was that the government viewed Indians hunting in the park as an incursion, whereas, to the Indians, the white man's laws regarding local game were not just unwelcome words, but unenforceable. What was deemed unspoiled wilderness to the white man was, to the Indian, simply the place his family and people lived, had *always* lived, sustained by deeply ingrained hunting practices. Although some whites entertained the myth that the tribes avoided the Yellowstone area because the geysers and hot springs held supernatural powers, the natives were actually much more practical: they used the hot springs for cooking and cleaning, and learned to take advantage of the fact that the springs warmed the surrounding earth and hastened the evaporation of snow from the grass, attracting herds of hungry deer, elk, and bison in winter.

In addition, the supplies guaranteed to local indigenous peoples by treaty were often meager or late, or had been pilfered by unscrupulous agents, and they had little choice but to fall back on hunting for sustenance. One ancient method was to set fire to parts of the forest, either with the immediate goal of driving animals from seclusion, or as a long-term strategy to clear wooded areas, since deer prefer meadows and fringe environments for browsing. In 1889, the Boone and Crocket Club, at the urging of Theodore Roosevelt, termed "the destruction of forests and of game caused by these Indian hunting parties . . . a serious evil," and demanded that new steps be taken to suppress Indian hunts and burning of the woods at Yellowstone. Early tourists were also a problem: neglecting camp fires whose sparks spread to the trees; vandalizing park attractions by cutting pieces off prominent rock formations as souvenirs; and, for sport, dropping branches, boots, and other objects into the geysers. Hunting had been allowed in the park during its first decade of operation, as there were few if any alternative means for tourists to get food; but in 1883, with the opening of hotels and restaurants, hunting was banned. This restriction emphasized an idea that was novel for its day: that a visitor's purpose in coming to the park would be to *view* wildlife, not shoot at it. Among sport hunters there was a surprising degree of acquiescence to the policy, partly because it appeared Yellowstone would serve as a safe breeding ground for wildlife, some of which would inevitably meander out of the park and become legal prey.[19]

Market hunters, however, continued to work the park, now illegally, as poachers. Hundreds of thousands of elk had been killed for their hides in Yellowstone during the 1870s, and even with tightened regulations, the park was far too sprawling an environ to be effectively policed: the poachers could easily slip in and out, securing buffalo heads and beaver pelts that, in turn, could be sold for a profit in nearby towns. The reality was that open-and-shut poaching cases were rare, and always difficult to prove. There were frequently no eyewitnesses, and the fact that the accused (and his circumstances) were often familiar and sympathetic to local judges and juries inclined the latter toward leniency. No doubt some officials hesitated to even report or prosecute poachers because they feared neighbors' retaliation, and few residents would testify against the accused. This rigid insularity took years to break down.

The unwritten truth about game law enforcement was that it often failed to even take itself seriously. The cost of a few illegally slain animals seemed to hardly warrant the expenditure in policing large swaths of land and prosecuting offenders. Virginia had established a deer hunting season in 1699, but did not hire game wardens to enforce it until 1916, 217 years later. Many places—Maryland in 1730, South Carolina in 1769, Kentucky in 1775—went on the books against poaching, but a crucial innovation didn't arrive until 1879, when New York State transferred the onus of prosecution from an illegal act of hunting to possession of an animal killed out of season, the latter being far easier to substantiate.[20]

Congress, sympathetic to the problems at Yellowstone, in 1883 made funds available for ten assistant superintendents to guard against illegal hunting, poaching, timber theft, and other provocations. These new officials, however, mostly political appointees, were far from the "mountain men of Montana . . . faithful and fearless in the performance of their duty" for whom Grinnell had advocated in the pages of *Forest and Stream*. Most lacked familiarity with the terrain and were soon overwhelmed by the harsh winters; nor were they prepared for the resolve and lethal character of some of the poachers. As Grinnell feared, the "old style of slaughter [was] kept up." Elk and deer hides were the basis of a lucrative business in the towns outside the park, while a potential windfall awaited a poacher who could emerge from Yellowstone with an intact buffalo head for sale. The situation was so egregious that even the greatest buffalo hunter of them all, Bill Cody, called for stronger measures.[21]

Unfortunately, without better laws there was little downside to the poacher's life at Yellowstone. The only penalty for the crime was expulsion from the park, which given its vast size was unenforceable and likely meaningless, and even when local Wyoming constables were added to the policing force, it soon emerged they were not above a bit of "poaching" themselves, using their badges to scam tourists into paying bogus fines. In one incident, an overzealous constable arrested visiting US congressman Lewis E. Payson of Illinois, chairman of the House Committee on Public Lands, on a trumped-up charge of not properly dousing a campfire.

For Sheridan, there was an obvious parallel to the law enforcement challenges he'd faced while representing federal authority in the postwar Reconstruction South—unpopular new laws, a restive population, a vast territory that defied governance, and unreliable local police whose sympathies tended to be with their white neighbors. Seeing at Yellowstone a similar lack of respect for the law, Sheridan in 1886 ordered in federal troops as the best way to "keep out skin hunters and all other hunters." In October of that year, a cavalry unit led by Captain Moses Harris marched into the park. It was termed a "temporary assignment," but the army would remain until 1918—the next thirty-two years.[22]

Despite the army's presence, some poaching of both game and timber continued, as it was almost impossible to dislodge the regional sentiment that those living near Yellowstone were entitled to its game for food and income, and its trees for firewood and building supplies. A breakthrough came on March 13, 1894, when army scout Felix Burgess and a Private Troike, patrolling on skis and snowshoes, caught poacher and market hunter Edgar Howell in the act. "Howell made his killing out in a little valley," Burgess recounted,

> and when I saw him he was about 400 yards away from the cover of the timber . . . His hat was sort of flapped down over his eyes, and his head was toward me. He was leaning over, skinning on the head of a buffalo. I thought I could maybe get across without Howell seeing or hearing me, for the wind was blowing very hard. I ran up to within 15 feet of Howell, between him and his gun, before I called to him to throw up his hands, and that was the first he knew of any one but him being anywhere in that country.[23]

"I see I was subject to the drop," Howell later confirmed, "so I let go of my knife and came along." Burgess signaled for Private Troike to come in from the trees and assist in taking Howell into custody. They marched him to the nearest park hotel, where Howell, "dirty, slouchy, and unkempt" after weeks trekking in the winter wilderness, "seemed to enjoy the square meals of captivity," polishing off two dozen pancakes in one sitting.[24]

Burgess's commanding officer, Captain George Anderson, recognized the significance of the arrest: because the poacher had been caught red-handed and there was no doubt as to his guilt, his case might serve as an example for reluctant policy makers of how brazen poaching was in the park and what few options existed in the way of punishment. By coincidence, *Forest and Stream* contributor Emerson Hough was at Yellowstone researching a multipart series for the magazine along with photographer F. J. Haynes, and the duo wrote up and documented the story of Howell's capture. The article was accompanied by disturbing photographs of Howell and one of his buffalo victims, and Hough made sure to include the equally troubling fact that poaching had reduced the park's buffalo herd from five hundred animals to fewer than two hundred.

Grinnell had long believed that poaching in Yellowstone could only be put down with strict enforcement, and he wasted no time using the Howell saga as an advocacy weapon, traveling to Washington to have his voice heard as editor of the nation's leading outdoor sports magazine. He personally disliked lobbying, but the Howell case was simply too ripe, too inviting as potential leverage, not to be used at once to press for better policing at Yellowstone and nationwide antipoaching laws with teeth. "So long as these lewd fellows of the baser sort, who lack only daring to be horse thieves and rustlers, know that they will not be punished for their invasions of the Park, ten regiments of troops could not protect it from their raids," *Forest and Stream* opined, "but let it once be known that punishment will follow swiftly on the heels of capture, and they will give the Park a wide berth." What gnawed at Grinnell was that although Howell was alleged to have killed eleven buffalo, the worst the law could do was expel him from Yellowstone and confiscate his gear, worth $26.75—a mere rap on the knuckles, given the severity of his crime and the fact that the buffalo trophies he had extracted were valued at $2,000. As Captain Anderson bemoaned, "There is no law governing this park except the military regulations. There is no punishment that can be inflicted on this lowdown fellow."[25]

The story of the bold and unrepentant poacher Edgar Howell, as told in Hough's *Forest and Stream* article (which castigated Congress as "ignorant and indifferent" on the need for real laws in the park), was picked up by city newspapers, and galvanized a country already concerned about the iconic buffalo's eradication. Grinnell, shrewdly activating the Boone and Crockett Club members' considerable political clout, worked closely with fellow member John

F. Lacey, a Republican congressman from Iowa. Convincing Lacey of the need to confront lawlessness in the nation's first national park was not difficult, as the congressman himself had been held at gunpoint during a stagecoach robbery there in 1887. The bill he and Grinnell managed to steer through Congress, the National Park Protective Act (known as the Lacey Act of 1894), provided jail sentences of up to two years and fines as high as $1,000 for any-one cutting timber, mining, or killing wildlife, including buffalo, in the park; made it unlawful to take game out of the park; and allowed officials to confiscate vehicles or equipment used for that purpose. It also created a sitting magistrate to hand down punish-ments. Previous versions of the bill had been floated unsuccessfully in the Senate, but now, with aroused public opinion supporting the measure, it passed both houses of Congress and on May 7, 1894, was signed by President Grover Cleveland, himself a hunter and angler. "The Howell buffalo slaughter marks an epoch, the turning point, let us hope," wrote Hough, "in the long course of a cruelly wasteful indifference on the part of the United States government in the matter of one of the most valuable possessions of the Amer-ican people."[26]

THE VICTORY OVER THE YELLOWSTONE POACHERS WAS A TRIUMPH for the fair chase ethos toward wildlife, and a milestone on the road toward the banishment of unethical or purely profit-driven hunting. Fair chase proponents now turned their attention from the continent's largest and most hardy creatures to its most frag-ile. Some blamed Marie Antoinette, whose brother Joseph took to calling her "Featherhead" for the elaborate bird plumage with which she adorned her tresses, for the necessity of the effort. The colorful plumes added height and color to her *poufs*, the piled hair-style which she popularized in June 1775 at the coronation of her husband, Louis XVI. The new queen's example inspired among fashion-conscious European women an enduring fetish for avian ornamentation, a look that, in somewhat moderated form, returned a century later on both sides of the Atlantic. About 1885, "the

MRS. ERNEST THOMPSON SETON.

Grace Gallatin, suffragist, hunter, and author, in the kind of fashionable "bird hat" that brought on the "Plume Wars." This grassroots effort on behalf of winged creatures led to the establishment of the Audubon Society. (Library of Congress)

idealized female silhouette shifted attention away from the full-ness of the lower body (exemplified by the crinoline and bustle) to the upper body, neck and head," explains scholar Robin Doughty. "Feathers upon enlarged hats and bonnets lent height to upper features and provided dignity and elegance."[27]

Of course, the use of feathers as ornaments did not originate in 1885, or even at Versailles. Men and women had long used plumes decoratively to add panache to their appearance. The word *panache* was itself derived from *pinna*, the Latin term for "tuft" or "feather," denoting confidence and swagger, and was associated with King Henry IV of France, who wore a white feather on his helmet to remain visible to his troops in the rush of battle, and whose motto was "*Ralliez-vous à mon panache blanc!*" ("Follow my white plume!"). By the late nineteenth century, however, colorful feathers of wild birds, called aigrettes by milliners, an allusion to the egret (whose plumes were most prized), were the source of a million-dollar international trade, boosted by newspaper advertise-ments and fashion spreads in women's magazines such as *McCall's, Ladies' Home Journal, Harper's Bazaar*, and *Vogue*.[28]

The feather fetish, like sport hunting, reflected the late nine-teenth century's enrapture with the out-of-doors. Birds, angelic and readily anthropomorphized, were seen as quasi-spiritual beings; *their* society, unlike ours, had remained pure, and books and prints depicting and honoring them sold briskly in America. England had gone down this path before in a related outdoors vogue known as the fern craze, instigated by the 1840 publication of *A History of British Ferns*, by Edward Newman, followed by the invention (by Nathaniel Bagshaw Ward) of the Wardian case, a glass case for pro-tecting ferns indoors in the damp British climate. A precursor of the terrarium, the Wardian case was soon a fixture in many upper-mid-dle-class British households, while fern-leaf decor also proliferated on plates, sofas, ceilings, and wrought-iron garden furniture.

While the fern craze inspired collecting expeditions by elite young people to the English or Scottish countryside, it was the busi-ness of bird plumage that came to represent huge profits. London was a global clearinghouse for the items, and New York its manu-facturing center, where approximately eighty-three thousand peo-ple, mostly women, were employed making and fashioning hats. In the most elaborate designs, their creations were arrayed with rib-bons, silk flowers, bird plumes, and sometimes even whole birds: a small stuffed owl might join pieces of dried fruit and animal fur; a nest of hummingbirds, finches, or warblers could be tastefully arranged beneath a large plume. Advised one fashion periodical of the feather's importance, "the extremely softening effect is ever desirable, especially for ladies no longer young."[29]

But by the mid-1880s, achieving this "softening effect" required the hunting and slaughter of about 5 million birds each year, including egrets, osprey, peacocks, pheasants, ducks, herons, par-rots, and grouse, as well as smaller birds, such as jays, humming-birds, finches, orioles, and larks—all told, about fifty US species. The most popular and also the most lucrative item was the white plume of the snowy egret, known as "little snowies," a water bird whose carcass could produce as many as forty to sixty plumes. Of these the most prized were the "nuptial plumes" that both male and female egrets displayed during courtship. For this reason, the birds were killed in the spring during breeding season, when their feathers were most deeply colorful and the recent hatching of eggs kept the parents faithful to their nests and thus easier to find.

Hats themselves were a de rigueur accessory for fashionable women, with designs suited for every kind of weather and even different parts of the day. But feathered hats abounded. In 1886, New York–based ornithologist Frank M. Chapman, later president of the American Museum of Natural History, conducted an informal survey as he took two long strolls through the Ladies' Mile shopping district of Manhattan; of 700 ladies' hats observed, 542 were festooned with feathers. Represented were 40 different bird species, including 23 waxwings, 15 snow-buntings, nine Baltimore orioles, 21 golden-winged woodpeckers, and 16 quail, as well as smaller numbers of bluebirds, warblers, owls, and one pileated woodpecker.[30]

The harvesters of bird plumes tended to be rural whites living along the streams, wetlands, and backwaters of Florida, Louisiana, and the Carolinas. As destructive in their work as the western buffalo men, they slaughtered whole heron and egret rookeries, leaving eggs and chicks to die or be eaten by crows. "Here and there in the mud lay the lifeless forms of eight of the birds," wrote naturalist T. Gilbert Pearson of a kill site. "They had been shot down and the skin bearing the plumes stripped from their backs. Flies were busily at work, and they swarmed up with hideous buzzings as we approached each spot where a victim lay. This was not the worst; in four of the nests young orphans could be seen who were clamoring piteously for food which their dead parents would never again bring to them."[31]

A related problem for concerned naturalists was that, in addition to atrocities committed for the sake of plumes, wild birds were also being harvested in vast numbers for food. One Dallas resident reported leading a torch-lit assault on a robin roost along the Trinity River in which he and six other men used shotguns to kill 10,157 birds in two hours ten minutes. In neighboring Louisiana, residents gathered 120,000 robins and brought them to market for only five cents per dozen, a dozen considered just the quantity required to fill a bird pie. Other small songbirds as well, such as finches, orioles, blue jays, and snow buntings also turned up in big-city food stalls.[32]

Game birds as well were dying in increasing numbers as sport hunters benefited from the technical sophistication of the double-barreled or repeating shotgun, which gave the hunter at least a second shot, if not multiple chances, to zero in on a fleet winged target. A five-shot Spencer was introduced in 1882; Winchester brought out the pump shotgun in 1893; and both types were soon replicated by other makers. With the widespread availability by the late 1880s of smokeless gunpowder, which increased the velocity at which shotgun pellets departed the gun barrel, hunters also gained the advantage of not having to wait until smoke cleared before taking a following shot. "A man feels master of the copse with a double-barrel; and such a sense of power, though only over feeble creatures, is fascinating," observed British naturalist Richard Jeffries in 1885. To get an idea of this increased lethal efficiency, William Hornaday, who questioned the gun makers' endless ratcheting up of firepower, compared the accuracy rate for a single-shot muzzle loader (10 percent); a single-shot breech loader (30 percent); a double-barrel breech loader (50 percent); a repeating rifle (60 percent); a pump shotgun (90 percent); and an auto-loading shotgun, which cocked again by its own recoil (100 percent). By 1911, there were sixty-six gun and ammunition factories in the United States, and in the following year alone, Americans bought 775,000,000 shotgun shells. "Is it not high time," asked Hornaday, who had himself already sworn off hunting, "for American sportsmen to cease taking their moral principles and their codes of ethics from the gun-makers?"[33]

Such overall improved technology, however, was popular in the hands of the burgeoning ranks of weekend hunters who, thanks to increased access to remote wetland areas, were better able to reach the feeding grounds of migratory birds and other fowl. With the extensive use of artificial decoys, as well as live disabled "hostage birds" set afloat to fool migratory fowl into landing, recreational bags of flying prey were often staggering—dozens, scores, hundreds of creatures shot to death. "The idea that in order to enjoy a fine day in the open a man must kill a wheel-barrow full of birds, is a mistaken idea," Hornaday scolded. "The Outing in the Open is the thing—not the blood-stained feathers, nasty viscera and Death in the game-bag. One quail on a fence is worth more to the world than ten in a bag."[34]

One abomination used by market hunters was the punt gun, which was capable of firing the equivalent of ten shotgun shells at once. So named because its size necessitated that it be lain across the punt of a boat before aiming, the weapon could fire a full pound of shot, scattering it instantly over unsuspecting flocks resting on water. Ignoring the fair chase edict that winged creatures were only to be targeted while in the air, the punt gunners blazed away indiscriminately; hundreds of birds could be killed in a day, in an hour.

To conservation-minded opponents of the plumage industry and other wanton bird slaughter, possible extinction was of immediate concern. The great auk, the Pallas cormorant, the Labrador duck, and the Eskimo curlew had all recently vanished, while the Carolina parakeet and once ubiquitous passenger pigeon were at the brink.

Given the former ubiquity of the pigeon, its imminent loss was a forceful lesson about the potential human impact of hunting. For despite being found only in central and eastern North America, passenger pigeons had until recently been the world's most numerous land bird; "beautiful wanderers," John Muir memorably called them, journeying in flocks so large they flowed "from horizon to horizon in an almost continuous stream all day long . . . like a mighty river in the sky." Eyewitness accounts of these mass migrations, which blotted out the sun for hours at a time, might be dismissed as fantasy or hallucination if they were not so frequently reported. In the early 1800s, ornithologist Alexander Wilson noted one flock almost 300 miles long, which he estimated contained more than 2 billion birds; so numerous were they that the tree branches where they lighted to feast on beechnuts, chestnuts, and acorns often snapped under their collective weight.[35]

Following the Civil War, due to the capability of the telegraph to alert and transport hunters to massive pigeon nestings,
the shooting and netting of these birds became both large-scale
and routine. From the famous 1878 Petoskey Nesting in Michigan,
which covered 150,000 acres, an estimated 1.5 million pigeons were
slaughtered and shipped to markets in major cities, 350 birds to a
barrel. At market, the birds sold to household shoppers for two
cents apiece, and were served at restaurants in a variety of dishes;
the squabs—pigeons under four weeks old—considered especially
succulent.

The persistent harvesting of the pigeons certainly was the primary source of their eventual disappearance, although experts point
to the fact that human settlement and clearing was slowly destroying the birds' habitat. It's also known that among species accustomed to swarming together in such large numbers—overcoming
all potential predators in what scientists term *predator satiation*—
even a partial reduction in the size of the flock can prove devastating to the whole, causing what appears as a mysterious, sudden
collapse. But for most people, it seemed impossible that extinction
could claim a species long known for swarms so plentiful they dark-
ened the sky. Perhaps the pigeons had all flown to South America, it
was said, or had gone far out to sea. For years, well into the twentieth century, hopeful isolated sightings were reported, some by ship
captains—the birds were in the Gulf of Mexico, off the coast of
Peru. The American Ornithological Union (AOU) conducted a two-
year "reward campaign" in 1910–1911 to honor any legitimate evidence of the birds' existence; the rewards went unclaimed. In 1914,
the last surviving passenger pigeon, a female named Martha, died
at the Cincinnati Zoo. Her tiny body, secured in a 300-pound block
of ice, was sent to the Smithsonian.[36]

BIRD STUDY AND PROTECTION GROUPS, SUCH AS THE NEW YORK
Association for the Protection of Game Birds (founded in 1844),
the Nuttall Ornithological Club (1873), and the AOU (1883),
tended to be peopled by specialists and dedicated birders. Grinnell, in the pages of *Forest and Stream* on February 11, 1886, put

forth a proposal for a broader membership group, one that would have a more activist bent. "Very slowly the public are awakening to see that the fashion of wearing the feathers and skins of birds is abominable," he wrote. "There is, we think, no doubt that when the facts about this fashion are known, it will be frowned down and will cease to exist. Legislation of itself can do little against this barbarous practice, but if public sentiment can be aroused against it, it will die a speedy death." He suggested that the group have no membership fees and that its name honor John James Audubon, a man whose work uniquely combined natural science and art as well as hunting, and who as an artist helped establish the idea of birds as more than flesh and feathers, but a wild and beautiful essence. Grinnell had lived near the Audubon family as a child on the far upper west side of Manhattan and attended a school run by the great birder's widow, Lucy Audubon. Like both William Hornaday and the young Theodore Roosevelt, Grinnell was a self-taught taxidermist; during a period after college when he worked in his father's financial business, he would have a friend bring him fresh specimens of unusual birds from the city markets each day so that he might dissect and study them at night.[37]

The inaugural issue of the Audubon Society's magazine, which appeared later that year, sounded a note of sorrow, as movement on the plumage issue had been slow to gain traction. "When the [Society] was first organized, it seemed a comparatively simple thing to awaken in the minds of all bird-wearing women a sense of what their 'decoration' involved," wrote New England poet and bird-lover Celia Thaxter. "We flattered ourselves that the tender and compassionate heart of woman would at once respond to the appeal for mercy, but after many months of effort we are obliged to acknowledge ourselves mistaken." Thaxter's indictment, which ran under the headline "Women's Heartlessness," concluded, "I would the birds could all emigrate to some friendlier planet peopled by a nobler race than ours, where they might live their sweet lives unmolested, and be treated with the respect, the consideration, and the grateful love which are their due . . . for we have almost forfeited our right to the blessing of their presence."[38]

By fall 1888, Audubon claimed fifty thousand members, but the managerial aspects of running the young organization proved too much for Grinnell, whose time was already spread thin among the Boone and Crockett Club, *Forest and Stream*, and other responsibilities. The project was suspended for several years, while the plumage crisis only deepened. It was then, as historian Jennifer Price has observed, America's "first real national grassroots conservation crusade" began. In 1896, local Audubon chapters began to spontaneously form in Massachusetts and Pennsylvania, the organizers and members mostly women, adamant that something be done. "A dead bird does not help the appearance of an ugly woman, and a pretty woman needs no such adornment," proclaimed Harriet Hemenway of Boston and her cousin Miss Minna Hall, who founded the Massachusetts Audubon Society and rallied the society ladies of Beacon Hill to the cause in a series of meetings and tea parties. The subject of a well-known oil portrait by John Singer Sargent, Hemenway came from a family of abolitionists and had once caused a scandal by inviting the educator Booker T. Washington to stay in her house when local hotels refused him. Walking the New England woods in a pair of tennis shoes to look for interesting avian life, she may have been America's original eccentric bird-watcher. The Audubon Society Hemenway led soon had nine hundred women members, who, within a year, in 1897, had used their influence to lobby successfully for a state law banning trade in wild bird feathers.[39]

It was a hopeful moment. That same year, *Century Magazine* ran the first comprehensive, illustrated article describing dinosaurs to the general public. Thanks to the Bone Wars and much exhaustive digging, it was by now clear that what lay underground or embedded in the hills and cliffs of the American West pointed to a very consequential prehistory—one of glacial movements, vanished seas, and faunal extinctions—the knowledge of which could not but influence contemporary attitudes and, hopefully, policies toward wildlife. To recognize the modern decline in animal populations, to contemplate the writings of Darwin on evolution and Agassiz on the Ice Age, and to consider the proof that immense mammals no one alive had ever seen had once walked the earth, led any reasonable mind to a new appreciation of life's impermanence and fragility. Opposing the unregulated hunting of birds for profit and sport required little further deliberation.

As Hemenway's success demonstrated, progressive causes were a sphere in which women, particularly educated women of means, could be both instrumental and effective. They were, it was thought, better attuned to be the moral conscience of the times, and the cause of conservation, which addressed wayward consumerism and greed, as well as animal protection, fit the spirit of the Progressive moment. Tapping existing female networks associated with women's clubs—popular since the 1860s and devoted to literature, temperance, and settlement houses, as well as campaigns to open museums, parks, and kindergartens—Audubon groups soon formed in other states with an average of 80 percent female membership. In this case, a powerful motivating force for female activism was the fact that female fashion had encouraged this morally reprehensible abuse. But as many reformers pointed out, a concern for America's birds was not only aesthetic; birds have always played a vital ecological role in controlling insect pests, to the betterment of all growing things, not the least human agriculture and human health. In the Dakotas in the mid-nineteenth century, settlers noticed that when prairie chickens or plovers were killed in great numbers, their crops suffered more damage from grasshoppers and other insects, the very bugs the vanquished birds routinely ate. By 1874, a year of severe grasshopper devastation on the plains, the folly of destroying nature's own check against such invaders became undeniable. "The great and inestimable service done to farmer, gardener and florist by the birds is only becoming known by sad experience," concluded a Kansas newspaper. "Spare the birds and spare your fruit; the little corn and fruit taken by them is more than compensated by the quantity of noxious insects they destroy. [They are] the farmer's best friends."[40]

Congressman Lacey of Iowa, who had been integral to the 1896 effort to protect wildlife in Yellowstone, joined together in 1900 with the Audubon clubs, *Forest and Stream*, and farmers to enable

passage of a second Lacey Act, which used the commerce clause of
the Constitution to prohibit the interstate shipment of wild species
killed in violation of state wildlife protection laws. The legislation
was approved by Congress and signed into law in May by President
William McKinley.

A few years later, Theodore Roosevelt, now the president,
explored another means of protection. In Florida, coastal fishermen
were in the habit of eliminating brown pelicans, which they considered pests, as the birds, with their enormous bills, were expert scoo-
pers of fish. Roosevelt, however, took a special liking to the birds
(they were known for being comfortable around humans, no doubt
contributing to how easily they were being slain). In 1903, perhaps
inspired by the private example of E. A. McIlhenny, head of the
Tabasco pepper sauce company, who in 1892 set aside a large protected zone for the snowy egret on Avery Island, Louisiana, Roosevelt established the Pelican Island National Wildlife Refuge off
the Atlantic coastal town of Sebastian, the first of fifty-two wildlife
refuges he would create during his presidency.

On paper, bird protection and the antiplume crusade seemed to
be making gains, but as ever, it was one thing to make a law, another
to have it enforced. It was particularly difficult to implement regulations aimed at safeguarding marsh birds and rookeries, as the
targeted birds were found in out-of-the-way places, access to which
was known most intimately by local hunters. Not willing to await
government action, the Audubon Society decided to hire its own
wardens—an idea endorsed by influential New York birder William
Dutcher, long active in the AOU and head of the Florida Audubon
Society. But some of the wardens hired to combat plume hunters in
the remote outback of southern Florida met intense hostility. They
were verbally and physically abused, or had their property stolen or
destroyed; some abandoned their posts or, under unexplained circumstances, disappeared. Near Charlotte Harbor, the bloodstained
hat of Audubon warden Columbus MacLeod was located, as was
his boat, which had been weighted down and sunk; his body was
never found. In South Carolina, warden Pressly Reeves was shot
and killed in an ambush; his killers could not be identified.

The best-documented case involved Florida warden Guy Bradley, himself a former plume hunter. "I used to hunt plume birds, but
since the game laws were passed, I have not killed a plume bird. I
make this statement upon honor," Bradley assured Dutcher upon
his hiring in 1900. Bradley's past and local knowledge fitted him
well for the job. After patiently explaining the new bird laws to his
neighbors, he established an informal network of coastal watchers
to alert him if plume hunters came around. But he was despised
as a traitor and, working largely alone, was extremely vulnerable.
On July 8, 1905, he witnessed Walter Smith, a Confederate war veteran, and his two sons, shooting in a rookery; Bradley had arrested
members of the family before, and Smith had warned Bradley there
would be trouble if he took either of his sons into custody again.
When the warden confronted the trio, the elder Smith was true to
his word, and shot and killed Bradley in cold blood.[41]

In court, Smith claimed that Bradley had fired first and that
he had only shot in self-defense, but a weapons expert brought in
by the Society testified that Bradley's gun had not been fired at all,
and Bradley's friends and family pointed out that, as he was a crack
shot, had he pulled the trigger, he would have been very unlikely
to miss his target at such close range. The case, observed by the
national press, had the feel of a small-town feud, pitting family
against family. Local sentiment was largely on Smith's side, and he
was acquitted, although it was not unexpected when Bradley's relations immediately went to the killer's house and burned it to the
ground. "A young and sturdy man, cut off in a moment, for what?"
Dutcher wrote, eulogizing the murdered warden. "That a few more
plume birds might be secured to adorn heartless women's bonnets?
Heretofore the price has been the life of the birds, now is added
human blood. Every great movement must have its martyrs, and
Guy M. Bradley is the first martyr in bird protection."[42]

Dutcher alluded accurately to the movement's inevitability, for
bird-friendly laws and rules had already begun to fall into place.
While legislative efforts in the 1870s to defend the buffalo had been
shamefully abandoned, a generation of rising concern for the eradication of species made a significant difference. Between 1895 and

1905, thirty-seven states adopted bird protection laws that distinguished game birds, such as swans, ducks, and geese, from protected
species, such as shore birds, egrets, and herons. In 1905, the same
year Dutcher was named the first president of the National Audubon Society, thirty-three additional states passed further restrictions. In New York State, the Audubon Plumage Bill of 1911 put
a ban on the sale of all native birds and slammed shut the domestic feather trade, while in 1911–1912, New York, Massachusetts,
and California all banned the sale of wild game for the market.
In 1913, President Woodrow Wilson signed the Underwood Tariff
Bill that closed off the importation of plumes from other countries,
and finally, the 1916 Migratory Bird Act (the Weeks-McLean Law)
extended federal safeguards to nongame shore and migratory birds.

The winning of the Plume Wars, along with the efforts to salvage a remnant population of American buffalo and the designating of secure wildlife refuges and other wilderness tracts, were
triumphs for the early conservation cause. Hunters were leaders
in all three endeavors, extrapolating from the spirit of fair chase
the means to adjust human actions and policies toward wildlife.
Critics often point out that hunters' interest in conservation is
motivated by the desire to preserve shootable game—that is, to
keep animals alive for a time so as to kill them later in sport; but
that sells short the hunting community's dedication in this regard.
There will always be people unhappy with the sport of hunting,
but there's no denying that, unique among most other large public
endeavors, it has nurtured a consciousness of equilibrium and an
ethics of restraint. Meant initially to guide the lone hunter's behavior, it has shown itself useful and adaptable in shaping communal
decisions regarding man's place in the natural world.

*Chapter Eleven*

# What Is Nature,
# What Is Man?

SINCE ITS BEGINNINGS, SPORT HUNTING IN AMERICA HAS HAD IMPLI-
cations for land use and conservation. Expanded federal authority in Yellowstone Park, while pushing back on poaching, also
offered an early example of how complex even well-intended wildlife conservation efforts can be, to the extent of having detrimental
consequences—for hunters as well as animal life, animal habitat,
and the human economy. When US troops in the park suppressed
the Indians' traditional forest burning practices, which ensured
ruminants had access to short-grass grazing places, tall growth
instead filled in the former clearings, denying sustenance to elk and
deer, while also allowing dead plant material to collect so that when
accidental fires did occur, they were more severe. Troops also killed
predators, such as mountain lions and wolves, a policy required for
the safety of tourists and helpful to neighboring livestock owners,
but this resulted in a significant increase in the elk population, one
that put a strain on the natural food supply.[1]

Law replacing custom, traditions rudely disrupted—this was how the coming of conservation could appear at ground level. Nowhere was this transformation more evident than in the great hunting grounds of the Adirondacks. The area's gift of isolation and pristine beauty in such close proximity to the large cities of the East Coast had made it an attractive retreat for the outdoorsman, and increasingly his family, too. And whereas the first generation of Adirondack travel writers in the 1850s, such as Thomas Headley, had focused on the region's tranquility and pine-scented bliss, William Murray's (in)famous 1869 guidebook had successfully touted tourism and recreation. The Park Street cleric, it was said, had "kindled a thousand campfires" in the region. By 1875, more than two hundred hotels had opened, as well as new stagecoach and steamboat services to take people to them; by 1900, more than twenty-five thousand visitors were invading the region each summer (as compared with fewer than 3,000 before the appearance of Murray's book).[2]

The word *vacation* came into greater usage at this time, as the fortunate "vacated" their stuffy city lodgings each summer for the sport and repose of the Adirondacks. But their blissful leisure came at the expense of the local residents who, if they could not find a niche in the tourist economy as guides or hotel workers, were left to deal—as hunters, loggers, farmers—with a brace of new conservation laws and the creation of large, private estates. In the eyes of authorities and new property owners, yesterday's logger became today's trespasser, game hog, or timber outlaw. Few were surprised in September 1903 when headlines brought news of a murder: the victim, a New York City millionaire long at war with his neighbors over their disputed use of his land.

Much had changed in these mountains since the halcyon days of Emerson's poetic jottings at Follensbee Pond, and not simply the influx of major commercial development. Philologist George Perkins Marsh's seminal 1864 book, *Man and Nature, or, Physical Geography Modified by Human Action*, had offered a startling critique of man's impact on the environment here, warning against the overcutting of timber for its ruinous effect on the soil, and citing the

Adirondacks as a vulnerable locale in need of protection. Anticipating the conservation movement by as much as a generation, Marsh was "the first to go beyond the Romantics and argue that forests should be preserved, not because they were aesthetically pleasing, but because they were necessary for human survival," writes historian John F. Reiger.[3]

A public servant as well as a lawyer and scholar, Marsh served three terms in Congress in the 1840s, where he opposed the extension of slavery and the Mexican War; from 1851 to 1853, he was US minister to the Ottoman Empire. In 1856, he authored *The Camel: His Organization, Habits, and Uses, with Advice for His Introduction into the United States*, a book describing the potential efficiency of an animal he called the "ship of the desert" for use in the American Southwest. After stints as Vermont's fishing commissioner and railroad commissioner (he proposed that a "gallows-car" be attached to every train for the explicit purpose of hanging corrupt railroad presidents), he was made America's first ambassador to Italy by President Lincoln in 1861, a position he would hold until his death in 1882.[4]

During Marsh's extensive travel in the Middle East and southern Europe, he noticed something that few had given serious regard—a pattern of environmental degradation, decimated wildlife, flooded wetlands, and diminished soil fertility brought about by short-sighted agricultural practices and poor forest stewardship. He feared that similarly negligent habits were at work in his own Vermont, in the neighboring Adirondacks, and elsewhere in America. Just as the Old World had been damaged irrevocably, he warned, so might similar neglect harm the United States, for Americans, he knew, suffered from the same misplaced faith that the earth was inexhaustible and would continually renew itself. Most worrisome, the consequences of human negligence did not reveal themselves until it was far too late to reverse them. This myopia could only be addressed if people were willing to act on the *anticipation* of a potential problem, and he was convinced the Adirondacks deserved immediate attention because the region served as the watershed of numerous rivers, including the Hudson. Marsh shredded the notion that anyone who owned land had also a right to profit from exploiting its natural resources; such "freedom" could do tremendous harm. Instead of parceling out the public domain and selling it into private hands, or to railroads or large industry, he argued, why not secure it for the public good? To keep the Adirondacks from large developers, and also limit potential harm from local residents (who he feared were unable to manage their own land in ways sympathetic to the public weal), he suggested Albany proclaim the region the property of New York State.

Marsh's book was in its own way as epochal as Darwin's *On the Origin of Species*, which had been published five years earlier, and a large influence on the thinking of Charles Hallock and George Bird Grinnell, both of whom revisited and enlarged upon Marsh's ideas in *Forest and Stream*. Marsh's ideas would later resonate with twentieth-century ecologist Aldo Leopold, who would see Marsh's premonitions confirmed in the devastation of the Dust Bowl of the 1930s. But in his own day, Marsh's arguments regarding the wise use of the commons were widely seen as impractical, even rash. Many of his contemporaries thought *Man and Nature* a pitiable detour from his respected work in linguistics and ethnology, and friends urged him to return to the scholarly footing he knew best. Marsh had a ready reply to such concern: "Wherever I go, I find the mud-piles better worth study than the superstructure of the social edifice."[5]

One official who did appreciate Marsh's warnings about the Adirondacks was Verplanck Colvin, a topographical engineer who supervised a critical New York State land survey. Colvin was an innovative administrator as well as an exacting scientist, the man who established both the precise height of Mount Marcy (5,343 feet) and the fact that Lake Tear in the Clouds was the indisputable source of the Hudson River. In 1870, gazing out from atop Mount Seward, another Adirondack peak he scaled, he witnessed the damage being done by unsustainable lumber clear-cutting, and prepared a convincing lecture on the risks of deforestation for state policy makers. As a result, he was appointed head of the Adirondack Survey, and in that capacity in 1873 warned that poor forest stewardship could ultimately endanger the water supply that flowed out of the mountains; he urged the legislature to create an Adirondack forest preserve.

Support for the idea came from sport hunters. An 1872 state advisory report on the region's future emphasized the importance of "the field sports of the wilderness," noting that they "are remarkably exhilarating, and strengthen and revive the human frame." Channeling Frank Forester, the report reminded legislators that "it is to their eager pursuit of field sports that metropolitan Englishmen owe their superiority in physical power, with that skillful use of firearms, independence, fearlessness, cool presence of mind, and ability which they possess to bear the fatigues of war and exigencies of military service." The New York legislature, backed by a coalition of sportsmen looking to save hunting grounds and downstate industries eager to protect the Adirondack watershed, closed off all sales of state lands in 1883, and two years later declared the Adirondacks a state forest. A state constitutional amendment in 1902 officially created the 6-million-acre Adirondack Park.[6]

As actions to maintain the region as a pristine wilderness advanced, hunting lodges and resorts proliferated. One of the first large inns to open was Paul Smith's, on Saint Regis Lake, in 1859. By 1900, this impressive edifice boasted 255 rooms, a bowling alley, a direct wire to the New York Stock Exchange, and a guest list that would eventually include P. T. Barnum and Presidents Grover Cleveland, Calvin Coolidge, and Theodore Roosevelt. Such establishments, including the Prospect House in Blue Mountain Lake, were, despite their elite clientele, kept deliberately woodsy, with a minimum of amenities, although, to be sure, the accommodations at the upper end tended to be deluxe. One was described as "a sort of Waldorf Astoria amid lakes and mountains," convenient from Grand Central Station. The close architectural cousins to these resorts were the "Great Camps," large rustic private homes often used as hunting lodges, usually with lakefront access, and built as a series of large capacious rooms sharing a common roof. Their designer was William West Durant, who combined elements of the Swiss chalet, precepts of Japanese architecture, and aspects of both the British Arts & Crafts and American Craftsman movements. With their large stone fireplaces and interconnected spaces, the Great Camps were well suited to the region's harsh elements and isolation. Built on a spectacular scale, they appealed to the very wealthy—Alfred Vanderbilt, J. P. Morgan, and railroad magnate Collis Huntington, among others, as well as New York mayor Seth Low.[7]

The popularity of hunting in the region led to the innovative Adirondack Guide Boat, a commodious deep-keeled vessel that allowed a guide to fit clients, gear, and game. It was rowed with locked oars, not paddled, enabling stationary positioning as well as fast traverse of Blue Mountain Lake or any larger body of water. Made from local pine, spruce, and cedar, the skiff's shallow draft was designed for the region's variety of waters—streams, lakes, and rapids—and its hull was light, to ease the portages guides were expected to perform. In the decades before trains and automobiles allowed extensive access to the region, these boats, in the hands of such skilled guides as Mitchell Sabattis, were a passport to hundreds of secret and otherwise unreachable bays, inlets, and shorelines. The craft had a "sneak paddle" that guides could deploy for imperceptible movement when working in close to shore, especially in the proximity of live game.

Along with these changes, the mountains also experienced efforts at hunting reform. Henry Bergh aligned his ASPCA against the notorious regional custom of hounding frightened deer into a lake, which he termed "water butchery." Although sportsmen had long railed against the practice on ethical grounds, Bergh was the first to suggest it should cease because this manner of killing game animals tainted their meat. "It is an undeniable law of nature," he wrote, "that the treatment of an animal at or previous to its killing is imparted for good or evil to its blood and tissues." Comparing it to the inhumane methods of the packinghouse, he asked:

> Can there exist a doubt that the abuse which cattle receive during their long voyages by rail is imparted to their flesh, and may not many of the diseases we suffer from be the consequence of such abuse? Half-starved, thirsting, and terrified by blows and shouting, its blood boiling with fever, the creature is

driven to the slaughter house and killed, and the next day, perhaps, its flesh is put upon the table for consumption.[8]

The sporting press added its voice to the call for change. Among
others, one *Forest and Stream* piece related how several men aided
by dogs had sprung "an antlered monarch" from dense brush into
the open, but after driving him over a peninsula and through two
lakes without getting off a decent shot, the so-called hunt ended only
when a man in a row boat pulled alongside "the noble fugitive, seized
him by the horns and ignobly drowned him by holding his head
under the water." Sickened by such cowardly acts, and armed with
a petition signed by hundreds of sportsmen, Bergh helped nudge the
state to legislate against hounding. A bill was enacted in June 1885,
but in response, resort owners stormed Albany, protesting that the
restrictions would ruin the regional allure for amateur hunters (for
whom chasing a deer into a lake was often the sole method of killing
one). In May 1886, they forced the law's repeal. Theodore Roosevelt,
along with zoologist and Adirondack naturalist C. Hart Merriam,
had better luck a decade later, attaining in 1897 both a ban on
hounding and jack-lighting, and a regulation against shooting water-
fowl before they took wing, laws soon copied by other states.[9]
For many native Adirondackers, of course, the rapid pace of
"modernizing" change in the mountains, and even the beneficial
reforms Bergh and others had sought, did not represent progress so
much as the reality that their customs and livelihoods were newly
subject to outside scrutiny and control. Once considered romantic
figures, even local hunting guides might now be suspected of poaching. As veteran guide Alvah Dunning explained, in times past,

nobody said a word if a poor man wanted a little meat an'
killed it, but now they're savin' it until the dudes get time to
come up here an' kill it an' some of 'em leave a deer to rot in
the woods, an' on'y take the horns ef it's a buck, or the tail ef
it's a doe, just so's they can brag about it when they go home,
an' they'd put me in jail ef I killed a deer when I needed meat. I
dunno what we're a-comin' to in this free country.[10]

A deer driven into an Adirondack lake is pursued in *A Good Chance*, by
Arthur Fitzwilliam Tait. This method of increasing a hunter's odds was
common but thought unsportsmanlike by many, and it was eventually
outlawed. (Library of Congress)

Whereas visiting sportsmen often did not need the meat of the
animal they killed, locals did, and they could resent what seemed to
be the stylish constraints of "the chase," as well as those game laws
that seemed to favor hunting as sport. The divide bred a deep insularity and culture of silence within rural communities. Neighbors
refused to bear witness against neighbors. To authorities investigating game law violations, the locals' sudden "ignorance" of others'
blatant activities, even their identities, was astounding. "Every con-
ceivable evasion is resorted to, and all local influences are brought
to bear to screen offenders against the State from justice," reported
a state commission in 1888. Meanwhile, forest rangers on patrol,
whether on foot or by boat, were occasionally fired upon, and it
was surely very small comfort that, as the commission reported,
"The shots are fired out of bravado, and not aimed to kill." In 1876,
a hunting party led by William A. Wheeler, New York congressman

and soon-to-be vice president under Rutherford B. Hayes, was fired upon, on suspicion that the visitors had cut the fishing nets belonging to a local family. No one was hurt, but the incident put a scare into owners of the large resorts. Stories making their way back to the city, of yokels firing at or near visiting sportsmen, could only depress hunting tourism. At one point, the residents changed tactics and began "policing" the forests to confront sport shooters they suspected of taking too much game. A number of city men met in the woods by rough-hewn vigilantes were warned in stark terms not to come back.[11]

If there was anything worse than the entitled sport tourists, it was the owners of private estates who erected fences, closed off large swaths of formerly open hunting lands, and hired private security to deter trespassers. In 1903, both New York financier Orando Dexter, with 7,000 acres near Waverly, and his neighbor William Rockefeller, cofounder of the Standard Oil Company, who held a 52,000-acre estate at Bay Pond, received anonymous threats. Dexter, age forty-nine, a graduate of Harvard and Columbia Law School, was heir to a news publishing fortune, a bachelor who was socially reticent despite his substantial wealth and connections. He had little curiosity about or concern for his Adirondack neighbors. What he did have was a very good head for mathematics and business. "If my son had a fault," his ninety-year-old father would lament, "it was his desire to add money to money, property to property." Dexter prosecuted anyone caught hunting or fishing on his domain, and in every way sought to bully his neighbors into submission rather than meet them halfway, denying them the traditional road and hunting access they'd enjoyed, and even closing off the blueberry fields where they'd romped as children. For thirteen years, he had been engaged in a vicious dispute with neighbor and lumberman Joe Alfred, rejecting Alfred's plea for use of an old logging road to be able to run his business. Eventually the courts upheld Alfred's right to use the road, but Dexter continued to issue threats—toward Alfred, trespassing hunters, or anyone who troubled his holdings.[12]

Dexter's routine was to drive into town at about one o'clock each afternoon to visit the post office and then enjoy a leisurely buggy

ride home while he perused his mail and magazines. On September
19, 1903, he departed for town with an overseer, Azro Giles, who
rode ahead, and a stableman named Bert Russell following behind.
Out of a desire for privacy, Dexter's carriage, which he drove himself, was not always in view of the two escorts. Suddenly, a short
way from the Dexter home, Russell heard two rifle shots; whipping
his horse vigorously onward, he arrived to find Dexter bloodied and
hanging out of the wagon. Russell propped him up against a tree,
demanding, 'Who shot you?' but the victim was already dead, slain
by a single bullet that went through the back of the thick wooden
wagon seat, entered and then exited his body, and wound up in the
hip of the carriage horse. The round was a regular soft-nosed .38,
common to rifle hunters. There was an investigation, and dozens of
residents were questioned by the sheriff, but the righteous silence of
the area's populace prevailed. The region's vast uninhabited tracts,
its dense forests and meandering waterways had historically offered
a promising place for people—and facts—to stay permanently lost.
One news account went so far as to imply it wasn't only potential
witnesses and informants holding out, but that "Mr. Dexter had
been involved in such a marl of litigation and had incurred so many
enmities" that even the local police know "much more about the
circumstances than they are willing to divulge."[13]

Rockefeller and other New York City owners of Adirondack
lands hurriedly gathered in the city to discuss the threat represented by the assassination, while the victim's father, Henry Dexter,
announced a $5,000 reward for any information leading to a convic-
tion. But even so substantial an offer proved insufficient to draw out
anyone with inside knowledge. "I was afraid to go up there," Dexter
senior said. "I begged [my son] again and again to give up his fight
against those outlaws. I told him they would kill him, and now they
have done it—shot him in the back." For the two opposing forces in
the Adirondacks, the crime, which was never solved, seemed only to
confirm the worst expectations and urge deepening entrenchment.
Locals saw it as fair warning to arrivistes who turned themselves
into feudal lords, while Dexter's fellow estate owners simply hired
more men with guns.[14]

IT WAS NO COINCIDENCE THAT ALONGSIDE ASPCA REFORM EFFORTS regarding sportsmen's ethical responsibilities and the increased concern over threats to wildlife, there developed an enhanced notion of animals as individuals—sentient beings that not only deserved a reprieve from man's cruelty, but likely had "the same faculties and emotions, in a diminished degree, as man." Darwin's ideas on the link between animals and humans also influenced this change. But how great were the similarities? Hunters would be the first to say that the fox was brilliantly evasive; bull elk, proud and domineering; and retrievers, capable of friendship, joy, and sadness. But did animals reason?[15]

The question came up for public debate in 1903 after the *Atlantic* published naturalist John Burroughs's strong critique of nature writers Ernest Thompson Seton and William J. Long, accusing them of irresponsibly endowing animal characters with human traits. Seton was the author of *Wild Animals I Have Known* (1898) and *Lives of the Hunted* (1901); Long wrote books for children, most recently, in 1902, *School of the Woods*. Both were working around the edges of what would later be called ethology, the study of animal behavior and awareness. Seton believed that it was important to highlight animals' individuality so as to show that, even within the same species, not all were alike. "The real personality of the individual and his view of life are my theme," he wrote, "rather than the ways of the race in general, as viewed by a casual and hostile human eye."[16]

What differentiated Seton's and Long's tales from animal fables was that they were presented as actual accounts, based on natural history, in which animals demonstrated an unprecedented level of individual agency. Seton wrote of an especially large wolf, Lobo, who, with his mate, a white wolf called Blanca, terrorized the cattle ranges of northern New Mexico, and who was so clever that he gathered all the poisoned baits left by man into a heap and then shat upon them. Seton's world also included a crow named Silverspot who led instructional drills for the younger members of his flock. Another of his heroines was Vix, a mother fox, who taught her kits how to fool a curious squirrel into approaching by playing dead. In one memorable passage, Vix evades a pack of hounds by riding on top of a sheep, thus disguising her scent, and then finishes off her pursuers by leading them onto a railroad trestle just as a train appears. Long, in a similar vein, had kingfishers catching and then releasing fish into small pools so their offspring could learn fishing, a porcupine rolling itself up into a ball and hurtling itself down a hill for fun, and a partridge that held roll call for its young. His most controversial tales featured animal "surgeries," in which creatures dressed their own wounds by applying splints of mud and twigs to broken legs or wings.

Burroughs, in "Real and Sham Natural History," took vehement exception, denying that animals possess humanlike qualities of reason, and insisting that their behavior is instinctual. "The crows do not train their young. They have no fortresses, or schools, or college, or examining boards, or diplomas, or medals of honor, or hospitals, or churches, or telephones, or postal deliveries, or anything of the sort," he wrote. "Nature is not benevolent. [She] makes no exceptions, never tempers her decrees with mercy, or winks at any infringement of her law . . . It is a hard gospel; but rocks are hard, too, yet they form the foundations of the hills." While imaginative animal stories may stir more public interest in wildlife than a dozen scientific monographs, Burroughs conceded, "no pleasure to the reader, no moral inculcated, can justify the dissemination of false notions of nature." He suggested that Seton's *Wild Animals I Have Known* should have been called *Wild Animals I Alone Have Known*, and derided the book's stories as "true as romance, true in their artistic effects, true in their power to entertain the young reader . . . but true as natural history they certainly are not." As for Long's claim of animal surgery, Burroughs was joined by William Hornaday in dismissing such accounts as fantastical. Animals did not use twigs to construct crutches and slings for their own injuries, Hornaday asserted, and would likely tear off any bandage applied by man, as they have no concept of such things as being good for them.[17]

Seton did not respond publicly to Burroughs's criticisms, possibly because he had been the target of an unfortunate public controversy once before. In that instance, the concern wasn't his sentimentality for animal life, but the opposite. He had submitted for exhibition in the Paris Grand Salon of 1892 a painting he called *The Triumph of the Wolves*, which showed a pack of wolves gnawing at the remains of a dead hunter, one animal clasping a human skull in its teeth. Widely criticized and deemed in poor taste, it was refused by the salon, and wound up exhibited the following year in a dark corner at the Chicago World's Fair. This time around, he kept mum, and when he and Burroughs met at a Manhattan dinner party hosted by Andrew Carnegie for New York writers, they enjoyed a mutually enriching conversation about the great outdoors that ended with Burroughs praising Seton's talents as a naturalist.

Long, however, kept the fight alive, replying in a later issue of the *Atlantic* that Burroughs erred in making the illogical assumption that all the creatures of one species were alike. They were individuals, Long asserted, each with its own singular traits and preferences, and thus stories depicting their unique characteristics were legitimate. Many people with a keen interest in wildlife, including Theodore Roosevelt, had applauded Burroughs for laying into Seton and Long (Roosevelt would later call them "nature fakers"), but Long's rebuttal raised an interesting question: if animals could have qualities unique to them as individuals (and anyone who spent time in their company knew animals *did* possess individualized habits, anxieties, tastes, even "personalities"), how airtight were conclusions made about any animal species?

The debate over nature fakery, now more than a century old, has never fully abated. If anything, it has become more sophisticated as advances in observational technology and methodology have allowed biologists to better understand how communication and cooperation occur within animal groups, from whales to fish to finches, and that they "reason" in ways humans may only minimally comprehend. While Long's tales of animal twig and leaf "bandages" remain dubious, biologists have in recent decades examined the premise that the basis of human altruism is descended from animals' tendency, in some species, to come to one another's aid when injured or in danger. Carl Akeley's *Wounded Comrade*, a

1913 sculpture depicting two elephants guiding an injured comrade to safety, a scene the renowned artist and taxidermist witnessed in Africa, is only one of many substantiated examples.

Of course, when Roosevelt thrust himself into the debate by referring to some writers as "yellow journalists of the woods [who didn't] know the heart of the wild things," and insisted that as a hunter he had a more authentic sense of animal behavior, Long howled. "The idea of Mr. Roosevelt assuming the part of a naturalist is absurd . . . every time [he] gets near the heart of a wild thing he invariably puts a bullet through it." So well known was Roosevelt's love of the chase, in fact, that in 1902 his *refusal* to kill an animal became national news. He had been hunting in Mississippi with that state's governor, Andrew Longino, when the party cornered a black bear; guides offered it to the president but Roosevelt demurred, saying he would not deign to shoot a creature that was already subdued. Reporters were accompanying the president, and on November 16, a *Washington Post* cartoon appeared that showed the nation's First Sportsman "pardoning" the bear. A few hundred miles to the north, a Russian immigrant named Morris Michtom and his wife, Rose, managed a candy store in Brooklyn and had a side business making stuffed animals. To commemorate Roosevelt's sportsmanlike act, they created a huggable plush toy that they named "Teddy's Bear." The president had never liked the nickname "Teddy," but he approved the Michtoms' use of the term when he learned of it, and in any case had little choice, as the Teddy Bear was already on its way to becoming an iconic children's companion.[18]

WHAT WAS A MAN, AND HOW DID THE HUNT IMPROVE HIM? FOR Roosevelt, the chase was an "arena for manly exertion; the stalking of prey, the reconnoitering and negotiation of difficult terrain, all rudiments in the nurturing of warrior skills and the instinct to explore and conquer." It was not only a means of invigoration, of being in nature, nor a toughening-up of youth for battle, but an integer of national virtue. One could contrast the imperialistic success of the British, who had long cultivated their hunting culture, with that of the Spanish, Portuguese, French, or Belgians, who had ultimately been disappointed in their expansionist endeavors, perhaps because they lacked strong hunting traditions, or had allowed what they had to atrophy. Roosevelt would have concurred with the sports magazine that averred that each American boy taught to hunt was "a soldier in the rough before he knows enough to stand to attention," but he saw the program in larger terms, the chase as an apprenticeship readying all America to support the national defense as well as the country's continued growth and dominance. It was a view he came to personify in 1898's Spanish-American War, the country's first large imperialist military adventure, when fervent patriotism suddenly became a blinding thing, sensational and jingoistic. During the war, Roosevelt rode up Cuba's San Juan Hill at the head of his "Rough Riders," a term he had borrowed from Buffalo Bill's Wild West, and came down a hero and into the White House as vice president to William McKinley.[19]

Not all admired Roosevelt's creed of manliness or his notion that the hunter was the "archetype of freedom." Educational reformer John Dewey, sociologist Thorstein Veblen, and philosopher and psychologist William James all thought Roosevelt's gun fixation immature: Dewey perceived in the obsession with stalking and killing animals a "hunting psychosis"; Veblen thought sports generally a form of "arrested spiritual development"; while James considered Roosevelt a permanent adolescent. "He treats human affairs," James complained, "from the sole point of the organic excitement and difficulty they may bring, gushes over war as the ideal condition of human society, for the manly strenuousness which it involves, and treats peace as a condition of blubberlike and swollen ignobility, fit only for huckstering weaklings." The *Nation's* founder and editor, E. L. Godkin, concurred that Roosevelt's "bully!" outlook was "essentially a boy's view." John Muir asked the president, when the two hiked and camped together at Yosemite in 1903, "When are you going to get beyond the boyishness of killing things?" But as historian Pamela Haag points out, "When [Roosevelt] imagined an American of the right type—still hardy despite urban life . . . still hard despite the softening forces of modernity—that American had a gun." This faith was as personal as it was consistent. Shot in the chest by a would-be assassin at a Milwaukee auditorium in October 1912, the ex-president, then a candidate for reelection, carried on with his remarks, assuring the audience, "It takes more than that to kill a Bull Moose."[20]

Roosevelt's worship of the boy as hunter and the hunter as tomorrow's conqueror led him into a contretemps with the Boy Scouts of America (BSA) as the United States mobilized for the First World War. From their inception in 1910, the Scouts had been a laboratory for adult notions about manliness and the life skills young men required. Indeed, the BSA drew its inspiration from the same influences that had nurtured sport hunting—a helping of British can-do spirit via founder Robert Baden-Powell, a hero of the Boer War; the legacy of the American frontiersman, thanks to artist Daniel Carter Beard, who in 1905 founded the Sons of Daniel Boone, in which boys dressed in fringed buckskin and emulated the legendary Kentuckian; and the youth of Ernest Thompson Seton's Woodcraft Indians, schooled in the lore and wisdom of the Native American.

The three groups, combined under the BSA banner, offered urban boys outdoor skills, an appreciation of nature, a code of good conduct, and Progressive ideals of one's obligation to parents and community. The governing triumvirate of Baden-Powell, Seton, and Beard, however, would not long survive. Seton's devotion to Indian mysticism clashed sharply with the outlook of Chief Executive James E. West, a hardboiled former YMCA officer who, according to Seton, had "never seen the blue sky in his life." West insisted on adding the phrase *brave, clean, and reverent* to the Boy Scout law, and steered the group toward a less than subtle militarism. This was the issue that ensnared Roosevelt. When initially formed, the Scouts had stood for international peace and cooperation, but as early as 1911, there were signs of a growing rift prompted by the Remington Arms Company's beginning to sell a "Boy Scout Special" rifle that came with a bayonet attached. There was considerable grumbling about this, and Roosevelt only stirred the pot when he noted that the Scouts made boys "good citizens in time of peace, and incidentally . . . fit them to become good soldiers in time of war." That same year, Brig. General William Verbeck, head of an upstate New York military academy, broadsided the BSA in a speech at the Waldorf Astoria, complaining that since the Civil War, the nation had misplaced its martial spirit, and that, as an example of how dire the situation had grown, a cabal of socialists, suffragists, and female schoolteachers now "opposed all use of military terms by the Boy Scouts." He warned of the risk of failing to train boys to shoot accurately over great distances, for in modern warfare bombs and bullets came from afar. "No more can the marksman [wait to] see 'the whites of their eyes,'" he declared; "before that they are wiped off the earth."[21]

When war came to Europe in 1914, the Scouts' official periodical, *Boys' Life*, audaciously sounded an antiwar theme; in one allegorical graphic, British and German soldiers fight as a Boy Scout assists a female figure labeled "Civilization" away toward "Peace." Condemnation was swift. Leonard Wood, army chief of staff and author of a book entitled *The Military Obligation of Citizenship*, resigned from the BSA national council, while an incredulous Roosevelt accused the Scouts of being "part of the wicked and degrading pacifist agitation of the past few years." Many early supporters were driven away by Roosevelt's rhetoric, but the Scouts eventually capitulated to the sweeping patriotism that brought the United States into the war, gaining a lasting reputation for social and political conformism, and in 1916 introducing merit badges for marksmanship.[22]

ROOSEVELT WROTE PASSIONATELY ABOUT HIS LIFE AS A HUNTER AND ranchman in the West, and through his designations of wildlife refuges and national forests, left an impressive legacy of dedication to America's fauna and wilderness. But the dynamic hunter of big game had another major role to play on behalf of the American sportsman—paving the way for access to Africa, where roamed the *biggest* big game on the planet—with a much publicized presidential safari in 1909–1910. Actually, Roosevelt undertook his journey just after leaving the White House, but the ambition, size, as well as the cultural significance of the expedition, befit a head of state.

Like nearly everything to do with hunting in the nineteenth century, the British had been there first. The heroic memoirs written by elite colonial British hunters, and the countless trophies they brought home, had reaffirmed the kingdom's mastery of the far reaches of empire and sparked a public infatuation on both sides of the Atlantic with the glamorous risks of stalking elephant and lion in the African bush. The prototypical British big game hunter was Roualeyn George Gordon-Cumming. Perceiving no shortage of game in 1840s Africa, he became an unapologetic killer, shooting thirty hippos over the course of a three-day trek; and on another occasion, slaying eight elephants. London's Crystal Palace Exhibition of 1851 was his coming-out, where he exhibited no fewer than nine wagons of hunting trophies and did brisk sales with his memoir, *Five Years of a Hunter's Life in the Far Interior of South Africa* (1850). He later ran his own London exhibition space, where he welcomed the public to see his huge collection of heads and horns, and lectured prolifically (and profitably) across England, often heightening the effect of his hunting tales with live musical accompaniment.

British big game hunters who came in Cummings's wake—such men as Lord Walsingham, Frederick C. Selous, Denis Lyell, and Richard Meinertzhagen—could not have differed more from the Daniel Boone–like figures who scouted the lonely forest trails of North America. The British shooter in Africa tended to be well born and educated, and did not walk alone or with a single guide but, rather, outfitted with pith helmet and safari jacket, led a retinue of supply-laden porters, gun bearers, tent boys, skinners, guides, and translators. Some were soldiers of fortune inspired by the challenge of jungle and beast; a few, such as Frederick Lugard, Alfred Sharpe, and Frederick Jackson, were imperial governors, enhancing their political authority with impressive kills. Many were young gentlemen lured to Africa by the opportunity to live as a great lord and owner of vast property, something no longer possible in Britain, while others became intoxicated by money-making schemes, smuggling, or the glory of military adventure. Ewart Grogan spent two and a half years walking from Capetown to Cairo in 1897–1900, dodging every jungle danger imaginable, wrote a popular account of it, and returned to England and fame. Denys Finch Hatton, glamorized by Robert Redford's portrayal in the film *Out of Africa*, became a professional guide and the lover of Baroness Karen Blixen (the writer Isak Dinesen) before dying in the crash of a bush plane in Kenya in 1931. Frederick Selous spoke several tribal languages and took major trophies of virtually every African mammal. With his erect profile, slouch hat, and neatly trimmed beard, he was a symbol of the British sportsman as man of action, and became immortal when, at the outbreak of the First World War, he talked his way into military service despite being sixty-four years of age, only to be killed by a German sniper. He was the model for Allan Quartermain, the hero of the H. Rider Haggard novel *King Solomon's Mines* (1885) and other Haggard yarns.

These "big shots," as they were known, were served by Rowland Ward, an English taxidermist and wildlife publisher who maintained offices in Piccadilly as well as record books of big game–related weights and measurements, urging on further accomplishments afield while nurturing the home crowd's appetite for souvenirs. "Horns were everywhere" in Victorian England, as one historian notes, to the point that the country began to be overrun with animal trophies. Several large English hunting lodges became so stuffed with heads, antlers, and skins that they were opened as museums for touring schoolchildren, while the wealthiest hunters simply built annexes on their estates to hold the inventory (most of which their twentieth-century descendants were glad to donate by the truckload to the Natural History Museum).[23]

One key difference between hunting in America and Africa was that in the latter many more of the intended prey were capable of mauling careless hunters to death. One small churchyard in Nairobi shown to Roosevelt and other American visitors held the graves of seven white "masters of the chase" who had been killed by lions. White deaths from wild animals of course paled next to the tally of black victims. Almost every large safari included incidents of native porters or gun bearers being clawed or worse by large cats or other game, although whites "tended to be phlegmatic about the deaths of African trackers." As many as 1,500 Tanzanians were devoured

by one particularly nasty pride of lions in the 1940s, a ghastly reality echoed in the work of twentieth-century paleo-anthropologists
whose examinations of fossil cave deposits in South Africa led
them to conclude that early man was himself frequently hunted
and eaten by large predatory cats. Veteran hunters agree that once
lions develop a taste for human flesh, they come to prefer it to other,
four-legged creatures on offer, and in most cases humans are easier prey. "Why fool around with Cape buffalo and zebra," as one
hunter asked, "when man is such a pushover?"[24]

Seasoned African hunters know that no matter how certain one
is of a well-placed shot, a wounded leopard, elephant, or rhino is
still an enormous threat. "All big game are very good at killing you
if you give them even a fraction of a chance," hunter and author
Peter Capstick has said. "The typewriter hasn't been invented that
can adequately portray what it's like to be next to a hundred furious
elephants at close range with no place to hide." The risk came not
only from predictable sources, but from the unexpected ones: a croc
bursting from the still water and opening its jaws over the gunwale
of a river canoe; an annoyed ostrich dealing a wounding kick; a
captured hyena pup impulsively closing its teeth on a human hand.[25]

One African denizen that confounded even the boldest British
hunter was the monkey, which for its humanlike movements and
behavior—including a noticeable "human" sadness upon being
shot—was often hard for men to eat. "Monkeys made excellent
roasts," it was recounted, "but some found something extremely
disgusting in the idea of eating, what appears, when skinned and
dressed, so like a child.'"[26] Instead, many small monkeys were
brought back to England to be kept as pets or exhibited in menag-
eries as "little people," dressed in nightgowns or pajamas, although
they fared poorly in the chill, damp British weather, and most lived
only a short time.

While the dangers of the African hunt could not be mitigated,
the difficulty of access could. In 1903, the Uganda Railway was completed, extending 581 miles from coastal Mombasa inland to Lake
Victoria. An engineering marvel and symbol of British know-how,
it was dubbed the Lunatic Express for the hubris of its conception

and improbable route—through warring tribes, across swollen rivers, and into the neighborhood of some very aggressive lions. With
thousands of Indian laborers employed in building roadbed and
laying track, as well as porters and servants, the lions "treated the
project as one extended buffet table," bringing work to a halt for
several weeks in southern Kenya. The animals proved incorrigible,
dragging numerous workers from their tents to be devoured, before
eventually being tracked and killed.[27]

Roosevelt was one of the first American hunters to take advantage of rail access to the forbidding interior. With him on his 1909–
1910 safari was his nineteen-year-old son Kermit. Like his dad,
the boy had not been athletic as a child, but in recent years had
become a fitness buff and, with his father's tutelage, a skilled shot.
The ex-president pronounced him "tougher than whipcord." The
Roosevelt party arrived in Mombassa in April, and embarked on
a trip that would lead to Port Florence on Lake Victoria, across
British East Africa—today southern Kenya, Congo, Uganda, and
southern Sudan—then, on to the Belgian Congo and the Nile, ending in Khartoum. Too restless to remain inside the slow-moving
train, Roosevelt preferred to sit up front on the cowcatcher as they
steamed inland.[28]

As befitted a world-renowned hero famous for his love of hunting, Roosevelt's safari was widely followed in the press. Coming a
decade after the Spanish-American War, in which he had played a
notable role, his African adventure seemed a kind of encore demon-
stration of America's new global reach. The trip was financed by
Andrew Carnegie, as well as by a $50,000 advance from *Scribner's
Magazine* for writing Roosevelt would submit mid-adventure,
and which would later be gathered in a book. He was also to collect specimens for the Smithsonian Institution and the American
Museum of Natural History. The expedition itself was large even by
safari standards, more like a small army, consisting of five hundred
porters and dozens of wagons and men, as well as extra skinners
and taxidermy gear so that valuable specimens could be preserved
on the spot. In the end, it gathered 25,151 specimens, everything
from hippos, warthogs, and Cape buffalo, to birds, reptiles, and

fishes. Roosevelt and Kermit together killed 512 animals, including 17 lions, 11 elephants, and 20 rhinos. Some captured animals wound up at the National Zoo in Washington; trophy heads went to either the National Collection of Heads and Horns at the Bronx Zoo, or the Smithsonian.[29]

Roosevelt's natural history pretensions were the target of some derision back home, as to many it appeared he simply enjoyed shooting things. Certainly his own writing about the hunt did nothing to disguise his joy at the excitement of the kill, and he was not above describing in graphic detail the impact of his bullets on flesh, bone, and sinew. Mark Twain, distressed by the president's seeming obsession, was skeptical that other Americans thought him manly, suggesting Roosevelt was "still only fourteen years old after living a half century." But the president deflected criticism of the large number of animals taken, saying, "I can be condemned only if the existence of the National Museum, the American Museum of Natural History, and all similar zoological institutions are to be condemned."[30]

In photographs taken of the African jaunt, many by his son, the fifty-two-year-old Roosevelt appears heavy in his garb. The porters he'd engaged called him Bwana Tumbo, "Mister Stomach" in Swahili; while Kermit was Bwana Merodadi, "Dandy Master." When the ex-president asked the natives what the name Bwana Tumbo meant, they diplomatically told him it was Swahili for "the man with unerring aim." In turn, Roosevelt largely shared the prevalent condescending view of the safari's black helpers, although the irony, as in all such treks into the African interior, was that "bwana" was fully reliant on his native hirelings—for his safety and his survival. There were countless dangers in the bush—sunstroke, disease, intense thirst, snakebite, things that came out of the water (Roosevelt, like Winston Churchill, had a serious fear of crocodiles); however, the worst potential calamity was the mutiny of an expedition's bearers. The wise bwana made sure to distribute generously the best cuts of meat taken in the hunt, and to rule his movable city with a firm yet compassionate hand. To his credit, as Roosevelt had demonstrated convincingly in the American West, he did not distance himself from a hunt's grittier aspects, nor was his bravado a show. In Africa, he got in close to large, dangerous prey to wait for the ideal kill shot, kneeling calmly behind his cover, polishing his glasses, while others in the company discreetly retreated to safer ground. After his first elephant kill, he impressed the bearers by eating pieces of its heart grilled on a stick.[31]

Far less successful for its authenticity was the effort to use the new medium of motion pictures to showcase the Roosevelt expedition. *Roosevelt in Africa*, by British filmmaker Cherry Kearton, was released in April 1910, before Roosevelt had even returned to the United States. Unlike the president's own well-received written dispatches, the film proved a major disappointment. It contained no actual hunting sequences and consisted mostly of poorly filmed images of wildlife, Roosevelt, and natives milling about before the camera, and one still photograph of a lion interspersed with tribal dancing and ceremonies. One deft critic used Roosevelt's own "nature faking" insult in reference to the production, while a theater manager embittered by a half-filled house complained that "anybody could take a .22 rifle and go out in the sagebrush in Idaho and get more excitement hunting jackrabbits."[32]

The release of *Roosevelt in Africa* came at a time when the medium of film was so new there were still many unresolved questions as to what should constitute a movie made for public viewing, what moral standards would be adhered to, and, in the case of a documentary travelogue like Roosevelt's, how much the viewer might expect to be educated as opposed to entertained. An answer of sorts came when William N. Selig, an enterprising film producer in Chicago, released a simulation of the Roosevelt hunt that he produced in a Chicago studio, using a vaudevillian who resembled the president, a geriatric lion purchased from a zoo, and a cast of local black "porters" and "gun bearers." The resulting *Hunting Big Game in Africa*, unlike its documentary counterpart, was a hit, with profits abundant enough to enable Selig to establish a movie studio in Los Angeles as well as a game farm that he used to make several more canned but profitable wildlife movies.

Of course, Selig's efforts, though entertaining, were almost exclusively sham. The lure of capturing the true exotic Africa and its large wild animals on film remained unaccomplished. But it was an attractive prospect, both artistically and financially, as American audiences were tremendously curious about a place so otherworldly. As Selig had demonstrated, the field was wide open to innovation. All one had to do was get to Africa with a camera.

RISING TO THE OPPORTUNITY WAS CHARLES "BUFFALO" JONES, THE veteran Kansas buffalo hunter, cattalo hybridist, and free spirit, who had no experience in making movies but was justified in his belief he knew how to hunt animals better than anyone else. He embarked for Kenya in spring 1910 with two expert cowhands, Marshall Loveless and Ambrose Means, as well as several equally skilled "cow-ponies," determined to make the ultimate cowboy film—one that would demonstrate that even wild animals of the Dark Continent could be subjugated by the lasso. After a life-time as a Plains hunter, Jones, now age sixty-five, had "broken his rifle" and forsaken the shooting of animals: he vowed to capture, not kill, the lions, warthogs, and rhinos that Roosevelt's entou-rage had slaughtered. Roosevelt, who had linked his expedition with the higher interests of science, had nonetheless been as tro-phy fixated as the British, harvesting a substantial tally of game. Jones instead sought to introduce the virtues of "wildlife conserva-tion." The *New York Globe*, an anti-Roosevelt paper, made much of this implied rebuke to the trigger-happy former president, who "has been slaying wild beasts, [while] Buffalo Jones has been rop-ing the critters in true wild western style." Jones and Roosevelt, who were friends, had hunted together in Yellowstone and, both being active in the mission to save the buffalo, treated the matter good-naturedly. Asked by a reporter whether Jones's men would really manage to rope ferocious jungle animals, Roosevelt cheer-fully observed, "I wouldn't be surprised if they do. Those cowboys are a reckless care-for-nothing bunch."[33]

The Jones expedition, with a dozen trained horses, twenty-one hound dogs, and a British filmmaking crew, landed at Mombassa in early March and proceeded by train to Nairobi. To the delight of an exuberant crowd, they paraded through the streets of the town, giving demonstrations of their roping skills, including lassoing some of the residents: natives were enticed for one rupee to attempt to run past the cowboys without being roped, and those who managed to do so received an additional rupee. Once in the bush, the team lost no time proving it meant business, capturing a cheetah, a giraffe, a zebra, and a hartebeest, as well as a surprisingly speedy warthog ("Travelingest hog I ever see," remarked one of the cowhands). Jones proceeded to brand the captured animals with his personal "BJ" insignia. Roping a lion proved the biggest challenge. After numerous attempts, the men finally cornered a lioness that managed to hide among some bushes and rocks where a horseman could not approach. After she mauled several of the dogs that tried to dislodge her, Jones resorted to hurling firecrackers in her direction, forcing her to flee into the open. A Keystone Cops–like series of chases ensued, in which the mounted cowboys chased the lioness and she in turn pursued them; fortunately, lions become winded relatively soon, and she was not as quick at stops and sudden turns as the well-trained ponies. The men finally managed to "toss twine" around one of her feet, and wrestled her into submission.[34]

Back home, Jones delivered his captured lioness to William Hornaday at the Bronx Zoo and spent several weeks exhibiting film of his adventures with an accompanying lecture, including at Carnegie Hall and the Brooklyn Academy of Music. Once he returned to Kansas, however, he began to feel restless. He missed the excitement of being the colorful, quotable cowboy, the homecoming hero who had done the impossible, and began to long again for the limelight, contemplating another roping project more outrageous than the first. A circus boss had mentioned to him that there would be considerable interest in anyone who could bring back a live African gorilla that could be exhibited in America, something that had never been done before. Young gorillas brought to the United States in 1897 and in 1911 had both died within days. Imagining the prestige and profits that would reward such a feat, Jones began to plan his return to Africa. Finding backers was not difficult. There was much curiosity about the world's most elusive creature, which was still so poorly understood that some speculated it was a kind of primitive human being rather than an animal. It was rumored that male gorillas either forcibly or consensually mated with native African women, and it was assumed by white Americans—who could read in almost any daily newspaper an account from the South of an alleged sexual offense committed by a black "beast"—that white women would hold an irresistible appeal for jungle gorillas (a theme echoed in the classic 1933 film *King Kong*). "If Old Man Gorilla is an animal, ropes and human cunning will capture him," wrote one William Mougey, who helped organize funds for the Jones venture, "but if he is, as many claim, of the same origin as ourselves, it may be necessary to use firearms to prevent some terrible revenge from him." When Hornaday expressed doubt that a gorilla could be taken alive, Mougey replied, "Buffalo Jones is not to be daunted by any such conclusion," adding:

> It is a well-known fact that the gorilla is passionately fond of music and will not leave the vicinity of a camp as long as the music continues, so Mr. Jones has taken advantage of his weakness and provided several talking machines with the records of the sweetest songs by women, and these, he is confident, will bring the old rascal up to the camp. It is also well-known that the gorilla is a greater fool than the old fool over women, and many native women have been carried off by him and kept for years in his den. This fondness for the fairer sex may prove the downfall of the gorilla, just as it has of many a man.[35]

Mrs. Eagle M. Smith, daughter of cowboy Ambrose Means, later told an interviewer that someone had offered Jones the staggering sum of $250,000 if he produced a live adult male gorilla. "The alleged reason for the large amount of money was because some research unit wanted to see if a male gorilla would mate with a woman."

Despite the best efforts of Jones and his entourage in the deepest jungles of the Congo, however, playing recordings of female vocalists singing Stephen Foster's "Jeanie with the Light Brown Hair" and other soothing favorites, local male gorillas were insufficiently curious, and failed to emerge. The Jones party did encounter and tangle with both a young female gorilla and an older male, but as Hornaday had warned, they were intractable and impossible to capture, and to Jones's regret, his party had to shoot and kill both creatures. The expedition spiraled downward from there as Jones contacted malaria and eventually had to be evacuated, while the outbreak of war in Europe later that summer of 1914 and the curtailment of ship traffic across the Atlantic complicated the return home of his crew, supplies, and specimens. He never completely escaped the lingering effects of the disease. When he passed away in Topeka in 1919, the local coroner entered as the cause of death: "Jungle Fever."

Both Theodore Roosevelt and Buffalo Jones had recognized the potential of combining the exciting new medium of motion pictures with the heart-stopping thrill of big game hunting. Through their publicized hunts, Americans gained an exposure to exotic animals, places and peoples, along with a glimpse of anthropology and natural science. Unfortunately, both Roosevelt's documentary and Jones's animals-and-lassos film came off as a bit slumbering. The true heirs to the emerging concept of capturing the exotic on screen proved to be an unlikely couple from the small-town Midwest, Martin and Osa Johnson. During 1907–1909, Martin had served as cook on a transpacific voyage by author Jack London and his wife and, once home, began showing a film and a series of slides he had made of the South Seas journey along with an exhibit of artifacts and photos. Occasionally he held "men's only" programs at which he exhibited images of native women and described the sexual customs of the Polynesian islanders. In 1910, he met teenaged Osa Leighty of Chanute, Kansas, who worked as a performer in his South Seas show, singing faux-Hawaiian songs; they married that same year.

The couple traveled the Orpheum Vaudeville Circuit with the South Seas images for six years, then struck out on their own in 1917, confident that new travels would yield even greater show material. One of their first independent ventures was a film of the natives of the Solomon Islands, where, according to the Johnsons, they were captured by a tribe of cannibals called the Big Nambas and destined for the cook pot, until some gallant British sailors materialized and secured their release. The resulting film, *Among the Cannibal Isles of the South Pacific*, earned impressive profits on its release in 1918; the Johnsons, later returning to the islands, screened the movie for the amazed natives, who were alternately thrilled and terrified to see themselves onscreen. Moving images of big city crowds also unnerved them, although they were said to be delighted by an extended film clip of a pie fight that Charlie Chaplin had sent along.

The couple soon heard from their stateside booking agent, however, who wired, "The public is tired of savages. Get some animal pictures." This presented a significant challenge. Wildlife photography of any kind, but particularly moving images, is difficult and requires tremendous patience. The Johnsons found it harder than their work with relatively cooperative Big Nambas, but eventually, with the help of a special 35 mm camera designed by Carl Akeley, which Martin customized to shoot slow-motion footage, they began to develop a stylized method. "The Akeley," as the camera was known, had been invented by its namesake out of Akeley's frustration with unwieldy film equipment unsuited to capturing live animals in motion. Pancake-shaped and designed to pivot easily on a tripod, it had a long focus lens and a specially designed shutter whose rotation, made possible by the camera's round shape, was larger than that of any other motion picture camera. This flexibility allowed the operator to better capture moving objects on film, without blurring. (The camera was used subsequently on Hollywood film sets, as well as by news organizations and the US army.) With assistance from Akeley and an endorsement from the American Museum of Natural History, the Johnsons undertook a series of filmmaking visits to Africa that produced *Trailing Wild Animals* (1923), *Simba: King of the Beasts* (1928), *Across the World with Mr. and Mrs. Johnson* (1930), and *Congorilla* (1932).[36]

Martin was the filmmaker of the duo; Osa was in charge of expedition organizing and, having been taught to hunt by her father, shooting the animals, or at least appearing to do so on-screen. She was reputedly a good shot and there was plenty of footage of her bringing down big game, although a later biographer revealed that a local hunter and marksman, an ex-pat American named Charles "Bud" Cottar Jr., often kept her covered while Martin filmed her stalking big game. By the time of their fifth African trip in 1933–1934, the Johnsons' operation had attained new levels of sophistication: they shot *Wings over Africa* (1934) and *Baboona* (1935), both of which, for the first time, featured aerial photography of the vast African plains and forests, and panning shots of enormous herds of animals in motion (spooked into running by the noise and appearance of the aircraft). It was stunning footage, riveting to American audiences. *Baboona* also secured itself a lasting place in film history when it was screened for passengers aboard an Eastern Air Lines flight on January 3, 1935, becoming the first-ever in-flight movie.

In the depths of the Great Depression, the Johnsons offered an identifiable saga of Yankee optimism and technological triumph—small-town adventurers in the most exotic places on earth, with guns and cameras and flying machines, gaining Hollywood legitimacy and public acclaim on their own terms. What truly "sold" the films was the visual juxtaposition of Osa, a petite white woman with girl-next-door appeal and a large gun, posed against the backdrop of wild Africa, with its excitable and occasionally frightening natives (at least as depicted by Western filmmakers) and its colossal elephants, rhinos, and other animals not before seen in their natural habitat. There was, of course, a great deal of contrivance in the Johnson films—dramatic sequences stitched together from random clips, the use of native beaters to drive wild animals into camera range—but if viewers noticed, they didn't mind. During the interwar years, these popular motion pictures of animals and indigenous peoples were among the most daring footage ever glimpsed in American movie theaters; in retrospect, they seem a kind of blueprint for much of the animal cinematography that followed, as well as the raft of animal and nature programs enjoyed by millions on cable television today.[37]

ONE CHARACTERISTIC THAT DATES THE WORK OF THE JOHNSONS and other early wildlife filmmakers is its condescending and racist depiction of native peoples. The seeming backwardness of the tribesmen is often played for humor, and even though they are being photographed where *they* live, they appear largely as extras in support of the primary story of brave white moviemakers/hunters interacting with fierce and potentially troublesome animals. For white Americans in the 1930s, however, the images and narration conformed to prevalent ideas about white superiority and the obvious virtue of the colonial experience in sub-Saharan Africa, as well as reflected widely held notions of racial and ethnic differences in American intellectual and popular discourse. The pseudo-science of racial and ethnic determinism known as polygenism, the belief that the world's many human "races" had distinct and separate origins and thus dissimilar attributes, had grown more respected and ubiquitous in recent decades. It emanated from prestigious universities and the pages of prominent magazines, emphasizing race and ethnicity as absolute determinants of character and how fit one was to be a productive member of society. One of the best-remembered products of this cultural derailment was *The Passing of the Great Race, or The Racial Bias of European History* (1916), a booklength rant about the alleged threat to the world's "Nordic people" from the rising darker and Slavic races. It was written by Hornaday's colleague Madison Grant, an attorney, Boone and Crockett Club member, and cofounder of the Bronx Zoo.

Grant was a devoted conservationist and big game hunter, active in safeguarding giant redwoods as well as populations of bears, eagles, and moose (he thought the latter's prominent nose made it look Jewish). Like Hornaday, he believed Nordic peoples, or as they were also known, Anglo-Saxons (a term that had lost its original meaning and now referred to a white person of northern European stock, or simply a white American), needed protection from extinction no less than did the buffalo. Roosevelt, in a 1905 speech, had used the phrase *race suicide* to describe the risk that birth control might lower birth rates among white women; the term was picked up by others to express alarm about an inevitable decline of people of northern European background in America. Grant's book, which was acclaimed by Roosevelt and numerous critics, joined a trend in fear-mongering titles about unwanted migrations, racial rankings, and the feared marginalization of Anglo-Saxons, such as Homer Lea's *The Day of the Saxon* (1912) and Lathrop Stoddard's *Rising Tide of Color* (1920). As Jedediah Purdy points out, many Boone and Crockett Club elites tended to perceive hierarchies in nature— a nobility of elk, buffalo, and pronghorn, and even rankings among forest denizens, such as Norway pine or giant redwoods. "For these conservationists, who prized the expert governance of resources, it was an unsettling short step from managing forests to managing the human gene pool." Grant's book influenced US immigration policy of the 1920s and later came to be quoted by Adolf Hitler, who was said to have also written Grant a fan letter. The only prominent challenge came from Columbia University anthropologist Franz Boas, who labeled Grant's shopworn views "dogmatic assumptions which cannot endure criticism."[38]

*The Passing of the Great Race* is justifiably infamous, but the incident that lives on most vividly in histories of the period is Grant and Hornaday's 1906 zoological and anthropological experiment of putting a Congolese Mbuti pygmy named Ota Benga on exhibit at the Bronx Zoo. The account of how Benga was brought to America will always be somewhat hazy, largely because the white man responsible, American explorer and businessman Samuel Phillips Verner, so often varied the telling. It appears the pygmy, who was in his mid- to late twenties, slight of build, and stood just under 5 feet in height, was one of several recruited, hired, or (in Benga's case) purchased from slavery by Verner, to appear as part of the University of Man exhibit at the 1904 Saint Louis World's Fair, which included Inuit, Filipinos, Zulu, and legendary eighty-year-old Apache medicine man Geronimo. The inclusion of live ethnic "villages" or other ethnographic demonstrations in public exhibitions was not new; they dated from at least 1815, when "the Hottentot Venus," Saartjie Baartman, a young Khoi-San woman from what is now South Africa, was exhibited and led virtually naked in and out of her cage in early nineteenth-century London, the key sensation Baartman's substantial rear end, apparently a Khoi-San trait. The Empire of India Exhibition in London in 1895 featured a "replica village" with human participants, and there were several live ethnic villages at the Columbian Exposition in Chicago in 1892–1893.

The pygmies proved to be among the most popular exhibits for the 18 million people who attended the Saint Louis Fair during its seven-month run, and Benga quickly warmed to his role, charging five cents a look to visitors desiring to see his "cannibal" teeth, which were carved to sharp points as a traditional native decoration. The group was repatriated to Africa by Verner after the event closed, but Benga either felt unsafe in his home country or was promised a generous reward to remain in America with his white mentor. At first, he lived in the American Museum of Natural History, where he learned some rudimentary English, but he became depressed residing in a large musty building away from nature, and was prone to act out in unexpected ways. Once, the story goes, he was asked to "seat" a female guest at a fund-raising reception and, pretending to misunderstand, hurled a chair at her.[39]

Hornaday had previously considered arranging a habitat exhibit at the Bronx Zoo that would include African aborigines, so he was more than willing to temporarily host Benga there. Benga, by his own choice, was soon abiding in a large cage at one end of the Primate House. At the zoo, as in Saint Louis, he proved to be something of a ham, mugging for onlookers, winning applause by pretending to communicate with birds and monkeys, and using the tips he earned to buy soft drinks and cigarettes. He was soon drawing substantial crowds who found his antics humorous, although as a reporter dispatched by the *New York Times* observed, "There were laughs enough in it, but there was something about it which made the serious-minded grave." To emphasize that Benga's presence was not frivolous but represented serious anthropological interest, Hornaday placed a sign outside the cage:

"Our race, we think, is depressed enough, without exhibiting one of us with the apes," complained black New York clergymen in protest of the public display of the Congolese pygmy Ota Benga at the Bronx Zoo in 1906. (Library of Congress)

THE AFRICAN PYGMY, "OTA BENGA"
AGE, 28 YEARS.
WEIGHT 103
HEIGHT, 4 FEET 11 INCHES.
BROUGHT FROM THE KASAI RIVER, CONGO FREE STATE,
SOUTH CENTRAL AFRICA, BY DR. SAMUEL P. VERNER
EXHIBITED EACH AFTERNOON DURING SEPTEMBER.[40]

In retrospect, Hornaday and Grant were probably trying to do the impossible in reading anthropology into what, particularly due to Benga's showmanship, must have seemed closer to vaudeville. But even if staging a living habitat exhibit at a world's fair was acceptable, the placing of a human being in a cage at a zoo was perhaps applying the theories of evolutionary racism a bit too literally, and the combination of monkey house, African man, and the delighted laughter and heckling of white patrons finally proved too much. New York's black community, decidedly not amused, vehemently protested so demeaning a spectacle. "We are frank enough to say we do not like this exhibition of one of our race with the monkeys. Our race, we think, is depressed enough, without exhibiting one of us with the apes. We think we are worthy of being considered human beings, with souls," declared the Reverend James H. Gordon, superintendent of the Howard Colored Orphan Asylum in Brooklyn and, according to the *Brooklyn Eagle*, "one of the most eloquent Negroes in the country."[41]

Samuel Verner, the man most responsible for Benga's presence in America, assured the ministers that "the public is the only beneficiary" of the African's residence at the zoo,[42] while Hornaday insisted he presented Benga "purely as an ethnological exhibit . . . I hope my colored brethren will not take the absurd position that I am giving the exhibit to show the close analogy of the African savage to the apes. Benga is in the primate house because that was the most comfortable place we could find for him." In frustration, Gordon and his colleagues visited City Hall to petition Mayor George B. McClellan Jr. to have Benga released to the guardianship of Rev. Gordon, but McClellan refused even to receive them. Hornaday, after first assuring a colleague he did not intend to "be browbeaten by a Committee of negro ministers who are only anxious for newspaper notoriety," finally agreed to allow Benga to freely wander the zoo grounds like any other employee. The result, however, was more unwanted commotion, as children followed him around, grunting like apes, and their parents scolded him that if he would not stay in a cage, he should go back to Africa.[43]

In response, Benga became unruly. He was accused of wounding a tourist with his bow and arrow; two days later, an attendant playfully sprayed water on him from a hose, leading Benga to strip off his clothes and then pull a knife on a zookeeper who demanded he get dressed. All this was too much for Hornaday, who was disappointed his purely educational intentions had been so badly misunderstood, and that zoo patrons took his exhibit to be some kind of sideshow. "Enough! Enough!" he exclaimed on the morning of September 17. "I have had enough of Ota Benga, the African pygmy. Ring up the Brooklyn Howard Colored Orphan Asylum. Tell them that they can get busy tinkering with his intellect. I'm through with him here."[44]

Benga was duly released to Rev. Gordon, and resumed his study of English at the orphanage, where he was also instructed in the lessons of the Bible; but on account of his chain-smoking and independence of mind, he eventually came to be seen as a bad influence on the other more youthful residents. In 1910, arrangements were made to resettle him in rural Lynchburg, Virginia, where he was employed on a tobacco farm. Changing his name to Otto Bingo, he had his "cannibal" teeth capped, wore Western clothes, and became popular with local children, to whom he taught forest skills. It was his custom there to relate his incredible life story to travelers and other interested parties in exchange for sandwiches and root beer. Despite these relative comforts and his many young friends, Benga, now age thirty-two, began to dream of returning to Africa; with war raging in Europe, however, there was little hope of booking travel across the Atlantic. In March 1916, he lit a bonfire in the woods, removed the caps from his teeth, and shot himself in the heart. "Evidently," Hornaday unkindly reflected upon hearing the news, "he felt that he would rather die than work for a living."[45]

OTA BENGA, HOWEVER, WOULD NOT BE THE LAST PRIMITIVE MAN to emerge from the forests of the past with something to teach the modern world. On August 29, 1911, workers at a slaughterhouse in Oroville, California, saw a disheveled individual they at first assumed was a tramp or a drifter, hanging around the property. He wore no shoes and only rags for clothes, and appeared emaciated; he refused to speak when approached. Sheriff's deputies could get no information from him and, assuming he was a drunk, a vagrant, or perhaps an escaped lunatic, put him in jail. Only after many days, with the arrival of anthropology professor Thomas T. Waterman from the University of California (UC), did the mystery begin to unravel.

The stranger who had walked out of the woods, Waterman pronounced, was something of a living miracle, likely the last surviving member of California's Yahi Indians, who had lived in seclusion for so many decades that most people considered them a folk legend. A series of violent conflicts with white settlers beginning in about 1865 had decimated the tribe, and the remaining twenty or so members retreated deeper into the wilderness and entered a "Period of Concealment" in which they avoided all contact with the outside world. In 1908, a surveying party stumbled upon a Yahi encampment and "Ishi," as the man Waterman met in the jail called himself, had fled. For three years, he had lived alone in the woods before arriving, half-starved, at the Oroville slaughterhouse.

What made Ishi (the name was simply the Yahi word for "man") particularly fascinating to Waterman and his UC colleagues was that it was quite possible he was the last Native American who had lived his entire life without contact with whites. Into an age of technological wonderment, of automobiles, street lamps, and telephones, had stepped an indigenous man out of the Stone Age, so primitive that he had never worn shoes. Everything that could be learned about him was of profound anthropological import. Ishi, in turn, found California at the dawn of the twentieth century dizzying. He was awed by the ability to get water by turning a knob, to produce light with a switch. Typewriters amazed him; toasters were mysterious; he was fascinated by streetcars, for their sheer size, loud gong, and hissing air brakes, and was endlessly curious about window shades, not understanding where the shade went. He had heard trains before from his forest sanctuary, but did not realize they ran on a track, so now when one approached, he ran and threw himself on the grass or hid behind a bush, despite attempts to reassure him.

A less amusing result of his long seclusion was that Ishi had no immunity to many diseases and, often sick, in September 1912 he was placed under the care of another UC educator, Dr. Saxton Pope. It was a fortuitous encounter, for it was soon apparent the two men had something in common besides keeping Ishi well: a great love of hunting. Pope was enormously curious to know the ancient hunting practices of the Yahi, and it was evident Ishi, a master bow and arrow maker, took pride in his tribal hunting methods and was flattered to be asked to share them.

The first principle of the hunt, Ishi taught, was patience. Incredible patience, the kind most whites would not comprehend. He would secret himself for hours at a place where he knew there were rabbits or squirrels, and employ an extensive vocabulary of animal calls that he produced with only fingers and lips to entice them to appear. "Not only could Ishi call the animals," Pope recalled,

> but he understood their language. Often when we have been hunting he stopped and said, "The squirrel is scolding a fox." At first I said to him, "I don't believe you." Then he would say, "Wait! Look!" Hiding behind a tree or rock or bush, in a few minutes we could see a fox trot across the open forest. It seemed that for a hawk or cat or man, the squirrel has a different call, such that Ishi could say without seeing what molested his "little brother." Often we have stopped and rested because, so he said, a blue jay called far and wide, "Here comes a man!" There was no use going farther, the animals all knew of our presence.[46]

Pope credited Ishi with awakening his interest in archery, a sport and hunting method Pope associated with Anglo-Saxon history and folklore. The English longbow, a 6-foot weapon carved from a yew tree and capable of sending an arrow more than 200 yards, had proved a formidable as well as a democratic weapon, one used by yeoman and nobleman alike. Native American hunters, of course, had their own traditions, and young Indian boys achieved such proficiency with the weapon they considered it an embarrassment if their arrow pierced a squirrel anywhere but directly in the head. Under Ishi's quiet mentorship, Pope became a dedicated advocate of the bow, arguing in numerous writings that high-powered guns robbed sport hunting of its deepest essence. "He who shoots with a bow, puts his life's energy into it," he wrote, "and when he speeds his whispering shaft and strikes his game, he has won by the strength of arm and nerve."

Women in particular were drawn to the aesthetic appeal of the use of bow and arrow. A popular turn-of-the-century illustration was that of an athletic-looking young woman posed at full extension, bow taut, arrow notched, a slim "Diana" in silhouette. And while bow-women were sometimes alleged to favor the sport because its greater degree of difficulty reduced the likelihood of taking prey, their participation was in no way ornamental or squeamish; they shot rabbits and deer (even, in one report, a wolverine), and ably field-dressed their kills.

As Ishi's disciple, Pope assumed the obligation to successfully demonstrate that Indians like Ishi, armed only with bow and arrow, had been able to kill large predators. In the years following Ishi's death from tuberculosis in 1916, Pope and his friend Art Young, using bow and arrow exclusively, killed a moose, a large brown bear, and a Rocky Mountain bighorn sheep, the latter animal among the most difficult prey to bring within bow range because of its keen sense and the remote heights it inhabits. "We have come to the belief that no beast is too tough or too large to be slain by an arrow," Pope wrote in triumph, and to further nail shut the argument, went with Young to Africa, where they shot with arrows a variety of creatures, including jackals, hyenas, and lions. Pope expected that a result of his work would be that hunters, upon discovering the intense *realness* of the bow hunt, its greater physicality and feeling of authenticity, would leave off hunting with guns altogether. That did not happen. But his dream of establishing the bow and arrow as a respected sport hunting weapon has certainly been fulfilled; it continues to gain in popularity. "So long as the new moon returns in heaven, a bent beautiful bow," predicted J. Maurice Thompson, like Pope an early advocate, "so long will the fascination of archery keep hold of the hearts of men."

ISHI HAD MADE A SENSATIONAL IMPRESSION BY STEPPING OUT OF THE forest; in 1913, a white man from Boston decided he had something to prove by going back in. To show that progress had not shorn modern man of his innate talent for survival, Joseph Knowles announced his intention to enter the wilderness without food, tools, matches, or even clothes, and live for two months with none of the comforts or benefits of civilization, as had man's earliest ancestors. On August 4, before a knot of reporters, he stripped naked and ran off into the woods of northern Maine, promising to leave a birch-bark record of his experience under a stump periodically, where it could be retrieved for publication in the *Boston Post* and other US papers. Within days, he reported that he was eating fish he had caught by hand and grilled over a fire made by rubbing two sticks together; had ambushed and strangled a deer with his bare hands; and had attained a pelt for warmth by beating a bear to death with a log.

Exactly two months later, on October 4, Knowles emerged dressed in nothing but his bear skin. A medical team carried out a prompt examination and declared him to be in better shape than when he'd started the experiment. His accomplishment in so successfully revisiting man's original condition was celebrated in the press as well as in a quickie book that overnight sold thirty thousand copies.

The *Boston American*, however, a rival to the *Post*, soon declared it all a fraud. The plan, it appeared, had been cooked up by freelance reporter named Michael McKeogh, who knew Knowles as a braggart who, after a few drinks, liked to regale listeners with tales of his wilderness exploits. McKeogh, listening in one evening, thought of a way to put Knowles's boasts to profitable use. During his time in the Maine woods, the *American* discovered, Knowles had had access to a cabin, food had been left for him, and McKeogh, not Knowles, had been leaving the birch-bark communiqués. The bearskin, an investigation showed, was perforated by two small bullet holes, casting doubt on Knowles's account of how he came by it.

On thus being exposed, most pranksters might have slunk away quietly, but Knowles doubled down. He purchased a small captive bear and, gathering several friends as witnesses, led the animal on a leash into the woods, where (he and they claimed) he clubbed it to death, proving he was capable of such a feat. Having thus sown confusion about the legitimacy of the Maine debacle, Knowles abruptly left for the West Coast, where the Hearst-owned *San Francisco Examiner* approached him about repeating his experiment. But by now, war had broken out in Europe, and with daily reports of the horrible obliteration of battalions at the front, readers were less interested in whether one man could survive in the woods of Northern California. The war, with its poison gas and bombs upon bombs and bodies sinking into the mud, ultimately had far more to reveal about humankind than any newspaper stunt ever could. Resolved, unflatteringly for the time being, it appeared, was the question of man's nature.[47]

# Chapter Twelve

# The Trophic Cascade

LEGEND TELLS OF A HUNTER, HUBERT, WHO WAS HIKING ALONE IN the Ardennes one gloomy day in the eighth century when he met a pure white deer whose antlers were an illuminated crucifix. In some versions of the story, the deer not only startles Hubert with its odd appearance, but engages him in a conversation about species preservation, asking why he and other hunters persist in killing the forest's hardiest deer while leaving weaker ones to breed. It's well known that Hubert thereafter became Saint Hubert, the guardian of hunters, but less so that, heeding the deer's words, he also went on to advocate for the more intelligent and selective harvesting of wildlife.

Hubert's tale is not unique. A nascent wildlife preservation ethos appears in most early hunting cultures, from South Asia's reverence for the elephant, which dates at least to the twelfth century BC, to Native Americans' traditional regard for the breeding cycle of the plains buffalo. Laws governing the taking of deer in America appeared as early as 1699, and by the first half of the nineteenth century, voices as diverse as ornithologist Alexander Wilson, artist George Catlin, and naturalist Henry David Thoreau were warning that the country's resources of wildlife and supporting habitat were not inexhaustible. Such concern was present in British hunting through much of its history, in the nascent American fair chase ethos of Frank Forester and Natty Bumppo, and would be articulated often and with especial eloquence by Charles Hallock and George Bird Grinnell in the pages of *Forest and Stream*. Inherent to the sportsmen's club movement of the 1870s, it soon after entered public discourse in relation to news of the impending extinctions of pigeons, buffalo, and other creatures.

Although many individuals are associated with the origins of modern conservation in America—Grinnell, Theodore Roosevelt, William Hornaday, Harriet Hemenway and Florence Merriam Bailey of the early Audubon Societies, among others—the movement's most visible representative was Gifford Pinchot. Appointed head of the U.S. Forest Service by President Roosevelt in 1905, Pinchot, a Yale-trained forestry expert, is credited with coining the term *conservation* and with advocating a philosophy of "wise use," the idea that natural resources should be utilized to provide the greatest possible good for man and nature alike. A countervailing view was voiced by John Muir, who, echoing Thoreau's belief that "in wildness is the preservation of the world," held that the very character of wilderness demanded it remain untouched. This dichotomy, between a human stewardship of nature and the notion that its virtue lies in its being left alone, has animated discussion of habitat and wildlife protection issues ever since.[1]

Another seminal figure in refining conservationist ideas was Aldo Leopold. Like Pinchot a graduate of the Yale Forestry School, Leopold joined the U.S. Forest Service in 1909 and was sent to the Southwest on an early federal predator control effort. The project was effective, bringing an estimated population of three hundred wolves in New Mexico down to about thirty, but Leopold would eventually describe his work as naïve. Approaching a wolf he had mortally wounded, he became mesmerized by "the fierce green fire" that flickered in its eyes even in the last moment of its life. "I was young then and full of trigger-itch," he later recalled. "I thought that because fewer wolves meant more deer, that no wolves would mean hunters' paradise. But after seeing the green fire die, I sensed that neither the wolf nor the mountain agreed with such a view."[2]

Initially faithful to the concept of wise use, Leopold slowly developed a Thoreau-like regard for wilderness, swayed in part by his attendance at a Hornaday lecture in which the famous taxidermist remarked that out of concern for the precipitous decline of many game animals, he had forsaken hunting. Leopold was a thinking man's hunter; he valued the sport as a reminder of the human-animal food chain, as a way to honor the nation's frontier heroes, and for its singular challenge to man's character, since each hunter was expected to heed game laws and behave ethically even when alone and unobserved. While he was not prepared to give up hunting, he understood why conservation was a logical adjunct to the pastime. Conservation offered a set of guidelines for governing society's relationship with wildlife, what he would later term "game management," a structure that mirrored the idea of fair chase, which bound the individual hunter responsibly to his sport and to his prey. "Twenty centuries of 'progress,'" he wrote,

> have brought the average citizen a vote, a national anthem, a Ford, a bank account, and a high opinion of himself, but not the capacity to live in high density without befouling and denuding his environment, nor a conviction that such capacity, rather than such density, is the true test of whether he is civilized. The practice of game management may be one of the means of developing a culture which will meet this test.[3]

The Winchester Repeating Arms Company—aware that hunters needed a steady source of game to hunt—enlisted Leopold and other hunters in 1911 to sponsor a group dedicated to stabilizing wild animal life. Seeing promise in the organization, which came to be known as the American Game Protective Association, Leopold urged the formation of a local New Mexico chapter and went on to report on regional wildlife populations for the group. He soon came to appreciate the enormous complexity of conserving natural resources, as there were a bedeviling array of forces and

counterforces with which to contend. Any attempt to remedy dwindling wildlife stocks, for instance, would have to include an *ecological* appreciation of natural systems, considering depreciation
of habitat, levels of predator species, local farming practices, and
the availability of sustenance for wildlife. The Greek word *ecology*,
which translates roughly as "home knowledge," appears initially
in 1860 in the writings of influential German zoologist and artist
Ernst Haeckel. Leopold's use of the term dated from about 1920,
and he gave it broad meaning to include the complex interwork-
ing of wildlife and their habitat—soil, trees, food sources, land—as
well as man's encroachment through settlement and agriculture.

While Leopold recognized that conservation and game management required trade-offs and judicious planning, his thinking
turned increasingly to wilderness that would receive no "improvements" from man, nor be developed and used under the precepts
of "wise use" conservation—it would be allowed to remain forever
wild. Thoreau's had helped inspire this philosophy, but any actual
policy based on the idea was still fairly radical. It recognized, if not
exactly agency, an inherent *selfness* to the wild, a quality of being
that preceded and would succeed man and was oblivious to his
interests. Wilderness might be physically immense, but as a concept
it was infinite. It was larger than the lifetime of any one person, and
no one had the right to intrude on its processes. "The privilege of
possessing the earth entails the responsibility of passing it on, not
only to immediate posterity, but to the Unknown Future," Leopold
asserted. "God started his show a good many million years before
he had any men for an audience . . . it is just barely possible that God
himself likes to hear birds sing and see flowers grow."[4]

In his book *Game Management* (1933), and later as a professor
at the University of Wisconsin, Leopold more fully articulated the
idea of man's place in nature. Synthesizing Native American beliefs
about the respectful bond humans must have with their surroundings if they are to rely on them, and the virtues of wilderness cited
by Thoreau and Muir, Leopold proposed a *land ethic*. In effect,
land was to be respected for its importance in the ecology of a place,
while man, rather than dominate his environment, would perceive

himself as part of it. "A thing is right when it tends to preserve the integrity, stability, and beauty of the biotic community," he wrote. "It is wrong when it tends otherwise." This view, later revived by Wallace Stegner, Edward Abbey, and Rachel Carson, among others, would become a cornerstone of the modern environmental movement. Leopold's hope that thoughtful wildlife and conservation management would succeed not solely as a set of official policies, but as values widely adopted and shared, was borne out eventually by the dawning of Earth Day environmentalism, a crusade for which Leopold's posthumously published memoir, *A Sand County Almanac* (1949), became required reading.[5]

Although he remained opposed to the market slaughter of game and other gross abuses of nature, Leopold thought it foolish to believe that America's backcountry was or could be populated only by environmentalist hikers and bird-watchers. It was people with diverse interests—hunters, fishermen, resort owners, land and timber developers—whose input would spell the fate of forests and wild fauna. As a hunter, he sought to transpose the values of fair chase to the larger issues of conservation and wildlife restoration work, a linkage by now fairly ingrained in the sport, thanks to the preaching of Hallock, Grinnell, Roosevelt, and others. It was the shared concern of hunters that bred an actual government commitment for wildlife preservation in the Federal Aid in Wildlife Restoration Act of 1937, introduced in Congress by Senator Key Pittman of Nevada and Representative William Robertson of West Virginia, and thereafter known as the Pittman-Robertson Act. It established an 11 percent tax on ammunition and other hunting gear, the money from which, known as "PR funds," would be distributed annually to the states and used by them for wildlife research, maintenance of wild areas, transplanting wildlife, and hunter education programs.

The idea of saving the sport of hunting within the context of saving wildlife has proved a durable one. While the US Forest Service, the Bureau of Land Management, and the wildlife specialists of the Department of Agriculture are supported through annual appropriations, state wildlife agencies are funded largely from fishing and hunting license fees and money passed along from

Pittman-Robertson and the Dingell-Johnson Federal Aid to Fish-
eries Act, which similarly taxes the sale of fishing equipment. The
oft-cited advantage of these taxed-at-point-of-purchase funds is
that they are not vulnerable to political sea changes in Congress or
state legislatures. In economic times, both good and bad, the funding remains stable, and cannot be downgraded due to diminished
government coffers. Pittman-Robertson has been amended several
times, such as to extend the tax to bows and arrows, and, in the
1970s, when interest in hunting ebbed, to tax nongame shooting.
Hunting groups are justifiably proud of the accomplishments of this
program, for the funds are credited with enabling the restoration of
elk, white-tailed deer, cougar, and other once diminished species,
and for making needed habitat protection possible.

IF THERE IS ONE THING THAT TRANSCENDS ALL THE DIFFERENT PER-
spectives on hunting and man's relationship to nature, it would be
the beauty and mystery of deer. More ethereal than other living
fauna, perfect in their form, ghostlike in their ability to quietly
vanish and reappear, the deer is frequently judged the most graceful of all earth's creatures. However, as prolific breeders, historically adaptable to cohabiting with humans, America's 30 million
deer are also a tremendous nuisance and often the focus of intense
debate.

From Landseer's heartrending tableau of an orphaned fawn in
*The Random Shot* to Walt Disney's *Bambi*, the deer is perceived as
beauty, sweetness, and vulnerability incarnate, a hunter's foil whose
inevitable death troubles the ordered universe. An admired example of nineteenth-century deer-death trauma was Charles Dudley
Warner's 1878 tour de force *A-hunting of the Deer*, which relates
the "thrill" of the hunt from the point of view of a madly fleeing
doe, desperate to distract hunters from her newborn. In the essay,
mother and fawn are startled one morning by the distant but certain
sound of an approaching dog pack; quickly feeding her offspring
and admonishing him to lay low and stay put (baby deer have no
scent, a biological miracle that allows them to escape detection by
predators, so long as they remain hidden and perfectly still), she

leads the hounds away from the fawn's hiding place. We run with her as she circles, doubles back, and even sprints through a village. "In a panic, frightened animals will always flee to humankind from the danger of more savage foes," Warner writes. "Perhaps the trait is the survival of an era of peace on earth; perhaps it is a prophecy of the golden age of the future." But such a promise of interspecies peace does not come soon enough for the doe, who, utterly fatigued, attempts to swim across a lake. Here, sluggish in the water, she is trapped by baying hounds and two hunters in a boat armed with gun and oar. "To paddle up to the swimming deer, and cut his throat, is a sure means of getting venison, and has its charms for some," Warner closes his account. "Even women and doctors of divinity have enjoyed this exquisite pleasure. It cannot be denied that we are so constituted by a wise creator as to feel a delight in killing a wild animal which we do not in killing a tame one."[6]

What Warner's compelling parable of maternal sacrifice was to Victorian America, the animated Disney film *Bambi* became for the moviegoing twentieth century. The story originated in the 1923 novel *Bambi: A Life in the Woods*, by Felix Salten, a Viennese Jew who was a prolific author, theater critic, and cultural figure. He was also a hunter who believed that, for the deer he killed, sudden death by bullet was preferable to the alternatives, and that those who criticized his "blood sport" would always remain at a remove from nature, while he became its intimate friend. Salten's novel sold thousands of copies in Europe and was published in 1928 in America, where it became a Book-of-the-Month Club selection; Walt Disney acquired the film rights in 1937, a year after Hitler banned all of Salten's writing and a year before the author fled to Zurich.

The Disney animation studio was in the midst of its incredible run of hit features—*Snow White and the Seven Dwarfs* (1937), *Pinocchio* (1940), *Fantasia* (1940), *Dumbo* (1941)—and devoted innovative effort to *Bambi*, such as filming wild deer at their browse and bringing live fawns to the animation workshop so artists might better study their anatomy and movements. The studio also experimented with imposing the faces of human babies onto the cartoon deer to make them appear more relatable.

Due in part to these meticulous efforts, and its seductive musical score, the film's telling of a young deer's coming of age amidst the forest's benign creatures, a loving mother, a remote but powerful father, and a particularly murderous breed of men with guns, has likely exercised a more lasting impact on the public's impression of hunting as a sport than any other artistic representation in history. "The message of 'Bambi' . . . is appealing above all to the men and women of tomorrow who are now our children," acknowledged the July 1942 issue of *Audubon Magazine,* upon the film's release. "To a child, in his simplicity, the life of an innocent, harmless and beautiful animal is just as precious as that of a human being, so many of whom do not appear altogether innocent and harmless and beautiful." The images and the emotions the film conjures are so embedded in our culture as to have become common referents; "Bambi" is part of our language. For seventy-five years, hunters and their spokesmen have tried, with agonized futility, to denounce the character and the film as portraying an anthropomorphized fantasy world no real deer inhabits. "Those [cartoon] animals don't procreate or eliminate wastes or eat one another," one sports writer complained. "They gaily romp and play their lives away. People never knew or don't want to know that death is as quotidian in the wild as sucking air in and blowing it out."[7]

*Bambi* was only the beginning of Disney's production of alluring wildlife fare. Two other Salten works also inspired Disney films: *Perri* (1957), about the adventures of a female squirrel; and *The Shaggy Dog* (1959), a Fred MacMurray comedy based on Salten's *The Hound of Florence* and starring a shape-shifting canine. The studio's animated and feature films, its documentaries, and its popular Sunday evening television show throughout the 1950s and 1960s, depicted Mother Nature "as a kind old grandma who provides a peaceful and idyllic existence for her charges," charged *Montana Outdoors.* "Little mention was made of nature's stern realities—of the survival of the fittest, the constant struggle for food and cover and the rule of fang and claw. Many viewers began to feel that wild animals live in perpetual harmony in enchanted forests, a vision of freedom, peace and beauty that was missing from their own lives." The article went on to argue that since all attempts to abolish hunting were doomed anyway, people on both sides of the question should divert their energies from misleading distractions such as *Bambi* to something useful, like preserving wild habitat.[8]

The "nature fakers"—to borrow Theodore Roosevelt's expression—of the early twentieth century were blasted for imparting thoughtful planning and other anthropomorphized behavior to animals. One reason *Bambi* managed to resonate so powerfully— and the same might be said of other animations featuring a hunting dynamic, such as Daffy Duck, or Bugs Bunny and his shotgun-toting nemesis Elmer Fudd—is that as "'toons," they make no pretense of representing actual nature reporting. To the extent that the story of Bambi and his friends offers a rosy distortion of life in the wild, it does so in a child's medium that has from its origins been inhabited by adorable animals that look, act, and talk like children. But *Bambi* deviates from the familiar type; the grown-up animals speak like concerned adults, while the human hunters are not inept Elmer Fudds, but determined, methodical killers; and unlike other cartoons, with their standard visual joke that animals walk away from a shotgun blast with nothing more than a blackened face or ruffled tail feathers, in *Bambi* they die. By both playing to and manipulating the viewer's expectations, *Bambi* exposes man as a heartless stranger, dead to the love and grace of the natural world. This, of course, is much the opposite of how hunters view themselves, and might explain why the film's universal popularity so grates on sportsmen.

Hunters may not be alone in their aversion to Disney's creation. To America's farmers and many suburban gardeners as well, deer are far from lovable cartoon creatures or even good neighbors: they are eating machines, munching 8 to 10 pounds of vegetation per day and exacting a burdensome toll on crops and flowerbeds. And their predawn food raids are hard to defend against, as a deer can move silently and almost invisibly through a cornfield and even leap an 8-foot fence if something delicious awaits on the other side. Farmers unwilling to accept the sustained loss of valuable crops to foraging deer can obtain an agricultural damage mitigation shooting permit, known as an "Ag tag," which allows them to shoot deer as pests out of season. They can also make their land more viable for the leasing of hunting rights, by planting designated areas with special treats deer love, such as clover, alfalfa, canola, turnips, rye and oats, or prepackaged seed mixtures sold as "Pure Attraction," "Autumn Buffet," and "Oatrageous." "You'll be ready to harvest the deer as they harvest their last mouthful," promises one manufacturer.[9]

When they're not consuming the nation's growing things, deer still cause trouble. They are, in fact, the deadliest animal in America, more dangerous than pit bulls, alligators, or rabid raccoons combined, each year causing 1.1 million vehicle crashes, killing two hundred people and injuring as many as ten thousand. Almost every driver who routinely travels rural highways after dusk will eventually have the experience of hitting, or narrowly missing, a deer; inevitably the driver reports that the animal seemed to instantly materialize "out of nowhere." In rural, heavily forested areas, such as northern Wisconsin and Michigan's Upper Peninsula, auto body repair shops rely on income from autumnal vehicular deer collision damage much as Macy's anticipates Christmas.

In communities with excess deer populations, concerned residents are often left to sift through various possible solutions, from increased hunting to deer relocation, or sterilization. "Relocation" has an appealing, nonlethal sound. It can, however, be expensive to implement, time consuming, and fail to deliver satisfactory results. For one thing, as deer are widely unwanted, it's often hard to secure a willing relocation site. There's also the deer's adjustment to new terrain, new kinds of disease, predators, and other dangers to encounter, any of which can doom the animal's chances. The larger issue, conservation experts say, is that deer capture and relocation cannot hope to compete with deer's high reproduction rates, the evolutionary result of deer having evolved over many millennia as high-value prey. At one enclosed reserve in Michigan, 10 deer multiplied to 212 in just six years. And where deer populations are culled, that much extra uneaten food becomes available to the deer that remain, who then thrive, resulting in higher fertility rates, more multiple births, and soon, a restored animal population. Original levels have been seen to return within just a few years.[10]

Deer birth control or sterilization are similarly often thwarted by the sheer number of animals involved and the painstaking work of capture, treatment, and release. It's far easier to shoot a deer than to capture it. Yet towns that import professional marksmen to thin deer herds are also frequently disappointed. The terms *marksman* or *sharpshooter* may suggest cool efficiency, but the intended victims are also expert—at making themselves scarce—which ultimately brings things back to the need for the deer to be tracked, preferably by those familiar with doing so: *hunters*. Indeed, given the paucity of other options, it appears that hunters are the only choice for combating deer overpopulation in a setting that lacks nonhuman predators. Authorities still often resist this step, however, for it requires them to open a special hunting season; it also brings the sport hunting culture to sleepy suburban towns, *those people* who drive four-by-fours, wear camo, and carry guns. Residents may embrace the objective but not the means.

Hunters have themselves been known to express discomfort with localized special seasons, as they can feel cast in the role of exterminators. As historian Jan Dizard points out, hunters may deride animal rights people for sentimentalizing deer, but they, too, have strong emotions invested in the pursuit of a beautiful, noble wild creature, and dislike the perverting of that quest. In addition, even the worst suburban "nuisance" deer is often semitame, accustomed to browsing freely around gardens and homes, so the very act of "hunting" such animals can feel demeaning. The worst scenario, from a hunter's perspective, is to get a good-looking deer locked in the scope and edge one's finger toward the trigger, only to notice at the last moment that the target is wearing a brightly colored kerchief. Homeowners sometimes can't help "adopting" an individual animal that's made itself familiar through diurnal visits to the backyard shrubbery, and will tie highly visible pieces of fabric around the deer's neck during hunting season, much as they have been known to do to safeguard their children. Deer predate mankind by at least 30 million years. It's not hard to imagine—on account of their resilience and adaptability, and ironically, also our great regard for them—that they will be quietly at their dawn browse long after we've gone.[11]

ALDO LEOPOLD'S PREDATOR CONTROL WORK IN NEW MEXICO IN 1907 was designed to preserve declining wildlife populations from ravenous wolves. But as the region became settled and elk and other wild prey were replaced by domestic sheep, cows, chickens, and horses, the wolves and other predators took the change in menu in stride. By 1915, with ranchers complaining that they were losing half a million livestock animals to predators each year, Congress was pressed to begin keeping such "gangsters of the wild" in check as an economic necessity. For the first time Washington, DC, allocated funds for a predator control program designed to protect livestock.

Initially a cash bounty system was established, an American tradition dating back to the seventeenth century, when Massachusetts offered a bounty on wolves and, in Pennsylvania, William Penn offered cash for the scalps of bears and weasels. But historically, bounty inducements have also been problematic, as fraud frequently leads to kill evidence being reused to claim multiple bounties, or animals with bounties on their head being raised for profitable slaughter. In the Southwest, shooters tended to reap the easiest rewards by eliminating low-level predators such as hawks or coyote pups, while shunning the pursuit of such apex predators as wolves, fox, cougar, or bear, whose killing would require considerable time and effort. In response, the government began hiring hunters on salary.

A particularly rugged breed of men responded to the call, exemplified by the legendary Ben Lilly, who guided hunts for Theodore Roosevelt, slept in a tree "as if he had been a wild turkey," and was renowned for such folksy gems as "Anyone can kill a deer; it takes a man to kill a varmint." Convinced God had dispatched him to eradicate "malefic creatures," he once informed a bear in his grasp: "You are condemned, you black devil. I kill you in the name of the law." But by the mid-twentieth century, the Ben Lillys of the world were no more, state and federal agencies having adopted more "scientific" predator control programs, using poisoned baits, gassing coyote pups in their dens, and shooting animals from aircraft. Today, a unit of the Department of Agriculture called Wildlife Services spends $127 million each year to kill a staggering number of wild animals—70,000 coyotes, 20,000 prairie dogs, 42,000 feral hogs, and more than 700,000 red-wing blackbirds, among many others. Wildlife Services operates largely at the behest of the livestock industry, which claims financial losses in the tens of millions of dollars each year from predator assaults on cattle, goats, sheep, and chickens, and from farmers bothered by bird and small animal crop devastation. The agency also deals with bird hazards to aircraft, nuisance geese, deer damage to orchards, and country roads flooded by the work of beavers. The government prefers to handle these control efforts because, in its own words, "if such work is left up to the angry and frustrated individuals experiencing the damage firsthand, some of those people are likely to respond drastically."[12]

Biologists and nongovernmental organizations concerned about species loss and animal rights, such as the Natural Resources Defense Council (NRDC), however, argue that nonlethal forms of control, such as guard dogs, fences, and warning devices, can be equally effective at deterring predators. The National Wildlife Foundation in the 1990s established a fund to compensate livestock owners for losses to predators, and Montana has experimented with wolf stamps, which can be purchased by nonconsumptive users (nonhunters) to encourage research and nonlethal controls. Perhaps most important, these programs bring new stakeholders into policy making as regards predator reintroduction and protection, although they do not always find willing partners among ranchers, who tend to "own" the issue, worry fiercely about its impact on their bottom line, and resent outside advice.

Thus, many public arguments over predator control quickly reach a familiar impasse—urban environmentalists and animal rights groups advancing "green," "nonlethal," citified policies unacceptable to rural inhabitants. One may feel concern for mountain lions, wolves, or bears pressured by loss of habitat, value them as emblems of wilderness, or believe they play a useful role in maintaining bio-diverse systems, but farmers and rural dwellers who worry about damage to livestock, or even the safety of their children waiting for a school bus along a country road, feel justified in holding a far less hospitable and less romantic view of these animals. Debate over the reintroduction of predator species will always look different depending on where one sits.

"We seem to kill predators out of mindless, even primordial antipathy, rather than for any good reason," observes historian Richard Conniff, although often there seems to be a sliding scale of humane concern for targeted creatures based on their level of threat but also their likability, with feral hogs at the bottom, pretty much friendless. Some predators, however, including coyotes, wolves, and bear, have human defenders who insist their crimes are exaggerated. The Humane Society of the United States (HSUS) points out that there has not been a single documented fatal wolf attack on a human in the last century, while Oklahoma senator Gil Graham once termed the coyote "the most unjustly accused of all animals." Yet the government continues to eradicate coyotes with extreme measures, including semiautomatic weapons, poisons, and aerial tracking.[13]

Naming animal species as predators can work as would an effective promotional campaign to make them more huntable. In the past decade, almost thirty thousand mountain lions have been killed as trophies, chiefly in the western states of Idaho, Montana, Colorado, and Utah, according to the HSUS, often with the aid of non–fair chase technology, such as hound packs outfitted with radio collars, cell phones, and all-terrain vehicles. Although the risk to humans of a mountain lion attack is quite small—since 1890, fewer than twenty people are known to have died from such an attack in the United States—the anecdotal reports of such incidents are unsettling, and that fear allows a relatively small constituency of big game hunters to preserve the right to take these animals in large numbers.[14]

Like wildlife conservation itself, prey and predator issues can be subject to wishful thinking, the faith that if just the right formula could be found the earth and its living flora and fauna might return to some harmonious equilibrium. Wilderness, however, never is or can be in a perfect or permanent state; it is always volatile and subject to constant yet inconsistent, natural stresses, some beyond human perception. New forms of competition may arise between predators, or among prey species, as well as from disease, hunting, agriculture, or the construction of malls and new homes. A blight infecting trees impacts the insects that rely on them, as well as the small animals or birds that rely on the insects; as a result, antelope or elk might relocate, taking such predators as coyotes or wolves with them, thus altering an ecosystem. In a phenomenon known as trophic cascade, first described by Aldo Leopold, predators by their increase or decrease can have profound effects on numerous other species; for example, if more wolves means a corresponding decrease in deer, there are fewer deer to vigorously rub their antlers against the bark of young trees, destroying them; the resulting lack of dead trees inhibits beavers from constructing dams, which in turn intensifies erosion along streams, the consequence being fewer reptiles, butterflies, or wildflowers. On the other hand, if wolves are decimated, that's one less check on deer-borne disease, as wolves tend to harvest weak and sick animals, removing them from the herd to the benefit of the ecosystem.

Much remains to be learned from such chains of events. When, in an effort to allay public fears of cougar attacks, Washington State issued permits to hunt them, many were killed, but biologists were soon informed, to their surprise, that reports of attacks had ticked upward. They remained baffled until they realized that the slower, older cougars, the mature adults who had a stabilizing effect on the entire cougar population, were the ones the hunters had managed to shoot, leaving only younger, more aggressive animals. "When the senior cougars are removed, chaos ensues," reports science writer Virginia Morell, "just as it would if all the adults in our society were suddenly killed and only teenagers were left to handle the affairs." A related program involving wolves, also in Washington, found that eliminating the older generation forced younger animals, less skilled in finding prey, to become more indiscriminate in their search for food, and thus more of a threat to domestic sheep and other farm animals. While it was long axiomatic among hunters and wildlife specialists that culling older animals from a population made it healthier, such observers as Morell now believe elders perform a crucial role in animal groups, providing discipline, helping to safeguard breeding, and teaching the young to avoid contact with humans.[15]

One of the most emotional public debates about predator management involves grizzly bears, *Ursus horribilis*, apex predators and an ultimate icon of American wildlife, as celebrated as they are feared. "Their nature is savage and ferocious and their haunts to be guarded against," cautioned eighteenth-century North American explorer Edward Umfreville. "The number of maimed Indians to be seen in this country exhibits a melancholy proof of their power over the human species." Nor were the brute's attributes lost on Lewis and Clark, the first official American explorers of the trans-Mississippi West, who dubbed it "grizzly." "These bear being so hard to die rather intimidates us all," Meriwether Lewis wrote in his journal in 1805. "I must confess I do not like the gentleman and had rather fight 2 Indians than one bear." Yet there has long been a deep and abiding fascination with the animals, as evidenced by the throngs who greeted the arrival of Samson at Barnum's Museum in New York City in the late 1850s, a 1,500-pound grizzly brought east by the mountaineer John "Grizzly" Adams. One of the largest of his species ever taken alive, Samson was immortalized as the model for the state flag of California.[16]

The bear's plight in ways mirrors America's shifting views of conservation/ecology. Venerated by Native Americans and respected by white settlers and ranchers for their strength and ferocity, bear were nonetheless detested and destroyed by ranchmen, where possible, as voracious killers of livestock. Certainly the most damning thing that can be said about them, however, is that they are known to attack, kill, and eat people. Even as statistics show that grizzly attacks on humans are rare, there are always enough confirmed victims, and horrific, publicized accounts of such events, to sustain a high level of concern. "The ever-present risk of jumping one of these death dispensers was enough to chill to the marrow the most courageous pioneer who ever lived," noted one account of the early

West, a sentiment still likely to be shared by hikers or hunters in the northern Rockies or Alaska.[17]

Hunters prize trophies of the grizzly's pelts and claws, but unlike black bears, which live mostly on fruits, berries, and acorns, grizzlies have never been considered good eating, as their own diet often includes carrion. In the early twentieth century, Yellowstone Park administrators turned both grizzlies' and black bears' penchant for eating human garbage into evening performances for park visitors, complete with bleacher seating, as, without fail, the animals arrived at dusk to plunder hotel and restaurant food waste. The garbage show was eventually curtailed, but the bears continued to draw tourists to the park, abetted by the national celebrity in the late 1950s of two Hanna-Barbera cartoon bears, Yogi and Boo-Boo, fictional denizens of "Jellystone Park." The era was characterized by low gasoline prices and the ubiquitous family trip west, a rite of passage that involved a station wagon loaded with children, Dad at the wheel, Mom studying the AAA map, and an obligatory stop "to see the bears" at Yellowstone, where visitors, despite official warnings, fed and photographed the animals that came begging at open car windows. An official reevaluation of human-bear relations did not come until August 1967, when on one night, in separate incidents 20 miles apart, two young female summer employees in Glacier National Park were dragged from their sleeping bags and mauled to death by grizzlies presumably attracted to nearby trash bins.

By 1975, only 136 grizzlies remained in the Yellowstone ecosystem, leading to the animal's being placed on the endangered species list. Today, however, thanks to restoration efforts, there are seven hundred grizzly bears in the system, and the bear is safely off the list. Such a change in status will mean that neighboring states may once again declare limited hunting seasons for the animals, and because of their reputation as an ultimate western trophy, it is expected the delisting will make the bears popular targets, although officials and watchdog groups will attempt to ensure that they are not hunted back into endangered status. Support has grown over the years for the bear's presence in the Rockies as essential aesthetically, echoing naturalist Enos A. Mills's admonition of a century ago: "The imagination will be alive so long as the grizzly lives."[18]

It's likely that the presence of grizzlies in the wild, and wilderness itself, will long retain its special meaning. But just as Americans' attitudes toward the grizzly and other predators did not remain static, so also did their view of wilderness evolve. To the early colonials, it was a forbidding wasteland; during the early nineteenth century, a sublime and alluring place of God-glorious waterfalls and birdsong. The Gilded Age sportsman perceived in it renewal as personal as a hunter's first step at dawn; in the thoughts and words of the first conservationists, it became, as William Cronon observes, "a highly attractive natural alternative to the ugly artificiality of modern civilization," notable in that it represented the human capacity for restraint. Cronon reminds us that the very concept of wilderness is man-made (we, after all, are who define and protect it); and that believing it to be a place where nature exists in some pre-Edenic balance is "a product of the very history it seeks to deny"—namely, the eradication of its prior human inhabitants. "To the extent that we celebrate wilderness as the measure with which we judge civilization," he warns, "we reproduce the dualism that sets humanity and nature at opposite poles. We thereby leave ourselves little hope of discovering what an ethical, sustainable, *honorable* human place in nature might actually look like."[19]

*Chapter Thirteen*

# The Guns of Autumn

THE AMERICAN SPORT HUNTER BY THE LATE NINETEENTH CENTURY honored the code of fair chase, killing animals only under conditions in which they had a chance to flee, a sensibility that helped transform hunting's spokesmen into leaders of the early conservation movement. It has proven to be such a consistent standard that modern hunting practices would likely be recognizable to Frank Forester and Charlie Hallock. Conscientious twenty-first-century American hunters respect the game they pursue and are sincere in their devotion to a sport that brings them into nature as few other things do. Most observe game laws and are scrupulous about gun safety, and a growing number harvest wild game not as trophies but for reasons of dietary preference and cost. Through their Pittman-Robertson taxes, license fees, and volunteer conservation programs, they also help to maintain healthy wildlife habitats.

However, many outside the hunting community have become less patient with even the most ethical forms of fair chase hunting and decry it as grossly *unfair*: the hide of the swiftest fleeing animal, after all, is ultimately defenseless against a bullet fired from a high-powered gun, or an arrow delivered by a compound bow.

Killing animals under any circumstances is unjust, animal rights advocates argue, because animals possess a moral right to their life just as we do to ours. But special contempt is reserved for those who kill for sport or recreation, and has been since at least 55 BC, when the audience in a Roman arena protested the slaughter of eighteen elephants in a staged "hunt." Cicero, who was present, was led to ponder, "What pleasure can a cultured man get in seeing . . . a noble beast run through by a hunting spear? . . . The whole affair was attended by a sort of pity, and a feeling that these huge animals have something in common with humankind."[1]

Human attitudes toward animals are being transformed today by what scholar Kimberly Smith has termed a "the process of ethical extension." From family to tribe, from neighborhood to nation, man grows in his discernment of his impact on, and his connectedness to, the greater world. Since the Enlightenment, the rights we extend to others have grown substantially to include men, women, and children, the disabled, the environment, even man-made structures. In theory at least, the lives of all human beings have become inviolable. But can such moral perception and grace be extended to non-human creatures as well? This recognition would supersede the humanitarian approach to modern animal welfare pioneered by Henry Bergh and his fellow nineteenth-century reformers, and surpass the more modern well-meant demand that animals raised and kept for slaughter be allowed a "cage-free" or even "free-range" life. It is, rather, a leap of ethical consciousness to the understanding that man no longer be considered the center of the biological universe, and that far greater humility need characterize his dealings with nonhuman beings. "The autonomy of nonhuman nature seems to me an indispensable corrective to human arrogance," William Cronon writes. "Any way of looking at nature that helps us remember . . . that the interests of people are not necessarily identical to those of every other creature or of the earth itself is likely to foster *responsible* behavior." Even the animal rights movement and its agenda of animal protection is insufficiently progressive for philosophers and animal ethicists Sue Donaldson and Will Kymlicka. That animals are entitled to live their life free of torment, confinement, and pain, in other words, should be obvious and inarguable. How much better might it be to not merely avoid harming animals, but fully accept their interconnectedness with us, and constructively engage them as "neighbors, friends, co-citizens, and members of communities."[2]

Of course, while human consideration of animals' role in the world has become more enlightened, no one believes we'll arrive anytime soon at an enchanted age for animals. What can be said is that increasingly the distinct otherness of the "brute creation" seems more intriguing, more pleasantly enigmatic. We treasure animals' steadiness as well as their eccentricities, and are enriched by them—the companions we consider family, the "liminal wildlife," such as squirrels, birds, and chipmunks, that we encounter daily in city parks and backyards, or the wild animals that live deep in the woods or in the sea, which we seek out at times but that, for the most part, please us simply by the fact of their being: it's enough to know they are there. Then there are the billions we think of not so much at all, the doomed, muffled phalanx, the living assembly line of animal protein with hooves or wings (appendages they hardly need). Our knowledge and tolerance of this world of unimaginable suffering weigh upon us and are sources of profound anxiety.

It is one thing to recognize that animals deserve our respect and protection and have a right to the life they were intended by nature to live, and to vow that we, with growing sensitivity, are groping toward ways to end the abuse they suffer. But how do we square such noble aspirations with the reality of the country's meat industrial complex, a system supported by the 96 percent of Americans who eat meat at least once a week, and which some critics have described as nothing less than the largest infliction of pain and suffering on living beings ever carried out in human history? That's a claim that deserves serious reckoning. Ironically, in terms of their proliferation, industrial animals must be considered the most "successful" on earth; while it is estimated that the world contains about 40,000 lions, 500,000 elephants, 50 million penguins, and 200 million dogs, a census of factory farms would find 1 billion domesticated pigs, 1.5 billion domesticated cows, and 20 billion chickens.

What this means is that all the world's animals that live in the wild, or in zoos, as house pets or beasts of burden, taken together, would still constitute a minority compared to those "meals-in-waiting," the living agricultural products whose entire (and very brief) life takes place entirely along the industrial farming production line.[3]

Moral arguments against this system seem unlikely to change it, despite the advent of some "humanely raised" or "free-range" alternatives, and while experts theorize it could eventually collapse from ecological and economic stresses, it is for the moment too efficient, affordable, and ingrained. We devote far more thought to choosing between "Buffalo-style" wings and Jimmy Dean Sausage Crumbles than the system that produces them. Someone clicking TV channels at almost any time of day will find with ease a nature show featuring hushed narration and wild animals in their natural environment, but the nauseating undercover footage of what passes for normal at industrial farms, as ethicist Peter Singer comments, "is limited to the briefest of glimpses as part of infrequent 'specials' on agriculture or food production. The average viewer must know more about the lives of cheetahs . . . than he or she knows about the lives of chickens or veal calves."[4]

That's a bit unfair to the many ongoing and successful efforts humans have made on behalf of other living creatures, from closing down captive whale shows and puppy mills, to fostering the ethical raising of poultry and cattle and the proliferation of animal rescue and neutering programs. But given the vast numbers of food animals suffering in factory cages, progress is bittersweet. Regardless of our best intentions or conscientious dietary and lifestyle choices, we live in a world of animal displacement and misery. "While the animal advocacy movement has won some battles over the past century," say Donaldson and Kymlicka, "it has essentially lost the war." Our current methods of animal agriculture constitute tortures even Hogarth did not imagine, and are in a way more horrendous for being unseen.[5]

Hunting, of course, has always been about food politics, and the sport has welcomed in recent years a surge of new interest from so-called do-it-yourself (DIY) or adult-onset hunters. Some DIYers are former vegans who have come to embrace "hunting their own dinner" as a way to more honestly align obtaining meat protein with principle. Others pursue it as a means of self-sufficiency. Whatever the reason, DIY hunters have thought it through; they are probably the world's most conscientious eaters, or at least the most self-aware. "I like to know where my food comes from," Anthony Licata, editor of *Field and Stream*, explained at a 2016 forum. "I like to know that my meat is organic, that it's free range, that it's lived a humane life. And for me, there's no better way to know that than through hunting. I'm very proud when I feed my family that meat."[6]

Were we even "meant" to eat our fellow creatures? Biographer and essayist Plutarch reminded his fellow Greeks two thousand years ago that humans have "no curved beak, no sharp talons and claws, no pointed teeth," and he dared them to try and "kill *yourself* what you wish to eat—but do it yourself with your own *natural* weapons, without the use of butcher's knife, or axe, or club." Many biologists since Plutarch's time have echoed his complaint: while animal carnivores have a set lower jaw for stability and sharp incisors for tearing meat, human teeth appear designed for munching fruits and grinding vegetables, our hands designed to pluck fruit from trees. Yet paleoanthropologists concede that proto-humans at some point recognized that plant nutrients were stored in the bodies of herbivores, creatures that could with crude, sharp weapons be stalked and slain, the takeaway being more efficient, high-caloric, high-protein meals. There's evidence that the iron and vitamin B-12 found in meat products are essential to human health. We are "behavioral omnivores–that is we eat meat," writes wellness activist Kathy Freeston, "but our evolution and physiology are herbivorous, and ample science proves that when we choose to eat meat that causes problems, from decreased energy and a need for more sleep to increased risk for obesity, diabetes, heart disease, and cancer." But absolute agreement on this subject, in lieu of greater scientific certainty, remains elusive.[7]

If your primary concern is for animal welfare and wildlife conservation, however, it's hard to escape the trauma that any type of domestic farming wreaks on the environment. One reason DIY hunters themselves cite for joining the chase is the awareness that any type of agriculture, however green or organic, inadvertently destroys animal lives. "One may . . . abhor all meat-eating on the grounds of cruelty," writes hunting scholar Mary Stange, "but in a single sunny afternoon, a farmer plowing a field wreaks more carnage, in the form of outright killing and the destruction of nests and mating areas, not to mention the impacts of pesticides and herbicides on wildlife, than the average hunter does in a lifetime." Tovar Cerulli, whose well-regarded book *The Mindful Carnivore* describes his awakening to the virtues of the hunt, reflects that "the mere fact of living, I had begun to realize, linked me to larger webs of life and death. Regardless of what I did, whether I liked it or not, I had an impact. No matter what I ate, habitats had already been sacrificed. No matter what I ate, animals would be killed." As Kentucky-born novelist Barbara Kingsolver recalls, "I've watched enough harvests to know that cutting a wheat field amounts to more decapitated bunnies under the combine than you would believe."[8]

If humankind's presence alone causes animals to die, it might lend credence to the hunter's claim that as man is already deeply involved in animal destruction, hunting is simply its most honest manifestation. "Hunting made me realize that there's a lot that has to happen before that piece of meat gets to your plate," observes Georgia Pellegrini, a professional chef and author of *Girl Hunter: Revolutionizing the Way We Eat, One Hunt at a Time.* "As a chef, I wanted to participate in that process because it makes the experience more meaningful. You think about the ingredients differently, you think about the experience of eating it differently, and you have more control over how the animal was treated." Most DIY hunters cite the importance of this closeness to the killing process. They rebel against eating industrial meat, in part, because of how thoroughly that system severs all human relationship with the animal world. "The supermarket," notes naturalist Richard Nelson, has become "an agent of our forgetfulness."[9]

DIY can also be economical: one shot, one elk, and the family freezer is well stocked for a year. However, the self-sufficiency argument has its limits. Unless one lives near the woods and inherited granddad's shotgun, hunting can require a great deal of specialized equipment and clothing and involve travel to remote areas, particularly as former access to nearby hunting grounds is limited by sprawl, loss of habitat, and landowners' fears about liability. When one weighs the costs—weapons, ammunition, permits, camo, warm clothes, game calls and other gadgets, plus motels, gas, and processing—DIY in the end may not necessarily offer a substantial savings over the shrink-wrapped ground chuck down at Kroger's.

HUNTERS ARE EQUALLY AWARE OF THE SPILLOVER INTO THEIR PAStime of the ongoing debate about the place of guns in American life. Despite opinion polls that consistently show that the public appreciates the difference between "the gun scourge" and fair chase, the intensity of the nation's Second Amendment furor cannot help but impact a sport that centers on high-powered weapons. Hunting, its participants will tell you, is a single-shot sport, and many hunters have no use for and even disdain for military-style semiautomatics, the "ugly" guns that potentially contaminate hunting's image. Yet, the weapons industry and sport hunting have had a long kinship, as technology proven at Creedmoor and at other competitive shooting events often led to military innovations, and, vice versa, when hunters' demands based on prey and ease of use contributed to factory design improvements. In return the National Rifle Association (NRA) took both its frontier motif and the notion of guns as a "natural right" largely from the idea of the American as pathfinder/hunter (a faith so unqualified, the Bill of Rights had not bothered to protect hunting explicitly). And nineteenth-century gun makers, aided by an abundance of good hunting art and the arrival of high-quality color lithography, proved adept at promoting the gun not solely as a useful tool but as the hunter's most faithful companion—indeed his *only* friend in a tough spot.

The results were memorable print and calendar advertisements by Smith and Wesson, Winchester, Remington, Colt, and others that used the innate power of hunting narratives to sell weapons and ammunition. The detailed artwork had to possess a high degree of accuracy, as hunters are absolute sticklers for it; exacting attention was given to representations of wild animals, dogs of various breeds, natural surroundings, and especially the featured weapon, down to the precise rendering of year and model. These works included *nostalgia art*, such as the panoramic *The Days of Bison Millions*, by Carl Rungius (the so-called Rembrandt of the moose); Charles M. Russell's evocative sunlit buffalo in *When the Land Belonged to God*; or reprints of such perennial favorites as George Catlin's and Alexander Tait's mid-nineteenth-century images of white men and Indians together riding down buffalo on horseback. There was also *animal combat art*, along the lines of Edwin Landseer's classic *None But the Brave Deserve the Fair*, in which two bucks crash antlers on a stormy mountain ridge as a harem of does looks on; and *predator-prey art*, showing a cougar about to pounce on an unsuspecting deer or hungry wolves circling a wounded buffalo. There was a lot of what might be termed *devoted hound art*, best represented in the work of artist Bob White, who depicted robust-looking hunting dogs in close-up, flushing and retrieving quail; also *heroic animal art*, which might capture a bighorn sheep or wild horse poised on a precipice overlooking a majestic vista. There was an abundance of *hunters' fraternity* scenes—men sharing moments of anticipation before the chase or eating a hurried breakfast around a campfire, as in *A Good Time Coming*, by Tait, or padding cautiously forward together on snowshoes with rifles at the ready, as in Winslow Homer's *Deer Stalking in the Adirondacks*. "Diana" images of women hunters, arrow notched and bow extended, had their vogue, as did a popular calendar print entitled *Prairie Girl*, featuring a wholesome Annie Oakley type holding a rifle or large revolver.

The most compelling style was doubtless *predicament art*, showing a hunter's close scrape with a mountain lion or grizzly. As its name implies, predicament art featured a suspended "uh-oh moment," a stare-down between hunter and prey, in which the hunter's ability to react was in question; the picture pointedly offered no resolution, other than a guarantee that the hunter's gun, for which he was cautiously reaching (and which clearly bore the manufacturer's name), would be key to his survival. A master in

The sudden appearance of a bear startles two hunters in *A Call to Action* by prolific western illustrator Philip R. Goodwin. Such "predicament art" was common in early-twentieth-century hunting ads, implying the necessity of a reliable gun. (The Athenaeum)

this realm was Philip R. Goodwin, known for the semicomical *A Rude Awakening* (1906), showing an enormous moose standing in the weeds above a groggy hunter who is just emerging from beneath the upturned canoe where he'd spent the night; *The Right of Way* (1907), which shows a stubborn-looking black bear and a porcupine meeting in the middle of a felled tree that's lying across a creek; and *The Interrupted Shot* (1924), in which a prone shooter already targeting some grazing elk is surprised by a mountain lion who has eyes for the same prey.

The predicament themes could appear dire, as in *The Last Cartridge* (1902) by Dan Smith, wherein a hunter, having just killed a cub bear with a pistol, now wields the tiny weapon in uncomfortably close quarters against the cub's enraged mother; or in Philip Lyford's chilling 1916 illustration *Mountain Lion Attack*, in which a nature photographer armed with only a pistol and encumbered with a heavy camera is trapped between a 1,000-foot drop and a vicious cat that suddenly springs from above. The theme of a looming grizzly is used artfully in *Dangerous Bend* (1915) by Newell Convers Wyeth, as two hunters in a small boat peer nervously around a large boulder where a huge dark bear waits in ambush.

One kind of predicament art took as its subject the hunter taking aim from a precarious height. Easily the best known is *A Chancy Shot* (1912) by Harry C. Edwards, in which a man, perched on a high ridge, sheer drops on every side, mountain goats grouped in the middle distance, gingerly reaches down for the rifle his partner is handing up to him. Initially used by Remington to sell its Model 14 ½ slide-action rifle, the print was so popular that Winchester and Savage also bought rights, simply slugging in their brand on the rifle stock.

During the Second World War, print ads for hunting weapons took on a distinctive cast. Many depicted a GI, his face grimy from battle, deriving momentary reassurance from noticing that the gun in his hands resembled one he had used to hunt deer back home. By the early 1950s, Cold War anxieties bred a cult interest in the rugged historical figures Daniel Boone and Davy Crockett, both of whom were featured in movies, on television, and in toys, hats, and comic books marketed for children; the trend may have begun with a popular 1946 Remington ad of a hunting father and son stopping to admire a Boone graffito on an ancient tree trunk. As the approving ghost of Boone himself smiles down from above, Dad says, "You couldn't choose a better hero, lad, than the American frontiersman!"

The homecoming of a generation of military veterans, young men taught to shoot and handle firearms, helped swell the ranks of American hunters, as well as those of the NRA. The organization purchased land in New Mexico to be used for its shooting competitions, and emphasized in its promotional materials its role as a watchdog of American gun safety. Throughout the 1950s and 1960s, a small modest decal denoting NRA membership was a common sight in the rear windows of cars in suburban parking lots, connoting other civic-minded organizations, such as the Civil Air Patrol or the YMCA, rather than the fierce advocacy group the NRA would become.

However, a small insurgency of members who desired a more fundamentalist stance on Second Amendment rights would soon change the group's direction. It was a revolt initiated in part, according to historian Scott Melzer, by the political assassinations of the 1960s, which brought a chorus of support for gun control measures from the public and elected officials. Feeling threatened, the NRA aggressively pushed back. There had been gun control laws before, such as the 1911 Sullivan Law that demanded New Yorkers obtain a police permit to own a weapon, and the 1934 National Firearms Act, which banned automatic weapons, such as machine guns. But never before had the idea of gun ownership been so directly challenged. Much was made of the fact—in the press and ultimately in the halls of Congress—that Lee Harvey Oswald had, for $12.78, bought the Italian Carcano rifle he'd used to kill President John F. Kennedy through a mail-order advertisement in the NRA periodical *American Rifleman*. In response, a proposed Gun Control Act lingered in Congress for years and was only passed in 1968 after the traumatic back-to-back murders of Martin Luther King Jr. and Senator Robert F. Kennedy in April and June, respectively, of that year. Even then, the bill was so weakened by NRA advocacy that its chief accomplishment was to restrict the ability to obtain a gun by mail order.

For decades, the federal judiciary's reading of the Second Amendment was that it protected a collective right to gun ownership, reflecting the founders' preference for a militia of armed yeomen instead of maintaining a standing army. The amendment, as Richard Hofstadter wrote, "was, in effect, a promise that Congress would not be able to bar the states from doing whatever was necessary to maintain well-regulated militias." At the time the amendment was drafted, the American victory over the British in the Revolutionary War stood as proof that a militia of citizen soldiers could defeat a European standing army (an opinion that came to be revised after the War of 1812). However, many read the amendment's protection as fundamentally an individual right. By the twentieth century, no one thought much about militias any more, and most Americans, due to the lingering twinned ethos of the frontier and of the self-sufficient individual, and decades of zealous product sales and promotion by domestic gun manufacturers, remained steadfast in the belief that one was entitled to possess a firearm, whether for hunting, target shooting, or personal security. The self-defense rationale only deepened after race-related violence in Detroit, New York, and other urban areas in the 1960s; conservatives declared a crisis of law and order. Eventually, a breakaway group led by NRA board member Harlon Carter, a former head of the US Border Patrol, and the author of *Guns & Ammo* magazine articles such as "Anti-Gun Hysteria Prelude to a Police State," began to insist the association act to safeguard gun rights at all costs from any threatened congressional reforms.[10]

The NRA also jumped quickly on the defensive in reaction to a ninety-minute CBS documentary, *The Guns of Autumn*, a highly critical view of sport hunting that aired in early September 1975. After word leaked that the show would "take hunting to the wood shed," the NRA began its campaign of indignation even before the film aired, and successfully convinced several advertisers, including Datsun, Carnation's Coffee-Mate, and Teledyne Aqua Tec Waterpik, to cancel their sponsorship. The resulting program was, if anything, even more offensive than the gun lobby had feared. "If one were planning to portray the glories of love between woman and man in a television documentary, then devoted the entire show to the antics of a drunken clod in a bordello, one would achieve the same level of truth," griped *New York Times* sports columnist Nelson Bryant. "[The show] was powerful stuff and the fragment of the hunting scene it portrays is accurate, but because it is only a fragment the final result is propaganda." The *Daily News* concurred, labeling the program "disgusting, deceitful, biased and unprofessional journalism."[11]

Produced by veteran television documentarian Irv Drasnin, the film did offer a most unflattering view of the sport, showing a group of louts and their hounds treeing and then shooting bears drawn to a town garbage dump, then a close-up of people skinning one bear while someone remarks of the dogs gnawing on it, "We feel that they deserve a chew." In other troubling scenes, men blast away mindlessly at birds and ducks, and a wounded fallow deer screams in pain and clings to life as hunters shoot it seven times at close range, before one of them takes the antlers in hand for a manly trophy pose.

Such images naturally only confirmed the worst suspicions of those already disposed to dislike the sport. "Strong men wept. More than one woman left the room, looking sick. Children up past their bedtime were suddenly hurried away, sobbing," reported syndicated television critic Harriet Van Horne, who termed what she and her living room full of friends had seen "an orgy of killing, American-style . . . the savage murder of noble beasts by ignoble beasts." A colleague at the *Times*, critic John O'Connor, offered the conclusion that "man no longer hunts because he has to but because he likes to," and that the "once-noble contest between man and beast has evolved, with the help of some sophisticated technology, into not a hunt but an execution."[12]

By coincidence, on the very day of the show's broadcast, September 5, Lynette "Squeaky" Fromme, a member of the Manson Family, armed with a Colt .45, had made a botched attempt in Sacramento to assassinate President Gerald Ford. The incident had the effect of reminding the country that it was dangerously at risk of gun violence, and lent immediacy to the images brought to the TV screen in *The Guns of Autumn*. The reaction to the documentary hinted at the deepening of entrenched and divided opinion regarding hunting, for in an age of the casual violence of a Manson Family, an endless war in Vietnam, and the threat of nuclear war, many viewers related easily to Drasnin's vision that shooting animals to death for sport was a cruel anachronism. The network, however, reported that most of the forty thousand letters it had received about the program disparaged its antihunting bias.

The liberal assault on hunting and, by extension, armed citizens, made explicit in *The Guns of Autumn*, represented the very sentimentalism the NRA's Harlon Carter was determined to overcome. "We may well be the first people in history to [become] the victims of sentiment over reason," he warned. "One must not be too impressed by the ultra-sensitive, the over-sympathetic people. One must not be too impressed that today their tender souls recoil at the death of an animal or a bird." A little more than a year later, at an NRA convention in Cincinnati, Carter's forces ripped control of the association from the group's elders and redirected it permanently toward a noncompromising absolutism on gun rights.[13]

The NRA's bellicose defense of universal gun rights sometimes becomes entangled with a defense of hunting, but while hunters appreciate the right to acquire weapons of their choosing, they generally don't share the gun lobby's deep paranoia or its insistence that one must be armed to repel home intruders or combat tyranny. In response, gun makers have in recent years pushed the sale of guns designed for self-defense rather than sport hunting, such as pocket-size pistols and tactical weapons, while some gun rights advocates have gone so far as to disparage sportsmen as "Fudds," for cartoon character Elmer Fudd. Hunters do tend to be more accepting than gun owners generally of the idea of regulation, which in their sport means permits, license fees, training courses in weapons handling and shooting safety, and limits on the taking of game. In addition, the nature of hunting, a sport that necessitates quiet, stealthy movement, a reliable sense of place, and a clear head, cannot help but bring a heightened awareness of gun safety. "Hunters are accustomed to following nuanced gun laws . . . so we understand that common sense regulation doesn't mean an end to bearing arms," writes Oregon-based hunter and author Lily Raff McCaulou. "We should be helping lead the national conversation about gun control, because we are uniquely suited to move the debate away from polemic and toward effective compromise."[14]

However, even respected hunting spokesmen can incur the wrath of the gun rights community, as Jim Zumbo, hunting editor of *Outdoor Life*, discovered in February 2007. Disturbed to learn that hunters were using the military-style AR-15 to shoot prairie dogs, Zumbo wrote in an impassioned blog post:

Excuse me, maybe I'm a traditionalist, but I see no place for these weapons among our hunting fraternity. I'll go so far as to call them "terrorist" rifles. . . . Sorry, folks, in my humble opinion, these things have no place in hunting. . . . We've always been proud of our "sporting firearms." . . . To most of the public, an assault rifle is a terrifying thing. Let's divorce ourselves from them. I say game departments should ban them from the prairies and woods.[15]

The response from the nation's gun owners, led by their powerful lobby, was a vociferous howl of protest. Remington canned Zumbo as a spokesman, the Outdoor TV hunting channel suspended him, and his magazine terminated his employment. "The reaction—from tens of thousands of owners of assault rifles across the country, from media and manufacturers rooted in the gun business, and from the NRA (of which Zumbo was a 40-year member)—has been swift, severe and unforgiving," reported the *Washington Post*. "Despite a profuse public apology and a vow to go hunting soon with an assault weapon, Zumbo's career appears to be over." The disgraced editor managed to win his way at least partially back into the gun crowd's favor through a new public friendship with über-gun enthusiast Ted Nugent, and his refusal to support an assault weapon ban proposed by Michigan senator Carl M. Levin—a ban, ironically, inspired by Zumbo's strongly worded plea.[16]

VINTAGE SPORTSMEN'S CALENDARS OF THE CHASE'S THRILLS AND risks seem quaint today, in comparison to modern hunting videos, many accompanied by pounding heavy-metal soundtracks, which proliferate on television and the Internet. The link between the traditional and more cutting-edge era may have been forged in 1965, when ABC-TV's *Wide World of Sports* discovered that viewers were hungry for a program devoted to rugged outdoor endeavors, predominantly big game hunting and fishing. The resulting spin-off, *The American Sportsman*, slotted into Sunday afternoon programming, where it often followed a football or baseball game, became a surprise hit. Hosted initially by Joe Foss, war hero, former governor of South Dakota, and future president of the NRA, and later by sportscaster Curt Gowdy, the show featured a catchy theme song with the enticing lyric "Follow me, and find contentment . . ." and a roster of weekly celebrity hunters and anglers, including Bing Crosby, Robert Stack, Andy Griffith, Redd Foxx, Cliff Robertson, and William Shatner. It remained on the air for twenty-one years.

With today's much more diverse cable and online media on offer, a viewer can choose to be informed, entertained, and even titillated by hunting. One can learn how to select camouflaged garb for ambushing turkeys; ways to persuasively "bugle" back and forth with an elk ("tell the elk a story"); methods for quartering and pan-frying a squirrel; or how to deploy a special flashlight designed to highlight a blood trail in the dark. There's a robust trade in over-the-top testosterone-fueled safari videos with such provocative names as *Death Rush: Greatest Hippo Charges Ever*, and cable shows featuring bikini-clad young women shooting alligators, as well as more sober documentary-style accounts of veteran guides tracking bear, bighorn sheep, yak, or black rhino. Many home-produced YouTube hunting videos, with their backwoods settings, modest production values, and all-too-human protagonists, are frequently compelling cinema verité.

The past decade's most talked-about development in hunting television and videos has been the advent of women as the medium's brightest stars. Perhaps this is no surprise; women are the fastest-growing segment of the hunting community, having increased by 20 percent since 2006. Some attribute the increase in part to the popularity of such films as *The Hunger Games* or *Avatar*, in which female leads excel with bow and arrow. Although women's participation in sports overall has grown in the past quarter-century, the hunting industry, always worried about flagging interest in the sport, has gone out of its way to be encouraging. States have stepped up, offering Becoming an Outdoors Woman (BOW) work-shops covering a range of outdoor skills, including archery and the use of shotguns and rifles.

Women new to the sport have generally shown themselves to be as skilled and accomplished as any man, whether with rifle or bow, and the producers of the programs (many of whom are also the stars), cannily exploit their own youth and vivaciousness as well as the freshness of their pioneering role in a male-dominated endeavor. The potent visual impact of an attractive woman with a high-powered weapon confidently bringing down large game is, for the almost exclusive viewership of male hunters, significant to say the least. Melissa Bachman, one of many female hunters with a devoted following, is a former high school pole vault champion and star of *Winchester Deadly Passion*, who uses her toned upper body to good effect by going to full extension with her hunting bow. The appeal of this classic "Diana the Huntress" pose, not lost on magazine illustrators more than a century ago, lives on today on such Internet sites as Bow Hunting Hotties. Yet the programs of Bachman and other sportswomen are also convincing of women's brawn and vigor in the field. Bachman explains her tactics to the camera like the veteran hunter she is as she stalks and kills prey with a variety of weapons; there is no doubt she is capable of butchering the game she kills. "Self-sufficiency," hunter-chef Georgia Pellegrini reminds us, "is the ultimate girl power."

Many of the leading women shooters have sponsorship, endorsement deals, and global reach. Along with Bachman's *Passion*, viewers can choose among *Larysa Unleashed*, with former New York City accountant turned hunter Larysa Switlyk; or follow the pursuits of Michaela Fialova of Czechoslovakia, a.k.a. "the Sexy Hunter"; Eva Shockey, the second woman (after Queen Elizabeth II) to ever grace the cover of *Field and Stream;* or Theresa Vail, Miss Kansas 2013 and a devoted hunter. Switlyk and Fialova have both been featured in competition with other women on the reality TV show *Extreme Huntress*; Shockey became an overnight hero in 2014 when she replied to criticism of her trophy images by creating a line of T-shirts that read "I'll Never Apologize for Being a Hunter."

Because of women's proven acumen at the sport and the tremendous potential they've shown for marketing it, the old hunters' fears that women on hunting trips bring bad luck or scare away game with their incessant chatter have been swept into the gut pile of history. Most of the celebrity women hunters, however, and a few who innocently stumbled into the limelight, have been the targets of a distinct form of harassment—fierce and often obscene online denunciations of their posing in trophy pictures with big game they have felled. *New York Magazine* has dubbed such images of attractive women proudly straddling their trophy animals as "the near-perfect outrage-generating viral item." Trophy photographs of any privileged American smiling proudly alongside a slain creature in Africa can probably be expected to offend someone, but why is special enmity reserved for the female hunter? Is it because women have succeeded at a chivalrous sport long reserved for men; is there revulsion at the evidence that women, the givers and nurturers of life, can also enjoy the thrill of taking it; or simple dismay on the part of male hunters at what some perceive as the glitzy turn their sport has taken?[17]

Bachman, who aroused worldwide contempt for a picture of her posed proudly with her rifle atop a magnificent-looking lion, has been the subject of petitions seeking to ban her from return-ing to South Africa. Texas Tech cheerleader Kendall Jones, at age nineteen, was attacked for her overly chipper manner in posing with and climbing on top of large animal kills she made on safari. (She replied to her critics by printing T-shirts that read "I Hunt. It's Legal. Get Over It.") Big-hearted San Diego bow hunter Jen "Jen the Archer" Cordaro, who started a program called Bring a Kid Hunting, became the focus of a petition on Change.org, claiming, "She brainwashes children into believing that murdering animals is a positive activity in the world . . . She must be stopped." One *Extreme Huntress* winner, Rebecca Francis, received death threats and was labeled "the Beauty Pageant Killer" in April 2015 after an image appeared on social media of her posing far too cutely with a slain giraffe. British comedian Ricky Gervais reposted the image to his 8 million followers with the message, "What must have hap-pened to you in your life to make you want to kill a beautiful ani-mal and then lie next to it smiling?" In general, the shooting of giraffes—stately, gentle, otherworldly herbivores adored by chil-dren (and recently declared to be threatened with extinction)—tends to upset people. Francis, however, insisted that she had been asked to kill the bull giraffe by local villagers because he was very old and they wished to harvest the meat. Many poorer Africans rely on so-called bush meat—meat from nondomesticated mammals, as well as reptiles and birds. A similar explanation came the next year from Ely Gourdin, the father of twelve-year-old Aryanna Gourdin of Utah, who was photographed posing triumphantly atop a giraffe and a zebra she had killed; the child received no fewer than seventy-three thousand hostile online messages, to which her father responded by pointing out the meat from the giraffe had fed "800 orphans."[18]

Lately, the contempt for video huntresses has spread to big game trophy seekers generally. Each year, 18,500 foreign hunters, most of them Americans, pay thousands of dollars to kill African trophy animals in South Africa, Zimbabwe, Zambia, Namibia, and Botswana. In South Africa, the hunting is chiefly on private game ranches, of which there are nine thousand, but elsewhere in Africa, where many hunts are staged on communal lands, residents (theoretically at least) receive a portion of the tourist dollars paid for official permits, and benefit more generally from community services made possible by the revenue derived from the sport. The tourist hunters buy expensive licenses to hunt specific kinds of prey or make direct payments to private game preserves, where their "luck" is better; prices range from $42,000 for an elephant, $9,400 for a hippopotamus, and $6,000 for a sable antelope, to $350 for a warthog. The shooter usually donates the meat to the local village and departs with his or her significant trophy head, horns, or skin. Many such trips are arranged through Safari Club International (SCI) and other trophy-hunting services. Hunters often single out one particular species of animal they want, although many repeat visitors vie to collect what the SCI calls the African Big Five—lion, leopard, elephant, Cape buffalo, and rhino—all of which, with the exception of the buffalo, are threatened with extinction. "Kill all five and your name is enshrined in the record books," Wayne Pacelle, president and CEO of the Humane Society of the United States (HSUS), says sarcastically, "and what much of the world thinks of as a killing spree is, at least in the small fraternity of the Safari Club, treated as a lifetime accomplishment." Additional club competitions include Bears of the World, Cats of the World, and Spiral-Horned Animals of Africa. For advanced hunters, there is the African 29 Club, and also an elite fraternity of SCI World Hunter of the Year awards that go to those who have bagged three hundred species of animals on six continents.[19]

Even when hunters pay the appropriate fees, the desire to bag their animal of choice can lead to poor decision making and the abandonment of the fair chase ethos. The most newsworthy recent hunting scandal was the July 2015 killing of Cecil, a distinctive-looking, black-maned lion lured from its sanctuary in Zimbabwe's Hwange National Park and shot by Walter Palmer, a Minnesota dentist. It was reported that Palmer, who paid $55,000 for the license to kill the lion, and his guide Theo Bronkhorst, attached elephant meat to their truck as bait as they drove outside the boundary of the park. Cecil was tempted by the bait to leave the park, the guide illuminated him with a spotlight, and Palmer shot the animal with an arrow. Badly wounded, Cecil suffered through the night until Palmer found him the next day and killed him with another arrow. When he and Bronkhorst realized the animal was wearing a radio collar, indicating it was part of an ongoing study, they failed to report the incident but, as Pacelle writes, "tried to cover up the killing by moving the collar away from the kill site and then destroying the tracking device."[20]

Zimbabwe initially vowed to extradite Palmer for prosecution, but ultimately did not do so or charge him with a crime. However, as a result of the international outrage over Cecil, who was a favorite of wildlife watchers and tourists who visited Hwange Park, Palmer had to shutter his suburban Minneapolis dental practice and go into hiding. In December 2015, the US Department of the Interior listed African lions as threatened or endangered, hampering American hunters, who had been killing about seven hundred of the animals per year. The airlines KLM, Lufthansa, and Virgin Atlantic already had rules in place forbidding the shipment of animal trophies as baggage, but in the aftermath of Cecil, the HSUS lobbied other airlines to cease allowing their planes to be used as "getaway vehicles for the heist of Africa's wildlife." With media and public pressure on the airlines to act, the no-trophy rule was soon adopted by Delta, American, United, Air France, and many others. This ban thwarted one of the primary rewards of the expensive safari hunt, as between 2005 and 2014 Americans alone had brought home approximately 565,000 animal trophies, chiefly from South Africa. "Trophy hunting," concluded Virgin Atlantic founder Richard Branson, "feels like a relic of a bygone era when people were conquerors, rather than stewards of their environment."[21]

The economic equities as well as the conservation issues involved in big-ticket hunting in Africa would be fairly byzantine under normal circumstances, but become hopelessly complex with the added mix of lucrative poaching, official corruption, national political instability, and the multitude of stakeholders and advocates. For every comment about how trophy hunting in Africa helps manage animal populations and provides funds and food to hungry villagers, other voices claim that too many at-risk animals are killed, that the trophy money is siphoned off by corrupt local officials before it reaches the people, and that the true recipients of the tourist hunters' dollars are the whites who own the private preserves. Many respected conservation groups, such as the World Wildlife Federation and Save the Rhinos International, support trophy hunts. They point to what happened after Kenya banned such sport hunting in 1977: once the animals lost their value as trophies, there was no point in hiring security to protect them, and 60 percent of the large mammals living outside the country's national parks began to disappear, killed by poachers, farmers who consider them a nuisance, or villagers concerned about animal marauding and attacks. But animal protection organizations have praised the Kenyan ban for making the country's animals less skittish around humans, thus improving wildlife watching and other nonhunting tourism, which many reformers favor as a more humane but still profitable alternative to killing Africa's animals.[22]

Encouraging nature photography in lieu of hunting, Pacelle suggests that African wildlife be viewed as "living capital," noting, "You can watch a lion a hundred times . . . 500 times. You can monetize that each time, aggregating more dollars for the economy, for rural communities, for the government. You can shoot the animal only once. Many more people want to just see exotic animals in their natural habitat; it's fewer who insist on shooting them and bringing home a trophy." Kenya has fifty-one national parks and reserves, which create almost $50 million a year in entrance fees and much more in related spending on lodging, food, and guides; such spending supports 300,000 jobs. However, photo tourists tend to flock to the large preserves where there are many animals, while locations deeper in the outback that may hold special appeal to hunters don't receive as many nonshooting Western visitors. Botswana, which banned trophy hunting in 2013, reports that as a result of the ban, wild animals have fewer elephant carcasses to scavenge, and so steal livestock—and even an occasional sleeping human—in greater numbers.[23]

It remains unclear which voices will have the greatest legitimacy and sway in proposing and carrying out long-term decisions affecting African wildlife. The continent's hunting-conservation system is sprawling enough that it may desperately need reform in one locale yet function quite smoothly somewhere nearby. And given the variability of the health of wildlife species, the economic and nutritional stresses on rural African villagers, and the presence of undemocratic regimes in the region, devising uniform policies will be difficult. It is very much an open question as to whether Africa will find the means to rely on alternatives to cash-bearing American hunters.

WHILE IN MONTANA IN 1886 TO GATHER BUFFALO SPECIMENS, William T. Hornaday brought to earth a 1,800-pound bull. In removing the hide, he discovered embedded in it four bullets of different sizes, none of which had come from his gun. It was not uncommon to find a blunted old bullet nestled in the flesh and bones of a buffalo, but Hornaday could not help marvel that the creature had lived for months, perhaps years, with four separate wounds, from four different hunters, and had thus survived as many attempts on its life. As Hornaday's urgent collecting trip had been made in response to a fear the American buffalo would soon be extinct, his appreciation of the tough, walking-wounded buffalo he had felled was that much more poignant.

In general, however, the wounding shot is a shot that is not supposed to happen. The savvy and conscientious hunter knows to hold out for a shot to the heart or lungs of the prey, one that kills quickly and certainly, often within seconds. Sport hunting, after all, cannot really be defended without the utmost effort to give the prey a humane death, a death distinctly unlike the one it would suffer, say, in a slaughterhouse, from starvation, or in the jaws of a predator. The idea of the One Clean Shot is revered and universal, and when things do go wrong in the field, the hunter faces an ethical dilemma. The hunter's code dictates that a wounded animal must be tracked until it is located so that it can be mercifully put down, an obligation that can use up hours and miles and is particularly onerous in fading light, inclement weather, or over difficult terrain. "Perhaps the most unsatisfactory thing we know of is to shoot a moose, and certain that he is wounded mortally, to be forced to follow him a whole day before finding him dead," observed Charles Hallock. It is little wonder that a hunter's prayer implores, "Lord, let me kill clean. And if I can't kill clean, let me miss clean."[24]

To address this unwanted situation, such target ranges as Creedmoor and Wimbledon created "running deer" mechanisms in response to shooters' complaints that stationary target practice inadequately prepared them for shooting accurately in the wild. The deer silhouette was made of sheet iron and suspended from a pivot that gave it a slight dancing motion as it traversed a narrow rail track. To reinforce the desired objective of locating the animal's vitals, shots that banged off the silhouette's "haunches" earned the shooter a punitive fine (and usually the mirth of onlookers). Of course, firing at a moving animal is never ideal. What shooters look for is the clear shot at an animal's broadside, ideally as it is standing still. They aim just behind the shoulder, where the major organs are located. To do this at 100 yards calls for calm precision, a good eye, and a steady trigger finger. If the deer is moving, particularly at an angle or against a camouflaging backdrop, the task is considerably harder, and most hunters will not take such a shot for fear of an inconclusive result.

Ernest Hemingway, on safari in Africa and unable to sleep one long night due to a broken arm, fell into a reverie that his pain must be what a wounded bull elk feels if it takes a bullet in the shoulder but gets away. "In that night I lay and felt it all," he recalled, "the whole thing as it would happen from the shock of the bullet to the end of the business and, being a little out of my head, thought perhaps what I was going through was a punishment for all hunters." He soon recovered, but the troubling fantasy of inhabiting the wounded elk's world haunted him, and he vowed to hunt and kill as cleanly as possible evermore, "and as soon as I lost that ability I would stop." On another occasion, he was nearly incapacitated by regret when, after he shot and missed the vitals of a massive sable bull, the wounded animal bucked and fled, and could not be found. "Tonight he would die and the hyenas would eat him," Hemingway knew,

> or, worse, they would get him before he died, hamstringing him and pulling his guts out while he was still alive . . . I felt a son of a bitch to have hit him and not killed him. I did not mind killing anything, any animal, if I killed it cleanly, they all had to die and my interference with the nightly and seasonal killing that went on all the time was very minute and I had no guilty feeling at all . . . But I felt rotten sick over this sable bull . . . It was my own lousy fault . . . It came from over-confidence in being able to do a thing and then omitting one of the steps in how it is done.[25]

The increasing popularity of bow hunting—up from 8 percent of all hunters in 1970 to 33 percent today—offers what some view as a possible remedy for errant wounding, as the weapon requires that hunters get closer to their prey. Many enjoy what feels like the greater authenticity of the sport, its anachronistic purity, and the fact that it calls for superior tracking, calling, and hunting skills. Professional hunter Rebecca Francis switched from rifle to bow and arrow several years ago because killing animals at long range no longer seemed in the spirit of fair chase. She prides herself on being able to stalk so closely to prey, as she did a herd of elk, "I could see their eyelashes when they were blinking." Few people ever have such a relationship, she notes. "It's you and God's creation. It's as close to God as you can get."[26]

Historically, there has been pushback from gun-bearing hunters as well as animal rights advocates that bow and arrow bring a greater risk of wounding animals who will then die a slow, lingering death. Boone and Crockett Club chairman Samuel Webb worried in 1951 that "the average man is not skillful enough at dispatching an arrow and will make pincushions of the animals," and an Oregon Humane Society officer complained more recently, "They can talk as much as they like about sportsmanship of the bow, but it's too much of the Middle Ages for hunting today." Studies performed in Texas, Michigan, Iowa, Minnesota, and elsewhere since the 1980s concur that deer are wounded by arrows at a far higher rate than those shot by hunters using guns. Wildlife author Adrian Benke explains that because arrows often "rainbow" in their trajectory, unlike bullets, which fly in a more or less linear path, the archer may have greater difficulty placing a shot with a high enough degree of accuracy to ensure instant death. In addition, he writes, animals will "jump the string" upon hearing an arrow's release, thus moving the hunter's "target zone" of heart and lungs, increasing the likelihood of a wounding shot. Also, with the time needed to notch an arrow, draw back, aim, and release, there's less chance of a quick follow-up. Bow hunters dispute these limitations, insisting that with the advent of high-tech compound bows, the speed and lethal accuracy of a hunting arrow have hugely improved. They also note that the greater proximity of hunter to game limits cases of "mistaken identity," in which rifle hunters firing at tremendous distances accidentally kill cows, horses, mules, dogs, or other unintended victims. Some also point out that the precision and maximum stealth required by the sport discourages the abuse of alcohol, and the lewdness and "jackassery" that can characterize other, especially younger, shooters.[27]

Hunters are famously meticulous about measuring and recording the weight and length of trophies, as well as statistics such as the precise number of tines on a deer or elk's antlers (the two leading hunter associations, Boone and Crockett, and Pope and Young, are particularly devoted to this), but there's little data on wounded animals and missed shots, probably because it's a subject no hunter likes to discuss. And of course, there's hardly any accounting of the frequency with which a hunter passes on a target. "Many's the time have I forgotten to shoot, and let the stately deer go by unscathed," wrote journalist Charles Wilkins Webber in 1856. "With such moods upon me, I could not bear to hurt the lovely creatures; it seemed as though a voice of our mother nature chide me: 'Shame! Shame! To slay the beautiful.'"[28]

Most hunters insist that nothing comes close to the experience of the chase and kill, what author Paul Shepard calls the "ecstatic consummation," and that wildlife photography or trail hiking, rewarding as those outdoor experiences may be, can never replace the tradition of the chase, one that so powerfully links man to nature and reinforces his own manhood, ultimately sending him back to the modern world reinvigorated. However, as in Hornaday's example—and this was true for Thoreau, Seton, Leopold, and others—hunters, as they come to know better the world's terrible fragility, and sense their own mortality, often express less desire to put animals to death. They might in retrospect consider fortunate the novice hunter who, gripped by anxiety, simply cannot squeeze the trigger. Buck fever, as it is known, is the tendency, especially of first-timers, to freeze up or shoot badly when confronted with a large, breathing wild animal, which suddenly, preposterously, a hunter is expected to kill. Sometimes a creature's humanlike movements, features, or expression are the inhibiting factor; the majesty of a great antlered stag, king of all he surveys, may also intimidate, or as George Bird Grinnell once reported, so might the

unanticipated yet absolute perfection of a lone mountain goat on a
precipice high overhead, silhouetted against a sunset sky.[29]

IN 1846, SEVENTEEN-YEAR-OLD LEWIS HECTOR GARRARD OF CIN-
cinnati embarked on his first western adventure, his head full of
John Frémont, Frank Forester, Kit Carson, and James Fenimore
Cooper, seeking his own "grand sensation of liberty." Joyfully he
took his first solo hunt in a small wood above a river in Kansas,
where he fired enthusiastically but ineffectually at a woodpecker.
Within moments a heavy hand fell on his shoulder, and Garrard,
startled, looked up into the face of a very unhappy Indian. "You
bad," he said. "You shoot, you scare me."[30]

As Garrard's worried new acquaintance was aware, hunting is
unique among sports in that it holds the gravest of consequences
for nonparticipants. Statistically, the number of hunting accidents
may be low—about one thousand per year, somewhat less than
one hundred of which prove fatal—and proportionately the number is not high compared with other forms of recreation, such as
skiing or scuba diving, but what distinguishes it is its interper-
sonal aspect: hunting mishaps have victims—often other hunters, sometimes passersby, who may suffer serious wounds from
"perpetrators'" sloppiness or ineptitude. Most involve careless
weapon handling, such as shooting oneself in the foot when stepping over a fence or log with a loaded gun, or what some call a
"Dick Cheney," accidentally wounding a hunting companion, as
the former vice president did on a Texas bird shoot in 2006. In the
past two decades, there has been a rise in the number of falls from
tree stands (which increasingly come with safety straps), in which
a hunter dozes off while awaiting a deer and drops as much as 20
feet to the ground. All hunting misfortunes, with their ready-made
tabloid headlines—"Man Blames Remington Defect for Loss of
Leg"; "Dad Shoots Son, Self"; "Guide Caught in Elk Stampede"—
tarnish a sport built on participant safety, and because they tend
to occur in remote places, subsequent explanations or excuses
may be unsatisfying. "Scarcely a week passes," Frank Forester
complained of some of his more careless fellow woodsmen, "but

we see that some unhanged idiot has had, as it is glibly termed, the misfortune to blow out the brains of his sweetheart, wife, or child."[31]

Such mishaps are as old as the chase itself. Peleus, one of the Argonauts and the father of Achilles, mistakenly speared his host while a guest in a ceremonial boar hunt. King William II of England was killed by another hunter's arrow in summer 1100. According to Marco Polo, the apostle Saint Thomas, kneeling in prayer at a monastery in Chennai while on a mission to spread Catholicism in India, was slain in error by an archer firing at a flock of peacocks. Emperor Maximilian I so loved the hunt that he met with his aides and ministers while on horseback, and often, took both rod and gun in hand so as to fish and hunt simultaneously. Such distractions perhaps contributed to the deaths of two of his three wives— Mary of Burgundy, whose horse reared and collapsed on top of her while hunting in March 1482, killing both her and the couple's unborn infant; and, in 1510, Bianca Maria Sforza, known as Bianca of Milan, who also died in a hunting mishap. As Vice President Cheney discovered, for public figures, the scorn for hunting carelessness easily becomes political embarrassment. Such was the case, in the seventeenth century, of George Abbot, the archbishop of Canterbury, who accidentally shot a gamekeeper with a crossbow. Although the Crown pardoned him of the charge of homicide brought by his political rivals, he was humiliated by lingering gossip that so august a figure should have been indulging in hunting, an unseemly recreation for a person of his calling. He spent the rest of his life, friends said, in a state of contrite melancholy.

It is perhaps oddly fitting that America's first great frontier novel, James Fenimore Cooper's *The Pioneers*, opens with a hunting accident. The pompous Judge Marmaduke Temple is boasting of having slain a deer with his superb shooting when it's discovered that, in fact, the truer shot of the hunter Oliver Edwards, companion of Natty Bumppo, was what killed the deer, while the judge's own misdirected fire had wounded young Edwards in the shoulder. The device echoes in Nathaniel Hawthorne's story "Roger Malvin's Burial," in which a father kills his son, having mistaken him for a deer, in expiation for having abandoned his dying father-in-law to the elements in the very same spot years before. Hemingway gives the theme a baroque twist in "The Short Happy Life of Francis Macomber." The eponymous hunter, on an African safari with his wife, is humiliated when he shows fear while pursuing a wounded lion. His wife then sleeps with the handsome safari guide whose quick thinking had rescued Macomber from the lion. Angry with himself for his cowardice and at his helplessness in punishing his wife for her infidelity, Macomber throws himself vigorously into the next day's hunt for Cape buffalo. With the guide's help, he manages to kill several of the animals and, gaining confidence and swagger as he goes, exults aloud that he has discovered the secret to being a successful hunter (and man); it is simply to never be afraid. His wife, however, alarmed by Macomber's change of character, "accidentally" kills him with an errant shot.

The sport's more notorious accidents are those in which innocent bystanders are harmed. These often occur because someone with "trigger itch" ignores hunting's cardinal rule—that one clearly see and identify one's target before firing. On December 1, 2001, Michael Berseth of Chippewa County, Wisconsin, was hunting with his wife and some friends in woods near their home. He shot at a white-tailed deer but was unsure whether he had hit it, and was on his way to investigate when he saw a flash of white through the trees about 60 yards away. He quickly raised his gun and fired again. One of Berseth's neighbors, Deborah Prasnicki, had spent the afternoon wrapping Christmas presents and had taken her two dogs out for a walk; she was wearing a white scarf. Berseth's wife, Jane, attempted to revive Prasnicki with CPR, but to no avail, and he was subsequently charged with second-degree reckless homicide and negligent homicide. At trial, prosecutor Rachel Anderson told the jury that Berseth knew the area, knew there was a road there upon which someone might walk, and had fired carelessly. "Ladies and gentlemen," she reminded them, "when you're hunting with a firearm, you must be sure of your target." The jury, however, impressed by Berseth's expressions of remorse and moved by the fact that Prasnicki's sister, Sharon Jorgenson, had called the death "a tragic accident," voted to acquit. Jane Berseth told a reporter that her husband had gotten rid of his eight hunting weapons. "I just don't have an interest in it anymore," he said, sadly noting of the woman he had killed, "I will always think about her. For the rest of my life I will think about her."[32]

A more infamous case was the 1988 killing of Karen Ann Wood, a thirty-seven-year-old mother of twins living in a rural-suburban area near Bangor, Maine. On the bright, chilly afternoon of November 15, around three p.m., Wood stepped out of her home and strode from her backyard toward some adjoining woods. Sixty yards away, forty-five-year-old hunter Donald Rogerson saw the unmistakable movement of a deer and fired his rifle. Not sure whether he'd hit anything, he pumped another round into the chamber and fired a second time. Wood, who was wearing a pair of white mittens, died instantly, shot in the chest. Authorities later concluded, based on the fact that she'd left her young twin daughters alone in the house, that Karen was headed in Rogerson's direction, possibly because she had heard gunshots and wanted to ask him and other hunters to leave the area. The shooting garnered immediate national attention because of the sharp cultural divide it exposed. Maine, like some other largely rural states (its total population at the time was only 1 million), was experiencing the growth, not entirely welcomed by longtime residents, of sprawling housing subdivisions and exurbs. Karen and her husband, Kevin, were from out of state, and had recently bought their home in Hermon, an area that was still largely countryside. Was it unfortunate but naive of Karen to walk out of her house in hunting season while wearing colors associated with a deer? Many thought so. The *Bangor Daily News* termed Rogerson's errant shooting "a double tragedy," columnist Tom Hennessey suggesting that if Karen Wood "had been wearing one piece of orange blaze clothing, she'd be alive today."[33]

Rogerson, produce manager at Doug's Stop & Save in Bangor, where he had recently been named "Employee of the Year," was well liked in the community. Regular customers at Doug's made it a point to pause and share a few encouraging words. Still, he faced serious consequences. There was talk of his being charged with manslaughter, and his culpability seemed obvious. In addition to the usual error of an overeager hunter failing to visually identify his target, a game warden pointed out that Rogerson had only a buck permit that day, and thus would have needed to identify a suitable deer not only by the color of its tail but by the antlers on its head. But hunting was a deeply entrenched custom in Maine, "a tradition older than voting." In the 1940s, the state had refused to allow a premiere screening of *Bambi*, and at the time of the Wood shooting, as many as 250,000 people, a quarter of the population, had a hunting license. To no one's surprise, on December 5, a grand jury aligned with public sentiment and refused to indict Rogerson. Wood was deemed at greater fault—she was an outsider, unfamiliar with Maine's way of life, who had erred by going into the forest in hunting season without considering her clothing.[34]

The Karen Wood killing showed all that can go wrong when hunting becomes a literal flashpoint in the cultural clash between rural and exurban America. In the case of Chai Soua Vang, a Laotian Hmong immigrant who ran afoul of local custom in northern Wisconsin in 2004, what was revealed was the lethal consequences when hunting misunderstandings occur across lines of language and national culture. Forty-five-year-old Vang, a resident of Minneapolis, was a former National Guardsman and father of six who had gone hunting with several friends. Outside the small town of Meteor, they separated, and Vang soon wandered from public onto private property. Finding an unoccupied tree stand, he climbed into it, and sat cradling his SKS semiautomatic rifle. Soon several white hunters from a nearby cabin, including one of the owners of the property, noticing they had a "tree rat," approached and ordered him away. There had been problems in the past with Hmong hunters, who, due to cultural differences and historical reliance on hunting for subsistence in their native Laos, tended to disregard the fact that even open land in the United States can be private and off-limits.

Vang climbed down from the tree stand as ordered and was walking away when some of the whites began to verbally abuse him, calling him a "chink," "gook," and "Hmong asshole." One made a grab at the hunting license tag on his back, so as to get his number and report him. At trial, Vang said one of the whites fired a shot at his feet, although other evidence and testimony disputes this; what is known is that Vang, furious at being taunted, suddenly wheeled and fired twenty rounds, charging at the whites as they scattered, killing six people, including a man and his twenty-year-old son, and wounding two others. Four of the victims had been shot in the back, some multiple times. Ten months later, Vang was convicted of six counts of first-degree murder and three charges of attempted homicide, and was sentenced to life without parole. In subsequent years, increased efforts have been made by Hmong community service organizations in the Twin Cities to familiarize hunters with the laws of private property, regulations for taking game, and American hunting culture.[35]

HUNTING HAS ALWAYS HAD ITS OTHER, QUIET HUMAN SUFFERERS, and not just the hunter's spouse left behind and alone with the kids for the weekend. Many people have warm memories of being introduced to the sport as children by a thoughtful mentor—a father, uncle, or grandfather—and of learning to adore the rigors of the pastime and to value the time spent outdoors with family and friends. For others, the recollections are not as kind: they recall being wet, cold, and miserable and being made to do things that felt inherently wrong; they did not like thinking of animals as prey nor did they enjoy shooting them, and they hated it all the more because they understood that their disaffection for the sport disappointed people they ordinarily strived to please. Decades later, some recall vividly their horror at having to watch or take part in the skinning and butchering of a hunted animal. Hunting can have, and has had, a disturbing influence on those who see only death and cruelty instead of beauty.

Sir Edwin Landseer, the eminent Victorian painter whose work set the standard for nineteenth-century hunting art, came to be so haunted. The very fascination with the beauty and heroism of the hunt that animated his greatest canvases had as its companion for many years a darker compulsion toward the potential cruelty of the natural world. One troubling later work, *Man Proposes, God Disposes* (1864), depicted ravenous polar bears feeding on the human remains of the lost Franklin British Arctic expedition, a canvas so disturbing that the gallery in which it hangs at the University of London is still in the practice of draping it with a flag when the room is used for exams. Another, a gory 1869 canvas of white feathers, sharp talons and blood, *The Swannery Invaded by Eagles*, was thought in poor taste and was publicly disavowed by none other than Queen Victoria, who had knighted Landseer in 1850 and was one of his most loyal patrons. In 1872, after many years of meticulous artistry around the theme of animal death and nature's pitiless glory, and having battled depression as well as drug and alcohol addiction, he was declared insane by his family. When he died the following year, thousands lined London's streets to watch his funeral cortege pass.

On this side of the Atlantic in 1862, Sarah Lockwood Pardee married William, son of Oliver Winchester, founder of the Winchester Repeating Arms Company and one of the most successful gun salesmen in the world. Her and William's efforts to start a family were frustrated by numerous stillbirths, and their only child, a daughter named Annie, born in 1866, was stricken by an infant wasting condition known as marasmus, and died of starvation after five weeks. In 1880, in rapid succession, the family patriarch, Sarah's father-in-law, Oliver, passed away, followed a half year later by William, from tuberculosis, and then only two months later, by the death of Sarah's mother. Inheriting 50 percent ownership of the Winchester concern, Sarah Winchester was an exceedingly wealthy widow, although an understandably melancholy one, unable to escape the sense she'd been singled out to endure an inexplicable series of personal sorrows. Bereft, and on the advice of friends, she sought the counsel of a Boston psychic medium, a spiritualist who, like others of his faith, "imagined a universe orchestrated by cosmic justice." He shared with Sarah the insight that the Winchester family was cursed by the spirits of all the people and animals ever killed by Winchester rifles, a number that must figure in the hundreds of thousands. Death would claim her next, he warned, if she did not build a home large enough to accommodate all these unhappy souls.[36]

In 1884, she dutifully purchased a sizable farmhouse in San Jose, California, and immediately began making improvements, often at great expense and seemingly to no purpose, to add windows that opened onto walls, steps that led nowhere, balconies that looked across to other balconies, multiple cupolas, and an observation tower. Secret rooms, secret passages, trapdoors, and peepholes abounded. Sarah may have hoped to please the spirits with all these nooks and crannies, or to simply keep them occupied. "The ghosts are clever," she once said. "That's why I have to baffle them." Perhaps such measures brought comfort; more likely she slept fitfully, unable to open her eyes in the dark for fear of being surrounded by spectral deer, rabbits, and murdered Indians. She lived as a recluse, looked after by a small staff of trusted servants, rarely if ever receiving guests. Even Theodore Roosevelt was turned away when, being in the neighborhood, he tried to pay his respects. She continued expanding the house for thirty-eight years, until in 1922 it had grown to two hundred rooms, separated by some two thousand doors. It was then the spirits found her.[37]

Widow Winchester had lived and died in the fear she would never escape hunting and its victims. But some hunters dread the exact opposite—an afterlife that offers no opportunity to indulge in the chase. In the caves of Dordogne, archaeologists have found forty-thousand-year-old hunting relics interred with the dead, apparently on the chance that in the next world the departed encountered hunt-able game. The notion still held appeal in sixteenth-century France, where King Francis I so loved following the stags that he demanded not merely to be taken a-hunting when frail with age, but that once deceased, his remains also be occasionally carted along.

Closer to home, in Kentucky, renowned dog breeder "Wash" Maupin insisted, as he lay dying in January 1868, that he be loaded upon a mattress fitted to a wagon and driven into the field, so that one last time "he might hear the cry of the pack which had meant so much to him through life." And in 1923 came a report that a Mr. Bywaters, following a rousing good hunt over miles of Virginia countryside aboard his beloved horse, Pollock, "fell asleep, doubtless with happy dreams, and never woke again."[38]

Such "pleasant going home" tributes appear with some frequency in the literature of the chase—honoring those fortunate enough to draw their last breaths at life's optimum moment: the close of a successful hunt.

*Epilogue*

# A Complex Inheritance

IT WAS PROBABLY INEVITABLE THAT AMERICA'S FRONTIER WILDER-ness, beckoning exploration and settlement for three centuries, would nurture the modern world's greatest hunting culture. With skills and traditions taught by the land's original inhabitants, the hunt sustained the early arrivals and led pathfinder Daniel Boone into the forests of Kentucky. It became business, folklore, diversion, and sport, and in the 1840s assumed a hybrid character—Native American acumen and the woodcraft of the white backwoods marksman joined by the refinement of the British hunt, but shorn of the latter's exclusiveness and replaced by a democracy of access to forest and marsh. As the nation migrated into cities after the Civil War and distances grew shorter by rail, the chase was redefined as uniquely meaningful recreation, its value to reacquaint and rein-vigorate Americans with the out-of-doors, this time as masters of nature's dominion. In the West, meanwhile, the ability to subsist on wild game was vital; railroad men by the thousands relied on the buffalo ribs and haunches of deer supplied by Buffalo Bill Cody and his kind. The equation of gun and survival, in war and on the fron-tier, helped induce a devotion to armed proficiency—hunting and

marksmanship perceived as components of manhood, prepared-
ness, and martial adequacy. These concerns occasionally took on
risible imagery, such as in a ubiquitous magazine ad showing a citified gent drawing a conspicuously tiny pistol from his pocket to halt
a threatening grizzly. But the hunter with gun (and dog) became
iconic features of the national canvas, compelling a fascination with
the narrative of the hunt and its visual motifs.

With the hunt came its exploitation as a means of profit, and
here the pursuit's excesses first were recognized. As in all such
awakenings, many were slow at first to react to the dangers and
coalesce around ideas that would come to be known as the conservation movement; it was, significantly, the hunters who led the
way, their ethos of fair chase over time beating back market hunting
and poaching to become "the way we hunt." The example of Theodore Roosevelt, a conservationist whose love of the chase was never
in doubt, and the guidance of editor George Bird Grinnell, both
served to broaden conservation's appeal beyond sporting gentlemen. It was "in positing idealized masculine behaviors as 'proper'
[that] elite recreational hunters began to set standards of behavior
for other hunters, cleansing the fields of all who did not abide by the
sportsmen's ethic," historian Louis Warren notes. "This became a
key component of the conservationist movement, for "recreational
hunters lobbied lawmakers to pass game laws that effectively wrote
their own sporting ideals into legal statutes." Jan Dizard, who has
written extensively on the subject, concurs that "the promotion of
conservation went hand in hand with the promotion of the ideal
of the sport hunter—a person who understood the need to practice self-restraint, a person who took pains to become knowledge-
able about wildlife and nature more generally, a person who was
respectful of nature as well as the safety and well-being of others."[1]

The evolution of the American hunter from quasi-savage to
wasteful market shooter to ethically conscious sportsman was significant. Its result is that American hunters by and large accept the
private-public obligations of a managed approach to wildlife, but, to
the chagrin of antihunting forces, are frequently the gatekeepers of
conservationist policies. Their financial contributions in this regard

are as steady as their trigger fingers. The annual expenditures of America's 12.5 million hunters is roughly 3.5 to 5 billion dollars on taxable hunting merchandise, such as guns, ammo, gear, and licenses, of which between 200 to 500 million flows into state coffers for wildlife conservation through the Pittman-Robertson Act. When additional expenses are added in, such as apparel, travel, gas, and meat processing, the expenditures gross more in the range of $20 billion. Many also take a more active role in conservation; in Utah, for example, a state whose wildlife management efforts have been something of a model for other regions, this has included volunteer hunters' air-lifting mountain goats to better habitat, building migration tunnels for deer beneath highways, and creating improved feeding environments for endangered wild game. It is not entirely clear what if anything would replace hunters' interest, dollars, or contribution of time, given the nonhunting community's tendency to be ambivalent or inconsistent in support of wildlife causes.[2]

This has long been a sticking point, for while the man or woman on the street will almost automatically speak in favor of wildlife conservation in the abstract, historic attempts to shift the burden of funding to the nonhunting public have been unsuccessful. Part of the challenge is that multiple perceptions of "conservation" may coexist even among like-minded people, and conservation boards traditionally are dominated by hunters and wise use advocates. In the 1970s, A. Starker Leopold, Aldo Leopold's son and a professor of zoology and biology at the University of California, Berkeley, decried the fact that his state's game commission was composed exclusively of political appointees, hunters, and fishermen and did not therefore reflect accurately the feelings of the general population. He warned that "the country's entire conservation movement, including hunting, will be badly weakened unless we can find a common ground to mobilize the wildlife interests of pro-hunting and anti-hunting groups into a cohesive front." Hunters, however, resisted the idea of including so-called nonconsumptive users on the grounds that people who have never hunted or fished don't truly grasp wildlife issues. "Too many preservationists have the Disney complex," said one. "They look at animals like they are a bunch of cute little playthings . . . and base their decisions on emotions rather than facts."[3]

Outside groups have the most success impacting policy through ballot initiatives that put questions involving hunted species directly to the state's electorate, which represents a far broader spectrum of opinion. Many wildlife supporters cite, as a turning point, a successful 1990 California initiative that attained a ban on mountain lion hunting. Since then, animal protection groups across the country have taken on trophy hunters, factory farms, and other animal-based industries in fifty-one statewide ballot campaigns, winning two thirds of the proposed bans in areas as diverse as bear-baiting, steel-jawed traps, airborne shooting of foxes and wolves, greyhound racing, gestation crates, and cockfighting. Prohunting groups and animal industries have occasionally retaliated by increasing the qualifications for ballot initiatives or denying animal rights forces legal access to the process. The estrangement is painful and unnecessary. "Oddly enough it is hunters, environmentalists, and non-consumptive users of nature who actually have lots in common," observes Bernard Unti of the Humane Society of the United States (HSUS). "All of their interests are threatened by some of the same things—loss of habitat, loss of species, threats to wetlands and watersheds, climate change, not to mention public indifference to these issues, what some call 'nature deficit disorder.' So the need for unity is pretty apparent, but unfortunately, due to fear and misunderstanding, the will is not there."[4]

In the 1990s, several environmental groups sought legislation for a version of Pittman-Robertson that would tax nonhunting outdoor gear, such as knapsacks, tents, kayaks, and Coleman stoves, but the makers of such products hated the idea and support from consumers did not materialize. The Conservation and Reinvestment Act (CARA), an effort in 1999–2000 to get a bill through Congress that would benefit nonprey animals, won the backing of numerous hunting organizations but, embarrassingly, not that of non- or antihunting groups. And despite bipartisan support, the legislation failed to win passage.

As Unti notes, a core problem is that hunters and nonhunters typically distrust and talk past one another. If a person believes it is immoral to shoot and kill an innocent wild animal, no counterargument about hunting as a means of maintaining wildlife population levels or people getting back in touch with nature is likely to resonate. Encouraging both sides to recognize the other's validity and their shared concerns for wildlife would be a huge step forward.

It is, however, hard to imagine a time when hunting will not be controversial. Human pressures on wildlife habitat, changing views on animal rights, arguments over land use, gun rights, food politics, and disagreements about what does and does not constitute sport are bound to keep the issue alive. As much as it may displease those who term hunting "a coward's pastime," such as People for the Ethical Treatment of Animals (PETA), opinion polls suggest that most nonhunters accept sport hunting as a legitimate form of outdoor recreation. With that in mind, many who voice concern about the limitless proliferation of handguns and tactical weapons make an exception for the ownership of hunting rifles and shotguns.

Most of us reside somewhere along a very broad spectrum of hypocrisy regarding animal lives. Hunting for sport may seem abhorrent, but would one make an exception for killing "nuisance" animals, such as coyotes or feral pigs? Perhaps one deplores how cattle are raised for food but covets the feel of leather shoes, belts, or handbags. One might denounce the cruelty of coursing terrified rabbits with hounds, yet relish the excitement of "playing" a tarpon as it fights for its life at the end of a deep sea fishing line. Hunters will argue strenuously that killing a wild animal that has lived free its whole life with a single accurate shot is more humane than buying the meat of a creature that lived its life in a cage, was artificially drugged and fattened, and driven to its death on an assembly line. Of course, the individual who buys meat in a store may not feel directly implicated in taking an animal's life. As Matt Cartmill suggests, "Even the most enthusiastic lover of fried chicken may suspect that there is something wrong with a man who finds recreation in wringing the necks of pullets."[5]

Recreation appears to be the offensive aspect. The raising and slaughtering of food animals may be an atrocity, but for many people it seems a necessary evil in contrast to the deeply offensive idea of killing a living thing for sport. And if killing an animal for sport is unethical, then collecting a trophy of that kill to mount on the wall of the den is also unethical, as is posing afield with a dead animal for a trophy photograph. Even the hunter's traditional rationale that the sport reacquaints man with his inner nature, that "it's good to be a barbarian, [for] you know that if you are a barbarian you are at any rate a man," can't help but come across as self-serving, since an innocent animal life is taken to make each such a moment of personal soul-triumph possible.[6]

To their credit, hunters' groups, aware of the vehemence of "anti" voices and vigilant that bad press not diminish the sport's ranks, counsel members to remain polite but firm when countering criticism. It is a commonly held belief among devoted hunters that outsiders "don't get it," that they fail to understand the reasons hunters take pleasure in their sport or how conscientious they are about its impacts, but that they might begin to comprehend if matters were patiently explained. Not all hunters have that patience, but many do.

Certainly the most aggravating source of conflict comes from so-called "Sabs," well-organized and militant individuals who intentionally sabotage hunts. The modern prototype for this form of activism is the Hunt Saboteurs Association (HAS), founded in England in 1963; after proliferating across the United Kingdom with an initial focus on interrupting deer and fox hunts, the group and its tactics have in recent years expanded to Europe, Canada, and the United States. Its methods of disruption, often carried out by disguised individuals, include the blowing of horns and whistles; playing distracting recordings of barking dogs; firing guns into tree stumps or the ground to frighten away game; and vandalizing or booby-trapping bait stands or tree stands, the latter of which can result in serious injury to a hunter.

While hunters know there's little use arguing with a Sab, they are cognizant of how poor hunting optics hurt their cause, and their organizations often encourage efforts to soften hunting's image, or at least avoid some of its harshest imagery. A 1980s brochure from the Wyoming Game and Fish Department, *Play It Cool and Protect Your Hunting Privileges*, reminds those headed off for a hunting weekend to "be aware of your appearance in public" and avoid "walking into a store or café dressed as a 'Rambo' clone or wearing blood-stained clothes . . . don't display your game in a disrespectful manner. A dead deer strapped to the hood of your pickup with a cigar hanging out of its mouth may seem comical to some, but it is simply crass to many non-hunters."

Jim Willems, a sportsman writing in the Fall 2015 issue of *The Ethic, the Journal of the Pope and Young Club,* warned bow and arrow devotees: "If the only picture you have shows a lot of blood, don't share it. If all you have shows a deer in the back of a truck or hanging like a side of beef, don't share it. If the arrow is still in it, don't share it. Before you post a picture think about how your co-workers, your church friends and even your daughter's friends at school will feel about it." A Boone and Crockett Club tip sheet on the making of hunting videos warns against images of animals shot in the head, writhing in pain on the ground, or dying. Successful hunters should not straddle dead game on camera, use profanity, or appear inebriated; nor should the video include "hero shots" of successful hunters bare-chested or wearing sunglasses."[7]

Such fears are not unfounded. Trophy photos have proven to be the most predictable flashpoint between hunters and those who oppose the sport. Men and women in pursuit of large game, such as deer, elk, or mountain sheep, commonly "shop" for the animal upon which they elect to "spend" their permit; they may watch and wait for days for what they call "the shooter," the impressive, spectacularly antlered specimen they deem worth taking. When the bullet leaves the gun barrel and the desired beast staggers and succumbs, the hunter experiences a rush of adrenalin and emotion as he scrambles to touch and hold his long-awaited prize. Hunting videos are replete with such moments of celebration. But what hunters experience as triumph others view as prima facie evidence of hunting's perversity. Images of a jubilant human crouched next to or straddling a freshly killed animal, posed with its glazed eyes "look-ing" into the camera, strike many nonhunters as a sick attempt to suggest a partnership or brotherhood between killer and prey—winner and loser in a game well played. Joseph Krutch, author of 1957's *A Damnable Pleasure*, likely had such an image in mind as he wrote: "When a man wantonly destroys one of the works of man we call him Vandal. When he wantonly destroys one of the works of God we call him Sportsman."[8]

Perhaps less upsetting, but complex for other reasons, are animals memorialized by taxidermy, the result being a thing with a face that is no longer an animal but could hardly be called an inanimate object. Rachel Poliquen, a scholar who specializes in the subject, notes that "with the exception of big cats, which are often depicted snarling, mouths open, fangs exposed, most sporting trophies are crafted with calm expressions. [Their] docile features are meant to convey acceptance, as if the animal was at peace with its own termination, as if the animal acknowledged that a competition between two heroic rivals had occurred, and even more peculiarly, as if the animal acknowledged that by losing, it proved itself valiant, dignified, and worthy of the hunter's quest." She ponders what becomes of mounted heads when they are no longer with "their hunter-creator." For a trophy head always implies a story about the human who hunted and killed it, and without that context, the trophy becomes an unnerving cipher, and eventually unwanted clutter, as anyone who's ever unearthed a termite-bitten moose head in the attic will attest.[9]

To many, the question of hunting is not just about the barbarity of man, but about the rights of animals. Some dogs hide under the bed at the sound of thunder; most like to stick their head out the window of a moving car; cats are seen to eat cheese-flavored crackers; aquarium fish, skittish though they appear, have been known to enjoy the stroke of a human hand; octopuses squirt water at people they distrust. Individual animals vary in intelligence and behavior, and most species exhibit traits of memory retention and discernment. They play, evince pride or a loss of dignity, and "form lasting friendships, are frightened of being hunted, have a horror of dismemberment, wish they were back in the safety of their den, despair for their mates, [and] look out for and protect the children whom they love," writes animal activist Jeffrey Masson. "They *feel* throughout their lives, just as we do."[10]

To anyone who disputes that animals possess a range of emotions, animal rights advocates are quick to point out that much the same was once assumed about certain "lower peoples," including African Americans, Chinese immigrants, Jews, and Native Americans, well into the twentieth century. Because research in ethology, the study of adaptive animal behavior, is fairly recent, and observations in this field were for many years dismissed as anecdotal and thus impossible to substantiate, we are only beginning to appreciate the many ways nonhumans use clever and sophisticated methods of communication to hunt, migrate, survive, and experience pleasure. "At what point does an anecdotal observation take on scientific relevance?" asks Wyoming wildlife author Jim Hutto. "After ten observations? A hundred? A thousand? Ten thousand? Some scientists would say never; that if it can't be expressed in a number, it's not scientific. But I think, after you've observed these behaviors ten thousands of times, you can draw informed conclusions." The past decade has welcomed a trove of books, largely based on anecdotal evidence, that persuasively extol animal intellect, such as *The Hidden Life of Owls*; *The Genius of Birds*; *The Elephant Whisperer*; *Beyond Words: What Animals Think and Feel*; *The Cultural Lives of Whales and Dolphins*; and *What a Fish Knows*.[11]

We cherish animals, Michel de Montaigne observed, precisely because we see ourselves in them. It's a fascination that predates history. While we will never know if the animals depicted on cave walls were prey or predator, or simply neighbors, "what is clear, and what is significant," writes animal rights author Tom Regan, "is that the first painters were drawn, not to the sun or the moon, nor to the trees or the flowers, not even to the human form as their principal subject matter, but to other-than-human animals." Henry Beston, author of *The Outermost House*, who for a year lived and watched nature from his solitary perch on the beach at Cape

Cod, became inspired by the collective intelligence and "synchronous obedience" of flocks of birds, and began to ponder the "physic relation" that must function among and guide such creatures. "We patronize [animals] for their incompleteness, for their tragic fate of having taken form so far below ourselves. And therein we err, and greatly err," Beston wrote,

> for the animal shall not be measured by man. In a world older and more complete than ours they move finished and complete, gifted with extensions of the senses we have lost or never attained, living by voices we shall never hear. They are not brethren, they are not underlings; they are other nations, caught with ourselves in the net of life and time, fellow prisoners of the splendor and travail of the earth.[12]

If we accept that the dogs or cats or other animals in our care are sentient creatures with a sense of themselves and their surroundings, that they experience pain, loneliness, get bored or irritable, and have cherished places, favorite sensations and activities, why would we deny that such traits occur also in individual elk, wolf, or deer? Buffalo hunters on the Great Plains often commented on the powerful bond that existed between cows and their calves. A cow would risk her life to retrieve a wayward youngster or one who had lost its footing in a rushing stream; the calves in turn would remain by their mother's side even after she had fallen to a bullet, and follow mournfully behind as her remains and hide departed atop a hunter's mule. "There is something touchingly beautiful," concluded the western journalist Rufus B. Sage, "in such exhibitions of natural affection on the part of dumb brutes." As the eponymous four-legged hero concludes in Anna Sewell's *Black Beauty*, "Master said God had given men reason, by which they could find out things for themselves, but He had given animals knowledge which did not depend on reason, and which was more prompt and perfect in its way."[13]

Recent studies of animals' heightened sensory abilities have revealed some of the ways they are *more* sensitive to the world around them than we are. University of Montana biologist Erick

Greene reported in 2011 that despite human hunters' best efforts at stealth, small birds and animals quickly recognize and communicate man's trespassing footfall in the woods, confirming what the Native American bow hunter Ishi pointed out to his disbelieving white friend Saxton Pope a century ago. Such signals, known as seet calls, are heard not only by the sender's own extended family and species but by every bird, squirrel, elk, and deer within earshot, from the forest floor to the treetop canopy. The specific alarm calls can differentiate between threats, such as designating an oncoming ground predator or a circling hawk, and are produced in sounds that few people would recognize.[14]

When men or women, through inquiry or sheer happenstance, pause to observe nonhuman life more closely, they are often moved in powerful ways. This occurs even to those accustomed to taking animal lives. Wilderness author Grey Wolf, who claimed Ojibwe heritage but was actually an Englishman named Archie Belaney, was a devoted trapper until one day, in removing a dead female beaver from a trap, he saw the beaver's two surviving kittens struggling in the water, and pulled them out. "Their almost childlike intimacies and murmurings of affection," he would write, "their rollicking good fellowship with not only each other but ourselves, their keen awareness, their air of knowing what it was all about (made them seem) like little folk from some other planet, whose language we could not quite understand. To kill such creatures seemed monstrous. I would do no more of it."[15]

Similar reactions of shock and delight occurred among residents of Rockaway Township, New Jersey, when in 2014 they began to see a black bear walking upright on its two hind legs through their backyards. Nicknamed "Pedals," the bear, whose front paws appeared to have been deformed or incapacitated through injury, moved as fluidly and as casually as any human in an upright stance, so much so that even from nearby he appeared to be a person, albeit one dressed in a bear suit. Recalling the tradition of mythic beasts that walk upright—such as the werewolf or yeti—the effect of the bear's leisurely foraging was uncanny enough to lead witnesses to think twice about the usual separation between the human and nonhuman. The star of numerous homemade videos posted to YouTube, Pedals became an animal celebrity, attracting a substantial fan base as well as pledges worth more than $20,000 to have him relocated to a wildlife refuge. Unfortunately, as of 2010, New Jersey opened an annual bear hunt, and in October 2016 the upright bear was among 561 black bears shot to death during the weeklong season. Pedals's passing was noted in New York area media with sadness and dismay, although Bob Considine of the New Jersey Department of Environmental Protection, refusing to use the animal's name, chastised those who had "developed an emotional attachment," saying: "It is important to recognize that all black bears are wildlife. They are not pets. They're capable of doing damage, even in a compromised state."[16]

What Pedals's presence reminded us of, as he strolled suburbia's lawns and patios like the protagonist of a John Cheever short story, was that animals are not only like us, *we* resemble *them*. That shouldn't be surprising: we share 90 percent of our genes with chimpanzees, and 65 percent with chickens. And we certainly have no bragging rights as to endurance; humans have been perfecting themselves for 200,000 years; sharks have been around for 400 million. But what do we do with the knowledge that human life has an animal heart, and that individual animals deserve respect as separate beings? Some say that the more we embrace animal rights, the higher we raise the gate of compassion for all living things, including ourselves; and that wiser choices will ultimately be made on a range of biological, environmental, and moral issues. Thoreau, for one, saw the leaving off of eating animals as "the destiny of the human race, in its gradual improvement . . . as surely as the savage tribes have left off eating each other when they came in contact with the more civilized." Is the time approaching when we thank hunting for its several millennia of service to mankind, and with a heartfelt "job well done," bid it adieu? Might such an evolutionary advance usher in a new dawn of human awareness, a more egalitarian world?[17]

Hunters, among many others, might ask why we should cease killing and eating animals when in nature they do the same. The answer is that, cursed with powers of empathy, we know better. Unlike the owl swooping down to clutch a mouse or the wolf flushing a rabbit, we recognize and comprehend our animal victim's fear and pain—an awareness that leaves us no choice but to respond ethically, for ethics begins with the knowledge that our actions potentially harm another. Even then, there are limits to our understanding; for though many people will admit that one of their darkest fears is to be devoured by a wild animal (a vestige of our earliest ancestors' vulnerability to such a fate), we cannot really understand the anxiety a creature of prey experiences as it races for its life from a pursuing predator; nor does a wounded or sick animal share our consciousness that pain is often temporary and may ultimately cease.

Since we know animals can suffer, and that we can survive comfortably on nonmeat foods and stitch our clothing from something other than animal skins, the only ethical choice—and it is admittedly a very hard one—is to refuse to take part in hunting, slaughtering, and consuming of animals. "We are the most dangerous species of life on the planet," Wallace Stegner wrote, "and every other species, even the earth itself, has cause to fear our power to exterminate. But we are also the only species which, when it chooses to do so, will go to great effort to save what it might destroy." What makes the challenge of acting on this possibility so daunting, beyond the well-known intractability of human appetite and habit, is that it presents a supreme moral test, requiring, as Peter Singer says, "greater altruism on the part of human beings than any other liberation movement," for the simple reason that the animals are unable to bring about this transformation on their own.[18]

DEFIANT IN THE FACE OF PUBLIC CRITICISM OF THE SPORT THEY love, and concerned about the success of ballot initiatives brought by antihunting groups and potential restrictions on new hunting technologies, hunters have acted in recent years to bestow upon their pastime the same sort of constitutional guarantee that safeguards the right to bear arms. Vermont is far and away the trailblazer in this regard, having inserted a right to hunt and fish in its constitution in 1777, but nineteen other states, including Minnesota, Texas,

and Virginia, have done so since 1996, as have several others since
2000. In some states, the issue has been advanced by popular referendum. Despite the fact that the number of Americans who hunt
has declined in recent years, down to about 4 to 6 percent today,
support by nonhunters for hunting as an outdoor recreation has
remained steady at 70 percent or above, with 94 percent also saying
they support individuals' "right to hunt" so long as they obey hunting laws. It appears the felicitous words "Opening Day" will not
disappear from our vocabulary anytime soon.[19]

Most hunters still cite the profound restorative pleasure and
sanctity of close contact with nature as their reason for hunting—
some compare the experience to going to church—even as cell
phones and other technology, as well as loss of habitat, have diminished much of the historic solitude and physical challenge of the
chase. They hasten to remind others that their activities serve to sustain wildlife; that they respect game and make every effort to limit
animal pain; and either eat or share the meat of the animals they
slay. They're likely to mention that hunting is a positive social custom that teaches responsibility and builds character in the young.
The old adage "Hunt *with* your boy, and you'll never have to hunt
*for* him" remains a popular meme.

This is not to suggest that boosterish unanimity persists among
all hunters in the face of rapid advances in the sport. Just as the
nineteenth century saw sharp differences over the use of dogs to
drive deer into lakes, so do today's hunters debate the appropriate-
ness of trail cameras that allow hunters to stalk an animal using
photographic surveillance, infrared rifle scopes, hunting over bait,
bleating calls that emulate fawns and other newborns, and the
shooting of exotic animals and game birds raised in canned hunts.
As the global outrage over the killing of Cecil and the taking of
other African trophies suggests, public attitudes toward hunting,
even among hunters, are subject to change. Optimists perceive,
broadly, a growing regard for animal lives, but above all dangles
the ultimate prize, more of a dream, really, of a world in which
people see animals more as fellow citizens than as dinner. As
Thoreau once mused:

Can he who has discovered only some of the values of whale-bone and whale oil be said to have discovered the true use of the whale? Can he who slays the elephant for his ivory be said to have "seen the elephant?" These are petty and accidental uses; just as if a stronger race were to kill us in order to make buttons and flageolets of our bones; for everything may serve a lower as well as a higher use. Every creature is better alive than dead, men and moose and pine trees, and he who understands it aright will rather preserve its life than destroy it.[20]

Would such a change of heart be possible? Even if the implication of the hunting hypothesis is correct and we're forever stuck with instincts and behaviors developed in a time now indiscernible, has not humankind said good riddance to any number of primitive customs our ancestors held dear, or that were once thought useful, from human sacrifices to bleeding the sick? Some believe hunting to be of this category, and that change on an evolutionary scale may someday return it permanently to its past, "an antiquated, even childish pursuit, one that long ago held important meaning but today seems anachronistic." As Hornaday remarked in giving up a sport he loved, "We must awake, and arouse to the new situation, face it like men, and adjust our minds to the new conditions." Of course, real-world influences, not wishes, are what will likely affect the sport's decline—the shift of population into urban areas; a shortage of accessible hunting grounds; the end of the tradition of being able to hunt, with permission, on private property; and the fact that fewer youth under the age of seventeen are being introduced to the sport. This last is crucial, for studies indicate that if people are not exposed to hunting before they leave their teens, they are not likely to take it up as an adult, and without such generational continuity, it will be difficult to sustain the hunting culture. It remains to be seen whether these forces, along with other changes in the sport, might improve dialogue between nonhunting lovers of nature and adherents of the chase.[21]

For it's certain that hunting will endure, at least for the foreseeable future. "Hunting and sporting events involving animals have persisted for a reason," folklorist Simon Bronner reminds us. Insisting the hunt must disappear because it's "an irrational vestige of barbaric rituals" is as oversimplistic as defending it by saying "it has always been done." The vast preparation required, the walking under a heavy pack, the hours spent in concealment, the hunters who come home with no deer but return again and again to the woods, suggest a need for intimacy with nature lodged deep in the human psyche; "something," as Richard Nelson says, "that eludes the grasp of language and might be comprehensible only to those who actually experience the hunt." In the face of intensified public questioning of the sport, and the ever-greater expense and difficulty of hunting well, America's hunting cohort thus grows more serious, more self-aware. Increasingly mindful of their impact on habitat and prey species, more deeply absorbed with strategy and craft, they answer an impulse as timeless as it is ingrained: that the stalking of live prey renders nature spellbinding and consecrates one's own footsteps. Some will always find it so.[22]

# Acknowledgments

I was honored to be the recipient of a National Endowment for the Humanities (NEH) Public Scholar Program grant for 2015–2016, and greatly benefited from and appreciated the NEH's support. I am also grateful to the New York Institute for the Humanities at New York University (NYU), and its director Eric Banks, for providing me with office space through the institute's Fellow-in-Residence initiative. I wish to extend a large thank-you to the very generous Ta-Nehisi Coates; Adam Haslett; Alex Littlefield; David Mikics; David Oshinsky; Jon Weiner; and Brenda Wineapple, who provided references for fellowship applications on my behalf.

Researching any book is a major undertaking, and the assistance provided me by archivists and librarians was invaluable. Rebecca Gebhardt and staff of the Montana State Historical Society in Helena; Kellyn Younggren and her colleagues in the Special Collections Division at the Mansfield Library at the University of Montana in Missoula; and Mary Robinson and associates with the McCracken Research Library at the Buffalo Bill Center in Cody, Wyoming, were all giving of their time, resources, and attention. I'm also indebted to the staff at the Mountain Man Museum in Pinedale, Wyoming, and to director Jerry Pepper at the library of the Adirondack Museum in Blue Mountain Lake, New York. Closer to home, I came to rely on the archivists at the Rare Book Room of the New York Public Library; the New York Historical Society; the Brooklyn Historical Society; the Museum of the City of New York; and the Fales Library and Special Collections at NYU.

Special thanks to Chris Carling, chief marketing officer for Utah's Sportsmen for Fish and Wildlife, who welcomed me to the group's Western Hunting and Conservation Expo 2016 in Salt Lake City. I also wish to acknowledge the kindness of Greg Sheehan, director of the Utah Division of Wildlife Resources, who described the workings of the state's conservation efforts and the role of Pittman-Robertson Funds.

At the Humane Society of the United States, Bernard Unti and Nicole Paquette answered queries and suggested fruitful avenues for research. The HSUS does thoughtful and compassionate work in the fields of animal and wildlife protection, and its bimonthly publication, *All Animals*, is well worth a subscription.

Christopher Shaw, professor at Middlebury College and sage of all things Adirondack, who has visited the remote site of the 1858 Philosophers' Camp, offered valuable insight into the history of that unique event. David Braun and Andy Ward, curators of the G. A. Ruxton Memorial Museum (https:// ruxtonmuseum.org), shared their extensive knowledge of firearms history. In Brooklyn, Jason Dubow, David Mikics, Emily Steiker-Epstein, and Daniel Turbow all lent neighborly support.

I would be remiss in not voicing my appreciation of some of the writers and scholars who have preceded me, and whose works were both guide and inspiration. These include William Benemann, Matt Cartmill, Jan Dizard, Daniel Herman, Karl Jakoby, Richard Nelson, John Reiger, and Mary Zeiss Stange. For western lore and history, I am much indebted to the efforts of Brian Dippie, Richard Slotkin, Robert Utley, and Louis Warren. The story of the mountain men of the Rockies is memorably told in Bernard DeVoto's rollicking classic, *Across the Wide Missouri*. Tovar Cerulli and Lily Raff McCaulou were my informative guides to the world of adult-onset hunting.

At Basic Books, I was fortunate to have the collaboration and superb editorial leadership of senior editor Leah Stecher, as well as the conscientious support of Leah's colleagues: publisher Lara Heimert; project editor Sandra Beris; copyeditor Iris Bass; jacket designer Nicole Caputo; and book designer Jeff Williams. Thank you (again) to my friend, the talented Mindy Tucker, for the author photograph.

Finally, much appreciation to the two people without whose ideas and enthusiasm *The Fair Chase* would never have come to be—its acquiring editor, Alex Littlefield, and literary agent Stephanie Steiker of Regal Hoffman and Associates, who shepherded the project from proposal to completion with intelligence and grace.

# Notes

### Preface

1. The three hunting stories that I have adapted for the Preface are "An Adirondack Bear Capture" by "Glover" in *Forest and Stream*, June 2, 1894; Friedrich Gerstaecker, *Wild Sports in the Far West* (Boston: Crosby, Nichols and Co., 1859), 259–260; and David E Samuel, "Know Hunting: Truth, Lies and Myths," in *The Ethic: The Journal of the Pope and Young Club*, Fall 2015. Each adapted story contains some language taken directly from the original version.

### Introduction: The Nature of the Beast

1. C. K. Brain, "Raymond Dart and Our African Origins," essay in *A Century of Nature: Twenty-One Discoveries That Changed Science and the World*, ed. Laura Garwin and Tim Lincoln (Chicago: University of Chicago Press, 2003), 1; Raymond Dart, "Australopithecus Africanus: the Man-Ape of South Africa," *Nature* 115, February 7, 1925.
2. Quoted in Brain, "Raymond Dart," 4.
3. Sherwood L. Washburn and C. S. Lancaster, "The Evolution of Hunting," in *Man the Hunter*, ed. Richard B. Lee and Irven DeVore (Chicago: Aldine Publishing Co., 1968), 293.
4. See Robert Ardrey, *African Genesis: A Personal Investigation into the Animal Origins and Nature of Man* (New York: Atheneum, 1961); also Robert Ardrey, *The Hunting Hypothesis: A Personal Conclusion Concerning the Evolutionary Nature of Man* (New York: Atheneum, 1976); Matt Cartmill, *A View to a Death in the Morning: Hunting and Nature Through History* (Cambridge, MA: Harvard University Press, 1993), 14.

5. Cartmill, *View to Death*, 18; Mary Zeiss Stange, *Woman the Hunter* (Boston: Beacon Press, 1997), 47.

6. Quote from *Shooting Times*, November 30, 1962, in James Turner, *Reckoning with the Beast: Animals, Pain, and Humanity in the Victorian Mind* (Baltimore: Johns Hopkins University Press, 1980), 14; José Ortega y Gasset, *Meditations on Hunting* (New York: Scribner's, 1972), 139–141.

7. William Cronon, "The Trouble with Wilderness," in *Uncommon Ground: Rethinking the Human Place in Nature* (New York: W. W. Norton, 1995), 87.

8. See Statistica.com, "Hunting in the United States"; US Census Bureau data gathered by the US Fish & Wildlife Service; and "Hunting Statistics," Statistic Brain Research Institute, September 4, 2016. For approval stats, see 2006 American Sportfishing Association (77.6%), 2013 Responsive Management Nationwide Survey (79%), and 2011 National Shooting Sports Foundation (74%).

## Chapter One: The Prophet

1. Frederick E. Pond ("Will Wildwood"), ed., *Frank Forester's Fugitive Sporting Sketches* (Westfield, WI: F. E. Pond, 1879).

2. *New York Herald*, December 14, 1875; see also *The Newark Herbert Association to "Frank Forester," in Memoriam*, May 19, 1876 (Newark, NJ: Ward and Tichenor, 1876).

3. William S. Hunt, *Frank Forester: A Tragedy in Exile* (Newark, NJ: Carteret Book Club, 1933), 11.

4. Ibid., 13.

5. Ibid., 18.

6. Ibid., 22.

7. Henry William Herbert (HWH) autobiographical account sent to Evert Duyciknick, April 10, 1852, in Duyciknick Papers, Manuscript and Archives Collection, NYPL.

8. David W. Judd, ed., *Life and Writings of Frank Forester*, vol. 1 (New York: Orange Judd Co., 1882), 5; HWH autobiographical account.

9. Hunt, *Frank Forester*, 26.

10. Luke White, *Henry William Herbert and the American Publishing Scene* (Newark, NJ: Carteret Book Club, 1909), 6; E. N. Hornby, *Under Old Rooftrees* (Jersey City, NJ: self-published, 1908), 231.

11. Hunt, *Frank Forester*, 34.

12. Herbert to Algernon Herbert, April 7, 1833, in Stephen Earl Meats, "The Letters of Henry William Herbert" (PhD diss.), 1972, NYU Library.

13. Francis Brinley, *The Life of William T. Porter* (New York: D. Appleton and Co., 1860), 83.

14. White, *Henry William Herbert*, 33; first part of quote is from Ralph Waldo Emerson, "The American Scholar," in *Ralph Waldo Emerson: Selected Essays* (New York: Penguin Books, 1982), 102; the second is from Emerson, "Nature," in *Ralph Waldo Emerson: Selected Essays*, 35.

15. Rev. George B. Halsted quoted in *Frank Forester's Sporting Scenes and Characters* (New York: T. B. Peterson & Bros., 1881), 27.

16. Judd, *Life and Writings*, 6.

17. Frederick E. Pond, "Will Wildwood," in *The Life and Adventures of Ned Buntline* (New York: Cadmus Book Shop, 1919), 4–8.

18. HWH quoted in White, *Henry William Herbert*, 6, 28; HWH autobiographical account.

19. Herbert, Henry William, *Tales of the Spanish Seas* (New York: Burgess, Stringer & Co., 1847), 1–3.

20. Randy J. Sparks, "Gentleman's Sport: Horse Racing in Antebellum Charleston," *South Carolina Historical Magazine* 93, no. 1 (January 1992).

21. *Spirit of the Times*, February 1, 1840.

22. Norris W. Yates, *William T. Porter and the Spirit of the Times* (Baton Rouge: Louisiana State University Press, 1957), 80.

23. Frank Forester, *The Complete Manual for Young Sportsmen* (New York: W. A. Townsend Publishing, 1864), 26; Daniel Justin Herman, *Hunting and the American Imagination* (Washington, DC: Smithsonian Institution, 2001), 133.

24. See Pierson v. Post 3, Cai R 175 (1805) N.Y. Lexis 311; Hornby, *Under Old Rooftrees*, 227–228.

25. Emma Griffin, *Blood Sport: Hunting in Britain Since 1066* (New Haven, CT: Yale University Press, 2007); Frank Forester, "A Week in the Woodlands," *American Turf Register*, July 1839.

26. Forester, "A Week in the Woodlands." Tom Draw was modeled after Herbert's real Falstaff-like shooting buddy Tom Ward, a Warwick hotelkeeper and town constable. See Herbert to John Hasbrouck, February 1, 1854, in Meats, "Letters."

27. Forester, "A Week in the Woodlands."

28. White, *Henry William Herbert*, 29.

29. Letter from "J.L.," in *American Turf Register*, February 1840.

30. C. G. Hine, *Woodside: The North End of Newark NJ; Its History, Legends, and Ghost Stories*, chapbook published by the Newark Public Library, 1909.

31. Herbert and the NYSC are described in James B. Trefethen, *An American Crusade for Wildlife* (New York: Winchester Press, 1975), 73–75.

32. *Spirit of the Times*, February 8, 1846.

33. Ibid.

34. Herbert to George B. Halsted, March 19, 1844, in Meats, "Letters"; HWH autobiographical account; Herbert to William George Herbert, May 1858, in Meats, "Letters."

35. Hine, *Woodside*.

36. Ibid., Hornby, *Under Old Rooftrees*, 231.

37. Hornby, *Under Old Rooftrees*, 231.

## Chapter Two: When Good Queen Bess Met Daniel Boone

1. Griffin, *Blood Sport*, 55.

2. Ibid., 71, 79.

3. Herman, *Hunting and the American Imagination*, 20; Griffin, *Blood Sport*, 34.

4. William A. Baillie-Grohman, *Sport in Art: An Iconography of Sport During 400 Years* (London: Ballantyne & Co., 1913), 14.

5. Joseph B. Thomas, *Hounds and Hunting Through the Ages* (Garden City, NY: Garden City Publishing, 1937), 10.

6. James Lipton, *An Exaltation of Larks* (New York: Grossman, 1968), 5. Some of the first lists of hunting nomenclature appeared in the Egerton Manuscripts (1450) and *The Book of St. Albans* (1486). While the terms were in all likelihood rarely used, they were considered a mark of erudition among gentlemen.

7. Cartmill, *View to Death*, 62.

8. Nicholas Cox, *The Gentleman's Recreation* (London: Freeman Collins, 1686), 1–2, 19–20; Michael Kimmel, *Manhood in America: A Cultural History* (New York: Free Press, 1996).

9. Nicholas W. Proctor, *Bathed in Blood: Hunting and Mastery in the Old South* (Charlottesville: University of Virginia Press, 2002), 112.

10. Not surprisingly, given its elaborate rituals, pomp, and costuming, the fox hunt was subject to bemused treatment beginning in 1853 with the publication of *Mr. Sponge's Sporting Tour*, by Robert Smith Surtees, whose tales ridicule the sporting gentry. Surtees's literary gallop through hunt country follows the misadventures of society wannabe Soapey Sponge and his friends Lord Scamperdale, Mr. and Mrs. Jogglebury Crowdey, the twins Miss Jawleyfords, Lady Scattercash, Lord Mudlark, and a butler, Mr. Spigot. Mordant satire in the spirit of Thackeray's *Vanity Fair*, the book likely helped inspire Siegfried Sassoon's *Memoirs of a Fox-Hunting Man* (London: Faber & Gwyer, 1928) as well as P. G. Wodehouse and others who caricatured life in the English countryside.

11. *Forest and Stream*, July 13, 1876; Forester, *Complete Manual*, 25–26, 31–33.

12. Cox, *Gentleman's Recreation*, 19, 21.

13. William Elliott, *Carolina Sports, by Land and Water* (Charleston, SC: Burges & James, 1846), 250–251.

14. Thomas Bangs Thorpe, *The Big Bear of Arkansas* (Philadelphia: T. B. Peterson & Bros, 1846); see Introduction by William Porter, 7.

15. Brinley, *Life of William T. Porter*, 69; Yates, *William T. Porter*, 123; Thorpe, *The Big Bear*, 29.

16. Yates, 203.

17. Ibid., 130, 135, 185.

18. Thorpe, *The Big Bear*, 17–19.

19. Constance Rourke, *American Humor: A Study of Its Character* (New York: Harcourt Brace, 1931), 57.

20. Cartmill, *View to Death*, 74–75.

21. Richard Slotkin, *Regeneration Through Violence: The Mythology of the American Frontier, 1600–1860* (Norman: Oklahoma University Press, 2000), 299; *Forest and Stream*, October 5, 1876.

22. William Faulkner, "The Bear," in *Big Woods: The Hunting Stories* (New York: Vintage 1994), 13.

23. One scam perpetrated on unsuspecting customers was to advertise a captive "guyasticutus," collect admissions, then cry out that the creature had escaped, and in the resulting mayhem flee with the cashbox.

24. Eugene Current-Garcia, "Mr. Spirit and the Big Bear of Arkansas," *American Literature* 27, no. 3 (November 1955).

25. Richard Hofstadter, "America as a Gun Culture," *American Heritage* 21, no. 6 (October 1970).

26. Thomas L. Altherr, "Mallards and Messerschmitts," *Journal of Sport History* 14, no. 2 (Summer 1987).

27. John Filson, *The Discovery, Settlement and Present State of Kentucke* (1784), 65.

28. The moment was immortalized by several artists, most notably woodland painter William T. Ranney in 1849, in his magnificently lit *Daniel Boone's First View of Kentucky*. Abraham Lincoln, namesake grandfather of President Lincoln, went

through the Cumberland Gap with Boone in 1779; Robert Morgan, *Boone: A Biography* (Chapel Hill, NC: Algonquin Books, 2008), 60.

29. Filson, *Discovery, Settlement*, 80–81.

30. Quoted in Morgan, *Boone*, 430; Filson, despite using the techniques Boone had taught him to evade encounters with hostile Indians, vanished and was presumed killed in early October 1788 near the Great Miami River, when his surveying team was ambushed by a marauding band of Miami Indians. In the chaos of the attack, the whites split up. He was never seen again; Emerson, "Nature," 43.

31. George Pierson, *Tocqueville in America* (Gloucester, MA: P. Smith, 1959), 386; quoted in M. J. Heale, "The Role of the Frontier in Jacksonian Politics: David Crockett and the Myth of the Self-Made Man," *Western Historical Quarterly* 4, no. 4 (October 1973).

32. Heale, "Role of the Frontier"; *The Crockett Almanac 1840*, vol. 2.

33. *New York Herald*, May 9, 1836.


CHAPTER THREE: "LET US HAVE MORE HUNTERS"

1. Ralph Waldo Emerson, *The Early Years of the Saturday Club, 1855–1870* (Boston: Houghton Mifflin, 1918), 74, 421–425.

2. Ibid., 31; Louis Agassiz, *The Structure of Animal Life: Six Lectures Delivered at the Brooklyn Academy of Music in Jan/Feb 1862* (New York: Scribner's, 1866), 90.

3. Emerson, *Early Years*, 171; Moorfield Storey, *Ebenezer Rockwood Hoar, a Memoir* (Boston: Houghton, 1911), 148.

4. Letter from William J. Stillman to Charles Norton Eliot, September 1857, quoted in Ida G. Everson, "William J. Stillman: Emerson's 'Gallant Artist,'" *New England Quarterly* 31, no. 1 (March 1958); C. H. Burt, *The Opening of the Adirondacks* (New York: Hurd & Houghton, 1865), 13.

5. William Stillman, "The Philosophers Camp: Emerson, Agassiz, Lowell and Others in the Adirondacks," *Century Magazine*, August 1893.

6. Emerson, *Early Years*, 174.

7. Emmons was later invited to undertake a similar survey by the state of North Carolina; he was there when the Civil War erupted, and it was believed he was kept from returning home by Confederate authorities; he died at Brunswick, North Carolina, on October 1, 1863. See Albert Donaldson, *A History of the Adirondacks*, vol. 1 (New York: Century Publishing Co., 1921), 37.

8. Charles R. Simpson, "The Wilderness in American Capitalism: The Secularization of Nature," *International Journal of Politics, Culture and Society* 5, no. 4 (Summer 1992).

9. Philip Terrie, *Contested Terrain: A New History of Nature and People in the Adirondacks* (Syracuse, NY: Syracuse University Press, 1987), 45; Joel T. Headley, *The Adirondack, or, Life in the Woods* (1849), 2, 7.

10. Headley, *Adirondack*, 73.

11. William H. H. Murray, *Adventures in the Wilderness, or Camp Life in the Adirondacks* (Boston: Fields, Osgood and Co., 1869), 84.

12. Cox, *Gentlemen's Recreation*, 3; Henry David Thoreau, entry for November 12, 1851, *The Writings of Henry D. Thoreau: Journal*, vol. 3, ed. John C. Broderick (Princeton, NJ: Princeton University Press, 1981), 109; Henry David Thoreau, *The Maine Woods* (Princeton, NJ: Princeton University Press, 1972), 99.

13. Henry David Thoreau, vol. 2, *Writings, Walden Edition* (1906), 235–236; quoted in Charles R. Anderson, "Thoreau Takes a Pot Shot at 'Carolina Sports,'" *Georgia Review* 22, no. 3 (Fall 1968).

14. Emerson, *Early Years*, 73; Stillman, *Century*.

15. Elliot Gorn and Warren Goldstein, *A Brief History of American Sports* (Urbana: University of Illinois Press, 2013), 85.

16. Stillman, "Philosophers Camp."

17. Murray, *Adventures*, 10–11.

18. Edward J. Blankman, review of Murray's *Adventures in the Wilderness* in *New York History* 52, no. 4 (October 1971); William H. H. Murray, *Park-Street Pulpit: Sermons*, 279–280, quoted in David Strauss, "Toward a Consumer Culture: 'Adirondack Murray' and the Wilderness Vacation," *American Quarterly* 39, no. 2 (Summer 1987).

19. Thomas Wentworth Higginson, "Saints and Their Bodies," *Atlantic Monthly*, March 1858.

20. William H. H. Murray, *Music Hall Sermons*, second series, 124–125; in Strauss, "Toward a Consumer Culture."

21. Murray, *Adventures*, 11; Charles R. Simpson, "The Wilderness in American Capitalism: The Secularization of Nature," *International Journal of Politics, Culture and Society* 5, no. 4 (Summer 1992); James J. Walsh, MD, quoted in the journal *Woods and Waters* 14, no. 2 (Summer 1901), 8.

22. Murray eventually went back to his family's home in Guilford, Connecticut, and on March 3, 1904, died in the same room in which he had been born.

23. Warder H. Cadbury, *Arthur Fitzwilliam Tait: Artist in the Adirondacks* (Newark, DE: University of Delaware Press, 1986), 23.

24. Cadbury, *Arthur Fitzwilliam Tait*, 45, 81, 86.

25. Charlotte S. Rubinstein, "The Early Career of Frances Flora Bond Palmer," *American Art Journal* 17, no. 4 (Autumn 1985).

26. Currier & Ives published 7,500 lithographs during the firm's seventy-two years, 1834–1906. See Harry T. Peters, *Currier & Ives: Printmakers to the American People* (Garden City, NY: Doubleday, 1942).

## Chapter Four: Hunters Go West

1. Washington Irving, *A Tour on the Prairies* (London: John Murray, 1835), 69–70, 125, 241.

2. Ibid., 267, 276–277.

3. Ibid., 202.

4. Ibid., 235–236.

5. Ibid., 260–261.

6. Frederick Gerstaecker, *Wild Sports in the Far West* (Boston: Crosby, Nichols and Co., 1859), 43, 102–103, 120.

7. Ibid., 337.

8. Ibid., 276–277.

9. Ibid., 344.

10. Francis Parkman, *The Oregon Trail* (New York: Oxford University Press, 1996), 212.

11. William Benemann, *Men in Eden: William Drummond Stewart and Same Sex Desire in the Rocky Mountain Fur Trade* (Lincoln: University of Nebraska Press, 2012), 9.

12. More recently, the term *two spirit* has come into use in the Native American vocabulary; Benemann, *Men in Eden*, 9.

13. Benemann, *Men in Eden*, 87.

14. Ibid., 159–160.

15. Marshall Sprague, *A Gallery of Dudes* (Boston: Little, Brown, 1966), 22.

16. Bernard DeVoto, *Across the Wide Missouri* (Boston: Houghton Mifflin, 1947), 363.

17. Alvin Josephy, "First 'Dude Ranch' Trip to the Untamed West," *American Heritage* 7 (February 1956).

18. Ibid.

## CHAPTER FIVE: FOREST AND STREAM

1. *Forest and Stream*, June 4, 1874.

2. John F. Reiger, *American Sportsmen and the Origins of Conservation* (New York: Winchester Press, 1975), 39–40. As property values rose and fewer acres were available for hunting, some hunt clubs with extensive property became country clubs, welcoming golf links as an alternative gentlemanly pursuit. The first major golf tournament in America was held in 1894.

3. Terrie, *Contested Terrain*, 63.

4. Charles Brumley, *Guides of the Adirondacks: A History* (Utica, NY: North Country Books, 1994), 307.

5. *Forest and Stream*, February 3, 1876.

6. Charles Hallock, *An Angler's Reminiscences: A Record of Sport, Travel and Adventure* (Cincinnati: Sportsmen's Review Publishing Co., 1913), 2–3, 26.

7. Hallock, *Angler's Reminiscences*, 1; Hallock, "Wild Cattle Hunting on Green Island," *Harper's Weekly*, July 1860.

8. *Raleigh Progress* (undated) quoted in *New York Times*, October 11, 1863; *Hamilton (Bermuda) Royal Gazette*, September 22, 1863.

9. Hallock, *Angler's Reminiscences*, 2–3; *Forest and Stream*, August 14, 1873.

10. Monica Rico, *Nature's Noblemen: Transatlantic Masculinities and the Nineteenth-Century American West* (New Haven, CT: Yale University Press, 2013), 5–6.

11. Hallock, *Angler's Reminiscences*, 3; Charles E. Whitehead, "Game Laws," in Boone and Crockett Club, *Hunting in Many Lands* (New York: Forest and Stream Publishing Co., 1895), 358; Richard Nelson, *Heart and Blood: Living with Deer in America* (New York: Alfred A, Knopf, 1997), 104.

12. *Forest and Stream*, August 21, 1873.

13. Charles Hallock, *The Fishing Tourist* (New York: Harper and Brothers, 1873), 76; in Terrie, *Contested Terrain*, 70.

14. Hallock quoted in Gloria Swanson, "A Man Named Hallock" (originally published 1979), retrieved from City of Hallock website, http:// www.hallockmn.org.

15. *Forest and Stream*, August 26, 1875.

16. William Cole, "The Fresh Air Fund," *New England Magazine*, July 1896.

17. These included *The Scalp Hunters; or, Romantic Adventures in Northern Mexico* (1851); *The Boy Hunters; or, Adventures in Search of a White Buffalo* (1853); *The Quadroon; or, a Lover's Adventures in Louisiana* (1856); and *The Headless Horseman: A Strange Tale of Texas* (1866).

18. Kimmel, *Manhood in America*, 168; Forbush wrote *The Boy Problem* (1901); R. M. Ballantyne, *The Gorilla Hunters* (London: Thomas Nelson & Sons Ltd., 1908), 51–52.

19. Eric Mogren, "Miss Billie's Deer: Women in Bow Hunting Journals, 1920–1960," *Journal of Sport History* 40, no. 2 (Summer 2013),

20. "Miss Diana in the Adirondacks," *Harper's Weekly*, August 25, 1883.

21. *Boston Herald*, July 19, 1903; quoted in Ralph H. Lutts, *The Nature Fakers: Wildlife, Science, and Sentiment* (Charlottesville: University of Virginia Press, 2001), 19; Hallock, *Angler's Reminiscences*, 28.

22. Frances M. Roe, *Army Letters from an Officer's Wife* (New York: D. Appleton & Co., 1909), 42.

23. Mary Zeiss Stange, "Women and Hunting in the West," *Magazine of Western History* 55, no. 3 (Autumn 2005); *Russell County Record*, October 14, 1975, in Eugene D. Fleharty, *Wild Animals and Settlers on the Great Plains* (Norman: University of Oklahoma Press, 1985), 199.

24. Maxine Benson, *Martha Maxwell: Rocky Mountain Naturalist* (Lincoln: University of Nebraska Press, 1986), 81–86.

25. Mary Dartt, *On the Plains, and Among the Peaks* (Philadelphia: Claxton, Remsen, and Haffelfinger, 1879), 137.

26. *Forest and Stream*, June 29, 1876.

27. Michael Punke, *Last Stand: George Bird Grinnell, the Battle to Save the Buffalo, and the Birth of the New West* (New York: HarperCollins, 2007), 137.

### CHAPTER SIX: ARMING THE HUNTERS

1. Henry William Herbert, *Frank Forester's Field Sports of the United States and the British Provinces of North America* (New York: Stringer and Townsend, 1848), 29; cited in Russell Gilmore, "Another Branch of Manly Sport: American Rifle Games, 1840–1900," in *Guns in America: A Historical Reader*, ed. Jan Dizard, Robert Merrill Muth, and Stephen P. Andrews Jr. (New York: New York University Press, 1999), 105.

2. John W. Oliver, *A History of American Technology* (New York: Ronald Press, 1956), 277–278.

3. Sid Sidlo, "Technology in the Civil War: Cold Steel," *Cleveland Civil War Roundtable*, 2008, http://www.cleavelandcivilwarroundtable.com/articles.

4. Editors of *Outdoor Magazine*, *The Story of American Hunting and Firearms* (New York: McGraw-Hill, 1959), 109.

5. *Forest and Stream*, July 20, 1876.

6. Edward Ordway, "Reminiscences," *Annals of Wyoming*, June 1929, 153–155.

7. Letter appears in William Hosley, *Colt: The Making of an American Legend* (Amherst: University of Massachusetts Press, 1996), 12.

8. Gilmore, "Another Branch of Manly Sport," 118n16.

9. Frederick Whittaker, "The Story of Creedmoor," *Galaxy*, August 1876. The founders' criticisms certainly would not have extended to the sharpshooter units active in the war, such as those led by US General Hiram Berdan, which distinguished themselves at Gettysburg and other key battles. The allegations of poor rifle skills would seem to be at odds with the war's enormous death toll—620,000 in an 1889 estimate; 750,000 in a more recent survey—but two thirds of those losses are attributed to dysentery, typhoid, and other diseases. See Guy Gugliotta, "New Estimate Raises Civil War Death Toll," *New York Times*, April 2, 2012.

10. *Forest and Stream*, June 18, 1874; italics are mine.

11. *Chicago Inter-Ocean*, November 28, 1873.

12. *New York Herald*, September 27, 1874.

13. "The Story of Creedmoor," *Galaxy*, August 1876.

14. *New York Herald*, September 27, 1874; *New York Times*, September 28, 1874.

15. The Wild West 1883 program citation appears in Louis S. Warren, *Buffalo Bill's America: William Cody and the Wild West Show* (New York: Alfred A. Knopf, 2005), 223.

16. Edward Thomas, "Trap-Shooting in the Old Days," *Outing Magazine*, June 1915; see also *Forest and Stream*, August 26, 1875.

17. Zulma Steele, *Angel in Top Hat* (New York: Harper and Brothers, 1942), 218–219.

18. Hallock, *Angler's Reminiscences*, 26; *New York Times*, January 28, 1872; Steele, 219–221.

19. Steele, *Angel in Top Hat*, 223; *New York Herald*, January 10, 1872.

20. *New York Times*, January 12, 1872.

21. Larry McMurtry, *The Colonel and Little Missie: Buffalo Bill, Annie Oakley, and the Beginning of Superstardom in America* (New York: Simon & Schuster, 2005), 43–44.

## CHAPTER SEVEN: SPORTSMAN'S PARADISE

1. *San Francisco Chronicle*, March 31, 1878; collected in H. C. Merriam, *Way Out West: Recollections and Tales* (Norman: University of Oklahoma Press, 1969), 123–126.

2. *Kinsley (Kansas) Graphic*, May 18, 1877; *Saline County Journal*, April 17, 1873; Hutchinson *News*, January 23, 1873; Russell County *Record*, November 29, 1877; *Dodge City Times*, August 11, 1877; *Hays City Sentinel*, May 31, 1876; *Ford County Globe*, May 6, 1879; *Saline County Journal*, March 20, 1873—all in Fleharty, *Wild Animals and Settlers*, 148–151.

3. Richard Irving Dodge, *The Hunting Grounds of the Great West* (London: Chatto and Windus, 1877), 111–112; "Find Bones of Moose and Man," *Kevin (MT) Review*, July 19, 1923.

4. Arthur M. Stiles, "A Bear Hunt in Montana," *National Geographic Magazine*, February 1908.

5. Casper W. Whitney, "The Cougar," in *Hunting in Many Lands*, 238–254; see also Theodore Roosevelt, *The Wilderness Hunter* (New York: G. P. Putnam's, 1900), 32–33.

6. Roger D. Williams, "Old Times in the Black Hills," in Daniel Boone and Davy Crockett, *American Big Game Hunting* (New York: Forest and Stream, 1893), 79–83.

7. George Bird Grinnell, "In Buffalo Days," in Boone and Crockett, *American Big Game Hunting*, 196–197.

8. Letter from George Armstrong Custer (GAC) to Elizabeth Custer (EC), June 21, 1876, in Elizabeth B. Custer, *Boots and Saddles or, Life in Dakota with General Custer* (Lincoln: University of Nebraska Press, 2010, originally published 1885), 37–38, 312.

9. G. F. Ruxton, *Life in the Far West* (New York: Harper and Brothers, 1849), 97.

10. Dodge, *Hunting Grounds*, 342–343. The omnivorous diet of many natives made an exception for the wild turkey, which they disdained to eat as they feared doing so would make them run from their enemies, as the turkey does.

11. William E. Holston, "The Diet of the Mountain Men," *California Historical Society Quarterly* 42, no. 4 (December 1963); Lewis H. Garrard, *Wah-to-yah, and the Taos Trail* (Palo Alto, CA: American West Publishing, 1968), 22.

12. Dodge, *Hunting Grounds*, 173, 178.

13. DeVoto, *Across the Wide Missouri*, 36.

14. Benemann, *Men in Eden*, 157–158, 202; David L. Brown, *Three Years in the Rocky Mountains* (Cincinnati: Eberstadt and Sons, 1950), 8; in Benemann, 199.

15. See Randolph B. Marcy. *Thirty Years of Army Life on the Border* (New York: Harper and Brothers, 1866), 286; Bridger quoted in Charles G. Worrman, *Gunsmoke and Saddle Leather: Firearms in the Nineteenth Century American West* (Albuquerque: University of New Mexico Press, 2005), 59.

16. Brian Dippie, *Nomad: George Armstrong Custer in Turf, Field, and Farm* (Austin: University of Texas Press, 1980), x; *Forest and Stream*, September 10, 1874; *Forest and Stream*, February 18, 1886.

17. Elizabeth Custer, *Boots and Saddles*, 37–38.

18. Marcy, *Thirty Years*, 283–284.

19. *Turf, Field, and Farm*, September 21, 1867.

20. Robert Utley, *Cavalier in Buckskin: George Armstrong Custer and the Western Military Frontier* (Norman: University of Oklahoma Press, 2001), 137.

21. *Turf, Field, and Farm*, October 12, 1867; Gen. G. A. Custer, *My Life on the Plains* (New York: Sheldon & Co., 1874), 47.

22. Custer, *My Life on the Plains*, 50.

23. *Turf, Field, and Farm*, September 21, 1867.

24. Dippie, *Nomad*, xvi. Ironically, it was to Benteen that Custer dashed a last urgent message for assistance at the Little Big Horn; Benteen's inability to comply in time to avert the ensuing slaughter has long been a point of contention among Last Stand scholars; McMurtry, *Colonel and Little Missie*, 69; Utley, *Cavalier in Buckskin*, 61.

25. George Bird Grinnell, *Passing of the Great West: Selected Papers of George Bird Grinnell*, ed. John Reiger (New York: Winchester Press, 1972), 121.

26. Custer and Fetterman quoted in David Smits, "The Frontier Army and the Destruction of the Buffalo, 1965–1883," *Western Historical Quarterly* 25 (1994), 312–338.

27. Utley, *Cavalier in Buckskin*, 176.

28. *New Orleans Times*, February 14, 1872.

29. Donald E. Worcester, "Spotted Tail: Warrior, Diplomat," *The American West* 1, no. 4 (Fall 1964).

30. William Cody, *The Life of the Honorable William F. Cody, Known as Buffalo Bill* (Hartford, CT: Frank E. Bliss, 1879), 62–63, 162; William T. Hornaday, *The Extermination of the Buffalo* (Washington, DC: Smithsonian Institution, 2002, originally published 1889), 478.

31. *New York Herald*, January 14, 1872; McMurtry, *Colonel and Little Missie*, 77; Elizabeth Custer, *Boots and Saddles*, 106.

## CHAPTER EIGHT: BUFFALO BILL, CUSTER, AND TEXAS JACK

1. Turner, *Reckoning with the Beast*, 267–269.

2. *New York Herald*, September 2, 1843. Barnum's Hoboken scam may have inspired the expression that one who gets taken has been "buffaloed."

3. Frederick Eugene Pond, *The Life and Adventures of Ned Buntline* (New York: Cadmus Book Shop, 1919), 57, 70; Donaldson, *History of the Adirondacks*, vol. 2, 120.

4. Cody, *Life of the Honorable*, 263.

5. Henry Eugene Davies, *Ten Days on the Plains* (New York: Crocker & Co., 1871), 26. The honor was rescinded in 1916 when the military decided that civilians who had been given the award in the nineteenth century, even those attached to army units, were not eligible. However, the medals were restored in 1989.

6. Cody, *Life of the Honorable*, 320.

7. Custer, *My Life on the Plains*, 44.

8. *New York Herald*, June 30, 1874.

9. Grinnell, *Passing of the Great West*, 100.

10. Utley, *Cavalier in Buckskin*, 117; Letter from GAC to EC, September 28, 1873, in Elizabeth Custer, *Boots and Saddles*, 298; letter from GAC to EC, September 6, 1873, in Elizabeth Custer, *Boots and Saddles*, 292; *Turf, Field, and Farm*, October 17, 1873.

11. Donald F. Danker, ed., *Luther North, Man of the Plains: Recollections of Luther North, 1856–1882* (Lincoln: University of Nebraska Press, 1961), 184–188.

12. Grinnell, *Passing of the Great West*, 81–82.

13. Utley, *Cavalier in Buckskin*, 140. The following year the find was certified by the Newton-Jenney Geological Expedition; *Chicago Inter-Ocean*, cited in Peter Cozzens, "US Grant Launched an Illegal War Against the Plains Indians," *Smithsonian*, November 2016; Utley, *Cavalier in Buckskin*, 134.

14. Michael Griske, *The Diaries of John Hunton* (Westminster, MD: Heritage Books, 2005), 64–69.

15. Quoted in Robert Utley, *Frontier Regulars: The United States Army and the Indian, 1866–1891* (New York: Macmillan, 1973), 247.

16. Eugene M. Fusco, "The Last Hunt of General George A. Crook," *Montana Magazine* 12, no. 4 (Autumn 1962).

17. Quoted in Utley, *Frontier Regulars*, 239; James T. King, "General Crook at Camp Cloud Peak," *Journal of the West* 11, no. 1 (January 1972). The Indians refer to the fight that day as "the Battle Where the Girl Saved Her Brother," after an incident in which a young Cheyenne brave, Comes in Sight, had his horse shot out from under him, leaving him stranded in the whites' line of fire; his sister Buffalo Calf Woman swooped in on a horse and bade him jump aboard behind her; they both survived.

18. *New York Tribune*, July 6, 1876; *Forest and Stream*, November 2, 1876; Chief Washakie quoted in Henry P. Walker, "George Crook: The Gray Fox, Prudent, Compassionate Indian Fighter," in *Montana: Magazine of Western History* 17, no. 2 (Spring 1967).

19. *New York Herald*, August 3, 1876.

20. Paul Magid, *The Gray Fox: George Crook and the Indian Wars* (Norman: University of Oklahoma Press, 2015), 265; *New York Tribune*, July 6, 1876.

21. Magid, *Gray Fox*, 262; *New York Herald*, August 3, 1876.

22. Quoted in King, "General Crook."

23. Bourke diary, July 9 and 10, 1876; in King, "General Crook"; Grinnell, *Passing of the Great West*, 125.

24. In 1881 appeared a landmark book—Helen Hunt Jackson's *A Century of Dishonor*—which issued a sweeping moral indictment of America's treatment of native tribes since the colonial period. The author sent a copy to every member of Congress. It inspired the establishment of Indian rights groups and created extensive public sympathy for the natives and their vanishing way of life. See McMurtry, *Colonel and Little Missie*, 79.

25. *New York Herald*, July 23, 1876.

26. Cody, *Life of the Honorable*, 343–344.

27. Cody's triumph was soon tempered by the unhappy news that on August 2 his friend Wild Bill Hickok had been murdered while gambling in Deadwood, South Dakota. Superstitious poker players to this day refer to the cards Wild Bill was holding when he was shot—a pair of aces and a pair of eights—as the "dead man's hand."

28. Theodore Roosevelt, *Hunting Trips of a Ranchman* (New York: Modern Library, 1998), 38.

29. McMurtry, *Colonel and Little Missie*, 163–164.

30. *New York World*, May 13, 1894; Roger Hall, *Performing the American Frontier, 1870–1906* (New York: Cambridge University Press, 2004), 146.

31. Warren, *Buffalo Bill's America*, 540. See also Kevin Brownlow, *The War, the West, and the Wilderness* (New York: Alfred A. Knopf, 1978), 223–234.

## CHAPTER NINE: THE NEW TYPE OF GOODNESS

1. Bridger quoted in Norman B. Wiltsey, "Jim Bridger: He-Coon of the Mountain Men," *Montana* 6, no. 1 (Winter 1956).

2. A. J. Vaughn to Cumming, July 1856, in *Historical Society of Montana* 10 (1940), Helena, 192.

3. Sprague, *A Gallery of Dudes*, 148, 153.

4. William Thomas Dunraven, *Past Times and Pastimes*, vol. 1 (London: Hodden and Stoughten, 1922), 140.

5. Peter Pagnamenta, *Prairie Fever: British Aristocrats in the American West, 1830–1890* (New York: W. W. Norton, 2012), 179.

6. Ibid., 253.

7. British land ownership data is in Roger V. Clements, "British Investment and American Legislative Restrictions in the Trans-Mississippi West, 1880–1900," *Mississippi Valley Historical Review* 42, no. 2 (September 1955).

8. Badeau quoted in Pagnamenta, *Prairie Fever*, 286; *Forest and Stream*, January 14, 1975. McCarty was said to have returned to England to further organize the expedition, but there's no evidence that the hunt was ever conducted, at least not on the scale McCarty had proposed.

9. Michel de Montaigne, "On Cruelty," in *Montaigne: Selected Essays* (New York: Modern Library, 1949), 182.

10. Turner, *Reckoning with the Beast*, 9.

11. Jeremy Bentham, *Introduction to the Principles of Morals and Legislation* (1780); quoted in Peter Singer, *Animal Liberation: A New Ethics for Our Treatment of Animals* (New York: Ecco Books, 2002), 203.

12. Griffin, *Blood Sport*, 99.

13. Harriet Ritvo, *The Animal Estate: The English and Other Creatures in the Victorian Age* (Cambridge, MA: Harvard University Press, 1987), 131. The story of Bobby may be apocryphal in some of its details; stray dogs often lived in graveyards in England and Europe because they were fed and cared for there.

14. Charles Darwin, *The Descent of Man* (London: John Murray, 1871), 1.

15. Voltaire quoted in Virginia Morell, *Animal Wise: The Thoughts and Emotions of Our Fellow Creatures* (New York: Crown, 2013), 10.

16. Robert Sullivan, *Rats: Observations on the History & Habitat of the City's Most Unwanted Inhabitants* (New York: Bloomsbury, 2005), 79; *New York Tribune* cited in Steele, *Angel in Top Hat*, 298.

17. C. C. Buel, "Henry Bergh and His Work," *Scribner's Monthly*, April 1879.

18. Ibid.

19. Steele, *Angel in Top Hat*, 3.

20. Anna Sewell, *Black Beauty* (1877; repr., New York: Penguin Books, 2011), 189.

21. Buel, "Henry Bergh and His Work."

22. W. H. Goetzmann, *Exploration and Empire: The Explorer and the Scientist in the Winning of the American West* (New York: History Book Club, 1993), x.

23. Cody, *Life*, 280.

24. Discoveries of the secret past of the region also included finding evidence of mysterious past human civilizations. In 1874, western artist and photographer William Henry Jackson produced the first photographic images of the ruins at Mesa Verde, Colorado, site of the residence of cliff-dwelling Ancestral Puebloan peoples in the twelfth and thirteenth centuries.

25. Garrard, *Wah-to-yah*, 10.

26. Elliott, *Carolina Sports*, 232.

27. Grinnell, "In Buffalo Days," 159–160.

28. Hornaday, *Extermination of the Buffalo*, 430.

29. Grinnell, "In Buffalo Days," 163, 164.

30. Punke, *Last Stand*, xvi; quotations from the diary of buffalo hunter Matt Clarkson appear in Fleharty, *Wild Animals and Settlers*, 67.

31. *Rocky Mountain News*, December 21, 1873, in Fleharty, *Wild Animals and Settlers*, 259.

32. John G. Neihardt, *Black Elk Speaks: Being the Life Story of a Holy Man of the Oglala Sioux* (Lincoln: University of Nebraska Press, 1961), 181.

33. C. Kingsley, *South by West* (London: W. Isbister, 1874); in Fleharty, *Wild Animals and Settlers*, 255–256; E. N. Andrews, "A Buffalo Hunt by Rail," *Kansas Magazine*, May 1873, quoted in David A. Dary, *The Buffalo Book: The Full Saga of the American Animal* (Chicago: Sage Books, 1974), 87.

34. Fleharty, *Wild Animals and Settlers*, 185; see *Junction City Weekly Union*, April 25, 1869.

35. Sheridan and Sherman quoted in Smits, "Frontier Army," 312–338; see also Punke, *Last Stand*, 129–130.

36. C.M. Beeson, "A Royal Buffalo Hunt," *Transactions of the Kansas State Historical Society* 10 (1907–1908); Col. Henry Inman, *Buffalo Jones' Adventures on the Plains* (1899; repr., Lincoln: University of Nebraska Press, 1970, orig. pub. 1899), 91; Sitting Bull quoted in Smits, "Frontier Army," 338.

37. Harper's quote appears in *42nd Cong 2nd session Appendix to the Congressional Globe*, 179.

38. Letter from Hazen to Bergh, January 20, 1872; printed in *New York Times*, January 26, 1872; letter from Brackett to Bergh, January 30, 1872, printed in *New York Times*, February 7, 1872; letter from Bergh to Loring Moody, March 5, 1872, in Rare Books and Manuscripts Collection, Boston Public Library, as quoted in Lisa Mighetto, *Wild Animals and American Environmental Ethics* (Tucson: University of Arizona Press, 1991), 47.

39. Undated article in *Denver Tribune*, reprinted in *New York Times*, July 22, 1872; W. E. Webb, *Buffalo Land* (Philadelphia: Hubbard Brothers, 1872); graphic appears between pages 124–125 in Dary, *Buffalo Book*; *Forest and Stream*, December 25, 1873.

40. Henry Fairfield Osborn, "Preservation of Our Wild Animals," address to Boone & Crockett Club, January 23, 1904, quoted in Thomas L. Altherr, "The American

Hunter-Naturalist and the Development of the Code of Sportsmanship," *Journal of Sports History* 5, no. 1 (Spring 1978).

41. Punke, *Last Stand*, 130–131; see *Congressional Record*, March 10, 1874, 2106–2109; William T. Hornaday, *The Extermination of the American Bison* (Washington, DC: Smithsonian Institution, 1889), 513–521.

42. Douglas Brinkley, *The Wilderness Warrior: Theodore Roosevelt and the Crusade for America* (New York: HarperCollins, 2009), 150–151; Punke, *Last Stand*, 135–139.

43. Grinnell, "In Buffalo Days," 194–195.


CHAPTER TEN: "TIMES HAVE CHANGED, AND WE MUST CHANGE ALSO"

1. George Bird Grinnell and Theodore Roosevelt, *Trail and Camp-Fire: The Book of the Boone and Crockett Club* (New York: Forest and Stream Publishing, 1897), 332; quoted in Brinkley, *Wilderness Warrior*, 84; see also Brinkley, 31.

2. Kimmel, *Manhood in America*, 182.

3. Roosevelt, *Wilderness Hunter*, xiii; in Brinkley, *Wilderness Warrior*, 184.

4. *Forest and Stream*, July 2, 1885.

5. Reiger, *American Sportsmen*, 118.

6. Theodore Roosevelt, "Outdoor Pastimes of an American Hunter," quoted in Theodore Roosevelt, *Works*, vol. 3 (New York: Charles Scribner's and Sons, 1926), 125.

7. Memo about Origins of the Boone & Crockett Club, by Grinnell, March 11, 1919, in Box 3, Folder 3, B & C papers, Mansfield Library, University of Montana; *Forest and Stream*, January 17, 1889; in Reiger, *American Sportsmen*, 121.

8. Du Chaillu, Paul, *Explorations and Adventures in Equatorial Africa* (London: John Murray, 1861), 394.

9. Brinkley, *Wilderness Warrior*, 282.

10. Pat D. Tucker, "Buffalo in the Judith Basin," in Merriam, *Way Out West*, 69.

11. Hornaday, *Extermination of the Buffalo*, 464.

12. Inman, *Buffalo Jones' Adventures*, 47–48; in frustration, some later researchers tried introducing yaks into the cross-breeding mix, to no helpful effect. See Alvin Howard Sanders, "The Taurine World," *National Geographic*, December 1925; in Dary, *Buffalo Book*, 276. In the twentieth century, researchers with more sophisticated technology successfully created a mixed breed known as beefalo, which its promoters claim, is not only good-tasting but lower in cholesterol than domestic cattle.

13. Grinnell, "Last of the Buffalo"; Hornaday's 1889 survey found 1,091 buffalo. The numbers rose gradually, thanks to the cultivation efforts. In the United States and Canada, by 1910, there were 2,000; by 1922, approximately 12,000; in 1933, about 22,000; in 1972, roughly 30,000; and about 100,000 as of 1990 (Dary, *Buffalo Book*, 287).

14. Dary, *Buffalo Book*, 241.

15. William T. Hornaday, *Our Vanishing Wildlife* (New York: New York Zoological Society, 1913), x, 206.

16. *Forest and Stream*, June 19, 1876.

17. Baird quoted in Proctor, *Bathed in Blood*, xii; Scott E. Giltner, *Hunting and Fishing in the New South: Black Labor and White Leisure After the Civil War* (Baltimore: Johns Hopkins University Press, 2008), 50; *Forest and Stream*, October 19, 1882; Hornaday, *Our Vanishing Wildlife*, 113.

18. Anders Stephanson, *Manifest Destiny: American Expansion and the Empire of Right* (New York: Hill & Wang, 1996), 86; Remington quoted in Kimmel, *Manhood in America*, 151; Hornaday, *Our Vanishing Wildlife*, 100–102.

19. Quoted in Karl Jakoby, *Crimes Against Nature: Squatters, Poachers, Thieves, and the Hidden History of American Conservation* (Berkeley: University of California Press, 2001), 91; Punke, *Last Stand*, 150.

20. Nelson, *Heart and Blood*, 103.

21. *Forest and Stream*, March 13, 1883; Punke, *Last Stand*, 156.

22. H. Duane Hampton, *How the US Cavalry Saved Our National Parks* (Bloomington: Indiana University Press, 1971), 55; see also Jakoby, *Crimes Against Nature*, 97.

23. *Forest and Stream*, May 5, 1894.

24. Ibid.

25. *Forest and Stream*, March 24, 1894; *Forest and Stream*, May 5, 1894.

26. Jakoby, *Crimes Against Nature*, 126–127; *Forest and Stream*, May 5, 1894. Other than having some possessions confiscated and being briefly banned from the park, Howell managed through technical legalities to avoid punishment for his crime. Two years after the incident, he was hired by the park to help apprehend poachers. See Hampton, *How the US Cavalry*, 128–129.

27. Robin W. Doughty, *Feather Fashions and Bird Preservation: A Study in Nature Protection* (Berkeley: University of California Press, 1975), 17.

28. "Good King Henry," as his subjects called him for his many good works, has another avian connection; he is believed to have been the first public figure to publicly promise "a chicken in every pot."

29. Doughty, *Feather Fashions*, 23; Nancy C. Unger, *Beyond Nature's Housekeepers: American Women in Environmental History* (New York: Oxford University Press, 2012), 95.

30. Frank Graham, *Audubon Ark: A History of the National Audubon Society* (New York: Alfred A. Knopf, 1990), 23.

31. Ibid., 14.

32. Hornaday, *Our Vanishing Wildlife*, 106.

33. Turner, *Reckoning with the Beast*, 175; Hornaday, *Our Vanishing Wildlife*, 144–146.

34. Hornaday, Our Vanishing Wildlife, 4.

35. Lisa Mighetto, "Muir Among the Animals," *Sierra Magazine*, March/April 1985, 71–72.

36. David E. Blockstein and Harrison B. Tordoff, "Gone Forever: A Contemporary Look at the Extinction of the Passenger Pigeon," *American Birds* 39, no. 5 (Winter 1985).

37. *Forest and Stream*, February 11, 1886.

38. Celia Thaxter, "Woman's Heartlessness," *Audubon Society News*, Boston, 1886.

39. Graham, *Audubon Ark*, 12. The plume cause attracted several nationally known women nature writers, including Mabel Osgood Wright and Florence Merriam Bailey, founder of the Smith College Audubon Society, as well as her brother, C. Hart Merriam, head of the U.S. Department of Agriculture's Bureau of Ornithology and Mammology and the man whose positive review of Theodore Roosevelt's book *The Summer Birds of the Adirondacks* (1877) did much to establish the young Roosevelt's reputation as a naturalist. While a great deal of previous bird study involved examining stuffed specimens, Florence Merriam Bailey emphasized the value of observing

them in life; her book *Birds Through an Opera Glass* (1889), which describes seventy species of birds, helped set the standard for the modern American bird field guide. Suggesting that people use binoculars instead of a shotgun when out looking for wild birds, she went on to author several more regional handbooks, including the invitingly titled *A-Birding on a Bronco* (1896). Bailey's titles joined a veritable rush of books about how humans could relate to wild winged creatures: *Citizen Bird*, by Mabel Osgood Wright and Elliot Cues; *Bird Neighbors*, by Neltje Blanchan; *Bird World*, by Jenny Stickney; *Bird Friends*, by Gilbert Trafton; and *How to Have Bird Neighbors*, by S. Louise Patterson. See Peter J. Schmitt, *Back To Nature: The Arcadian Myth in Urban America* (New York: Oxford University Press, 1969), 34–36.

40. *Ellsworth (KS) Reporter*, May 3, 1877, in Fleharty, 134.

41. Jack E. Davis, *An Everglades Providence* (Athens: University of Georgia Press, 2009), 187.

42. Frank Chapman, ed., *Bird-Lore: Official Organ of the Audubon Societies*, vol. 7 (New York: Macmillan, 1905), 218.

CHAPTER ELEVEN: WHAT IS NATURE, WHAT IS MAN?

1. Jakoby, *Crimes Against Nature*, 119.

2. Tony Perrottet, "Where Was the Birthplace of the American Vacation?" Smith sonian.com, April 2013. By the 1870s, a number of sanitaria had been opened near Saranac Lake, the most notable one by Edward Livingston Trudeau, a doctor who had himself been cured of consumption by a stay at Paul Smith's Hotel in 1873.

3. Reiger, *American Sportsmen*, 84.

4. The army imported two boatloads of camels and tried them as beasts of burden in New Mexico and Arizona in the 1850s. The experiment was abandoned during the Civil War.

5. David Lowenthal, *George Perkins Marsh: Prophet of Conservation* (Seattle: University of Washington Press, 2015), xxxi.

6. First annual report of the Commissioners of State Parks of the State of New York, transmitted to the legislature May 15, 1873, Senate document 102, 1873 (Albany, NY: Weed, Parsons, 1874), 21, cited in Terrie, *Contested Terrain*, 63–64.

7. Charles Simpson, "The Wilderness in American Capitalism: The Secularization of Nature," *International Journal of Politics, Culture and Society* 5, no. 4 (Summer 1992).

8. *Forest and Stream*, February 18, 1886.

9. *Forest and Stream*, November 4, 1875; Steele, *Angel in Top Hat*, 227.

10. *Boonville Herald*, April 15, 1897; quoted in Jacoby, "Class and Environmental History: Lessons from 'The War in the Adirondacks,'" *Environmental History* 2, no. 3 (July 1997).

11. New York Forest Commission, annual report for the year ending September 30, 1888, Albany, Troy Press, 1889, xi; see also Jacoby, "Class and Environmental History"; and Forest, Fish, and Game Commission, Annual Reports of the Commissioner for 1907, 1908, and 1909 (Albany, NY: J. B. Lyon, 1910), 367; *Forest and Stream*, June 22, 1876; *New York Times*, September 22, 1903.

12. *New York Herald*, September 21, 1903.

13. Ibid.

14. Ibid.

15. Turner, *Reckoning with the Beast*, 162.

16. Ernest Thompson Seton, Introduction to *Wild Animals I Have Known* (Toronto: W. Briggs, 1898).

17. Cartmill, *View to a Death*, 150; John Burroughs, "Real and Sham Natural History," *Atlantic Monthly*, March 1903.

18. Long quoted in Ralph Lutts, *The Nature Fakers: Wildlife, Science, and Sentiment* (Charlottesville: University of Virginia Press, 1990), 113.

19. Kimmel, *Manhood in America*, 186; *Field and Stream*, July 1898; the new magazine would in 1930 buy and absorb *Forest and Stream*.

20. Theodore Roosevelt, *Ranch Life and the Hunting Trail* (New York: Century & Co., 1888), 83; quoted in Kimmel, *Manhood in America*, 183–184; Stephanson, *Manifest Destiny*, 105; Muir quoted in Mighetto, *Wild Animals*, 33; Pamela Haag, *The Gunning of America: Business and the Making of American Gun Culture* (New York: Basic Books, 2016), 261; Haag, *Gunning of America*, 455n.

21. *New York Times*, December 6 and 7, 1915. West and his allies returned fire by mentioning that Seton had argued against putting the Pledge of Allegiance in the *Boy Scout Handbook*, that his wife was a suffragist, and that Seton himself, British by birth and raised in Canada, was technically not even an American citizen. All were damning charges in the patriotic moment of 1915. Roosevelt quoted in David Macleod, *Building Character in the American Boy: The Boy Scouts, the YMCA, and Their Forerunners, 1870–1920* (Madison: University of Wisconsin Press, 2004), 178; *New York Times*, March 12, 1911.

22. Roosevelt quoted in Macleod, *Building Character*, 179–181.

23. John MacKenzie, "The Imperial Pioneer and Hunter and the Masculine Stereotype in Late Victorian and Edwardian Times," in J. A. Mangan and James Malvin, eds., *Manliness and Morality: Middle Class Masculinity in Britain and America, 1800–1940* (New York, St. Martin's Press, 1976), 181.

24. MacKenzie, *Imperial Pioneer*, 184. Research in the 1970s found that the badly damaged skulls of many newly discovered *Australopithecus* bore signs of fang marks from animal predators—leopards, saber-toothed tigers, and even hyenas—suggesting to investigators that these early prototypical men were themselves taken as prey by carnivores. See C. K. "Bob" Brain, *The Hunters or the Hunted: An Introduction to African Cave Taphonomy* (Chicago: University of Chicago Press, 1981), 271; Peter Capstick, *Death in the Long Grass: A Big Game Hunter's Adventures in the African Bush* (New York: St. Martin's Press, 1977), 14.

25. Capstick, *Death in the Long Grass*, 79, 87, 92.

26. Ritvo, *Animal Estate*, 31.

27. Capstick, *Death in the Long Grass*, 7. The lions were slain by Colonel J. H. Peterson, an engineer who was helping to build the railway, and whose memoir of the experience, *The Man-Eaters of Tsavo* (1907), became a best-selling and popular account of the confrontation between man and animal in Africa.

28. Jay Kirk, *Kingdom Under Glass: A Tale of Obsession, Adventure, and One Man's Quest to Preserve the World's Greatest Animals* (New York: Henry Holt, 2010), 194.

29. Totals appear in the pamphlet "Welcome Home, a dinner to Theodore Roosevelt, June 22, 1910 at Sherry's NY," Rare Book Room, New York Public Library.

30. Brinkley, *Wilderness Warrior*, 702–703; Bernard DeVoto, *Mark Twain in Eruption* (New York, Harper's, 1940), 10–18; Roosevelt quoted in Patricia O'Toole, *When Trumpets Call: Theodore Roosevelt After the White House* (New York: Simon & Schuster, 2005), 67.

31. Kirk, *Kingdom Under Glass*, 187.

32. Gregg Mitman, *Reel Nature: America's Romance with Wildlife on Film* (Seattle: University of Washington Press, 2009), 7.

33. Robert O. Easton, *Lord of the Beasts: The Saga of Buffalo Jones* (Tucson: University of Arizona Press, 1961), 165, 182.

34. Easton, *Lord of the Beasts*, 170.

35. Mougey letter of February 3, 1914, in Easton, *Lord of the Beasts*, 203–204.

36. Brownlow, *War, West, and Wilderness*, 468.

37. Martin Johnson was killed, and Osa injured, in the crash of a commercial plane in California in 1937; Osa carried on alone, returning to Africa to investigate pygmies. Her ghostwritten autobiography, *I Married Adventure*, was a blockbuster best seller in 1940. She later hosted television's first wildlife and safari show, *Osa Johnson's Big Game Hunt*.

38. Jedediah Purdy, "Environmentalism's Racist History," *New Yorker*, August 13, 2015; Pamela Newkirk, *Spectacle: The Astonishing Life of Ota Benga* (New York: HarperCollins, 2016), 44.

39. Phillips Verner Bradford and Harvey Blume, *Ota Benga: The Pygmy in the Zoo* (New York: St. Martin's Press, 1992); 158–169.

40. *New York Times*, September 9, 1906.

41. *New York Times*, September 11, 1906; Newkirk, *Spectacle*, 32.

42. *New York Times*, September 11, 1906.

43. Ibid.; Newkirk, *Spectacle*, 51.

44. *New York Times*, September 23, 1906; *New York Times*, September 25, 1906; *New York Times*, September 18, 1906.

45. Hornaday quoted in Bradford and Blume, *Ota Benga*, 220; see also Brinkley, *Wilderness Warrior*, 661.

46. Saxton Pope, "Ishi's Method of Hunting," from *Hunting with Bow and Arrow* (1923), 2–3; see http://www.archery library.com/books/pope/hunting with a bow and arrow, 2–3.

47. For an account of Joseph Knowles's adventure, see Richard O. Boyer, "The Nature Man," *New Yorker*, June 18, 1938.

## CHAPTER TWELVE: THE TROPHIC CASCADE

1. Pinchot is credited with introducing the term *conservation*, in 1907; he was inspired by the title *conservator* used by British officers in India.

2. Aldo Leopold, "Thinking Like a Mountain," in *Sand County Almanac and Other Writings on Conservation and Ecology* (New York: Library of America, 2013), 114–115.

3. Aldo Leopold, *Game Management* (1933; Madison: University of Wisconsin Press, repr. 1986), 423.

4. Leopold, quoted in Marybeth Lorbiecki, *Aldo Leopold: A Fierce Green Fire* (New York: Oxford University Press, 1999), 94.

5. Lorbiecki, *Aldo Leopold*, 84–85.

6. Charles Dudley Warner, "A-Hunting of the Deer," originally published in the *Atlantic* in 1878, also appears in *The Complete Writings of Charles Dudley Warner*, ed. Thomas R. Lounsbury, vol. 6 (New York: American Publishing Co., 1904). It was Warner, a close friend of Mark Twain's, who said, "Everybody complains about the weather, but nobody does anything about it," a quip often attributed to Twain.

7. Cartmill, *View to a Death,* 180–181. For discussion of a lost scene from the film in which Bambi and his father come upon the body of a dead poacher in the forest, which the stag uses to instruct Bambi that man is vulnerable as much as the forest animals, see Beverley Driver Eddy, *Felix Salten: Man of Many Faces* (Riverside, CA: Ariadne Press, 2010), 206, 314.

8. "Anti-Hunting a Wasteful Issue," *Montana Outdoors,* August 1977.

9. Tovar Cerulli, *The Mindful Carnivore: A Vegetarian's Hunt for Sustenance* (New York: Pegasus Books, 2012), 170; Al Cambrone, *Deerland: America's Hunt for Ecological Balance and the Essence of Wildness* (Guilford, CT: Lyons Press, 2013), 35.

10. Cerulli, *Mindful Carnivore,* 170.

11. Jan Dizard, *Going Wild: Hunting, Animal Rights, and the Contested Meaning of Nature* (Amherst: University of Massachusetts Press, 1994), 118; see also Jan Dizard, *Mortal Stakes: Hunters and Hunting in Contemporary America* (Amherst: University of Massachusetts Press, 2003), 193–194.

12. Editors of *Outdoor Magazine, The Story of American Hunting and Firearms* (New York: Outdoor Life/McGraw-Hill, 1959), 151; *New York Times,* September 18, 2016; ADC Fact Sheet, August 1990, USDA.

13. *New York Times,* September 18, 2016; Cleveland Amory, *Man Kind? Our Incredible War on Wildlife* (New York: Harper & Row, 1974), 340–341.

14. "Cecil 2: Trophy Hunting America's Lion," PDF publication from the Humane Society of the United States and Humane Society International, February 3, 2016.

15. Morell, *Animal Wise,* 266; Wayne Pacelle, *The Humane Economy: How Innovation and Enlightened Consumers Are Transforming the Lives of Animals* (New York: William Morrow, 2016), 200.

16. Edward Umfreville, *The Present State of Hudson's Bay* (London: Charles Stalker, 1790), 167–168; see Calvin Tomkins, "Ursus Horibilis," *New Yorker,* May 7, 1966.

17. Clipping from unnamed newspaper dated June 13, 1941, "Grizzly Bear Hazard to Men of Early-Day West," "bears" vertical clippings file, Montana Historical Society.

18. See "Grizzly Bears and the Endangered Species Act," National Park Service website, http://nps.gov/yell/learn/nature/bears.htm; Enos A. Mills, *Grizzly: Our Greatest Wild Animal* (Boston: Houghton Mifflin, 1919), 284; quoted in Michael J. Dax, *Grizzly West* (Lincoln: University of Nebraska Press, 2015), 25.

19. Cronon, "Trouble with Wilderness," 78–81.

## CHAPTER THIRTEEN: THE GUNS OF AUTUMN

1. W. G. Williams, ed., *Cicero, The Letters to His Friends,* vol. 2 (Cambridge, MA: Harvard University Press, 1929), 6; cited in Cartmill, *View to a Death,* 41–42.

2. Kimberly K. Smith, *Governing Animals: Animal Welfare and the Liberal State* (New York: Oxford University Press, 2012), xv; Cronon, "Trouble with Wilderness," 87; Sue Donaldson and Will Kymlicka, *Zoopolis: A Political Theory of Animal Rights* (New York: Oxford University Press, 2011), 24.

3. Yuval Noah Harari, "Industrial Farming Is One of the Worst Crimes in History," *Guardian,* September 25, 2015.

4. Donaldson and Kymlicka, *Zoopolis,* 252–253; Singer, *Animal Liberation,* 216.

5. Donaldson and Kymlicka, *Zoopolis,* 252.

6. Intelligence Squared debate, "Hunters Conserve Wildlife," held in New York, May 4, 2016, 41.

7. Plutarch essay on flesh eating, in *The Ethics of Diet: A Catena of Authorities Deprecatory of the Practice of Flesh-Eating,* ed. Howard Williams (London: F. Pitman, 1883), 47–48; Kathy Freeston, "Shattering the Meat Myth," *Huffington Post*, July 12, 2009.

8. Stange, *Woman the Hunter*, 120; Cerulli, *Mindful Carnivore*, 52; Barbara Kingsolver, *Prodigal Summer* (New York: HarperCollins, 2001), 322–323.

9. Kristen A. Schmitt, "More Women Give Hunting a Shot," *National Geographic*, November 4, 2013; Nelson, *Heart and Blood*, 281.

10. Richard Hofstadter, "America as a Gun Culture," *American Heritage* 21, no. 6 (October 1970). The individual self-defense interpretation of the amendment would not be acknowledged by the US Supreme Court until 2008, in *District of Columbia v. Heller*.

11. *New York Times*, September 7, 1975; *New York Daily News*, September 11, 1975.

12. Undated column circa September 1975 by Harriet Van Horne, syndicated TV critic, in antihunting clippings file, Mansfield Library, University of Montana; *New York Times*, September 14, 1975.

13. Harlon Carter, "Why Men Hunt," in *Arizona Wildlife Trophies* (Phoenix: Arizona Wildlife Federation, 1975), 15.

14. *New York Times*, October 8, 2017.

15. Jim Zumbo, "Assault Rifles for Hunters," see "Hunting with Zumbo," http://www.razoreye.net/mirror/zumbo/zumbo_assault_rifles/html.

16. Blaine Harden, "'Terrorist' Remark Puts Outdoorsman's Career in Jeopardy," *Washington Post*, February 24, 2007.

17. Kerry Howley, "Hunting Rebecca Francis," *New York Magazine*, July 27, 2015.

18. *San Diego Union Tribune*, January 29, 2015.

19. Pacelle, *Humane Economy*, 226; "Trophy Hunting by the Numbers," HSUS PDF, February 2016.

20. Pacelle, *Humane Economy*, 224.

21. James R. Ryan, "Hunting with the Camera," in *Animal Spaces: New Geographies of Human-Animal Relations*, eds. Chris Philo and Chris Wilbert (London: Routledge, 2000), 206; Pacelle, *Humane Economy*, 228; Richard Branson cited in *Africa Geographic Newsletter*, August 17, 2015.

22. Howley, "Hunting Rebecca Francis"; Pacelle, *Humane Economy*, 223.

23. Intelligence Squared debate, "Hunters Conserve Wildlife," held in New York, May 4, 2016, 24–25; Pacelle, *Humane Economy*, 223.

24. Hallock, *Angler's Reminiscences*, 50.

25. Ernest Hemingway, *The Green Hills of Africa* (New York: Scribner's, 1935), 147–148, 271–272.

26. Howley, "Hunting Rebecca Francis," and *New York Daily News*, July 30, 2015; statistics from US Fish & Wildlife Service 2011 Survey.

27. Samuel Webb to Allan Ames, April 2, 1951, Boone & Crocket Papers, Box 35, Folder 7, Mansfield Library; one test of archery skill involving five hundred participants revealed that only 12 percent could hit a 12-inch target three out of five times from a distance of 25 yards, suggesting that in the wild a hunter's chance of making a kill shot with an arrow from even that short range would likely be less than 60 percent; see Linda Hatfield, "Report on Bowhunting," http://www.animalrightscoalition.com/doc/bowhunting_report.pdf; Mogren, "Miss Billie's Deer."

28. Charles Wilkins Webber, *The Hunter Naturalist: The Romance of Sporting, or Wild Scenes and Wild Hunters* (Philadelphia: J. W. Bradley, 1851), 193.

29. Cerulli, *Mindful Carnivore*, 205.

30. Garrard, *Wah-to-yah*, 3.

31. Forester, *Complete Manual for Young Sportsmen*, 97.

32. "Jury Acquits Wisconsin Hunter in Woman's Shooting," March 29, 2003, http://www.CNN.com/2003/LAW/03/19/ctv.berseth.trial/index.html; "Jury Clears Berseth in Shooting Death," *Chippewa (WI) Herald*, March 28, 2003.

33. *New York Times*, September 10, 1989.

34. Edie Clark, "The Killing of Karen Wood," *Yankee Magazine*, November 1989; *New York Times*, September 10, 1989.

35. *Eau Claire Leader-Telegram*, November 21, 2014.

36. Haag, *Gunning of America*, xxiv; *New York Times*, May 31, 1970.

37. *New York Times*, May 31, 1970; Haag, *Gunning of America*, 277; *New York Times*, May 31, 1970.

38. Joseph B. Thomas, *Hounds and Hunting Through the Ages* (New York: Derrydale Press, 2001), 11–12.

## EPILOGUE: A COMPLEX INHERITANCE

1. Louis Warren, *The Hunter's Game: Poachers and Conservationists in Twentieth-Century America* (New Haven, CT: Yale University Press, 1997), 14; Dizard, *Mortal Stakes*, 22.

2. Insomuch as fair chase led to the conservation ideal, Dizard notes, it's to be regretted that no similar impulse became intrinsic to commercial fishing, farming, or extractive industries, as many costly environmental problems might have been lessened or avoided. See Dizard, *Mortal Stakes*, 22; "Financial Returns to Industry from the Federal Aid in Wildlife Restoration Program," Andrew Loftus Consulting and Southwick Associates, October 2015; also see Statistica.com, "Hunting in the United States; US Census Bureau data gathered by the US Fish & Wildlife Service; and "Hunting Statistics," Statistic Brain Research Institute, September 4, 2016.

3. *Los Angeles Times*, November 15, 1974.

4. Initiative and Referendum History-Animal Protection Issues (HSUS); interview with Bernard Unti, HSUS, October 7, 2016.

5. Cartmill, *View to a Death*, 241.

6. Roderick Nash, *Wilderness and the American Mind*, rev. ed. (New Haven, CT: Yale University Press, 1973), 153.

7. *The Ethic*, Fall 2015; Boone & Crockett Club Collection, Box 102, Folder 5, Mansfield Library, University of Montana.

8. Quoted in Eric G. Bolen and William Robinson, *Wildlife Ecology and Management*, 5th ed. (Hoboken, NJ: Pearson Publishing, 2003), 171.

9. Rachel Poliquin, *The Breathless Zoo: Taxidermy and the Cultures of Longing* (University Park: Pennsylvania State University Press, 2012), 143, 147–148. Poliquin does see a supreme value in one particular type of animal trophy, however, for "if a creature becomes extinct, no matter how much video footage and photographic images may have been amassed, nothing can ever compare to the physical presence of the animal, admittedly dead and stuffed, but a physical presence nonetheless. The

taxidermied remains of passenger pigeons, quaggas, great auks, and all other extinct species are precious beyond words. They are the definition of irreplaceable." See *The Breathless Zoo*, 4.

10. Jeffrey M. Masson and Susan McCarthy, *When Elephants Weep: The Emotional Lives of Animals* (New York: Delacorte Press, 1995), 232.

11. Hutto quoted in Al Kesselheim, "A Walk on the Wild Side," *Sun Magazine*, May 2017, 13–14.

12. Montaigne, "On Cruelty," 184; Tom Regan and Andrew Linzey, eds., *Other Nations: Animals in Modern Literature* (Waco, TX: Baylor University Press, 2010), 1; Henry Beston, *The Outermost House: A Year of Life on the Great Beach of Cape Cod* (Harmondsworth, UK: Penguin, 1928), 24–25.

13. Rufus B. Sage. *Letters and Scenes in the Rocky Mountains* (Glendale, CA: Arthur H. Clark, 1956), 19; Sewell, *Black Beauty*, 47.

14. See *Helena Independent Record*, November 3, 2011.

15. Grey Owl quoted in Amory, *Man Kind?*, 211. Grey Owl's real identity was not exposed until after his death in 1938.

16. Liam Stack, "Pedals the Walking Bear Said to Be Killed by a Hunter in New Jersey," *New York Times*, October 17, 2016.

17. Thoreau quoted in Herman, *Hunting and the American Imagination*, 152.

18. Wallace Stegner is quoted in Cronon, "Trouble with Wilderness," 97; Singer, *Animal Liberation*, 247.

19. See Statistica.com, "Hunting in the United States; US Census Bureau data gathered by the US Fish & Wildlife Service; and "Hunting Statistics," Statistic Brain Research Institute, September 4, 2016; for approval stats, see 2006 American Sportfishing Association (77.6%), 2013 Responsive Management Nationwide Survey (79%), and 2011 National Shooting Sports Foundation Survey (74% for hunting overall and 94% for the right to hunt). The wide acceptance of the use of guns for hunting, in preference to other uses, is heard even in the common refrain of gun control advocates that one "doesn't need a semiautomatic weapon to kill a deer." Case law has yet to affirm that hunting is protected by the Second Amendment.

20. Thoreau's quote is in "Chesuncook" (1858), from *The Maine Woods* (1864), collected in *The Writings of Henry David Thoreau*, vol. 3 (Boston: Houghton Mifflin, 1906), 134.

21. Dizard, *Mortal Stakes*, 35; Hornaday, *Our Vanishing Wildlife*, x; *Helena (MT) Independent*, March 11, 2005.

22. Simon Bronner, *Killing Tradition* (Lexington: University of Kentucky Press, 2008), 15; Nelson, *Heart and Blood*, 236.

# Index

PHILIP DRAY is a historian
who has written or
coauthored seven books
on American history
and culture, including
*At the Hands of Persons
Unknown*, which won the
Robert F. Kennedy Book
Prize and the Southern
Book Critics Circle
Award and was a finalist
for the Pulitzer Prize.
Dray lives in Brooklyn,
New York.

*Photograph by Mindy Tucker*